FITCHB P9-DCO-749

A16601908078

WITHDRAWN

FITCHBURG PUBLIC LIBRARY

THIS BOOK IS THE PROPERTY OF THE
ABOVE LIBRARY

GOOD CARE AND PROMPT RETURN IS THE
RESPONSIBILITY OF EACH BORROWER.

THE MODERN LIBRARY
of the World's Best Books

EIGHT
SPANISH PLAYS
of the Golden Age

*The publisher will be pleased to send, upon request,
an illustrated folder listing each volume in*

THE MODERN LIBRARY

EIGHT

❧ SPANISH ❧

PLAYS

of the

Golden Age

TRANSLATED, EDITED,
AND WITH AN INTRODUCTION, BY

WALTER STARKIE

LITT. D.

THE MODERN LIBRARY · NEW YORK

Play Index

© *Copyright, 1964, by Walter Starkie*

All rights reserved under International and Pan-American Copyright Conventions. Published in New York by Random House, Inc., and simultaneously in Toronto, Canada, by Random House of Canada, Limited.

Library of Congress Catalog Card Number: 64–10292

THE MODERN LIBRARY

is published by

RANDOM HOUSE, INC.

BENNETT CERF   DONALD S. KLOPFER

Manufactured in the United States of America
by H. Wolff Book Mfg. Co., Inc.

Designed by Jeanette Young

Dedicated
to the memory of
FÉLIX LOPE
DE VEGA CARPIO
(1562-1635)
on the occasion of the
quadricentenary
of his birth
NOVEMBER 25, 1562

❧ § ❧

✎§ Contents §✎

⤳ Preface ⤲

We have selected the following eight classical plays from the vast repertory of the Golden Age (*Siglo de Oro*) of Spanish drama, not only because of their literary excellence, but because they are characteristic examples of the complex Spanish art form of the *comedia* created by Lope de Vega (1562-1635), Shakespeare's great contemporary, whose quadricentenary we celebrate this year. The *comedia* combined with poetry the sister arts of music and the dance, and developed as an inspired improvisation, echoing the ancient epic poems and ballads of the Romancero—"Spain's perpetual plebiscite," as it was once called—and adapting itself in Protean fashion to the caprices and whims of the vociferous groundlings of the pit and women's gallery, or "stewing-pan."

In order to emphasize the minstrel origin of the Spanish drama we begin with an interlude-extravaganza, which we have freely adapted from one of the important episodes in the fourteenth-century autobiographical poem, "The Book of Good Love" of Juan Ruiz, Archbishop of Hita, Spain's greatest writer before Cervantes. Our English version may be performed by a *gangarilla*, to use the barnstorming term employed by the sixteenth-century vagabond playwright Agustín de Rojas, that is to say, three players, to whom we should add an extra actor behind the stage to be the ghostly *compère* and introduce the characters through a megaphone. The interlude, however, may alternatively be played, in the fourteenth-century manner, by a single actor, or *bululú*, who recites the whole interlude in *cante fable* style, as the wandering minstrels did in the square of Alcalá de Henares and Guadalajara.

We next come to the little sixteenth-century interlude by Lope de Rueda, whom Benavente calls the "Father of the Spanish stage," which is similar to a scenario from the Italian *commedia dell'arte*, with the part of Harlequin the stupid clown written out instead of being improvised. It should be acted in classical zany style, with plenty of *lazzi*.

In our English versions of Lope de Vega, Cervantes, Tirso de Molina, and Calderón, we have employed a stylized rhythmic pattern in an endeavor to convey the varying tempo of the Spanish *comedia* and to mark the contrasts between the arias and the recitatives.

In *Peribáñez and the Comendador of Ocaña* our version emphasizes the continual antithesis between individual and collective humanity: in Act I, with the village wedding, nuptial song and *folía* (a folk dance); in Act II, with its chorus of reapers contrasting with the grim purpose of the Comendador, his disguised lackey Luján, the innocent victim Casilda, and the tortured mind of Peribáñez; in Act III, with its grotesque parade of armed peasants in antithesis to the company of squires, all developing in strophe and antistrophe like a stylized ballet.

In *Pedro, the Artful Dodger*, on the other hand, our version emphasizes the picaresque-Gypsy characteristics of the hero Pedro, who is a legendary avatar rising out of the mists of the Middle Ages, and is the Spanish counterpart to the German Till Eulenspiegel. But the drama of Pedro and Belica, the Little Gypsy, is stressed collectively at different levels: first, by the stylized dialogue of the Mayor and rustic characters, and their grotesque dances; then at a higher level by Maldonado and his Gypsy dancers in their tribal *Zambra;* and at the highest level by the King and Queen (both stylized) and their courtiers, hide-bound by palace etiquette. The whole play, with its accompanying entr' acte interlude—*The Jealous Old Man*—is a "Midsummer Night's Dream," harlequinade and all, written by Cervantes, Shakespeare's *confrère* from southern Europe.

In our version of Tirso de Molina's *Playboy of Seville* we have accentuated the leitmotifs signalizing the ruthless energy of Don Juan Tenorio and his restlessness suggested by his frequent warnings to Catalinón to keep the horses saddled and ready for the road. In Tirso de Molina's masterpiece more than in any other *comedia* we have the essential dualism of Spanish *tragicomedia,* the alternating extremes, which have been called by the critic Dámaso Alonso, the Scylla and Charybdis of the Spanish soul. We have underlined this dualism in our interpretation of the interplay between Don Juan, the hero, and his servant clown.

In *The Mayor of Zalamea,* which is a masterpiece in form as well as in content, we have alternated prose and verse in an attempt to convey the contrast between recitative and aria in Calderón's drama.

As epilogue to our collection of Spain's Golden Age of Drama we have included our translation and description of the *Mystery of Elche,* the only example of a Spanish lyrical play which survives today as a sacred as well as popular ritual played annually on the Feast of the Assumption. It is a unique spectacle, combining thirteenth-century chant, with its Moz-arabic influences, and sixteenth-century polyphony, in the form of a complete music drama performed by the folk of Elche, "the Jerusalem of the West," amidst its palm trees on the Mediterranean shore.

WALTER STARKIE

University of California, Los Angeles
April 27, 1962

✑ *Introduction* ✑

THE
SPANISH THEATER
✖✁✁

THE MOST successful products of the Spanish genius have
been created as a result of the constant effort to give life and
perfection to individual qualities sprung from traditional roots
but ripened at a late season. Such fruits are esteemed for
their rarity; being no longer found in other countries, they
introduce elements whose efficacy has been missed. The best
examples are to be discovered in the Renaissance, the period
which was in other countries radically modernist, but in Spain
made a truce with traditionalism, thus avoiding, as far as
possible, a break with the Middle Ages. This break was
practically complete in other countries, but Spain remained
stanchly loyal to the great truths and beauties of the Middle
Ages, and strove to revive them, adapting them to the new
spirit of the Renaissance.[1] The Spanish Monarchy from Ferdinand and Isabel the Catholic, for the two ensuing centuries,
is conceived as a Renaissance state, which still supported the
medieval doctrine of universal Catholicism. The imperial idea
of Charles V was based upon a similar combination of principles. St. Ignatius watching over his arms the night of March
24, 1522, in front of the altar of Our Lady of Montserrat, in
order to become a Knight of Christ, gave life to the meta-

[1] R. Menéndez Pidal, *The Spaniards in their History.* Tr. W. Starkie.
London and New York, 1950, p. 135.

phorical idea of "Spiritual Knighthood" so dear to the Middle Ages, but he also gave a new meaning to asceticism in his foundation of the great religious order of modern times.

Other examples were the restoration of scholastic philosophy, which had such a long flowering under Vitoria, Soto, Maldonado and Suárez, and afterward extended its vast influence over other Catholic countries; the development of contrapuntal technique on traditional foundations in the fifteenth and sixteenth centuries with masters like the Andalusian Cristóbal de Morales and Francisco Guerrero from Seville, and Tomás Luis de Vitoria from Avila, all of whom had great influence in Italy and Germany. Finally mysticism, the *Romancero,* the Books of Chivalry and the Drama, all are further examples of late-ripening fruits, the slow evolution of some medieval types, which were very much appreciated outside Spain and exercised universal influence. All those achievements were accomplished with a broad sweep and continuous effort truly national in character. At the outset let us stress the significance of the Spanish epic poems, which, breathing the loftiest national spirit, were preserved in the prose of the chronicles, survived in fragmentary ballads that were sung by high and low throughout the Peninsula and beyond the seas, and became, as Menéndez Pidal says, the sum total of the nation's memories. Then came a great period of transformation when the traditional ballads were taken by the famous poets and woven into the texture of the new art form of the day—the drama.

We must not forget that it was the Church which put an end to pagan spectacles, and in the obscurity of the Middle Ages gave origin and birth to the modern drama. At first by forming part of the liturgy, in alternating chants, dialogues and choruses with some sort of scenic apparatus; then by amplifying and complicating these representations with the events in the life of Jesus Christ, of Our Lady, of the Saints, or of the heroes of the Old Testament. Then afterward by permitting, within or without the churches, these embryonic dramas to be enacted in the vulgar tongue, with great apparatus and with music, songs and other popular pastimes, the Church greatly facilitated their growth. And when, on account of the abuses which this tolerance necessarily produced, it closed its doors to every profane element, we see the modern theater created.[2]

MINSTRELSY AND THE DRAMA: JUAN RUIZ, THE ARCHPRIEST OF HITA

The *juglar* or minstrel played a great part in the development of Spanish drama. Mankind always needs the entertainer: once the vogue of his refined song passed away, the troubadour disappeared, but the "low-brow" minstrel still kept on wandering through the villages.[3] The minstrel always had a touch of the devil in him, and that was why the Church pursued him, and the worthy citizen, though admiring his talents, would call him disreputable. The tradition of the Roman *Mimus,* or wandering mummer, who was *infamis,* or outside the pale of law, descended to the *juglar* in Spain, and from him to the wandering actor and has lasted to our day. After the brilliant period of minstrelsy in the thirteenth and fourteenth centuries we find the whole tradition of the wandering singer and player summed up in the *Libro de Buen Amor* (The Book of Good Love) written by the Spanish Archpriest of Hita, Juan Ruiz, which we might call the "Golden Treasury of Minstrelsy." The Archpriest, who has been called the Rabelais of Spain, is closer in poetic genius to the Father of English poetry, Geoffrey Chaucer, who was his contemporary. Certainly he is the greatest figure in Spanish literature before Cervantes, and he deserves universal fame, for nobody has ever described the essence of wandering as did that portly, hirsute priest with the ferrety eyes. In his book which he meant to have passed from hand to hand, like a ball in a game played by fair damsels, we discover every type of song and ballad and hosts of vivid sketches of fourteenth-century life that needed only the presence of a minstrel-actor gifted with powers of *cante fable* to arouse the

[2] E. Cotarelo y Mori, *Bibliografía de las controversias sobre la licitud del Teatro en España.* Madrid, 1904, p. 9.
[3] The Siete Partidas of Alfonso X the Wise (1256-1263) frequently mention the mummer and his twin brother the *joculator,* or minstrel, as entertainers. J. P. Wickersham Crawford, *Spanish Drama before Lope de Vega.* Philadelphia, 1922, p. II.

enthusiasm of the audiences in village squares and baronial
halls. So popular, in fact, was the Archpriest that, as the
proverb went, "the man died but not his name" (*murió el
hombre mas no su nombre*), and even fifty years after his
death a wandering minstrel had only to shout in the plazas
of the Castilian villages: "*Agora comencemos del libro del
Arcipreste*" (Let us now begin from the Book of the Archpriest), for the crowds to gather from all sides around the
juglar, as if he had been the Pied Piper.

We have selected from this Golden Treasury of Minstrelsy
and adapted as *cante fable* the Dialogue between Don Melón
Ortiz and Doña Endrina, which is a sparkling picaresque or
libertine interlude, introducing as pivotal character the rascally old bawd, Trotaconventos (Toddle-Troll), the forerunner of La Celestina and the Nurse in Romeo and Juliet.
So vividly dramatic is this scene that it deserves its place in
our selection as a reminder of the important part played by
the minstrel in the evolution of Spanish drama. The Archpriest portrays himself: "More than average tall, sturdy, thick-
set, hairy, full-chested, bull-necked, black-eyed with thick
eyebrows, neat legs, small feet, sensuous lips, large ears, and
expansive nostrils." Adopting his autobiographical method
he identifies himself with the lovesick young Melón (Sir
Percy Pumpkin), who begs the good offices of the wily Trotaconventos (Toddle-Troll) to break down the resistance of
the sprightly widow. In our little extravaganza we have made
the Archpriest act as *compère* and present his characters.
Doña Endrina (Lady Sloe-Eyes) must have been a dainty
little minx, and she probably was also one of those who inspired the Archpriest's poem celebrating the beauty of little
women which survives today in the spirited translation by
Longfellow, to the eternal discomfiture of all Junoesque ladies:

> *A peppercorn is very small, but seasons every dinner
> More than all other condiments, although 'tis sprinkled
>   thinner,
> Just so a little woman is, if Love will let you win her,
> There's not a joy in all the world you will not find within
>   her.*[4]

[4] This version was published in *The Hispanic Anthology*. New
York, 1920.

THE FORERUNNERS

During the fifteenth century, as a result of the Renaissance, a profound change took place in ancient poetical traditions. In Italy the Renaissance had gradually penetrated into medieval forms of culture and had transformed them, but in Spain the Renaissance came as a revolution that was hostile to the poetical theories of the Middle Ages. The Spanish conquests in Italy from the time of Alfonso V of Aragon increased this tendency, and as a result we have an illustration of the saying: *Graecia capta ferum victorem cepit*. It was a decisive moment, for the art of the theater was springing to life, and everyone turned to Italy as the source of inspiration. Torres Naharro, Lope de Rueda, Timoneda and his followers devoted their energies to imitating Italian comedies and novels, while in lyric poetry, as Lope de Vega said, the native genius of Spain had disappeared owing to the craze for imitating the Italian muse. In the last third of the sixteenth century the only plays that rivaled the Italian-inspired drama were those of romantic character, such as the *Amadis* and *Don Duardos* of Gil Vicente and the *Duquesa de la Rosa* of Alfonso de la Vega, and it is significant that the Books of Chivalry were considered the obvious source of material for dramatists. But then came 1579, when the Sevillian dramatist, Juan de la Cueva, broke new ground by basing his play *La Muerte del Rey Don Sancho* on the most famous of national epic stories—the Siege of Zamora. It must have caused a sensation in the theater to hear the lines of the ancient ballad, which every member in the audience had known by heart from childhood. It was thus possible for the public, through its memories of the *Romancero*, to collaborate intimately with the actors on the stage, and this imparted to the characters in the play a vitality which had not existed previously in the theater. Thus, the year 1579, when the ballads were woven into the texture of the play for the first time, marks an epoch in the history of the Spanish theater. And Juan de la Cueva, in addition to that play, produced in Seville in the same year two further plays taken from the poetic tradition: *La Libertad de España por Bernardo del Carpio,* and the tragedy of the *Seven Infantes of Lara.*

LOPE DE RUEDA (1506-1565)

Although Juan de la Cueva and his followers had caused a revolution in Spanish drama, their plays were more in the nature of experiments, and we should consider them along with the works of two other pioneers of the Spanish theater in mid-sixteenth century, Torres Naharro and Lope de Rueda. Bartolomé Torres de Naharro, who was acknowledged later by Lope de Vega as one of the originators of the *comedia*, declared in the prologue to his *Propalladia* (1517) that there were two kinds of *comedia: comedia a noticia*, or plays that treat of events which have actually happened, and *comedia a fantasía*, or plays the action of which is the pure invention of the author. Torres Naharro was the earliest to write *comedias* in the manner which Lope de Vega afterward perfected and turned into the *comedia par excellence*.[5] Henceforth the term *comedia*, as used by Spanish dramatists in the "golden age" of their theater, is identical with our "play" or the German *Schauspiel*. As Morel Fatio says, *"Les drames les plus noirs de Calderón sont encore des comedias."* [6] Although Juan del Encina, the Court poet, musician, and dramatist of Ferdinand and Isabella at the end of the fifteenth century, was called "the Patriarch of the Spanish Theater" and was the predecessor of Torres Naharro and Juan de la Cueva, the title of Father of the Theater was given by Spain's most celebrated modern dramatist, Jacinto Benavente (1866-1954), to Lope de Rueda (1506-1565), because he was the first playwright to write directly for the popular stage. By birth a Sevillian, and a goldbeater by trade, he became a leading figure in the sixteenth century as a wandering actor-manager or *autor* as well as playwright, and toured from town to town in Spain. The earliest documentary notice about him is of the year 1554, when he represented an *auto* at Benavente in honor of Philip II, on his passage through that town on his way to England. *Autos*, incidentally, were in the early days little secular or religious plays: when in the sixteenth century the *autos* celebrated the Holy Eucharist on the feast of Corpus Christi and became abstract in form and akin to the English

5 H. Rennert, *The Spanish Stage*. New York, 1909, p. 275.
6 A. Morel Fatio, *La Comédie du XVII siècle*. Paris, 1885, p. 10.

Moralities, they were called *autos sacramentales*. Lope de Rueda's historic importance, however, lay in his invention of the *Pasos*, or short dramatic interludes, turning on simple episodes of daily life: an invitation to dinner from a penniless university graduate, an argument concerning husband and wife on the price they would charge for the olives in their garden which had not yet been planted. The merit of those vivid little scenes, which could even be interpolated in a full-length *comedia*, did not lie in their dramatic conception, but in their crisp dialogue, which is a treasure of popular speech, and rich in idiom. As Fitzmaurice-Kelly says of him: "Rueda had clearly read the *Celestina* to his profit; and his prose, with its archaic savor, is of great purity and power."[7]

We have included in our selection the interlude entitled *The Mask* (La Carátula), the second of the seven *Pasos* included in *El Deleitoso*.[8] It introduces the *bobo*, or simpleton, a stock character of the medieval farce that had appeared in the *autos* of Juan del Encina. As this little sketch with its rustic dialogue recalls the speech of our rural Irish plays we have translated it into the Irish idiom. The *paso*, however, bears a closer resemblance to a scenario of the masked and improvised *commedia dell'arte* with its stupid and clever clowns, Harlequin and Brighella, who spoke in Bergamask dialect. The highest tribute to Lope de Rueda was given by Cervantes at the end of his life, in 1615, in the prologue to the volume of his plays, and it is the more valuable as the hero of Lepanto had seen, when a boy, the primitive performances of the wandering actor-playwright's barnstormers in the public square in Valladolid or Alcalá de Henares:

In the time of this celebrated Spaniard all the properties of a theatrical manager were contained in a sack, and consisted of four white pelisses trimmed with gilded leather, and four beards and wigs, with four staffs, more or less. The plays were colloquies or eclogues between two or three shepherds and a shepherdess. They were supported by two or three interludes, either that of the "Negress," the "Ruf-

[7] J. Fitzmaurice-Kelly, *History of Spanish Literature.* New York, 1898, p. 169.

[8] Lope de Rueda, *El Deleitoso*, Matías Mares, Logroño, 1588.

fian," the "Fool" or the "Biscayan," and these four characters the said Lope de Rueda acted with the greatest skill
imaginable. At that time there were no *tramoyas* (theatrical
machinery), nor challenges of Moors or Christians, either
afoot or on horseback. There were no figures arising, or
seeming to arise, from the center of the earth through the
hollow of the stage, which at that time consisted of four
benches arranged in a square, with four or five boards upon
them, raised about four spans from the ground, nor did
clouds with angels or souls descend from the skies. The
furnishings of the stage were an old blanket drawn by two
cords from one side to the other, which formed what is
called the dressing-room, behind which were the musicians
singing an old ballad without the accompaniment of a
guitar.

The establishment of Madrid as the capital of Spain in
1560 is an important event in the history of the Spanish stage.
Up to that time the Royal Court had moved up and down
Spain, sometimes settling at Toledo, Valladolid, Seville, Granada and other cities. With the rapid growth of Madrid, the
capital, in wealth and population, it was necessary to find
a fixed place where the companies of strolling players might
perform. The creation of a permanent theater in Madrid,
however, was due to a body of charitable citizens who had
founded in 1565 a fraternity called the *Cofradía de la Sa-
grada Pasión*, to feed and clothe the poor and equip a hospital for women suffering from fever. They obtained the
privilege for representing all plays given in Madrid, and resolved to devote the funds there raised for the benefit of
their charity. Two years later, in 1567, another fraternity was
founded called the *Cofradía de Nuestra Señora de la Soledad*.[9]
The two brotherhoods purchased for the representation of
plays a number of *corrales* or courtyards of houses in the
neighborhood of the Puerta del Sol, including one in the calle
del Príncipe, which was called Corral de la Pacheca, as it had
belonged to a certain Doña Isabel Pacheco. In those yards,
which resembled the inn yards in England, where plays were
performed, the stage was set at the back, and the larger

[9] A. F. Schack, *Geschichte der Dramatischen Literatur und Kunst
in Spanien*. Frankfurt am Main, 1854, Vol. I, p. 264.

portion of the audience watched the performance standing in the courtyard, while the windows of the principal building and of the surrounding houses served as boxes for the well-to-do spectators.[10]

Such were the stage conditions when the actors of the *commedia dell'arte* arrived in Madrid in 1574, under the celebrated actor Alberto Nazeri de Ganassa, who was said to have invented the character of the second clown, or "zany," called Harlequin. He had been in France since 1571, where he and his company had been received with acclamation. In Madrid he presented his plays mostly in pantomime, it appears; he succeeded in the same year in obtaining the privilege of erecting a theater in the Corral de la Pacheca, where the stage, raised seats and *patio* were exposed to the inclemency of the weather. With the help of two carpenters, and using the boards and canvas of the Corral de la Pacheca, Ganassa built the theater with a roof covering the stage and the sides of the *patio,* and over the latter he stretched an awning to shade the spectators from the sun, and protect them from the rain. The *patio* or pit was patronized by the rabble—the *vulgo* or *gente de bronce*—who viewed the play standing. On account of the infernal clamor and din they made, they were called *mosqueteros* or musketeers. The same conditions obtained in France and England, and the boisterous rabble stood, as did the "groundlings," in the pit of the inn yards of London. So great were the crowds that thronged the *corrales* in Madrid on Sundays and feast days that the two fraternities determined to erect their own permanent theaters. The first one, in the calle de la Cruz, was opened in 1579, and the second, in the calle del Príncipe, in 1582. We should note, incidentally, that in 1576, three years before the building of the Corral de la Cruz in Madrid, the first genuine London playhouse, the Theater, was built by James Burbage, one of the Earl of Leicester's players, and in 1582 another theater, the Curtain, was erected close to the former in Finsbury fields. The Corral de la Cruz and Corral del Príncipe after 1584 were the only public theaters in Madrid and, as Rennert says, their glory in the annals of modern drama is surpassed only by the Globe and Blackfriars in London.[11]

[10] Schack, *op. cit.,* pp. 264-265.
[11] H. Rennert, *op. cit.,* p. 36.

LOPE DE VEGA (1562-1635)

It is a remarkable coincidence that the dramatic careers of the two great authors of the English and Spanish drama began about the same time, for Lope de Vega, who was born 1562, began to write for the public stage about 1585. Shakespeare, who was born in 1564, came to London in 1586. But whereas Shakespeare completely outshone all his English contemporaries, Lope de Vega was the first of a team of dramatists which included serious rivals for preëminence, such as Tirso de Molina and Calderón. Lope de Vega had his Earl of Southampton, but neither dramatist ever received any help or encouragement from his monarch.

Lope de Vega, it is true, wrote so vast a number of plays that he could never have hoped to revise them all, but Shakespeare never worried about the fate of his plays once they were in print, and as Collier says: "He never corrected a line of them after they were in type." [12] Lope wrote in 1606 of his plays: "If anyone should cavil about my *comedias* and think that I wrote them for fame, undeceive him and tell him I wrote them for money."

In 1582, when Madrid had two theaters and companies began to perform regularly, what was needed was a truly national poet, whose genius would revitalize the whole art of the theater. It was then that Lope de Vega, that "Monster of Nature" and "Phoenix of Geniuses," as he was called, appeared in the theater. Of Lope it may be said that he created the Spanish national theater, and built up an entire dramatic history of the country from the chronicles and epics, interweaving ballad phrases with his verses in such a way that the original cannot be separated from the new. This he could do all the more easily because the best Castilian ballads cut short the narrative, leaving only the dialogue. Lope de Vega was a case of miraculous precocity: when he was twelve years old he translated Claudian's *De Raptu Proserpinae,* and at seventeen he composed a play on the exploits of Garcilaso de la Vega and the Moor Tarfe, divided into four acts, but with several fragments of ballads interwoven into the action of the play. The ballads were venerated by the people as

12 J. P. Collier, *Shakespeare's Works.* Vol. I, p. 142.

records of the nation's history rather than enjoyed as poetry, but Lope de Vega was able to breathe into these legends of past heroes the magic of his genius, and transform them into drama. And what is still more remarkable is that his vast erudition, acquired later, and his enormous reputation among men of letters, did not in the slightest degree diminish this vivid and intensive feeling for traditional poetry. His heart was always open to the artless simplicity of folk songs, for they awoke in him deeper harmonies. Menéndez Pidal, with his rare acumen, points out how deeply suggestive was the technique employed by Lope de Vega in these plays based on traditional themes.[13] He made use not only of the traditional narrative elements, but also of the short refrains that were sung by the people. Sometimes the lines of the ballad conjure up the vision of the heroic age of León and Castile; at another, the allusions are allegorical and echo the chants of pilgrims on their way to far off Santiago de Compostela; or again, the author uses the refrains of the ballads and the proverbs to add salt and charm to the dialogue of his *graciosos*, as he called his clowns on the Spanish stage.[14]

Peribáñez and the Comendador of Ocaña

From Lope de Vega's "Ocean of Plays" we have selected *Peribáñez and the Comendador of Ocaña*, a play universally admitted to be one of his masterpieces. Never did he write more vivid scenes of rustic life describing the simple country folk at their daily tasks. It is a play redolent with thyme and verbena, and echoing songs and ancient ballads. Thus Lope de Vega did not draw the plot of *Peribáñez* from a historical incident, but from the fragment of one of the old ballads of the *Romancero*:

> *Más quiero yo a Peribáñez*
> *Con su capa la pardilla.*

[13] Lope de Vega's best plays are dynamic, moving onward in a series of short impressionistic episodes resembling the cinema. Menéndez Pidal uses the term cinedrama to describe Lope de Vega's use of rapid movement in his plays.
[14] R. Menéndez Pidal, *La Epopeya castellana a través de la Literatura Española.* Buenos Aires, 1945, p. 186.

*Que al Comendador de Ocaña
Con la suya guarnecida.*

(I love far more my Peribáñez in his plaid
Than the Comendador in his braided cloak.)

Lope had the genius to see what rich dramatic material could be extracted from the ballads and chronicles of Spain's past history, and through them he reached the ancient epic, because his dramatic genius led him straightway to the most poetic passages, which were those derived from the old rhapsodic poems. *Peribáñez* is also a social drama and stresses the fact that Honor is not the exclusive monopoly of the noble caste in Spain. Peribáñez, the peasant, is not noble by birth, but is noble in heart and soul, and when his feelings of honor and human dignity are violated, he is at once ready to avenge himself upon the powerful and aristocratic Comendador. Before the arrival of Lope de Vega, the outraged husband in the lower classes in Spain had generally been portrayed as a grotesquely comic character, but Lope in his *New Art of Writing Plays* (1609) laid down as a principle that cases of *pundonor* or "point of honor" were the most effective for the stage, as their appeal was universal.[15]

There is, nevertheless, a profound irony in Lope's treatment of the theme of honor in this play, and unless we understand this, we shall miss its moral significance: the Comendador, when he makes Peribáñez a captain, and gives him a higher social status in order to send him away from Ocaña and leave the coast clear for the seduction of Casilda in her husband's absence, enables the latter to avenge the affront and protect his honor as an equal. For Peribáñez, henceforth, possesses rights within the social structure which he uses to vindicate the sanctity of his hearth and home, and the moral of the play, which springs from the clash between contrasting personalities of the Comendador and Peribáñez, consists in

---

15 In the fourteenth and fifteenth centuries the municipal orders living on the Andalusian frontiers became strengthened owing to their struggles against the Moors. Every day witnessed situations where a farmer, as in Lope de Vega's play, might become a knight. This democratic spirit appears in many dramas of Lope.

the triumph of personal integrity within the pattern of the hierarchical society of Lope de Vega's day. The modern Hispanists Aubrun and Montesinos have shown that this play, as well as its companion play, *Fuenteovejuna,* is not, as it used to be considered in the past, a drama of class struggle, but a play embodying class relationships within the social structure of the monarchical society of those days, in which each individual was tested according to his hierarchical station in life.[16] As E. M. Wilson too says in his study of the images and structure of the play, the Comendador is not a criminal and a scoundrel like the Comendador in *Fuenteovejuna,* but a man overwhelmed by sinful lust, as by Nemesis, and driven to violate the code of honor of his caste.[17] This gives added poignancy to a play which reflects here and there the moral struggles which beset Lope all his life, and which are disclosed in the frank letters he wrote to his patron, the Duke of Sessa. Lope was a Don Juan burdened with a conscience, and after treading the primrose path of dalliance he was tortured by remorse, and his conscience left him no peace. It is said that he would flog himself till the whitewashed walls of his room were stained with blood, and he would devote himself to the care of the sick, the lepers and the poor, in an attempt to mortify his sinful flesh. His devotional moods deepened when sorrows came upon him. The death of his beloved son Carlos Félix was followed soon afterward by the death of his second wife in 1614. It was then that he wrote the *Four Soliloquies on Death,* which with his *Rimas Sacras* are among his most moving poems. It was in a moment of sadness and mystical yearning that he took holy orders. This, as Fitzmaurice-Kelly says, was his irreparable mistake. No man was less fitted to be a minister of religion. By an ironic stroke of destiny, worthy of the Greek drama of Aeschylus, during his last year he, this embodiment of Don Juan, became the victim of the sinister avatar, when his youngest and most beloved daughter, Antonia Clara (Antoñica, as he used to call her), was abducted from his home when she was barely seventeen, by a notorious

[16] C. V. Aubrun et J. F. Montesinos, *Peribáñez.* Paris, 1943, Introd.
[17] E. M. Wilson, *Images et Structure dans Peribáñez.* Bulletin Hispanique, LI, 1949, pp. 125-159.

libertine of the Royal Court, a widower who was called Tenorio (which was also the surname of Don Juan himself).[18]

Lope's contemporaries were never weary of celebrating his incredible industry, his invention and his "Ocean of Plays." His disciple and biographer Montalbán says that his pen never could keep pace with the rapidity of his thoughts. He wrote a play in two days, which even experienced copyists would find no mean feat to copy at that time. And at Toledo, on one occasion, he wrote, at a stretch in two weeks, fifteen acts, that is to say, five *comedias*. He was supposed to have written 220 plays by 1603, and by 1609 the total rose to 483; in 1618, it reached 800; in 1628, 1070; and in 1632, 1500. After his death his friend and disciple Pérez de Montalbán, in a posthumous panegyric, asserted that Lope wrote 1800 plays and more than 400 *autos*, bringing his total output to 2200. This would mean that Lope never wrote less than 24 plays a year, that he usually wrote 50, that the yearly average rose to 60 as he grew older, and that in the last three years of his life he wrote over a hundred—say, two plays a week. Most of Lope de Vega's plays have perished, and those that are extant today reach the number of 470.

MIGUEL DE CERVANTES (1547-1616)

The next play we have selected is *Pedro de Urdemalas* (Pedro, the Artful Dodger) by Miguel de Cervantes, which belongs to the second period of his dramatic works, and was included in the volume of eight plays and eight interludes which he published in 1615, the year before he died. It contains the celebrated prologue in which the veteran author, speaking in the mood of melancholy reminiscence, recalls his early thrills, when as a boy he saw Lope de Rueda, and describes the innovations he himself introduced in his early plays written in the eighties of the preceding century. When Cervantes had returned to Madrid in 1580 from his five years of captivity in Algiers, he discovered that his father's affairs had gone from bad to worse, that his deafness had isolated him from the world and that his mother and sisters had beggared themselves trying to raise ransom money for him and his

18 L. Astrana Marín, *Vida azarosa de Lope de Vega*. Madrid, 1935, pp. 404-410.

brother Rodrigo. Miguel was the characteristic ex-soldier, whose services to his country were forgotten when the war had passed, and he became in those days a denizen of Madrid's Grub Street, spending most of his days and nights haunting the tree-lined square of the Mentidero, or Liar's Walk, where the actors and the gossips of the city gathered and tore to shreds the reputations of their betters. He had at the time a "liaison" with an actress, Ana Franca de Rojas, by whom he had a natural daughter, Isabel Saavedra. To this early period belong his early dramatic efforts—*El Trato de Argel* (The Algiers Affair), 1580, *El Cerco de Numancia,* 1583, and *La Batalla Naval.* In those days he had high hopes of achieving success as a playwright, and in old age he refers to his innovations, such as reducing the *comedias* from five acts to three, and representing upon the boards the "imaginations and hidden thoughts of the soul and moral abstraction." [19]

In the *Journey to Parnassus* (1613) he refers to his former rosy hopes of success in the theater: "Of the money I make no account, but fame I would value, be it much or little, for it is a thing of exquisite delight, and no less importance, to see crowds of people issuing from the comedy, all in a fine humor, and the poet who wrote it standing at the door of the theater, receiving congratulations from all around." What happened in those early days was that Lope de Vega, then in his early twenties—that "Portent of Nature" (as Cervantes calls him) and Phoenix of Geniuses—appeared and swept away into lumber room the productions of Cervantes, Juan de la Cueva and all their followers. The one-armed hero of Lepanto saw all his hopes of popular recognition vanish when he watched the triumph of the younger poet, and he was to say later in the "Postscript" to the *Journey to Parnassus:* "When a poet is poor half of his divine fruits and fancy miscarry by reason of his anxious care to win his daily bread." The need for daily bread forced him to lay aside the pen. From 1587 for the next fifteen years he would have no time for literature, but his wanderings up and down Andalusia and La Mancha and his personal misfortunes and trials would spur him on to create his philosophy of kindly toler-

[19] Cervantes's memory played him false: Francisco de Avendaño as early as 1553 had written *comedias* in three acts.

ance and understanding of the follies of mankind. When *Don Quixote* took the world by storm in 1605, and the Knight of the Rueful Figure and his squire were celebrated all over the country, and their names were even used as nicknames at Court, Cervantes again found himself amidst the famous writers at the Royal Court at Valladolid. He then discovered that Lope de Vega, now his rival, would not forgive the sharp digs given to the latter's dramatic methods in Chapter 48 of Part I of *Don Quixote* through the mouth of the Canon of Toledo, and had said of the work to a friend: "Of the poets I do not speak, but there is none so bad as Cervantes, nor is anyone so foolish as to praise *Don Quixote*." When, however, toward the end of his life, Cervantes turned again to the theater and wrote the plays of his second period, he followed the lead of Lope de Vega, modified his style, and introduced the innovations of his rival, such as reviving the function of the *gracioso* or clown, which had been so prominent a feature of the drama of the patriarch of the theater, Juan del Encina, in the fifteenth century, and of Lope de Rueda in more recent times. It is in the prologue to the eight plays that he makes his *Gran Rifiuto*, good-humoredly denying the dramatic theories he had upheld in 1604 in *Don Quixote*, and in Act II of *El Rufián Dichoso* he says *mea culpa* in the dialogue between Comedy and Curiosity, where the former says:

> *I was good in days gone by,*
> *And even nowadays, if you*
> *Examine carefully, I'm not bad,*
> *Though I foreswear those solemn laws*
> *That I received as heritage*
> *From Plautus, Seneca and Terence,*
> *And other Greeks you know about.*

Pedro, the Artful Dodger (1611)

It was under Lope de Vega's influence that Cervantes wrote his last *comedia*, *Pedro de Urdemalas* (Pedro, the Artful Dodger), which Professor Valbuena Prat calls "the masterpiece of his theater." Lope de Vega, too, wrote a play entitled *Pedro de Urdemalas*, which he mentions in the second edition

of *El Peregrino en su Patria,* 1618. It was played in 1622 at
the Royal Palace in Madrid. In spite of this, it was for a long
time attributed to Montalbán, but the text is published in the
eighth volume of Lope de Vega's plays. It is in complete contrast to the play by Cervantes, for it is the legend of Pedro
de Urdemalas that appears, not the character himself, and
the lovesick heroine Laura disguises herself as Pedro whom
she has read about (perhaps in the play of Cervantes?) and
tries to copy his exploits. According to Cotarelo y Mori, the
first mention of this roguish folk hero Pedro de Urdemalas
occurs in *Almoneda,* a grotesque poem by Juan del Encina
in the fifteenth century, where he is credited with tricks
of all kinds, including sheep shearing, plucking eyebrows,
and collecting old wives' tales. Pedro, the Artful Dodger, is,
in fact, the Spanish Till Eulenspiegel, a rolling stone that
gathers no moss, with a zest for adventure and a nimble wit.
He is, too, "a snapper up of unconsidered trifles" like Auto-
lycus, with more than a touch of the picaroon and Gypsy.
Pedro, the Artful Dodger, in spite of being as poor as a
church mouse and obliged to have recourse to every wily
trick, honorable or the reverse, if he would hold his own in
the struggle for life, is as merry as a lark on a sunny morning.
His motto is the Gypsy one, "The Lord will provide," for
who knows what good fortune may turn up at the turn of
the road? And so every day tells its own tale: he pretends
he is blind to deceive the close-fisted widow with the shekels;
then a soul in Purgatory, in order to wheedle money out of
her for the benefit of the bodies of those in this world; he is
ready to be enrolled in the Gypsy tribe, when the chief tells
him he is to be bridegroom of the fair Belica; and he ends
up, finally, as an actor in order to have the illusion that he
is King, Prince, Pope, for as he says sententiously, "The profession of player comprises every state in human life." The
moral of the play, thus, is Shakespearean and expressed in
metaphors drawn from the stage. Man is "a poor player, that
struts and frets his hour upon the stage," and Pedro, the Artful Dodger, who has become Nicolás de los Ríos, the celebrated actor and producer (incidentally, the man who was
to produce Cervantes's play *Pedro de Urdemalas,* but died
suddenly of apoplexy),[20] follows his destiny, which is to play

[20] Nicolás de los Ríos was one of the most celebrated producers

many parts before the final awakening. And we are reminded of Sancho's answer to Don Quixote, when the latter had moralized on the parts men play in life: "A brave comparison though not so new, for I've heard it many a time, as well as that one about the game of chess, how so long as the game lasts, each piece has its special office, and when the game is finished they are all mixed, shuffled and jumbled together, and stored away in the bag, which is much like ending in the grave." When we reach Act III of the play we realize that it bears a close relationship to Part II of *Don Quixote*, and shows us the theater within the theater, in true Baroque fashion. But Cervantes, as Valbuena Prat observes, in contrast to Calderón who shows life as a play, presents Pedro, the Artful Dodger, in the process of living his illusions in the world of the theater, like Henry IV and other heroes of the Pirandellian drama. And the Protean Pedro, who has all the saving graces of serenity and detachment that are lacking in the tortured heroes of Pirandello, stands in antithesis to Belica, the foundling reared by the Gypsies in their tribe, who, when she is raised to a higher sphere, forgets her old companions and is arrogant and ungrateful. Pedro, who is the wisest man of the play, is entirely devoid of rancor or envy, and says to her:

> *Your claims and mine have reached fulfillment,*
> *But whereas mine were in fiction only,*
> *Yours were in real earnest.*

No play in the repertory of the Golden Age of Spanish drama possesses greater variety of themes than *Pedro, The Artful Dodger*: at one moment we are reminded of the *Little Gypsy*, the exemplary novel of Cervantes, at another of Lope de Vega's play *The Mayor of Zalamea*: we continually hover between different social levels. Sometimes we are with the

---

and authors of the time of Cervantes and Lope de Vega. He produced a number of the latter's plays. He was playing in Madrid in 1609, but died suddenly of apoplexy in 1610. The play was evidently written for Ríos, and the latter's death must have been a great disappointment to Cervantes. Ríos had an adventurous life and was a friend of Agustín de Rojas who introduces him as one of the main characters in his celebrated *El Viaje Entretenido*. Madrid, 1603.

Mayor and his rustics, sometimes with Maldonado and his Gypsies, and these characters then make way for the philandering King (who recalls the Duke of Illyria of Shakespeare) and his lovesick queen. From a characteristic rustic dance we follow Pedro, who is now a Gypsy preparing to accomplish the "Great Trick." First, he is disguised as a blind man; then he calls up the souls in Purgatory; then by moonlight we take part in the magic rites of St. John's Eve; and we realize that the whole play is a Midsummer Night's Dream written by Shakespeare's *confrère* from southern Europe.[21] As Joaquín Casalduero says in his fascinating interpretation, the play is based on fancy (*fantasía*) and wit (*ingenio*), and is treated as a burlesque with Baroque implications. The actor symbolizes the social world, and unity springs from the realization of our destiny.[22]

The Interlude of The Jealous Old Man (1615)

We have selected as our next example of Golden Age drama *El Viejo Celoso* (The Jealous Old Man), an interlude by Cervantes. It is dated 1615, and as Armanda Cotarelo says, it is the last of the interludes in date but the first of them in merit. In our judgment this little *tranche de vie* is an admirable foil to *Pedro de Urdemalas*, which, we have seen, fits into the category described by Torres Naharro as *comedias a fantasía*, but it is also linked with the former play by the fact that it also takes place during the festival of St. John, with its magic rites and superstitions, and the musicians at the end sing the following song:

> *On St. John's day if rain should fall,*
> *You'll have no wine and your loaves will be small;*
> *But if you fight on his day they say*
> *You'll live at peace for a year and a day.*

During the *siglo de oro* it was the custom to accompany a *comedia* with two *entremeses* or interludes, one between the

[21] As Klein says, "the scenes of this merry play fly like the skirts of the Gypsy dancing girls." *Geschichte des Spanischen Dramas.* Leipzig, 1872.

[22] J. Casalduero, *Sentido y Forma del Teatro de Cervantes.* Madrid, 1951.

first and second *jornadas* or acts and the other between the second and third. Caramuel, the first editor of the celebrated Luis Quiñones de Benavente (1589?-1651), a close friend of Lope de Vega, and author of nine hundred interludes, observed that the *entremeses* of Quiñones served the purpose of dispelling the tedium of the spectators between the acts: without them even the best *comedia* in the world would be in peril owing to the attacks it was liable to suffer at the hands of the unruly *mosqueteros* in the pit. Caramuel also adds that a manager who was plagued with a poor *comedia* could always insert a couple of *entremeses*, which would act as "crutches" and prop it up and prevent it from falling, and the author who had a good interlude up his sleeves, lent wings to his *comedia* and enabled it to soar higher.[23]

The word *entremes* (inter-missum) or French *entremets* (side dish), as applied to festal pieces accompanied by singing, is found as early as 1412 in Valencia, and Lamarca states that Valencia was the city that originated the *entremesos*, as they were called locally.

The greatest master of these short dramatic interludes was Cervantes, who perfected the vigorous, realistic sketches of Lope de Rueda, and produced little dramatic masterpieces, which can be compared to the etchings of Goya. Cervantes the writer, according to a modern Spanish critic, is the antithesis to Cervantes the man, for the former laughs when the latter weeps, and when in 1615 the hero of Lepanto wrote his last interlude, *The Jealous Old Man*, he was in the doldrums. In this interlude he depicts a jealous old husband who—like Carrizales, the rich old Indiano in *El Celoso Extremeño* (The Jealous Extremaduran), one of the *Exemplary Novels* (1613)—has been so foolish as to marry, at three score years and ten, a pretty young girl of fifteen. The plot of *The Jealous Old Man* is very ancient, and came originally from the medieval collection of thirty-seven tales entitled *Proverbiorum seu clericalis disciplina libri tres*, by the Sephardic Jew Moses, a native of Huesca in Aragón, who took the name Pero Alfonso when converted. The trick of the leather hanging concealing the lover, which was described by Pero Alfonso in his

---

[23] Caramuel defines interludes as follows: *"Entremes apud Hispanos est comoedia brevis in qua actores ingeniose nugantur."* Caramuel, *Rhythmia*. Campaniae, 1662.

eleventh example, *De Marito et Uxore,* was also used by the Archpriest of Talavera[24] in the fifteenth century in *El Corbacho,* and this is probably the direct source of Cervantes.

TIRSO DE MOLINA—FRAY GABRIEL TÉLLEZ (1571-1648)

The Playboy of Seville and the Guest of Stone (1630)

After Lope de Vega we come to Tirso de Molina, the second in order of the three great dramatists of Spain's *siglo de oro,* and one whose reputation has grown since the nineteenth century, when the dramatist Hartzenbusch only allotted him one volume of the Rivadeneyra edition, the same as was allotted Juan Riuz de Alarcón, Rojas Zorrilla, and Agustín de Moreto. Tirso is not, however, a bridge between the Lope de Vega cycle of dramatists and the cycle of Calderón, for his dramatic technique is exclusively that of Lope, though he differs from his master, owing to his psychological and descriptive characteristics.

Tirso de Molina should be studied not through isolated plays, but in his entirety in order to feel the full force of his genius, which was uneven in spite of many moments of undeniable greatness. His play *La Prudencia en la Mujer,* to give one example, was considered by Menéndez Pelayo to have topped the high-water mark of the Spanish drama.

We, however, felt impelled to select *El Burlador de Sevilla* (The Playboy of Seville) in preference to others by the master, because of the immense possibilities it offers to an imaginative producer. No Don Juan play has ever equaled Tirso de Molina's original in imagination, force and impressiveness, and it is true to say that he has given the world a character as universal as Don Quixote. Many studies on the Don Juan theme have been published by scholars in every country, and the consensus is that the character originated in ballad literature. Ramón Menéndez Pidal in an interesting study has analyzed the accounts of the legends in Spain, and

[24] For detailed criticism of this interlude and on *Pedro de Urdemalas* see A. Cotarelo y Valledor, *El Teatro de Cervantes.* Madrid, 1915, pp. 515-536 and pp. 389-430.

has himself collected ballads from Sepúlveda and Riaza in Castile, which lay stress on the insult to the dead and the invitation to join the living at a banquet. The legend presented itself, generally, in the form of a ballad describing how a young man finds a skull on the ground and sardonically asks it to dine. The skull turns up at the dinner and invites his host in return to join him next night in the graveyard.[25]

There are in Tirso de Molina's play three fundamental traditional traits which coincide with the original legends and ballads. First of all, Don Juan is the characteristic *burlador* or playboy with whom Lope de Vega had made everyone familiar through countless plays: dissolute, impulsive, boastful, flamboyant, and an arrant hoaxer—a playboy in the sense that Synge gave to the word in his *Playboy of the Western World*. Don Juan was not a blasphemer or an atheist like Leonzio, his Italian counterpart, but simply what the Spaniards call a *calavera* or rake. He was deeply Spanish in his attitude toward the hereafter, but simply banished the thought of it from his mind. Another essentially Spanish trait in the Don Juan legend is the identity of the statue with the dead man, and in the folk ballads the statue and the dead man alternate. The third Spanish trait in the tradition is the double invitation to dinner, which we find in Tirso de Molina's play, and in all the Spanish legends and ballads, but not in the Gascon stories or the German *Märchen*.

Although Don Juan's unbridled passions were what caught the fancy of the public in the theater, it was not what the author wished to emphasize, for he, being a theologian and a member of the Mercedarian Order as well as a man of letters, was chiefly concerned with the problem of salvation.[26] The

---

25 R. Menéndez Pidal, *Estudios Literarios*. Madrid, pp. 105-136. An excellent study on the sources of the play.

26 It is, however, most significant that Tirso de Molina in 1625 fell foul of the Junta de Reformación which had been set up in Madrid by the Conde Duque de Olivares to reform the abuses in the theater. The Junta, on account of "the evil example and tendency of his profane *comedias*," even urged his banishment to one of the remote monasteries, and his excommunication, "so that he may write no more *comedias*." This was the year when his *Condenado por Desconfiado* (The Doubter Damned), his celebrated Faustian drama on predestination, was produced by Roque de Figueroa.

question was whether a man could defy all moral principles and transgress all social laws and still be saved: could a man snap his fingers at life after death and trifle with divine mercy and expect to escape Hell? The answer given by the theologian Gabriel Téllez, alias the dramatist Tirso de Molina, was an emphatic no, and Don Juan, the Playboy, disappears with the Comendador and goes down to Hell following one of the most impressive scenes in all Spanish drama. As some critics have pointed out, Tirso in dramatizing the Nemesis of Don Juan had anticipated Schopenhauer's antithesis between Love and Death, and the doctrine that he who has enjoyed the maximum of beauty should suffer the most terrible of all deaths. On the other hand let us not forget that Don Juan also personifies the Renaissance doctrine of the individual's joy in life and his revolt against the ascetic melancholy, and the renunciation of the Middle Ages. Also, throughout the play runs an undercurrent of protest against the whole social system of the country, the abuse of privileges by the nobles, and the appalling corruption of the royal favorites.

The main fascination of *The Playboy of Seville* today arises from the clashing points of view, which are interpreted dramatically by that imaginative and introspective monk of seventeenth-century Spain who, if we may believe his contemporaries, used to shut himself up in his cell when he was writing his plays and gesticulate and shout the dialogue aloud to himself. And the play, as he has written it, shows that the cloistered monk must have had many a bitter struggle with his demons, for even as late as seventeenth-century Spain there was in the mind of all Spaniards a clash between the Western European and the Oriental attitude toward life. Western civilization had set woman upon a pedestal, and Dante in a celebrated sonnet invokes "the Ladies who have intelligence of Love":

Donne che avete intelletto d'amore.

His invocation was to spiritual love, which the people personified in the Blessed Virgin. Against this chivalrous idea of love arose the opposing spirit of Don Juan from the East. He was Oriental and Semitic in race, and according to his law man, not woman, was the center of the universe, an idea essentially Moorish and Arabic.[27] Woman in his plaything, and when he crosses into Paradise he will meet wonderful *houris*, but woman herself is not allowed to enjoy that paradise of men. When Tirso de Molina wrote *The Playboy of Seville*, he created his hero Don Juan Tenorio to be the prototype of the sinister libertine, and so we find Don Juan's descendants in literature ever since, for in addition to his libertinism, Don Juan had his Satanic pride, a far stronger vice, and the one that Baudelaire remembered in his great poem *Don Juan aux Enfers*, where he describes the lonely hero standing on Charon's ferry proud and unseeing:

> *Tout droit dans son armure, un grand homme de*
> *   pierre*
> *Se tenait à la barre et coupait le flot noir;*
> *Mais le calme héros, courbé sur sa rapière,*
> *Regardait le sillage et ne daignait rien voir.*[28]

Ever since Tirso de Molina, the enlightened monk, brought him on the Spanish stage in 1630, Don Juan, the gallant playboy, has been declining. Under Molière, later on in the same century, he loses some of his flamboyancy and becomes more of an abstraction, for he and Sganarelle are busy rehearsing the theories that were to dominate eighteenth-century France under Voltaire. In the eighteenth-century world, it is not literature or the drama which keeps alive the sinister Don Juan, but the divine music of Mozart in the opera *Don Giovanni* through the theme played on the trombones in the orchestra. In the nineteenth century, Byron's Don Juan is not the gallant but the victim of women who are in love with his fatal beauty. In all the nineteenth century there is only one exception: Zor-

[27] W. Starkie, Introd. to *Tiger Juan* by R. Pérez de Ayala. London, 1933, p. 34. R. P. de Ayala, *Máscaras*, Vol. II. Madrid, 1919, p. 256.
[28] Dr. Marañón considers that Tirso de Molina's model for the Playboy was Don Juan de Tassis, Count of Villamediana, whose mysterious assassination intrigued all the Spanish world in the early years of Philip IV's reign. He and his white charger were figures of romance, and he was reputed to be the Queen's lover. After his death in 1622 it was discovered that he was the leader of a group of homosexuals. See G. Marañón, *Don Juan*. Madrid, 1942, pp. 101-112.

rilla's Don Juan is a chip off the old block, but what happens
in the end? Instead of hurtling down to Hell, he is saved at
the point of death by the tears of Doña Inés, who resembles
Marguerite in Gounod's *Faust;* and when later on, under the
influence of the Nordic giant Ibsen, we discover in the pseudo-
romantic Spanish dramatist José Echegaray, not Don Juan, but
the Son of Don Juan, it is the son who pays for his father's
sins, for the fathers have eaten sour grapes and the children's
teeth are set on edge.

After Zorrilla's play Don Juan's decline becomes a *dégrin-
golade* until we come to Bernard Shaw, who takes the pa-
thetic avatar and gingers him up to point a moral in the new
Gospel of Creative Evolution. Don Juan becomes Doña Juana,
who pursues her masculine prey, and when she has married
him she treats him as a soldier treats his rifle. He is the pater
familias who will enable her to fulfill Nature's Life Force and
add to the population. Even in modern Spain, Don Juan is
as good as buried, for we find the Brothers Quintero writing
a play entitled *Don Juan Buena Persona* (Don Juan a Decent
Fellow) which might be laid on the tomb as the epitaph of
the once gallant hero.

PEDRO CALDERÓN DE LA BARCA (1600-1681)

In the personality of Calderón we find at once the greatest
antithesis to Lope de Vega. Whereas in Lope all is energy,
passion, folklore and improvisation, in Calderón we find aristocratic distinction, reflection and calm serenity. Whereas
much of the life of the *Phoenix* reads like a mixture of Casa-
nova's *Memoirs* and a picaresque novel, Calderón's life story
might be called "a biography of silence." [29] His life was peaceful and unruffled, though in his youth he sowed his wild oats
—as on the occasion when he and others stormed the convent of the Trinitarian nuns in Madrid (where Cervantes was
buried), while pursuing the actor Pedro de Villegas, who had
wounded his brother. The incident occurred in the winter of
1628-1629; the actor had taken sanctuary in the convent of
the Trinitarians, when Calderón and his companions, with the
judge, burst into the convent and disturbed the nuns, believ-

[29] A. Valbuena Prat is the foremost authority on Calderón today.
Op. cit., p. 21.

ing that they were hiding the guilty attacker. The incident would have died down but for the celebrated preacher Fray Hortensio Paravicino, who thundered against Calderón and his associates, accusing them of sacrilege. In revenge, the dramatist lampooned the preacher in his play *El Príncipe Constante*, which appeared in February 1629, with the result that the enraged cleric appealed to law. The incident is significant as an index to Calderón's peppery and rebellious character, in spite of his calm, severe exterior in later life. We also find in his play *The Purgatory of Saint Patrick* a similar incident of violation of the cloister, which was considered scandalous when the play appeared. As well as the hot-tempered, impulsive Calderón, we have the heroic Calderón during the Catalán War in 1640-1642 when as a knight of Santiago, he served in the cavalry under the Count-Duke of San Lucar, and was personally congratulated by the commander-in-chief for his valor. Nevertheless after the war he retired immediately from military service. It was soon after his retirement, in 1644 at the latest, that he wrote his famous play *The Mayor of Zalamea*, which reflects his misgivings about certain aspects of Spanish military organization.[30] Of his love life we know little, for he does not refer in his works to the death of his mistress, though his sorrow may have been the reason why in 1651 he became ordained a priest. After that date we note his tendency toward stoicism and pessimism, which is reflected in his plays, where we find the recurring phrases: *"Humo, polvo, viento y nada"* (smoke, dust, wind and nothing) and *"Así son las glorias del mundo"* (such are all the glories of the world), which the skeleton dressed in the mantle of Justice, says to Cipriano in *El Mágico Prodigioso*. This stoical pessimism of our author was shared by many artists as well as writers in the mid-seventeenth century, for we find it in the haunting, macabre pictures of Valdes Leal, especially in "Las Postrimerías," which he painted for the Hospital de la Caridad in Seville.

After the death of Lope de Vega in 1635, Calderón became the dictator of the theater, and from that day until his

[30] The play must have been written when the Spaniards still believed they could reconquer Portugal. It was first printed in 1651. J. Geddes, *El Alcalde de Zalamea*. New York, 1918, Introd. pp. xxii-xxiii.

The Spanish Theater

death, he reigned supreme. According to Professor Valbuena, one of Calderón's stanchest admirers, he is the great master of the Baroque era in the theater. If Fray Luis de Leon was the poet of the later sixteenth century and Cervantes of the period between the two centuries Calderón, embodying as he did the dramatic ideals of Lope, the decorative elements of Góngora's poetry, and the theological casuistry of the century is both universal and of his own epoch. But there are two periods in his works which have to be distinguished: the first, in which he follows the trend of Lope's dramas, contenting himself with modifying the technical ideas and style of his predecessor; the second, in which he is the master of his own muse and strikes out in a new direction. The Lopesque period of Calderón's work was in his youthful years, from 1630 to 1640. His creative period was in his mature years, after 1635. Only after that year do we discover the essential Calderón who, like an anchorite, renounced the rebellious ideas of his youth and with self-denial purified his style of all that he considered gross and excessive.[31]

The Mayor of Zalamea (1651)

Lope de Vega had written a play entitled El Alcalde de Zalamea concerning the peasantry of Extremadura; the hero of the play, Pedro Crespo, the Mayor, administers justice impartially to all. The two daughters of the Mayor elope of their own free will with two officers. The Mayor eventually captures the officers and forces them to marry his daughters. The King and Don Lope de Figueroa then arrive, and are treated with all the honors by the Alcalde, but Don Lope de Figueroa, who has heard of the escapade of the officers, asks to have them appear before him, as they have been guilty of a criminal offense. The Mayor then points to their bodies swinging from the balcony. The girls are sent by their father to a convent, and he promises to pay the dowry the girls need for admission into the Order. Crespo is appointed perpetual Mayor of Zalamea. Calderón, in spite of using many passages of Lope de Vega's play word for word, nevertheless adapted

[31] In La Vida es Sueño (Life's a Dream), 1635, Calderón anticipates the Discours de la Méthode of Descartes and his metaphysical meditations (1643).

it to suit his own dramatic technique. He evidently had vivid recollections of his own experiences under the colors, for in his adaptation of Lope's play there is a wealth of military atmosphere. He had witnessed many scenes of lack of discipline in the Catalán campaign of 1640, and he thus depicts most effectively the spirit of lawlessness among the troops of Philip II in the invasion of Portugal. He gives zest to the play as well as historical significance by his presentation of the great old warrior Don Lope de Figueroa, who was a link with Don John of Austria, and the campaign in Flanders as well as the Portuguese campaign. Don Lope shows his true mettle when he has to face the Mayor, Pedro Crespo, who has as strong a personality as he has. It is significant that Calderón modeled himself upon Lope de Vega when treating the subject of the peasantry with which he was unfamiliar. Nevertheless, Pedro Crespo is an admirably drawn character and impresses us by his honesty, integrity and sense of dignity. He is always more than able to hold his own against Don Lope de Figueroa. The minor characters, too, give color and variety to the play. Rebolledo, the swashbuckling adventurer, and his moll, La Chispa, come out of the picaresque novels, and so does the grotesque Don Mendo, the penniless hidalgo, and his servant Nuño, who plays the part of the *gracioso*. It is only in the characters of the Captain and the heroine Isabel that we find the *estilo culto* which followed in the wake of Góngora's later style. The Captain, who personifies the ideas of military caste and privilege, is a vigorous, well-drawn character, who recalls the Comendador in Lope de Vega's *Peribáñez*. His Góngoristic description of his method for winning a woman's love within a day is characteristic of the Baroque style of Calderón. Isabel, who, at the beginning of the play, impresses us by her modest dignity, loses some of our sympathy in the great scene in the third act when she describes in euphuistic style her tragic experiences, and we are forced to the conclusion that Calderón failed to create heroines who could compare with those of Lope de Vega or Tirso de Molina.

Calderón made his most valuable contribution to world drama when he joined the great dramatists of Western Man with his symbolic play *El Mágico Prodigioso* (which Shelley called "The Wonder-Working Magician") and his universal masterpiece *Life's a Dream*. Segismundo, the Spanish Hamlet, is the Cartesian hero of the period, and his two soliloquies are the two Solomonic columns that support the whole burden of the mighty drama.

THE DRAMATISTS, THE ACTORS, AND THEIR AUDIENCE

When comparing Spain's theater during the era of Philip III and Philip IV with that of England in the days of Elizabeth and James I, we discover many differences, in spite of similarities in general arrangement. In London boys always played women's parts until the Restoration in 1660, whereas in Spain, since the days of Lope de Rueda, actresses were a regular feature, especially in the provinces, and after 1587, owing to the competition created by the popularity of the Italian Columbines in the troupes of Ganassa and the Martinellis, women played at Court as well as in the two Madrid theaters. Lope de Vega wrote many of his plays to give opportunities to particular actresses to show off their talents.

Scenic arrangements were as primitive in Spain as in England, though after 1580 they had improved to such an extent that *comedias* could present upon the stage miraculous visions, artistically contrived scenes, alarums of war, and even actual horses.[32] According to Morel Fatio the plays representing the lives of saints—which became *de rigueur* after the closing of the theaters in 1598, when the theologians introduced restrictions—lent themselves to scenic devices which, though primitive, attracted the general public.[33] Nevertheless no attempt was made at optical illusion, and owing to the absence of a drop-curtain, the actors at the beginning of a play had to enter before the eyes of the spectators. There was, however, a curtain at the back of the stage, like the traverses of the Elizabethan theater, which could be drawn aside to represent a bedroom, a chapel, or a cave. The sides of the stage were also hung with curtains of green baize, according to Cervantes, which were arranged so that the public could see behind them. At the back of the stage there was a gallery (*lo alto del teatro*) which could represent the walls of

[32] Schack, *op. cit.*, Vol. I, p. 308.
[33] Morel Fatio, *Bulletin Hispanique*. Oct.-Dec., 1901, p. 481.

the city, the ramparts of a castle, or a mountain. The gallery, incidentally, ran along the back of the stage, and extended the gallery of the theater.[34] The Spanish stage, according to A. F. Schack, was not nearly so deep as the modern stage, but was as wide, and its decorations consisted of curtains hung at the side, leaving various entrances free. These represented a room, a hall, a street, or a forest, without any change, though sometimes in Lope's plays trees were represented on the stage or painted on canvas hangings at the sides. If the stage was unoccupied for a moment and persons came on through another entrance a change of scene had to be imagined by the spectator, though none was visible on the stage. Thus, descriptive dialogue was of utmost importance for indicating time and place. Only when the progress of the action could not well be otherwise indicated was recourse had to expedients of scenic arts, and such use was mostly left to the judgment of the theatrical director, the "author," as he was called in those days, as the poets gave only the most minimal stage directions.[35] It is important to note that Lope de Vega and his followers did not divide their *comedias* into scenes, nor did any of the older dramatists. The only division they made was into three acts. The breakdown into scenes was the work of later editors. Lope de Vega, who wrote for the stage for half a century, refers in his prologues to the various parts of his *comedias* to the innovations introduced by his rivals, one of which consisted in elaborate scenic appliances or *tramoyas,* and in the Dialogued Prologue prefixed to Part XVI (1623) of his plays says: "I have come to great misfortune and I suppose that this is due to one of three reasons: either because there are no good actors, or because the poets are bad, or because the public lacks understanding, for the directors avail themselves of machinery, the poets of the carpenters, and the auditors of their eyes . . . they are justly moved by this machinery to delight the eyes but not by the Spanish *comedia,* where the figures rise and descend so clumsily and animals and birds appear in like manner, which the ignorance of the women and the uncouth mechanics among men come

---

34 H. Rennert, *op. cit.,* p. 88.
35 H. Rennert, *op. cit.,* p. 88.

to see." Lope's complaint shows that the audiences had changed in the third decade of the seventeenth century, and the "many-headed" now went to see the play, not to hear it. Again in the Prologue to Part XIX of his *Comedias* (Madrid, 1623), in the dialogue between the Poet and the Theater, the former says: "Since they use *apariencias*, which they call *tramoyas*, I do not care to publish my *comedias*." Lope never concealed his scorn for the arts of the scene painter and the machinery. As Fitzmaurice-Kelly says, "Lope needed no scene painter to make good his deficiencies," and his opinions are echoed by the Canon in Chapter 48 of *Don Quixote*, Part I. It is significant that the word "appearances," which was the technical Spanish term for stage machinery, was current in England in the first half of the seventeenth century.[36]

In considering the production of the *comedias* in the *siglo de oro* it is also important to contrast the arrangement of the Spanish stage with the Elizabethan and the French of the period. The Spanish stage, though wider, did not project into the theater as did the Elizabethan, and its two sides were provided with the hangings already discussed. In France, on the other hand, at the Hôtel de Bourgogne (the only public theater in Paris during the second half of the sixteenth and the first thirty years of the seventeenth century), the stage setting was that of the Mysteries of the Middle Ages, which consisted of two parts: the mansions, and the free space between and in front of the mansions. The mansions, incidentally, were simply houses or buildings to which the action was transported during the play.

The attitude of the vociferous public in the theater had an important bearing on the evolution of drama during the Golden Age. The audiences in Spain in those days were as noisy, pitiless, and as hard to please as their descendants at the modern bullfight. The "musketeers" in the *patio* or pit constituted the most formidable part of the audience, and were especially feared by both author and actor, for their caprice decided the fate of the *comedia*. Shakespeare again and again voices his spleen against the rabble, but Lope is even more violent and scornful. In the prologue to the first

[36] J. P. Collier, *Annuals of the Stage*. London, 1831, Vol. III, p. 372.

volume of his *Comedias* (1628) he addresses the *vulgo* thus: "To you I address myself, wild beasts, for to the noble it is unnecessary; they speak for me better than I myself could do. Here are my *comedias:* treat them as is your wont; not as is just, but as is your pleasure, for they face you fearlessly and with contempt, and having passed the ordeal of your whistlings, they can now readily pass that of your noisy ravings. If they displease you I shall rejoice, for it will be a proof that they are good; if they please you, however, then the money they will have cost you will be, for me, a sufficient revenge for this proof of their worthlessness." Lope de Vega was not always so arrogant toward "the musty superfluity," for he confesses sadly in his *New Art of Playmaking* (1609) that the playwright must serve up to his public the subjects most likely to win their applause, and his words may be paraphrased in words written by Dr. Johnson in the following century:

> *The drama's laws the drama's patrons give,*
> *For we that live to please, must please to live.*

Even the Court poet Calderón did not consider it a loss of dignity to beg the applause of the "musketeers," and at the end of one of his plays, the *gracioso* begs the honorable public, in the name of all the actors, "pardon for all our faults." Nor were the women in the audience less disorderly or more charitable. The more respectable women who occupied the *aposentos*, or boxes, or went masked (as they also did in English theaters) behaved themselves decorously, but the horde of women who occupied the *cazuela* (stewing-pan), where men were not allowed to enter, were as vociferous as the pit, and a police officer was always stationed in that gallery to keep order. Like the "musketeers," the women in the "cage," as it was also called, pelted the actors with cucumbers, orange peels or anything at hand, to show their disapproval, and they generally came prepared with rattles, whistles or keys, and even the estimable Roque de Figueroa, an actor famed for his unruffled dignity, addressed them prayerfully from the footlights, thus showing the awe which even the most famous players felt toward these impudent wenches of the rabblement. As Rennert says, Roque's prayer, begging the indulgence of his auditors, is the best evidence of the character of this *vulgo,* before whom the works of the greatest dramatists of Spain were represented.[37]

The conditions we have described explain the many additions to the Spanish *comedia* in the seventeenth century, which became, as a result, the most complex sort of entertainment ever given in a playhouse.[38] The success or failure of a *comedia* generally depended upon the judgment of the mob, and this was conveyed by applause and the shouts of *Victor* in the case of success, and by whistles and hisses when the play was doomed. The managers, producers, authors and actors tried by every means to woo the favor of the public. This they did by reading the play privately to the chiefs of the various claques and procuring their approval. The leader, who was a cobbler, a sausage maker or some such ignorant member of the general public, sat surrounded by his claque, who yawned when he yawned, laughed when he laughed, and then, at the signal of his whistle, burst out all together in a chorus of catcalls and whistlings, overwhelming the play. To placate the unruly members of the audience it was customary to recite a *loa* or *introito,* which begged for their good will. This was either a monologue or a short sketch performed by a few of the cast. After that came the first act, but sometimes after the *loa* there was a *paso* before the first act, or a song and a dance; and between the first act and the second, and between the second act and the third, there were the *entremes* and the *sainete.* And in addition to these short interludes, which kept the rabble amused, there were *bayles* or dance numbers which were often elaborate ballets, and sometimes one of the actors or actresses, like La Chispa or Rebolledo in Calderón's play, would sing a *jácara* or popular ballad, either from the stage or from the women's gallery. According to Augustín de Rojas, the plays always concluded with a *bayle,* "for this sent the people home in a happy mood." [39] Ramón Pérez de Ayala, the distinguished novelist of modern Spain, once compared the performance of a *comedia* of the Golden Age to a succulent banquet: "First," he said, "we have the *loa* or *apéritif;* then the *jornadas* or acts

---

[37] H. Rennert, *op. cit.,* p. 120.

[38] M. MacGowan and W. Melnitz, *Golden Ages in the Theater.* Englewood, New Jersey, 1959.

[39] A. de Rojas, *Viage Entretenido.* Madrid, 1603, p. 126.

of the play, which are the *platos fuertes*, or joints; and between them we have the *entremeses* or *entremets;* and at the end, the *sainete* as dessert. We Spaniards are moderate in most matters, but when we start eating, we never stop until repletion is reached." And Somerset Maugham, in *Don Fernando,* has an enlightening remark to make on the peculiar qualities of Lope de Vega, whose *comedias* at their best are inspired improvisations. "His plays," he says, "can best be appreciated if you look upon them as operatic 'books' in which verse takes the part of music. He will write a bravura passage in which three persons, for instance, embroider upon an idea, each one ending his speech with the same refrain, so that you can almost hear the burst of applause that greets the ingenuity. Sometimes a character will present a theme in four lines and then enlarge upon it in stanzas, each of which ends with one of the four lines. It is as much a set aria as *La Donna è mobile.*"

The Mayor of Zalamea, too, in spite of its picaresque scenes with La Chispa, Rebolledo, the *gracioso,* Nuño, and the humorous interplay between the gruff Don Lope de Figueroa and his equally obstinate opponent, Pedro Crespo, the Mayor, is a serious play with an undercurrent of tragedy. That play, like *Peribáñez,* is a magnificent tribute to the exalted passion for honor which must be set among the enduring characteristics of Spain.

Summing up the Golden Age of the Theater in Spain, we must remember that great as the popularity of the drama was in Spain, and rapid as had been its rise, its decline and fall were almost equally rapid, and by 1650 the Spanish drama was clearly on the wane. The death in 1635 of the founder of the national theater, Lope de Vega, was such a serious loss that in a few years the magnificent structure began to totter. It is strange to find that by the middle of the century all the greatest dramatists, with the single exception of Calderón, were dead. Guillén de Castro died in 1631; Alarcón's death occurred in 1639; followed by that of Mira de Amescua in 1644; Tirso de Molina died in 1648, but he had ceased to write for the stage before Lope's death. Of the lesser lights of the drama, Montalbán died in 1638, and Luis Vélez de

Guevara in 1644. Calderón alone was still writing *comedias* after the middle of the century, for even his followers, Rojas Zorrilla and Moreto, had written their last plays by that time. As Rennert points out, at the close as at the beginning, the Spanish national drama exhibits a striking parallel to the English, which had also produced all that was best in it before the closing of the theaters in 1642, at the beginning of the Civil War.

A SURVIVAL

The Mystery Play of Elche

With the great modern men of the Spanish theater, whether playwrights such as Jacinto Benavente and Federico García Lorca, or musicians like Manuel de Falla, the theater became, as it always was in the Golden Age of the Spanish drama, a ritualistic performance in which the actors gave the impression of taking part in a dance, for all Spanish art seems to descend from the dance, and it is significant that in Spain today we find the dance and, indeed, drama as part of religion. In Seville at Corpus Christi, the religious dance of the *Seises* is performed in front of the High Altar of the Cathedral, and at Christmas time in the Cathedral of Palma in Majorca the ancient ritual dating from the fifteenth century of the *Canción de la Sibila*, or Song of Last Judgment, is sung dramatically by a little boy in the pulpit.

But the most interesting survival of ritual in drama is the Mystery Play of the Mediterranean town of Elche called the *Festa de Elche*, which is still performed in that town every year on the day of the Assumption of Our Lady, on the fifteenth of August.

The Mystery of Elche is the only example of a Spanish lyrical play of the thirteenth century which has survived to our time. It is thus an early forerunner of the music drama, for opera did not appear in Italy until 1600. It is the only sacred play which escaped unscathed from the Council of Trent (which forbade religious plays), and in it priests take part as characters. What makes the Mystery of Elche unique is that the thirteenth-century chant has been fused with polyphony of the sixteenth century, and a complete music-drama celebrating the passing of Our Lady and Her Assumption, is the result.

The Mystery of Elche is performed by the inhabitants of Elche every year; the words and music have been transmitted orally from father to son, century after century. The earliest *consueta* or text, according to legend, was found in a casket floating in the sea in 1370. Afterward there were four *con-suetas*, of which only one exists today, arranged by the Beneficiado Lozano in 1709. In spite of the *consueta*, most of the actors and singers sing by tradition, for they have not learned music. In modern days it is mainly due to the Alicantine composer Oscar Esplá that the music of the Mystery Play can be heard today in its full ancient tradition, and through his influence the work was declared a national monument of Spain.

The Elche Mystery Play finds an ideal setting in a city which has been called "the Jerusalem of the West," for it is encircled by thousands of palm trees which create biblical surroundings for the drama. The first performance is the general rehearsal, which takes place on the 13th of August, and music lovers may appreciate the details of the music and drama undisturbed by the great multitude which fills the church for the two acts of the drama on the eve and the day of the Assumption.

No drama in the world conveys more powerfully the sense of theater and ritual in one, as does this unique musical Mystery Play. For this reason we have included our translation of the text of the play in this volume. It seems to us that the *Mystery Play of Elche* is a precious illustration of how the Spanish theater has developed through the ages, and it should be remembered by those who look upon the theater as the inspiration of the people.

THE
GALLANT,
THE
BAWD,
AND THE
FAIR LADY

❧§❧

Interlude – Extravaganza

by

JUAN RUIZ

Archpriest of Hita

from

THE BOOK OF GOOD LOVE
(*El Libro de Buen Amor*)

❧§❧

DRAMATIS PERSONAE

Juan Ruiz, Archpriest of Hita, Compère
Sir Percy Pumpkin (Don Melón de Ortiz), a young man about
    town
Toddle-Troll (Trotaconventos), an old bawd
Lady Sloe-Eyes (Doña Endrina), a merry widow
Mother Mutterkin (Doña Rama)

PERIOD: The first half of the fourteenth century.

The first version of the *Libro de Buen Amor* comes from the
Toledo manuscript, 1330; the second, from the Salamanca
manuscript, dated 1343. The Archpriest was probably born
in the beginning of the last third of the thirteenth century
at Alcalá de Henares, and wrote his work in old age. He
made additions to the primitive version in 1343, when he
was in jail at the instance of the Archbishop of Toledo, Don
Gil de Albornoz. He died about 1351. We have used the
palaeographic edition of Ducamín, Toulouse, 1901.

SCENE 1.

The crowded market place of Alcalá de Henares.

ARCHPRIEST. *Sir Percy Pumpkin standing under the archway
  sees Lady Sloe-Eyes pass by.*
SIR PERCY PUMPKIN. Look at Lady Sloe-Eyes sailing through
  the square!
  What a beauty! Ah, what charm she has!
  What a lithe and slender figure, what a graceful swanlike
  neck!
  With her flowing locks, her rosebud mouth and dimples,
  She is the cynosure of all neighboring eyes,
  As she trips daintily along the sunny street.
  But when she shines on us those dark brown eyes like sloes,
  She pierces all our hearts with Cupid's seven darts.
  But hush! This is no fitting place to prate about my love;
  I'm trembling like a leaf, I can't control my hands or feet,
  I'm pale, and feeling faint, and just about to swoon,
  And my fear of those around makes me babble like a fool.
  I declare I scarcely know where on earth I am,
  Nor whether I am coming, nor whither I am going:
  No one but a fool would try to hold converse
  With a pretty lady in the market place:
  Who knows but the dog that barks behind the door
  May be loosely chained? what shall I do?
  My best plan is to humor her with a playful jest or two,
  And mask my subtle purpose, but in a cozy place
  I'll speak to her in earnest and unbosom all my thoughts.
ARCHPRIEST. *The young man with a sweeping gesture bows
  to Lady Sloe-Eyes and addresses her.*
SIR PERCY PUMPKIN. My lady, a niece of mine who is living
  in Toledo
  Commends herself to you, and sends you kindly greetings:
  If there were time and space, and you were so disposed,
  I should so like to meet you and get to know you better.
  My parents lately wanted me to wed
  A rich young heiress, only daughter
  Of Don Doubloon, the millionaire,

But I refused, and said I'd only wed
A girl of my choice who would win my heart.
(*Lowering his voice he says aside to her:*)
Hush! I was only jesting but now they have gone off,
And no one is near, I must confess, my lady,
There is no woman in all the world
I love as much as you: why for two years and more
I have been suffering all the pangs of love,
And, do believe me, they rack me day and night.
But nothing more I'll say, my pretty lady,
Till you give an answer to my stumbling words.
Do tell me truly what is in your mind,
And let us see within each other's heart.

LADY SLOE-EYES (*scornfully*). I don't care a rap for all you've
said,
Many Sloe-Eyes are tricked by philanderers like you,
All men are playboys and deceive the girls they meet;
And do not imagine I wish to hear your babble:
Go seek another victim, and fill her head with lies.

SIR PERCY PUMPKIN. How ferocious her ladyship when she
plays her wanton wiles!
Yet though our hands have fingers they are not all the same:
Neither are men alike, nor do their thoughts agree,
And my fur lining's black and white, yet it's all of rabbit
wool.
The just, alas, must suffer, as though they all were sinners
And another's fault may hurt many a guiltless man.

LADY SLOE-EYES. But I don't want another's fault now to injure
me.

SIR PERCY PUMPKIN. Do have a few words with me under
yonder arch.

LADY SLOE-EYES. Don't let these passers-by see you talking
to me here.

ARCHPRIEST. *Lady Sloe-Eyes walks slowly under the archway.
She is proud and debonair, though gentle and demure in
mien, and keeps her eyes modestly lowered as she walks.
Sir Percy then continues his conversation.*

SIR PERCY PUMPKIN. Be kind to me, my lady, and listen to
my tale:
I must blurt out my forlorn love and my despair.
Imagine I'm being flippant just to pass the time,

For I don't know what to do since you're so obstinate.
Yet I'll call God to witness, lady, and this earth as well
That every word I'm saying is the plain unvarnished truth;
But you are colder than the snow upon the mountain side,
And you're so young a girl that I am terrified,
For it's a risky thing to talk to one as young as you,
Who would sooner be playing ball than talking to a man.
But though youth is the season for frolicking and dalliance,
Mature age wins in judgment, for through experience we
learn.
So I beg you to be kind and meet me another day,
And I'm sure in the end you'll listen to my plea.
For though man doesn't eat the apple, nor even start to
nibble,
He gazes at the forbidden fruit, and its sight rejoices him
And so to have a vision of so ravishing a lady,
And converse with her enraptures a man's heart.

LADY SLOE-EYES. I see no dishonor if a young man and a lady,
Converse together, if there's reason in their talk,
But duennas and ladies must have their answers ready,
When any man would tilt in words with them.
This privilege I'll grant you as I would to any man,
So speak when you wish if my honor you will guard,
And I'll jest in words too, if you give me the chance,
But don't think I'll let you make a fool of me,
Nor can I now consent to stay with you unchaperoned,
For if a lady were observed alone with a gentleman,
It would blight her reputation and lead to her ill fame.
So if my chaperon is present, I'll have a talk with you.

SIR PERCY PUMPKIN. My lady, such a favor earns my deepest
gratitude.
I only hope with God's help the day will soon arrive,
When I can prove to you what a friend you have in me.
I'd say more, but I dare not, lest you might take offense.

LADY SLOE-EYES. Leave that to me, Sir Percy, I'll tell you
soon enough.

SIR PERCY PUMPKIN. My lady, promise me, if the day should
ever come,
When we can both agree, as I do fondly hope,
That you and I will seal our agreement with a kiss:
This is not much to ask, but I shall be overjoyed.

LADY SLOE-EYES. How often have I heard of ladies tricked
by kisses,
For kisses kindle mighty fires, in a lonely woman's heart,
And she's conquered, once she grants such favors to a man.
I'll not grant you kisses, but I'll let you take my hand;
My mother's on her way from Mass, so I must haste away,
In case she might suspect me of giddiness and levity,
But there'll be time this summer when we may talk together.

ARCHPRIEST. *With these words Lady Sloe-Eyes trips away,
and the lovesick Sir Percy murmurs to himself that this is
the finest day he has known since he was born.*

SCENE 2.

ARCHPRIEST. *Here comes Sir Percy Pumpkin in quest of his
old bawd, Mother Toddle-Troll.*

SIR PERCY PUMPKIN. In my predicament I'll have to go in
search
Of Mother Toddle-Troll, my darling old bawd:
As she is the queen of all the go-betweens,
She will give me help in my present plight.
She is, I know, a witch of Satan, and a whorish bawd,
One who peddles jewels, lays traps, and snares all and
sundry;
She's a bag full of tricks, and a flaming Troy as well,
Why, she'll set a town on fire and reduce it all to ashes,
Such a ruin she brings wherever she appears.
Watch her nose her way, as from house to house she goes,
Bartering gifts and samples, mixing with high and low;
In love affairs she's a gust of wind, blowing from the sierra.
Like a mill she whirls her sails, and makes the millstone
grind;
Look, here she comes, the peerless paragon of bawds.
(*Enter* MOTHER TODDLE-TROLL.)

SIR PERCY PUMPKIN. Welcome in God's name, dear Mother
Toddle-Troll,

You have come in the nick of time, for I now am most
    anxious
To entrust my life and fortunes to your care:
If you won't help me, my life is at an end.
I have heard many men sing your praises to the skies,
And how you always help all those who are in trouble,
That is why I now seek most urgently your help:

TODDLE-TROLL. Out with your story, man, and place your trust
    in me,
Put your cards on the table, and tell what's in your mind,
And I'll do all I can, and I'll be truly loyal;
The business of a go-between is one that needs discretion,
Why, we hide more deceits, more trickeries and rogueries
Than any hell kitchen or brothel in the town.
If the people only knew what trafficking of trollops
We plot and plan for you and others of your ilk,
What flaming rows and riots would break out everywhere;
For many weddings we arrange lead to years of penance,
And many tambourines we sell have bells that never jingle.

SIR PERCY PUMPKIN. I love a fair duenna more than any girl
    I've seen,
And she, unless I'm wrong, has a soft spot for me;
To avoid a host of troubles I kept the matter dark,
For I'm by nature timid, and I know by harsh experience
That in our community the slightest tittle-tattle
Swells into mighty rumor, which once it starts to simmer,
Takes long to die away, even though it be untrue;
For gossips out of envy spread their false reports,
And the mean always thrive on the lowest chicanery.
Wherefore go, I beseech you, as an envoy to my neighbor,
And speak to my lady soft words on my behalf;
Arrange this whole affair as best you can for both of us.

TODDLE-TROLL. I'll go right away to your pretty neighbor's
    house,
And cast such a glamour, and make the girl so pliant
With sugar and almonds that your heartburn will soon
    vanish,
But tell me, my son, who is the pretty lady?

SIR PERCY PUMPKIN. She is called Lady Sloe-Eyes.

TODDLE-TROLL.   I know her
    very well.

SIR PERCY PUMPKIN. But for heaven's sake, mother, prepare
 yourself for squalls.
TODDLE-TROLL. As the girl has been married I'm sure she
 will consent;
 When a jennet has been ridden once, she'll not refuse the
  saddle:
 And wax, though it's frozen stiff, and harder than stone,
 Once your hands have warmed it, and kneaded it as well,
 Will bend itself double a hundred times and more.
 So every widow bends, once she's caught by the glamour.
 Mark well, my friend, what all the proverbs say:
 "Once grist is in the mill, it is first come first served";
 And, "A message delayed means a man dismayed,"
 And, "A man forewarned is a man forearmed."
 So this is not the time for laziness and sleepiness,
 The duenna you're mad about is bespoken to another,
 And your rival at this moment is hot upon her trail,
 And his lineage is noble, and is equal to your own,
 But your pleas take precedence, in spite of all he has given
 And I am only lukewarm, as he is too niggardly
 For one who is so rich; but he sent me a pelisse,
 A handsome one it was, neither big nor very small:
 When your own gifts come later, if they're of such a size
 That they break all the records, you will win the prize.
 This duenna you mention is entirely in my power,
 Except with my approval no man will ever win her;
 For I know what she's thinking, and what she wants to do,
 And she follows my counsels more than her own wishes:
 But I've said quite enough for you to bear in mind.
 Such is a bawd's vocation, and I've plenty on my hands.
 Now if a little money you could give me on the side,
 Which I can hand to this girl and to the other lasses,
 I'll get to work and cast the glamour over all of them,
 And so bedevil and enmesh them by my subtle snares,
 That I'll land one and all of them into the bag.
SIR PERCY PUMPKIN. Dear Mother Toddle-Troll, I'll pay you
 right royally,
 And all my house and goods will be at your disposal.
 As a start, take this pelisse, and be off with you at once,
 And don't be a laggard, but get down to your job,
 And before you go, listen to my parting words:

If you put all your energy and your dexterity
Into this enterprise, I'll make this bet,
That personal profits and riches you will get.   (*Exeunt.*)

SCENE 3.

ARCHPRIEST. *Look at the old bawd Toddle-Troll departing*
in high glee, jingling her joybells and casting her evil eye
over women with her gems and rings and face towels, and
when she comes to Lady Sloe-Eyes's house she knocks at
the door and shouts: "Here are fine face towels: who will
buy them?" She knocks again at the door.

LADY SLOE-EYES. Come in, don't be shy.

(*Enter* TODDLE-TROLL.)

TODDLE-TROLL. Here's a ring, Lady Sloe-Eyes; slip it on your
    finger;
If you'll keep a secret I'll whisper a tale
In your ear which I heard from a mutual friend.

ARCHPRIEST. *Lady Sloe-Eyes is all agog and cocks her ear.*

TODDLE-TROLL. Young lady, I see you are locked in a cage;
You'll grow old, my honey, if you don't now and then
Take a turn in the market place. Why your pretty face
Will not dazzle a soul inside these four walls.
Now there's a gay bawdy house here in the city,
Where you could meet daily the pick of young men;
When I go there I watch those lads growing handsomer;
Nowhere could a girl find a choicer snuggery.
Although I am poor those lads treat me like royalty,
And Sir Percy Pumpkin's the flower of them all.
No one can touch him in breeding or property,
He sows his wild oats with the wildest of rakes,
But among steady fellows all think the world of him,
For he's gentle and lamblike, and no one, I'm told,
Has ever seen him clench his fists for a fight.
It is no small exploit, to win to his side
The mad by his wisdom, for this signifies

That though among the wise there is no wiser,
Yet when he is consorting with the madcaps
He just plays crazy, for no man that's wise
Goes mad just because he consorts with a loon.
Such thoughts often come when I jingle my tambourine.
I am sure you will find no one here who can vie
With Sir Percy, but don't think that he is a prodigal,
For he and his dad are as like as two peas,
Just as we fancy we see in a calf
The ox it will turn into; so do we judge
A man's disposition by the work that he does.
Now mark my words, dearie, this man, I believe,
Would marry you instantly if you were keen.
My matchmaking scheme with girl clients has been
To question them up and down as in a game,
So tell me your secrets and open your heart.

LADY SLOE-EYES. Tell me, my good woman, who is this great
    paragon?
How well off is he? Give me time to reflect.

TODDLE-TROLL. Who is he? you ask: he's a treasure, my lady,
God brings you this moment for your own pleasure.
He's a well set up young man, a neighbor of yours;
Believe me, dearie, not one of your suitors
Can be compared to him: why the day you were born
The white beans foretold you a wonderful destiny;
And then reserved this young man for your joy.

LADY SLOE-EYES. Cease all this sermonizing. I am positively
    certain
That prattling young man will yet give me the slip,
Many a time he comes here with his fatuous cajoleries,
But neither he nor you can sway me in the slightest.
A girl who is trusting and believes your lying tales,
And pins her faith on men who swear eternal love,
Binds herself hand and foot and gags her mind and heart;
Her tears soon make a sorry havoc of her face.
Stop pestering me, for I have a host of other troubles,
And many try to frighten me with gruesome threats of
    violence,
But I don't want to think of all those worries now.

TODDLE-TROLL. Mark my words, honey, since you became a
    lonely widow,

You are quite unprotected and no one is afraid of you.
For a widow who is left alone to face the world, I say,
Is more forlorn and lonesome than a stray cow that's at bay,
But that young man can always be your sturdiest champion,
And act as your bulwark against a sea of troubles,
Such as legal actions, threats of violence, moratoriums.
For many say that they intend to sue you in the courts,
And they will end by robbing you of all your goods and chattels,
Leaving you like a turkey that's plucked of every feather.
When your late lamented husband used to live by yonder arch
His house in the street shone peacefully in the sun,
But when the master of the house no longer rules the roost
The light of the home is quenched and peace departs forever.

ARCHPRIEST. *At this point the old bawd in more emotional tones begins to cast the glamour over Lady Sloe-Eyes.*

TODDLE-TROLL. Here you are, my daughter, a widow and a concubine,
As lonesome as a turtledove without a mate to care for her.
And this, I believe, is why you're thin and pale,
For where there are only women, there is nothing but bickering.
God bless the home where a good man rules the family,
And pleasure and happiness go hand in hand in harmony.
That is why I wish yonder youth could be your mate;
With him not many days would pass ere you would start to blossom.

LADY SLOE-EYES. It wouldn't look well for me to wed within the year,
For no widow remarries till her year of mourning's passed.
If I were now to wed, I'd be shamed before the world,
I'd lose all the legacy bequeathed to me, and win
But scant respect from the second man I'd marry.

TODDLE-TROLL. My child, the year has already run its course;
So follow my advice and take this man as groom;
And let us go to see him, and you will win the day,
Once he discovers he is closely linked with you.
Your omens, dearie, promise the brightest of all future.
What profit can there be for you in a widow's weeds.

Meandering with bowed head amidst the jibes of others?
Cast off your mourning, honey, and wed this very year!
This year's fateful swallow never gave a wiser counsel.
LADY SLOE-EYES. Stop! I shouldn't dare to do what you advise,
Or what that young man asks, so cease your provocations,
And plague me no more with your litanies of words;
They have fallen on deaf ears as I don't want to remarry,
Though over a hundred have begged me for my hand,
And now you are pestering me and driving me mad.

SCENE 4.

ARCHPRIEST. *Toddle-Troll, eager to enhance her service as
bawd, and to draw a fee from Sir Percy Pumpkin, toddles
off now to tell him that Dame Mutterkin, Lady Sloe-Eyes's
cantankerous old mother, has married the latter off to some-
one else.*
TODDLE-TROLL. My son, my best advice is forget what you
can't get;
What is the use of beating your head against a wall?
SIR PERCY PUMPKIN. Woe's me! how grim are the tidings you
now bring,
You wicked old killjoy, why did you tell me now?
No good you'll ever do will efface the harm you've done.
A plague upon you, gossiping, huckst'ring old bawd,
Who turn all topsy-turvy by your rogueries.
My limbs now tremble, my strength evaporates,
My life is ebbing, now all my hopes have fled.
Since my love has left me to wed another,
I don't care a fig for this poor life of mine;
As she'll not be mine, let death claim me now.
TODDLE-TROLL. In one brief hour a sorrow passes and a wound
is healed,
And after storms and lashing rains come the gentle breezes
And through the murky clouds there bursts the golden sun,
Our health and life return after days of suffering.

Comfort yourself, my son, and put your trust in me;
The rapturous joys of love are in the offing now,
Lady Sloe-Eyes is ours and will obey my word.
She will not hear of marrying anyone but you,
For all her thoughts are centered in yourself alone,
And if you love her madly, she loves you still more.

SIR PERCY PUMPKIN. Old mother, tell me, what do these words
    mean?
You act like a mother when her child is crying,
She pets and comforts him to stop his sobs.
Are you joking, and making a fool of me?

TODDLE-TROLL. A lovesick swain is just like a timorous bird,
Which has escaped the claws of a preying hawk;
Ever after it believes that the hunter's near,
Ready to pounce, and so it is afraid.

SIR PERCY PUMPKIN. Why can't you tell me whether she loves
    me now
Or ever will? A girl in love never hides
Her feelings, but betrays them by her sighs,
Her pallor, and her speech.

TODDLE-TROLL.   My dear young friend,
The girl's expression shows she is mad for you,
Why when I mention you I see her blush,
And lose her composure, though through weariness,
At times, she is silent, but she then entreats
Me to go on with my story, and I then
Pretend I can't recall, and she begins
To speak but stops and listens dreamily.
I note in her many signs of restlessness,
For she often throws her arms around my neck,
And we remain thus locked in our embrace:
We're always talking of you, but when someone
Arrives we change the conversation and
Her lips quiver slightly; she then blushes and
Turns pale once more, and her little heart beats faster.
She seizes my hand, and presses it in hers,
And when I mention your name she looks at me,
Sighing deeply and tries to restrain herself,
But her eyes gleam with excitement, and I'd wager
That she'll not sleep a wink when she lies with you,
And there are other details I have noted:

She never denies, but always says she loves you:
The fruit on the branch is ripe and about to fall,
And Sloe-Eyes will run here if Toddle-Troll but call.

SIR PERCY PUMPKIN. As you, mother, now raise my hopes so
    high,
Do not relax your efforts but press on,
For slackness loses many an opportunity
And many a victory is won by a trick.

TODDLE-TROLL. My friend, you may be sure that with my help
You will be comforted, for I shall trick
That minx of a duenna, and bring her to heel,
But now I must ask you to mark my words:
All I've received from you is a mere pelisse,
But if you want to nibble dainties, you
Must pay your score. There are men who sometimes fail
To carry out the promises they've made.
When ordering they're prodigals you find,
But when they are asked for cash they turn into misers.

SIR PERCY PUMPKIN. Have no fears on that score, mother
    Toddle-Troll,
What meaner action than to hoodwink the poor?
May God strike me dead if I ever swindle you!

TODDLE-TROLL. High-sounding words! but poor pot-wallopers
Always smell a rat when bigwigs promise the moon.
However now I'll test all your fine promises,
And I shall call on the lady, and I'll bring
Her to my house where she will speak with you.
But if I get you both beneath my roof,
I beg you to behave like a worthy man,
For she, poor girl, has a heart of gold,
And in one hour she'll give you all you want.   (*Exeunt.*)

SCENE 5.

ARCHPRIEST. *We now reach the house of Lady Sloe-Eyes. I
see the old bawd in the distance. She is puffing and blowing as she toddles along. Enter Toddle-Troll: she knocks*

at the door. It is Lady Sloe-Eyes's mother, the grim old
harridan Mutterkin, who answers the door.

MOTHER MUTTERKIN. Who calls?

TODDLE-TROLL. (*aside*). It is Mother Mutterkin.
Plague upon her!
My evil spirits won't let me alone!

MOTHER MUTTERKIN. What brings you here, my friend?

TODDLE-TROLL. I'm all worried and in the dumps!
That man says the most atrocious things,
And he hunts me all day as if I were a hind.
He demands the return of the ring he gave,
He says he is selling it, and as he's full of cash,
I don't understand what he wants at all.

MOTHER MUTTERKIN. I must then go and ask the neighbors
Who is this fine Sir Percy Pumpkin.   (*Exit.*)
(*Enter* LADY SLOE-EYES.)

TODDLE-TROLL. Thank God Beelzebub has whisked away
That grumpiest old harridan, your mother.
When she is with you none dare open their mouths.
Well, my girl, how are your affairs coming on?
You're buxom, and bonny as a morn in May.

LADY SLOE-EYES. What news do you bring me of that young
man?

TODDLE-TROLL. News is it? Why he's now as thin as a wraith,
And down in the dumps! There's no more flesh on him
Than you'd find on a lovesick cockerel
When Michaelmas has passed. Why wonder, child?
One who's so crazed with love can't hide his feelings.
But now my heart can understand,
And tears come into my eyes when I consider
How madly you must be in love with him:
He is forever present before your eyes.
Ever since you spoke to him he has been crazy,
And though you're silent you are even madder,
And the hidden fire of love is killing you.
Now tell me what is your real wish and pleasure,
But I must have the truth, and only the truth.
It is for you to decide now once for all,
For if I have to come here every day,
The whole district will soon get wind of it.

LADY SLOE-EYES. For this man's love I would risk anything,
  But I'm not free, for my mother watches me,
  And never leaves my side.
TODDLE-TROLL.   May a plague consume
  That wizened old hag who gives her daughter the pip,
  And may she soon be coffined and carted away,
  But Love is turbulent and breaks down doors,
  He slips past guards and leaves them all for dead;
  He brushes aside vain fears and vague suspicions,
  And the strongest locks spring open at his touch.
LADY SLOE-EYES. Alas, what troubles afflict a lover's heart,
  And allow no rest, such thoughts so torture me
  That I should prefer to die than suffer thus.
TODDLE-TROLL. Since you can't quench the flame that burns
      your heart,
  Obey the command of him who worships you,
  But don't imagine you can obliterate
  What you love most: that only Death can do.
  But now come with me to my house to rest,
  And we shall play ball and some other games,
  And I shall give you nuts and pears to eat,
  And nectarines and apples in profusion.
  From here to my house is but a step, and there
  You can slip on a flowing dressing gown,
  And relax to your heart's content. And so, my dear,
  I'll come to fetch you when the road is clear.   (*Exeunt.*)

SCENE 6.

ARCHPRIEST. *We are back in the house of Sir Percy Pumpkin,
  and here Toddle-Troll enters all bustling and bubbling with
  good news for Sir Percy.*
TODDLE-TROLL. How goes it, friend, are you in better fettle?
  No matter how poor a wizard I may be,
  I can unearth the serpent from her den!
  Tomorrow the duenna will come to speak with you:

And you may prove the truth of the ancient saying,
That the constant pilgrim always finds a meal.
Tomorrow when you're with her prove yourself a man;
Don't let her fancy that you are a cynic,
So speak and press your suit, when I'm not there
To prod you on, and mind you don't waste time;
So plenty of gab, make hay while the sun shines,
And leave her no peace, for as the saying goes:
"When they give you a heifer run with the halter."
Crave and entreat when you are wooing her,
But once her passion's kindled, then full speed ahead:
Better see her blush for shame, than have to watch
Disillusion's black looks steal across her face.

SCENE 7.

The House of Toddle-Troll.

ARCHPRIEST. *Today is the feast of Saint James the Apostle,
and it is midday, when the people are at dinner, and there
is not a soul in the streets. Lady Sloe-Eyes sets out from
her house and with her toddles along my old bawd Mother
Toddle-Troll. She leads the lady demurely towards her
house. My bawd out of the corner of her crafty eye spies
Sir Percy Pumpkin hovering in the offing. No sooner have
the pair gone into the house than up he comes, but finds
to his consternation that the door is locked and barred.
He knocks loudly.*

TODDLE-TROLL (*inside*). Hello! Who's there? What noise is
that? Is it a man or the wind? I think it's a man! I'm not
wrong! Do you see? Do you see? How the devil's on the
watch for the pitch black sin! Is it he? It isn't he! But it's
like him! I'm sure it is he! Of course it's Sir Percy Pumpkin.
I'd know him anywhere. I'd scent him like a bloodhound.
That's his face all right with his large lustrous calf's eye.
Lord, watch how he stalks his prey. He paws the ground

like a dog on the scent. Now he'll rage and rant, but he
can't pull the iron bolt on the door. Ye gods! He'll break
down the door: he's shaking it like an auction bell. Sure!
He wants to enter. Why don't I speak to him? Hello, Sir
Percy Pumpkin! Clear to hell out of this! Did the devil
bring you here? Don't break down my door! I earned that
door penny by penny from the priest in Saint Paul's. And
you, my lady, didn't you stick a nail in it for safety? I'll
open the door. Wait! Don't break it down! Now calmly
and quietly tell me what's your business. Then go away
from my door, bad 'cess to you! Don't be so violent! All
right! Come in and be welcome! I'll see what you can do.

SIR PERCY PUMPKIN. My Lady Sloe-Eyes—my darling! Toddle-Troll, you old hag! Was this why you kept your door
closed—Satan's baggage, and bad luck to you! On this most
auspicious of all days, fancy sporting your oak! Why God
and my good fortune had reserved the fairest of all women
for me.[1]

ARCHPRIEST. *Sir Percy Pumpkin disappears to join Lady Sloe-
Eyes within, where presumably the love affair reaches its
final consummation. What remains is the epilogue in which
Toddle-Troll moralizes in bawdlike fashion to Lady Sloe-
Eyes on the theme that it is no use crying over spilt milk.*

EPILOGUE

TODDLE-TROLL. This is what happens when my back is turned:
When I left the house you saw the nets close in.
What were you up to here alone with him?
Don't try to blame me for what has occurred,
You made your bed and you must lie on it.
Silence is your best plan, and mum's the word.
If a veil descends to cover the whole affair,

[1] At this point, after Stanza 877 of the original text, thirty-two
lines are missing from the manuscript, probably excised from the
original by some agelast censor.

You won't imperil your marriage later on,
And this is better than losing your good name,
For after all, you admit the harm is done.
Henceforth defend yourself with tooth and nail.
What is done, is done, and you'll stand your ground.
So hold your head high, let them insinuate:
If the gossiping magpie had not blabbed so much
They wouldn't hang her up for the folk to jeer.
Why punish yourself for the sake of a man,
When every man acts as Sir Percy did?

LADY SLOE-EYES. My curses on all you wicked old hags!
You have diddled and you've double-crossed us women:
Only yesterday you were prepared to help,
But today I am hooted, scouted and despised:
Time's out of joint, and my life's gone awry.
(THE ARCHPRIEST *moralizes in the following final words to
the public:*)

ARCHPRIEST. Wisdom and sense we may find among the sages,
For learning and science mature with the ages:
My old bawd's conscience at last was at rest,
And after the lawsuit her sentence was the best:
"A man, if he's wise, should never complain,
Especially when there is nothing to gain;
What we cannot cure we must wisely endure."
And as for fair Sloe-Eyes and Sir Percy I'll say:
They are happily married and blessing that day.

THE
MASK

❧❧❧

Rustic Interlude

by

LOPE DE RUEDA
(1506-1565)

❧❧❧

❧ DRAMATIS PERSONAE ❧

Alameda, Simpleton
Salcedo, his Master
(Salcedo also plays the ghost of Diego Sánchez)

The text used herein of *La Carátula*, the second of seven *Pasos*,
is based upon that contained in the edition of *El Deleitoso*,
printed in Logroño by Matías Mares in 1588.

Enter ALAMEDA *and his master* SALCEDO.

ALAMEDA. Are ye there, sir?

SALCEDO. I'm here: haven't you two eyes in your head?

ALAMEDA. Faith, sir, if I hadn't run into you, I'd never have found you, not even if I traipsed round and round oftener nor a dog that wants to lie down.

SALCEDO. Sure, that's not hard to believe, Alameda, where you're concerned.

ALAMEDA. If you didn't believe me I'd say you'd lost your wits; for I'm here to see you about something that has me mighty troubled in my conscience. But I must be rum!

SALCEDO. You mean mum.

ALAMEDA. I suppose I mean mum; I think that . . .

SALCEDO. Well say what you mean. This is an out of the way place, if mum's the word, and there's some secret you want to get off your chest.

ALAMEDA. Can anybody hear us, do ye tink? Look well; what I have to tell is dead secret; for as I was traipsin' around I didn't run into you, and then I sees 'twas yerself right enough, just as if they whispered your name in me ear.

SALCEDO. I believe you all right.

ALAMEDA. An' why would ye not believe me, an' I the grandson of a pastry cook?

SALCEDO. What's up?—out with it!

ALAMEDA. Whisht! Speak soft!

SALCEDO. Say what you have to say.

ALAMEDA. Is anyone listenin'?

SALCEDO. Haven't I told you there's no one about?

ALAMEDA. Do you know that I'm after findin' someting that'll put me on top o' the wurrld.

SALCEDO. Have you found something, Alameda? I'd like a share.

ALAMEDA. No, no: I alone found it, and I want to enjoy it alone, if me luck is in.

SALCEDO. Let us see what you've found—come on, show it.

ALAMEDA. Tell me, sir, have you ever seen a windfall?

SALCEDO. Yes, I have.

ALAMEDA. Well my find is worth more than that; more than twenty-five *maravedís*.

SALCEDO. Is that possible? Let us see.

ALAMEDA. And I don't know if I'll sell it, nor if I'll pawn it either.

SALCEDO. Show it.

ALAMEDA. Slowly then, slowly. Just have a squint at it.

SALCEDO. Ah! What a letdown! Is that all it is?

ALAMEDA. What? No good, is it? Well, I'm tellin' you, sir, that when I was out lookin' for wood, bless me if I didn't find near the wall o' de yard yonder dis bloody face. Now, tell me, sir: where dem faces come from?

SALCEDO. My dear Alameda, I don't know what to say, except that you'd have been better off if the lashes had dropped off your eyes than make such an unlucky find as you have this day.

ALAMEDA. Is it unlucky for a fella to find such a ting as dis?

SALCEDO. Unlucky, is it? I wouldn't be in your shoes for all the cash in Venice. Do you know who the sinner was who owned that face?

ALAMEDA. A sinner is he?

SALCEDO. I fancy I must know him.

ALAMEDA. I do too.

SALCEDO. Tell me, Alameda: have you not heard tell of Diego Sánchez, the caretaker whom the robbers skinned after taking all his money?

ALAMEDA. Diego Sánchez?

SALCEDO. Yes, Diego Sánchez. You can't deny that is the man.

ALAMEDA. So this is Diego Sánchez? Bad 'cess to the mother who bore me! Couldn't the Lord above have made me find a fine friar's wallet bulgin' with bread than de face o'one who's been flayed. God save us! Diego Sánchez! Diego Sánchez, is it? I don't suppose he'll let a word out of him, no matter how I yell. Now tell me, sir; what happened to the robbers? Were dey ever found?

SALCEDO. No; they've not been found: but, my dear Alameda, the police are dying to know who are the criminals.

ALAMEDA. And tell me, sir, am I then the criminal?

SALCEDO. Yes, my friend.

ALAMEDA. What will they do to me if they catch me?

SALCEDO. The least they can do to you when they find you is to put a rope round your neck, and hang you.

ALAMEDA. Hang me, is it? And afterwards they'll land me in de galleys—and I'm one who's a wee bit weak in the gullet and choke easily: I suppose, sir, then if dey hang me I'll lose me appetite.

SALCEDO. The one piece of advice I'll give you, friend, is to go to the shrine of Saint Anthony and take on the caretaker's job the other fellow held; in this way the police can do nothing to you.

ALAMEDA. Now tell me, sir, how much will I have to pay to get a poor box and a bell like that unlucky fella?

SALCEDO. No need to buy new ones. The town crier will be selling the ones belonging to the last caretaker, and you'll be able to buy them; but there is one thing I'm afraid of.

ALAMEDA. I'm scared of more then two hundred tings. But why are you scared?

SALCEDO. Some night when you're all alone in the shrine you'll be scared out of your wits by the ghost of that poor devil. But I'd prefer that than to have you putting the wind up all of us when we find you strung up by the neck like a dog on a churchyard wall.

ALAMEDA. And I'd be winded too, wouldn't I, sir? if they pressed me Adam's apple, divil a bit could I breathe.

SALCEDO. Well, my dear fellow, you'd better get a move on: if you don't hurry the peelers may catch you.

ALAMEDA. An' what in heaven's name am I to do with dis face or whatever it is?

SALCEDO. Better get rid of it: don't let them find it on you.

ALAMEDA. Well, I'll leave it and be off then; please God I'll make a good caretaker. So rest in peace and good luck to ye, Diego Sánchez. (*Exit* ALAMEDA.)

SALCEDO. Now that I've made that poor half-wit think this mask is the phiz of Diego Sánchez I'll play a trick on him with it: I'll go and wrap myself up in a sheet as best I can, and I'll bob up in front of him, pretending I'm the ghost of Diego Sánchez: what a lark it'll be! I'll get going quick. (*Exit* SALCEDO, *and enter* ALAMEDA, *dressed as a caretaker, carrying a lighted lantern and a bell.*)

ALAMEDA. Charity, gentlemen! just what'll buy a penny worth
of oil for me lamp! A Saint's caretaker has a dog's life, an'
no mistake: not a square meal to be had: only a crust of
bread now and then: I might as well be a warrener's pup
that's kept dyin'o' hunger so as he'll be quicker to pick up
the scent, an'he huntin': And mind ye, them dogs who used
to be pals o'mine, don't recognize me now that I'm togged
out in this caretaker outfit, and when dey see me beggin'
from door to door the crusts that were their standby, bless
me if they don't set upon me with their jaws open, ready
to gobble me up as a cuckoo does butterflies. An' de worst
of it all is that the shrine yonder is as silent as the grave:
not even the buzzin' of a fly! An' when I start tinkin' of
the soul o'that skinned caretaker it puts de fear of God in
me: An'no sooner do I hear a rustle, or a wee bit of a
sound than I hide me head under the blankets: why I declare I'm like a pot of rice on the fire wid de lid on it to
keep the gravy from escapin'. God in His infinite mercy
give us a hand! but sure He knows best, amen.

SALCEDO (*disguised with a mask*). Alameda!

ALAMEDA. Heavens above! They're after callin' me. Will anyone give us a copper or two for de oil?

SALCEDO. Alameda!

ALAMEDA. There are two Alamedas. There's Alameda, and
there's meself, God be with me!

SALCEDO. Alameda!

ALAMEDA. Holy Ghost preserve us! It must be someone
wantin' to give me alms.

SALCEDO. Alameda!

ALAMEDA. Go on, go on with your Alameda, Alameda! They'll
give me a puck in the eye wid a copper I suppose.

SALCEDO. Alonso de Alameda!

ALAMEDA. Yes, Alonso and all! Faith an' they know too well
the name I was given at the font. I don't like the look o'
dis. Who in heaven's name are you?

SALCEDO. Don't you recognize me by my voice?

ALAMEDA. Be your voice is it? I wouldn't like to: I'd know
you if I saw your face.

SALCEDO. Did you know Diego Sánchez?

ALAMEDA. It's he, it's he! but perhaps it isn't, an' it's someone
else. Sir, I knew seven or eight in this life.

SALCEDO. How is it you don't recognize me?

ALAMEDA. Are you one of them?

SALCEDO. Yes I am, for before they skinned my face . . .

ALAMEDA. It's de skinned fellow, it's de skinned fellow all right!

SALCEDO. I want you to recognize me, so here I am.

ALAMEDA. Why me? Well I forgive you. But Mr. Diego Sánchez, better wait for someone else to come along who'll know you better nor I do.

SALCEDO. I was sent to you.

ALAMEDA. To me? Look here, Mr. Diego Sánchez. For the love o' God, let me be! I give in, and I'm struck all of a heap.

SALCEDO. What's that you say?

ALAMEDA. I'm at the end of me tether.

SALCEDO. Do you now recognize me?

ALAMEDA. Ta ta ta ta, I do, ta ta ta ta, I recognize you right enough.

SALCEDO. Who am I then?

ALAMEDA. If I'm not mistaken, you're the caretaker whose face they skinned to rob him.

SALCEDO. So I am.

ALAMEDA. I wish to God you'd never been: And have you no face?

SALCEDO. I used to have a face before, but now it's one stuck on, bad cess to it!

ALAMEDA. Well what do ye want now. Mr. Diego Sánchez?

SALCEDO. Where are the skeletons of the dead?

ALAMEDA (*aside*). To de graveyard he's sendin' me. (*Aloud*) Do dey get deir meals dere, Diego Sánchez?

SALCEDO. Yes: Why do you ask?

ALAMEDA. What do dey eat?

SALCEDO. Cooked lettuce and mallow roots.

ALAMEDA. That's a foul diet, an' no mistake. What a number of fellows with the squitters must be dere! But why do you want to take me with you?

SALCEDO. Because you're wearing my clothes without my leave.

ALAMEDA. Here, take them, take them away, I don't want them.

SALCEDO. Now you'll have to come, and if they discharge you scot-free, they'll let you come back.

ALAMEDA. And if they don't?

SALCEDO. You'll then have to stay with the skeletons in the old cisterns: but there's something else.

ALAMEDA. What's that?

SALCEDO. You know that those who skinned me threw me in a stream.

ALAMEDA. Your lordship must have been cool there at any rate.

SALCEDO. What you must do is to go at midnight sharp to the stream and take my body and carry it to the San Gil's graveyard at the end of the town and shout in a loud voice: "Diego Sánchez!"

ALAMEDA. And tell me, sir, where do I go after that?

SALCEDO. Later on, later on.

ALAMEDA. Well, Mister, wouldn't it be better for me to go home to fetch an ass to carry your corpse?

SALCEDO. Yes, go quickly.

ALAMEDA. I'll be back in a moment.

SALCEDO. Hurry, I'll wait here.

ALAMEDA. Tell me, Mr. Diego Sánchez: how long is it from now to de Day of Judgment?

SALCEDO. God only knows.

ALAMEDA. Well you may wait until you know it.

SALCEDO. Come back quickly.

ALAMEDA. Don't eat until I return.

SALCEDO. So? Wait.

ALAMEDA. Blessed Virgin! The fella's followin' me. (*Exeunt.*)

PERIBÁÑEZ
AND THE
COMENDADOR
OF
OCAÑA

❧⬥❧

Comedia
in Three Acts
by
FÉLIX LOPE
De VEGA CARPIO
(1562-1635)

❧⬥❧

✺ DRAMATIS PERSONAE ✺

King Henry III of Castile
The Queen
Peribáñez, a peasant farmer
Casilda, wife of Peribáñez
The Comendador or Knight-Commander of Ocaña
The Condestable
Gómez Manrique
Inés
Costanza
Luján, a lackey
A priest, in the manner of the *gracioso*, or clown
Leonardo, a gentleman attending the Comendador
Marín, a lackey
Bartolo, a peasant farmer
Belardo
Antón
Blas
Gil
Benito
Llorente
Mendo
Chaparro
Helipe
A painter
A Secretary
An Alderman and a Councilman
Peasants and peasant women
Musicians
A page

The action of the play takes place at Ocaña and Toledo in 1406. The text of *Peribáñez y el Comendador de Ocaña* we have used is that published by Juan Eugenio de Hartzenbusch in *Biblioteca de Autores Españoles, Vol. XLI*.

ACT I.

The House of PERIBÁÑEZ *in Ocaña.*

Enter PERIBÁÑEZ *and* CASILDA *as bridegroom and bride:* INÉS *as patroness, the* PRIEST, COSTANZA, *musicians, peasants and peasant women.*

INÉS. I wish you both long years of happiness.
COSTANZA. If they be as I wish you'll never die.
CASILDA. My wish to serve makes me deserve your favors.
PRIEST. Although not wrong, such wishes are out of place.
    No wish of mine, Casilda, could compare
    With the nuptial blessings I read out to you:
    I invoked so many that not one remains
    For any friend or relative to ask.
INÉS. Your reverence, I'll simply wish them luck.
PRIEST. I put my faith in God who helps the good,
    But my niece you'll find a level-headed lass.
PERIBÁÑEZ. If she but be devoid of jealousy
    I'll doubt no more and end the argument.
CASILDA. Give me no cause, dear husband, and I vow
    You'll never find in me a jealous wife.
PERIBÁÑEZ. From me you'll never even hear the word.
INÉS. They say it was the sky above decreed
    That love should thus be burdened by this care.[1]
PRIEST. But now the time has come for both of you
    To sit and bless the day that made you one.
PERIBÁÑEZ. Joy in abundance fills my heart this day
    That God has given me so fair a bride.
PRIEST. You are right to ascribe that grace to God!
    For in this fairest kingdom of Toledo
    There is no face can rival hers today.
CASILDA. If by my constant love I can repay
    Your fondness, husband, you will still remain
    In debt to me.

[1] Blue, the color suggested by the sky, was taken by Spaniards as the symbol for jealousy.

PERIBÁÑEZ.   As long as you, Casilda
    Cannot in fondness ever hope to win,
    So may you fail to conquer me in words.
    I'd even lay Ocaña at your feet,
    And all the earth that Tagus bathes until
    It's Portuguese and enters the Spanish sea.
    A wood of olives laden with ripe fruit
    To me appears less beautiful, and fields
    That bloom with flowers in the month of May,
    Untrodden save by footsteps of the dawn.
    There's not a pippin ripening on the bough
    But would at once proclaim your eminence,
    Nor fair transparent oil within the jar
    That could so fill my senses with delight,
    Nor white wine mellowed for twice twenty years,
    Have more aroma than your fragrant lips;
    For as the rose smells sweeter to the lord,
    So does the peasant revel in his wine.
    But neither December's vines I weed and trim
    For autumn's sweet new vintage, nor May's showers,
    Nor waning August's heaps of wheat can vie
    With my delight at seeing in my house
    Before my eyes such a blessed antidote
    Against chilly winter and the summer heat.
    But now I must prepare my heart to be
    The fairest mansion wherein you can dwell
    In freedom, now that I deserve your love.
    Here you will live, and if a countryman,
    Through peace of soul, may be a king,
    You then, it's plain, are queen of this, my house,
    By law of God and human ordinance.
    As heaven then, dear wife, will make you blest,
    Let all who see you now say: "To the fair
    Casilda passes the luck of the ugly girl." [2]
CASILDA.   What can I say, when even a passing glance
    At you has all but bereft me of my soul?
    Never, when in the dance my feet began
    To tingle in rhythm, did I feel such thrill,

[2] According to the ancient proverb plain girls were lucky in marriage. One of Lope's plays was entitled *La Ventura de la Fea* (The Luck of the Ugly Girl).

Not even with shrill fife and rattling drum;
Nor myrtle and verbena on the morn
Of St. John's day, nor whoops the dancers gave,
Delighted me as do your loving words.
What well-tuned timbrel delicately played,
What psaltery can be compared to you?
What banner of procession with its cord
And tassels vies with your bespangled hat?
No feet new-shod delight me as your love,
You are the peer among a thousand lads,
A glorious Easter Cake on Easter Day,
With frosted icing, sweets and eggs and all.
Like a red fighting bull you chew the cud
In a green meadow; or like a new woven smock
You're borne 'midst jasmine in a gilded basket.
You're like the Paschal Candle, or the roll
Of baptismal marchpane wrapt in a hood of gauze,
But in the end you're like yourself, because
You have no real rival in the world.

PRIEST.   Enough of love; these youths all wish to dance
And choose their partners.

PERIBÁÑEZ.   Friends, who are old in love,
Pray pardon us.

A MUSICIAN. May your love go on growing.

(*The musicians sing and the peasants and maidens dance
the folía.*)[3]

MUSICIANS. *To you let flowering May*
  Fair greetings bring
  With murmuring stream:
  Let green alders raise their heads
  And blossoming almonds pledge their fruit.
  After dewy dawns,
  In the morning sun,
  Let lilies in profusion sprout

---

[3] According to Covarrubias in his *Tesoro* (1611) the *folía* was a
gay, noisy Portuguese dance in which numerous rustics took part.
It was accompanied by tambourines and other instruments. Some
of the dancers carried on their shoulders boys disguised as girls.
The dance was so lively that the performers gave the impression
of being mad. Hence the name *folía* which was derived from the
Italian *folle* (mad).

From their green spears.
On the mountain side,
Now snows have fled,
Let lowing kine
Browse on the sunny slopes
And crop the fragrant thyme.

FOLÍA. *May God shed blessings on our newly wed,*
And meadows greet them with a nuptial song.
Ice-bound mountains, beetling crags,
Gnarléd oaks and doughty pines
Speed the waters in their course
Thundering down into the vales,
Let sweet-throated nightingales
Warble their love to the green myrtles,
And birds with art build leafy nests.
May God bless our newly wed,
And meadows sing a nuptial song,
For today the two are one.

(*Voices and commotion within. Enter* BARTOLO, *farmer.*)

PRIEST. What is that?

BARTOLO. Can't you tell by the shout and the din?

PRIEST. I'll bet they have brought the young bull?

BARTOLO. A young bull is it? Faith, there are three of them!
But the spotted one they are bringing from the country—
Holy Moses! he has Spanish fire. More than an hour it took
to tie him up. He gave Blas two tosses, and no Italian ever
vaulted more lightly over the rope than he did. As for Antón Gil's mare, who had just been taken from pasture, she
voided all she'd chewed through her lacerated guts. No
laughing matter, I assure you; Tomás had his breeches
ripped off, but not one said a word, though the boy may
never grow a beard. Our Comendador, Lord of Ocaña and
its land, gallantly closed in to attack, braver than a hawk;
I swear to God if the bull had not been roped . . .

PRIEST. Could the beast get in here?

BARTOLO. Before, yes.

PRIEST. In that case then I'll go up to the terrace.

COSTANZA. Say a prayer, Your Reverence; there's no reason
for you to run away.

PRIEST. A prayer? What for?

COSTANZA. To give you courage to stand your ground.

PRIEST. You're wrong: some bulls don't understand Latin.
(*Exit.*)

COSTANZA. He is evidently going up on the roof—(*Voices within*)—the shouting is growing louder. Let us all go there: as the bull is roped he can't move away.

BARTOLO. That's true: the bull can't go beyond the length of the rope. (*Exit.*)

(*Enter* PERIBÁÑEZ, CASILDA, INÉS, COSTANZA, *peasants, women, musicians.*)

PERIBÁÑEZ. Would you like me to try a few passes?

CASILDA. Ah, no, my love, that is a ferocious beast!

PERIBÁÑEZ. Fierce or no, I'll grip the horns
And fell the bull to show my pluck.

CASILDA. It would be indecorous on your wedding day
To mention horns, and what bridegroom would face,
When newly wed, the horns of a fighting bull? [4]

PERIBÁÑEZ. Talking of proverbs there are two that trouble me:
"Jail not even for warmth," and, "Horn not even
As ink-horn," so I'll obey.

CASILDA. God help us, what is that?
(*Sound of voices within.*)

PEOPLE. What a misfortune!

CASILDA. Somebody has been hurt.

PERIBÁÑEZ. What? While we two were here?
(*Enter* BARTOLO.)

BARTOLO. I wish that beast had never left the wood!
I hope the lads will take no credit for this show.
God's curse on that bull. May you crop no more
In showery April than in swelt'ring August
And when you're mad with jealousy and face
Your rival, may he make mincemeat of you,
And when you ramble bellowing through the woods,
May the streams dry up and you be crazed with thirst
And may you die in the ring before the mob,
Hemmed in and goaded to a shameful death,
Not slain by a knight with lance or golden knife,
But hamstrung by a lackey with rusty blade,
And may you grovel, and your blood stain the dust.

[4] Casilda here delicately alludes to the popular belief that horns symbolized cuckoldry.

PERIBÁÑEZ. Now calm yourself and tell us what occurred;
Zamora's traitor never was so cursed.[5]

BARTOLO. The Comendador, our noble master,
Came proudly riding down the street,
Mounted on his sleek bay charger;
Black-spotted on its chest and back,
Bridled in silver, glaring fiercely,
Snorting and flecking with white foam
Its green and crimson emblem, on it came;
But master spies the charging bull,
Pulls down his cap, and flourishing his stick,
Spurs on his steed, which races like the wind,
Driving the crowd to right and left,
But suddenly gets tangled in the rope,
And down falls master in the midst of them.
His hurt is grievous and I fear for him:
Why am I telling this, when here they come,
Carrying him on their shoulders?

(*Enter the* COMENDADOR, *unconscious, carried by a number
of peasants on their shoulders; two lackeys,* MARÍN *and*
LUJÁN, *in buskins, cloak and cap, and others.*)

BARTOLO. The Reverend Father was here, so they'll be able to
give him absolution.

INÉS. I think he went away to hide.

PERIBÁÑEZ. Go up, Bartolo, and look on the terrace.

BARTOLO. I'll go for him.

PERIBÁÑEZ. Hurry.

LUJÁN. We two will go for a chair to carry his body, if God
has decided to take him.

MARÍN. Come, Luján; I'm afraid the Comendador is dead.

LUJÁN. I'm so afraid that my heart is pounding like mad.

(*Exeunt* LUJÁN *and* MARÍN.)

CASILDA. Pedro, I think he is recovering consciousness: go and
fetch water.

PERIBÁÑEZ. If the Comendador dies my days at Ocaña are
ended. A curse on our feast!

(*All depart except* CASILDA *and the* COMENDADOR. *He lies
in a chair, and she holds his hand.*)

[5] The reference is to the famous siege of Zamora in 1072 by King
Sancho, during which Vellido Dolfos entered and treacherously
killed the King. The incident is referred to in the ballads.

CASILDA. Oh, what a misfortune has befallen
One who is the flower of Spain!
Ah, gallant knight and valiant warrior!
Are you the one who with naked sword
Humbled the proud Moors of Granada?
Are you one who slew many men?
Has a hempen rope sufficed to kill
One whom the sword could not destroy?
Death herself wounds you with a rope,
This was your fate because you snatched
Glory from so many heroes.
Ah, my Comendador!

COMENDADOR. Who calls? Who is here?

CASILDA. Good news! He spoke.

COMENDADOR (*groans*). Alas! Who are you?

CASILDA. It is I, my lord. Do not be anxious,
Or cast down! you find yourself
Among those who wish you well.
Although, my lord, you may now be sorry
You ever chased that bull, remember,
In this house you are welcome.

COMENDADOR. All human treasure's gathered here,
I lay dead on the ground, or so I thought,
But when I recovered my senses I believed
I was in heaven: in God's name, I pray,
Do undeceive me: for surely a man
May fancy he's in heaven when he finds
An angel there like you.

CASILDA. Perhaps you're still hovering on the brink of death.

COMENDADOR. How so?

CASILDA.   Because you're seeing visions. If,
You're grateful now because you find yourself
Beneath my humble roof, I'd have you know,
That only today it has become my house.

COMENDADOR. Are you, fair lady, then the happy bride?

CASILDA. Not happy if this misfortune of yours
Should linger and increase because of me.

COMENDADOR. So you're already married?

CASILDA. Yes, and well matched, my lord.

COMENDADOR. Very few beautiful brides are.

CASILDA. My love had the ugly girl's proverbial luck.

COMENDADOR (*aside*). What a pitiful waste that so uncouth a
    yokel
  Should be the husband of so fair a bride!
  (*Aloud.*)
  Your name, I pray you?
CASILDA.   I am called Casilda.
COMENDADOR (*aside*). I am amazed at such perfection in
  One dressed in such attire. She is a diamond
  Enchased on lead. (*Aloud:*) Fortunate is the man
  A thousand times, on whom you bestow your charms.
CASILDA. It is not he who is well wooed, but I,
  Comendador, you may be assured of this.
COMENDADOR. Your spirit makes you just the wife for me,
  Do give me leave to shower gifts on you.
  (*Enter* PERIBÁÑEZ.)
PERIBÁÑEZ. There is no sign of the priest: what if the case
  Takes a more serious turn . . .
CASILDA.   You're wrong:
  Once more our Don Fadrique has his health.
PERIBÁÑEZ. So my love brings fair tidings.
COMENDADOR.   Aye, such is
  The wondrous power of this most heavenly gem.
  (*Enter* MARÍN *and* LUJÁN, *lackeys.*)
MARÍN. They say he has come to himself again.
LUJÁN. My Lord, your chair's here.
COMENDADOR.   Don't bring it beyond
  The door, I do not need it now.
LUJÁN.   Thank God!
COMENDADOR. If I'm restored to health, I hope to show
  By my reward how grateful I am to you
  For the generous welcome you have given me.
PERIBÁÑEZ. If I, sir, could exchange my health for yours,
  Believe me, I would do so.
COMENDADOR.   I am sure.
LUJÁN. How do you feel?
COMENDADOR.   I have a craving that I didn't feel
  When I entered this house.
LUJÁN.   I do not follow.
COMENDADOR. It matters not.
LUJÁN.   I'm speaking of your fall.
COMENDADOR. My life's in danger owing to a mad desire.

(Exeunt COMENDADOR *and* LUJÁN. PERIBÁÑEZ *and* CASILDA
remain.)

PERIBÁÑEZ. I think he is better.

CASILDA.   I was sorry for him.

PERIBÁÑEZ. The Comendador's fall seemed to me to be
An evil omen. Bad 'cess to the whole
Feast and the bull, and man who roped the beast.

CASILDA. That is nothing: he later spoke to me.
I think what has occurred is for the best,
For he may favor us if a chance arise.

PERIBÁÑEZ. It is now time, Casilda, for my love
To win love's guerdon and its recompense.
Now that we're in our own house you must be
Its ruler and mine also, though you know
That a woman when she marries must obey;
Such was God's ordinance for all the world.
All peace and happiness for both of us
I base upon that maxim, so I live,
My darling, in the hopes that you will now
Dispel my doubts and my anxieties.

CASILDA. What must a woman do?

PERIBÁÑEZ.   Listen to me.

CASILDA. Speak.

PERIBÁÑEZ. To adore your husband and to honor him
Is A, first letter of this alphabet.
As you are good, G is the letter,
Which is all I would ask from you:
The C will make you circumspect,
And S will make you sweet and sensible,
The letter F in life will prove
That you are firm and forceful,
And of stanchest faith.
The H bears tribute to your honor,
The I will make you illustrious,
And by your name shed luster on my house.
Through L you will be liberal,
And M will make you mistress of your children,
And one who will lament their faults.
With N you learn to answer "No"
To vain petitions,
And this "No" that few learn to use

Is contained in the letters N and O.
The P will make you pensive,
And Q describes your quest for men's esteem:
The R will give you sufficient reason
To banish undue folly.
The E will make you always eager
To seek my comfort;
The T will make you true.
The X good Christian, for it is
The first of all the letters
You must learn in life.
With Y and Z you must defend yourself
Against the vice of jealousy
That can destroy our plighted troth in love.
If you but learn by heart this simple song,
You will become the fairest flower of all
The county and I the noblest in the town.

CASILDA. To please you I shall learn
The letters of this alphabet,
But I beg you Pedro dear,
May I recite another one,
If this be not remiss?

PERIBÁÑEZ. Nay, I shall welcome it: recite.
I wish to learn from you.

CASILDA. Well, listen and be patient.
The first letter is A,
For arrogant you must not be;
And B should give you warning
Never to beguile me with lies.
C makes you my companion,
And D proclaims you a donor,
Generous because of my faith in you.
F means your mood is facile,
G bears a tribute to your gallantry,
H to your honesty, and I declares
You are devoid of base ingratitude.
L proves you liberal,
And M the finest man
That ever wedded wife did have,
For love's the peerless treasure.
The letter N proves you'll not be a ninny,

Or a plague your wife must bear.
And as for O it signifies
The hours that you will spend with me,
And P is precious for paternal
Counsels you must give to me,
And Q the quests that I must undertake
To make me worthy of your love.
With R you regale me, S you serve me,
And T shows my stanch tenacity
In clinging to you through thick and thin,
And V heralds love's deathless verity.
And as for X, I wish to imitate it thus
With open arms.
(*She kisses him.*)
As we are here this moment,
So let us be even after death.

PERIBÁÑEZ. I propose, my darling,
To learn this alphabet.
Do you want more?

CASILDA. My love, I hardly know
If I dare on our first day
To ask you a great favor.

PERIBÁÑEZ. My love is piqued.

CASILDA. Are you sure?

PERIBÁÑEZ. Yes.

CASILDA. Do listen.

PERIBÁÑEZ. Speak.

CASILDA. Assumption Day draws near,
And I have such a longing to see Toledo.
My object is not pleasure, but a devout
Wish to behold the image of Our Lady
That is borne in procession through the streets.

PERIBÁÑEZ. My wishes and yours, my love, are the same.

CASILDA. Let us then plan ahead our journey there.
The letter G proves how gallant you are,
And I now kiss your hands a thousand times.

PERIBÁÑEZ. Invite your cousins and we'll travel in style.

CASILDA. Do you wish to pamper me?

PERIBÁÑEZ. I want to buy . . .

CASILDA. Tell me.

PERIBÁÑEZ. A lovely costume.   (*Exeunt.*)

(*A room in the* COMENDADOR'S *house. Enter the* COMENDA-
DOR *and* LEONARDO, *his servant.*)

COMENDADOR. Leonardo, call Luján immediately.

LEONARDO. I have told him, but he was upset.

COMENDADOR. Call him again.

LEONARDO. I'll go.

COMENDADOR. Go.

LEONARDO (*aside*). I wonder what will be the end of this?
    Though he feels better he is more downcast,
    And groans though he is not in pain, and fills
    The air with sighs; this must be love, I reckon.   (*Exit.*)

COMENDADOR. Casilda, fairer and more radiant
    Than blushing dawn in the mantle of the sun,
    Or snowy peak that love alone can melt,
    With your white hands you culled in the fields of May
    All blossoms Zephyr quickens in Flora's bosom.
    I saw the green fields hail you with delight,
    For here and there fresh buds began to sprout
    When they felt the gentle touch of your white feet,
    And through your kindly care and husbandry
    Evergreen hope now burgeons in my heart.
    Lucky the husbandman whose eager hands
    Have reaped so ripe a harvest from your breast,
    And who one day to come, when his beard is white,
    Will see your sons on his heaped threshing floors,
    With such a bounteous harvest of ripe fruits,
    The sun would let you ride in his golden coach,
    Or in the wain that is made of twinkling stars.
    For his spade I would exchange my golden sword,
    And renounce my Ocaña for your humble home,
    The house at which the sun stops every day.[6]
    He is lucky to find such treasure in his bed.
    (*Enter* LUJÁN.)

LUJÁN. Pardon me: the bay horse needed my care.

COMENDADOR. I am done for, Luján, a thunderbolt has killed
    me;
    I still feel the effects of that swooning fit.

---

[6] This is a play on the meanings of *casa*, an ordinary house or
home, and "celestial house"—one of the twelve divisions of the
heavens through which the heavenly bodies pass every twenty-four
hours.

LUJÁN. So that fierce passion of yours still endures.
COMENDADOR. Just as fire seeks to soar up to its sphere,
    So does the fickle coward soul fly up
    Aspiring to such beauty: yes, Luján,
    I wish to become a friend of this good peasant,
    In whom honor sleeps less than in subtle courtier.
    What means must I use to achieve my plan?
    Would not the best plan be to say that I
    Intend to grant the wishes he expressed,
    And, perhaps, bestow on him some other favor?
LUJÁN. If I were cautious and foresaw the danger,
    I should win first the indulgence of the husband
    Before trying to lay siege to his wife.
    This fellow, though he is a decent man,
    And is honored among his equals, will
    Become unwary if you favor him,
    For there are husbands who less cautiously
    Defend their honor when they are indebted
    For favors given: indebtedness, my lord,
    Will make a man neglect his vital duties.
COMENDADOR. What favors shall I first bestow on him?
LUJÁN. If you consider favoring a peasant
    Your best plan is to give him a pair of mules,
    Which would be just like giving him Ocaña,
    For a mule is a peasant's greatest capital;
    And for his wife, gold earrings would be best.
    This, they say, was the plan Medoro used
    To win the heart of fair Angelica.[7]
    For Angelica's sake with blood of warriors slain
    Rinaldo drenches the fields of Agramante,
    And bold Roland, great baron of Anglante,
    Piles corpse on corpse upon the martial plain;
    While the wizard Malgesí shuns many a wound
    From the scepter's fury; watch Sacripante dash,
    And Ferragut, Spain's hope, fall to the ground!
    But while paladins deal strokes and counterstrokes,
    Medoro gives the lady high-heeled shoes,
    Choosing a pliant hour, and amidst the oaks,

[7] The following sonnet refers vaguely to incidents in Ariosto's *Orlando Furioso*, a work which influenced Cervantes in *Don Quixote* and Lope in his *Hermosura de Angélica*.

Or in the shade of cypress trees he woos,
Gathering so many rosebuds in that hour,
That for thirteen months she was his paramour.

COMENDADOR. The poet was quite skilful in portraying
The blatant triumph of self-interest.

LUJÁN. The wisest plan would be to make a gift;
That is the shortest and most secret way.
And personal favors are sure to betray,
For they are seen and noted by everyone,
And love reveals itself by hint or glance.
Diligent self-interest which deals in cash
Treads softly with feet wrapt in cotton wool.

COMENDADOR. Halt there! self-interest must win the day!

LUJÁN. It levels the mountains and it calms the seas,
Hereafter you will find that this is true.

COMENDADOR. Since you, Luján, served with me in Andalusia,
And I witnessed your honor and your courage,
I have been pleased to tell you of my pleasures
And inner secrets, for you are discreet
And can be trusted in all emergencies.
Who is wise, merits to be held in high esteem,
No matter where he is guided by his fortune;
And so I want to change your present duties.

LUJÁN. Let me know if there's any thing you need,
And of my affection you may rest assured,
Though I can't offer greater services.

COMENDADOR. Banish my lovesick thoughts.

LUJÁN. This is the only way.

COMENDADOR. Let us be off, and you go fetch the mules,
The finest pair the fellow has ever seen.

LUJÁN. Just clap the mule's yoke on that boorish neck,
And you'll see him arrive within the hour
His proud heart furrowed with his love of you,
On the watch for the harvest he now hopes to reap.
Remember, I pray you, that love like wheat
Produces no fruit until money is sowed.   (*Exeunt.*)

(*A room in the house of* PERIBÁÑEZ. *Enter* CASILDA, INÉS,
COSTANZA.)

CASILDA. It is not too late to start.

INÉS. The weather is fine, and the road is level all the way.

COSTANZA. In summer they often make the journey in ten

hours, and even in less. What fine clothes will you wear, Inés?

INÉS. They are shabby, and you see my figure.

COSTANZA. I am wearing a bodice full of trimmings of silver.

INÉS. With the jacket unbuttoned it looks very well.

CASILDA. I intend to wear one of velvet over a red skirt. That is the show dress of a married woman.

COSTANZA. Inés wanted to lend me a skirt, it belonged to Antón's wife. It was made of elegant cloth woven at Cuenca, where the finest cloth is made, but Menga, Blasco Gil's daughter, wouldn't let me wear it, saying that the color doesn't suit my complexion.

INÉS. I know of somebody who would lend you a finer skirt.

COSTANZA. Who?

INÉS. Casilda.

CASILDA. If you want my white linen skirt, it is becoming, or the green one, which is embroidered.

COSTANZA. You are generous and good-natured, but Pedro might scold you, and I don't want to make trouble, but thank you all the same.

CASILDA. My Pedro is not so bad-natured as you think, Costanza.

INÉS. Is your husband really affectionate?

CASILDA. Are you afraid we'll change so quickly?
In this village you will not find
So devoted a married couple,
Why we are both still nibbling
The icing off our wedding cake.

INÉS. Does he tell you how he raves about you?

CASILDA. He says little else, and I know
That I am all in a daze
From his billing and cooing.
At dusk when the evening star appears
Pedro comes home from the fields,
Hungry for his supper;
But first my heart whispers he is coming
And I rush to open the door for him,
Throwing down my sewing cushion,
(There's always someone in the village
Ready to buy my embroideries).
Pedro jumps off his mule,

And I throw myself into his arms;
I'm sure the poor hungry beast
Grudges us our long kisses,
And hearing it whinny Pedro says:
"As soon as the cattle are fed,
Miss Pretty Face, Pedro will go out again."
While he throws in the straw for them
He sends me out for barley;
I bring it and he sifts it,
And leaves what he will later use.
He then gives it all a stirring in the manger,
And among the animals he kisses me again;
For no place is too humble
For love to celebrate.
We then hasten away from the stall,
For the stew is boiling in the pot,
And hails us with simmering garlic and onion,
Our kitchen reeks, but we rejoice to hear
The pot's lid tapping its gay rhythms,
Which tempt us to trip to a rustic dance.
Then I serve him the meal on a spotless cloth,
But not on silver plates: though I wish that I could.
Instead, our painted plates from Talavera,
With their carnation pattern, feast our eyes.
I warm his plate of soup so cosily
That the lord of this our village,
The Comendador, I am sure, dines no better.
And Pedro has to pay the penalty,
For hardly a single mouthful does he eat,
But he gives me, his dove, the daintiest bit.
He drinks but leaves the half,
And I drain off the heel taps.
I then bring the olives, and if not,
The choice is dessert.
Dinner finished, hand in hand,
We give due thanks to God
For blessings we've received.
And we go off to bed,
Where dawn regretfully calls us,
When it is time for us to part.

INÉS. What a lucky little bride you are

To be so happily wed!
All that we're waiting for now
Is to start our journey.
(*Enter* PERIBÁÑEZ.)

CASILDA. Is the cart decorated?

PERIBÁÑEZ. As best we could.

CASILDA. May they all get in then?

PERIBÁÑEZ. I was sorry, Casilda, to see
That Blas's cart has a rug
And coverlet with coat of arms.

CASILDA. Ask some knight for me.

INÉS. You may ask the Comendador.

PERIBÁÑEZ. He was very kind to us,
And I think he would
Have given it to us.

CASILDA. What do we lose by going to ask him?

PERIBÁÑEZ. Wait a moment; when all is said and done
Why should we start without a coverlet?

INÉS. Let us then go and dress.

CASILDA. You can go and ask him for . . .

PERIBÁÑEZ. What, my Casilda?

CASILDA. A hat.

PERIBÁÑEZ. Not that.

CASILDA. Why? Is it extravagance?

PERIBÁÑEZ. We may be given the plumed hat of a lord
It would be windy for you; for me a burden.   (*Exeunt.*)
(*A room in the house of the* COMENDADOR. *Enter the* COM-
ENDADOR *and* LUJÁN.)

COMENDADOR. They are very fine.

LUJÁN. I have never seen finer beasts and I've seen many.

COMENDADOR. The earrings are missing.

LUJÁN. The owner said that the mules are three years old this
spring, and they cost the price you gave about a month ago
in the fair at Mansilla de las Mulas, and they are broken to
pack saddle.

COMENDADOR. Tell me how we can give them to her husband,
without arousing his suspicions?

LUJÁN. Summon him to your house and tell him that you are
grateful to him for his kind interest. It really makes me
laugh to see you appointing a man of my humble parts as
secretary to your affairs of the heart.

COMENDADOR. Don't become alarmed; when wooing
   A woman of humble parts, you must
   Obviously treat such an affair
   According to your own lights.
   If I were paying court to a lady I should
   Have given instructions to my secretary or steward,
   Or to a gentleman of my household.
   They would have gone in quest
   Of diamonds, chains, gems, pearls, clothes, satins,
   Damasks, velvets and other rare and exotic things,
   Even to the extent of ordering from Arabia
   The Phoenix; but since she is a peasant girl,
   I am obliged to reveal my plans to you, Luján,
   Though you are just my lackey: but in this business
   Of buying mules you are just the man I need,
   And so through you I treat my love in just the
   Same way as it treats me.

LUJÁN. Though your love affair, my lord, is ill-advised,
   The way you handle it is wise.

   (*Enter* LEONARDO.)

LEONARDO. Here is Peribáñez.

COMENDADOR. Who, Leonardo?

LEONARDO. Peribáñez, my lord.

COMENDADOR. What are you saying?

LEONARDO. I say that Peribáñez inquires for you, and I am sure you know him. Peribáñez is a farmer of Ocaña, a genuine Christian and a rich man, held in veneration by his equals, and if he wished to rise in this town, all who sally forth with their plow would follow his lead. For though he is a peasant, he is honorable.

LUJÁN (*aside to his master*). What makes you so pale?

COMENDADOR. By heavens! the mere report that the husband of a woman I love has arrived makes me tremble and turn pale.

LUJÁN. Will you not have the courage now to see him?

COMENDADOR. Tell him to come in; just as one who is in love
   Finds streets and windows, even iron bars
   Most pleasing to the eye, and in the maids
   Fancies that he sees their mistress' face.
   So I imagine I shall discover in her husband
   That beauty which has been my bane.

(PERIBÁÑEZ, *in cloak, enters.*)

PERIBÁÑEZ. Let me now bend the knee, my gracious Lord.

COMENDADOR. Oh, Pedro, a thousand welcomes!
Let me embrace you.

PERIBÁÑEZ. My Lord! such favor!
To a rough peasant, one
Of the humble folk in Ocaña;
Why such favors to a mere farmer?

COMENDADOR. You, Peribáñez, are not unworthy of honor.
You are a man of decent birth and habits
And because of your intelligence and wit,
You are the model vassal of my lands,
For this reason I owe you gratitude,
And still more, for I owe my life to you;
Without your help I should have lost it then.
What favor would you have me grant you now?

PERIBÁÑEZ. We men of good repute, as I claim to be,
Although we're poor, we all play the same part
As the noble gallants in the palace do.
My wife wants me to take her to the feast
Which, as you know, is held in the Cathedral
Of Toledo, in the month of August, and
All the Kingdom gathers in that shrine.
Her cousins, too, are going, but, my Lord,
Though I have at home some common woolen cloths,
I have no French tapestries of silk and gold,
No hangings embroidered with coat of arms,
Nor crowned with escutcheons and with feathered crests,
And so, I come to ask whether you, my Lord,
Would lend a rug and hangings to adorn
My cart, and I beseech you, make allowance
For my ignorance, and pardon one in love.

COMENDADOR. Are you happy, Peribáñez?

PERIBÁÑEZ. I would not change this homespun cloth of mine
For the grand cross of Comendador that you,
My Lord, wear on your breast, for I possess
An honored wife of no mean beauty, one
Who is a good and humble Christian.
I don't know whether her love equals mine,
Which is as great as woman ever had.

COMENDADOR. How right you are to love the girl who loves

You, both by divine and human ordinance.
And one whom you may cherish as your own.
Ho there! now give him the rug from Mequinez,
And eight more hangings with my coat of arms;
And as I now have a good chance to requite
The welcome I received in his house, when
I found life again, do give him the two mules,
Which I had purchased for the traveling car;
And to his wife the silver earrings take,
If the silversmith by now has finished them.

PERIBÁÑEZ. Even if in your name I kissed the ground
A thousand times, I could not ever pay
A tithe of what I owe for all you've given me.
My wife and I have been till now your fiefs,
Henceforth we are the servants of your house.

COMENDADOR. Go, Leonardo, with him.

LEONARDO.

                                    (*Exeunt.*)

COMENDADOR. Luján, what's your view?

LUJÁN.   Good fortune draws
    nigh.

COMENDADOR. This is for your ear: saddle my sorrel horse:
    I want to go to Toledo in disguise,
    For that peasant wench has bewitched my soul.

LUJÁN. Do you want to trail her?

COMENDADOR.   Yes, for she possesses me,
    Only the sight of her can cool my passion.

    (*The entrance to the Cathedral of Toledo. The* KING *and
    the* CONDESTABLE *enter with suite.*)

CONDESTABLE. Toledo rejoices and is ready to serve,
    Now that Your Royal Highness by your presence
    Favors the people; and their pleasure grows
    On this, the eve of that great festival.

KING. They may thank me for my desire to come.
    I'm an ardent lover of the city's splendor.

CONDESTABLE. And Toledo anxiously has done her best
    To show her affection and her gratitude.

KING. She is indeed eighth wonder of the world,
    Castile's fair crown, and finest ornament;
    She is the country's heart, my Condestable,

From whom the limbs receive the life that rouses
Them to vigor. She is in all eyes eminent.
Like Rome she is built on a mountain which
Subdued the seven hills, and has been famed
For many centuries. I leave with love
And admiration her basilica.

CONDESTABLE. This miracle, my Liege, even surpasses
The ancient holy shrine of Ephesus.
Do you propose to attend the cavalcade?

KING. I shall go to set an example by my faith
In the sovereign image, on whose day
I would beg all her prayers for my soul.
(*A page enters.*)

PAGE. The councilors from your noble city hall
Wish to do obeisance to Your Royal Highness.

COMENDADOR. Tell them to enter.

ALDERMAN. Toledo, my Liege, kisses these royal feet,
And wishing to reply to your just claims,
She called her nobles, and all citizens,
By common consent, for the campaign offer
A thousand men from all Toledo's Kingdom,
And forty thousand ducats.

KING.   I'm beholden
To Toledo for the services they give
Today, but we expect that from Toledo.
Are you both knights?

COUNCILMAN. Yes, we are knights.

KING.   Speak to the Condestable
Tomorrow, that Toledo may be told
How I pay my debt to her nobility.
(*Enter* INÉS, COSTANZA *and* CASILDA *with hats adorned with
tassels, and dressed as peasant women of the Sagra of Toledo; and* PERIBÁÑEZ *and the* COMENDADOR, *on the way.*)

INÉS. By heaven! I must see him.
Well we've come in time,
For the King is in the city!

COSTANZA. What a dashing youth!

INÉS. They call him Don Enrique the third. The third
They say makes the best go-between!
He is the son of the King, Don Juan the First,

And thus, grandson of the second Don Enrique,
He who killed the King Don Pedro, and was
A Guzmán through his mother, and a brave
Knight, though the brother was still braver, but
When they fell to the earth, then Fortune turned,
And unlocking their arms gave to Enrique
The dagger, which has now become his scepter.
But who is that tall man talking to him?
He is no less than the Condestable.

CASILDA. They, I suppose, are kings of flesh and bone?

COSTANZA. Of what were you thinking?

CASILDA. Damask or velvet.

COSTANZA. You really are a silly!

COMENDADOR (*aside*). Like a shadow I am following
The sun of that peasant wench,
And so foolhardily that I'm afraid
I'll be recognized by the King's suite.
But already he goes to the Alcázar.

(*Exit the* KING *and his suite.*)

INÉS. Hello! the King is going.

COSTANZA. So soon?

I have not yet been able to
Find out if his head is flaxen or red.

INÉS. Kings in our eyes, Costanza, owing to
Our deference, are like miraculous
Images, for every time we look at them
They seem to us to be of another color.

(*Enter* LUJÁN *with a painter.*)

LUJÁN. Here he is.

PAINTER. Which of them?

LUJÁN. My Lord, here is the painter.

COMENDADOR. My friend.

PAINTER. At your service.

COMENDADOR. Have you brought the card and paints?

PAINTER. Knowing your plan, I've brought
Paints and a card.

COMENDADOR. As soon as those peasant girls
Do settle down at their leisure,
Paint me the portrait
Of the middle one of the three,
Without their being aware of it.

PAINTER. I am afraid 'twill be a hard task;
  But I'm confident
  The likeness will be good.
COMENDADOR. Take heed of what I need:
  If this small portrait on the card
  Be a good likeness, I want you then to paint
  A full-size one with more space on a canvas.
PAINTER. Do you want it full-length?
COMENDADOR. Not so much: half-length will be sufficient,
  But with the same metal disks,
  The strings of beads, the smock and jacket.
LUJÁN. They are sitting over there to watch the people.
PAINTER. We now have an opportunity,
  And I shall paint the portrait.
PERIBÁÑEZ. Casilda, let us choose that seat over there
  To see the illuminations.
  It is said that they will bring oxen
  To the town hall this evening.
CASILDA. Let us go; for there we shall see them
  Without danger or disturbance.
COMENDADOR. You, painter, must portray the sky
  All edged with clouds, but draw
  A pleasant meadow covered with flowers.
PAINTER. She certainly is ravishingly beautiful.
LUJÁN. So fair that my master
  Is all covered with hair and
  Disguised as a savage.
PAINTER. The light will fail very soon.
COMENDADOR. Don't fear that; for she has
  In her blue eyes another sun!
  For you they are stars,
  But for me rays of fire.

ACT II.

Assembly room of a brotherhood at Ocaña.

BENITO. This is my view.

GIL.   Then sit down and make notes

ANTÓN. It's wrong to hold a chapter with so few.

BENITO. The meeting was already called since yesterday.

BLAS. Last feast, a thousand absences were marked.

GIL. Fellow members, now that our procession
Has been so honored and our Saint revered
It is a shame for our fine brotherhood
To lag behind when there's a remedy.
Such scant devotion reflects on all
Ocaña's folk and holds them up to shame,
For day by day throughout Toledo's realm
Devotion grows in pageants and processions
For old San Roque, our most blessed patron.
Why then, I pray, are we so niggardly
In spending money?

BENITO.   It was thoughtlessness.

(*Enter* PERIBÁÑEZ.)

PERIBÁÑEZ. If there is anything that I can do
Then here I am, if now it is not too late.

BLAS. Welcome, Peribáñez, we've missed your advice.

PERIBÁÑEZ. I fear that I can be of little help:
Hence all my hesitations.

BENITO.   Sit by me

GIL. Where have you been?

PERIBÁÑEZ.   I was at Toledo, where
I took my wife to see the festival.

ANTÓN. I'm sure it must have been a great display.

PERIBÁÑEZ. My friends. I truly do declare I saw
Heaven itself on earth when I beheld
The holy shrine, and image, which I swear
Has not in all the world its peer, unless
The heavenly sculptors do return to earth.
Who has not seen the original throned on high,
Can never match the one Toledo venerates.

The procession was held, as is the custom there,
But there was extra pomp and majesty,
Because the King was present at the feast.
He was passing through the city on his way
To Andalusia to wage the Moorish war.

GIL. Without your constant help, my friend, alas,
Our brotherhood goes wrong in a thousand ways.

PERIBÁÑEZ. I thought the other day I could have come
And walked in the procession of our saint,
But renounced when I was told Casilda's plans,
And until past the octave I could not
Prevail on her to join me.

GIL.   So the King
Was there.

PERIBÁÑEZ. Yes, and the Master of Calatrava.
A fine campaign they surely are preparing.
Not one Moor will they leave to tell the tale
Of those who live and quaff the waters of
The Betis, though I know how they meet our troops.
But a truce to all and tell me what's afoot.

BENITO. The business of San Roque's brotherhood,
And since you've come while we were about to name
A steward, Pedro, you're here in the nick of time
To undertake the post.

ANTÓN.   When Peribáñez came
I said the same.

BLAS.   Who will say nay to this?

GIL. For my part I agreed, and in the feast to come,
Let him take full responsibility.

PERIBÁÑEZ. Though now I am a married man and might
Refuse to undertake this post, I shall
Consent to become your steward, and I'll strive
To spur myself to serve San Roque well.

ANTÓN. I'm sure you'll do what's needful.

PERIBÁÑEZ. What's needed?

BENITO.   I'd move that a showier statue
Be made of our San Roque.

PERIBÁÑEZ.   A good idea.
What does Gil say?

GIL.   He's right. The statue's old.

PERIBÁÑEZ. And what does Antón say?

ANTÓN. A bigger one
Should now be made to inspire our devotion.
The dog of the present statue is all skinned,
And more than half the loaf of bread has gone.
The angel, I remind you, is broken, and
The two fingers with which he blesses us.[8]

PERIBÁÑEZ. Blas, what do you say?

BLAS. Pedro and Antón should go
Today to the city and search for a painter,
Who'll do up our old statue, for it is wrong
To waste our cash when we might mend the old.

PERIBÁÑEZ. Blas is right, for our brotherhood is poor;
But how can it be carried?

ANTÓN. On your ass
Or mine. Well covered with a sheet, it will travel safe.

PERIBÁÑEZ. Today we've talked enough. I must go to Toledo.

BLAS. I want to tell you there's no trickery
In the opinion I have given, and if you'll agree
That money must be spent to turn our Roque now
Into a huge St. Christopher, I, Blas,
Declare I'm ready to pay my fair share.

GIL. If such were needful we would all agree.

PERIBÁÑEZ. Let us go, Antón, I must greet my wife.

ANTÓN. I'll be waiting with the statue in the cart.

PERIBÁÑEZ. Casilda will say I am flattering her,
But though the chapter's mission is an excuse,
I fear I may annoy her if I leave
Ocaña for Toledo at harvest time. (*Exeunt.*)
(*A room in the house of the* COMENDADOR. *Enter the* CO-
MENDADOR *and* LEONARDO.)

COMENDADOR. Tell me what happened.

LEONARDO. If to win Inés
Will profit us, here's how it came about.
Inés to Ocaña from Toledo came
With your fair peasant doxy, and she was
Like dawn in attendance on the rising Sun,
But soft and less reserved. I wandered up
And down her street as often as I could,

[8] St. Roch (native of Montpellier), the patron against pestilence,
was very popular in Toledo. He is always represented with his dog
who brought him bread daily when he was stricken by plague.

But unobtrusively, for in such folk
You will always find maliciousness on show.
At the dance I managed to have a word with her,
I paid my court, but bashfully she replied.
Next day when on the threshing floor we met
I spoke to her and poured forth all my woes.
She then paid greater attention to my prayers,
And promised to give a kind ear to my love,
When I hinted that she might be my wife,
Though she feared what she had good cause to fear.
And I assured her, if she would consent,
That you yourself would even make the match,
But if she refused, then nothing would be done.
And so if you desire through Casilda's door to pass,
Only Inés will help you to achieve success,
For she is her cousin, and she's pert as well.

COMENDADOR. Ah, Leonardo, would that my good luck
    Could but discover a way to mollify
    The cruel harshness of that peasant heart!

LEONARDO. Is she then so ungrateful?

COMENDADOR.   I followed her,
    You know where, as a shadow does the sun.
    But when I showed her my face unconcealed,
    She gazed at me in terror as at death:
    Her face, now flushed, now pale, like driven snow,
    Did change as rage and scorn did surge in her.
    And I gazed at her with humble and loving eyes,
    Showing that her harsh looks were killing me.
    In her distracted state she was even lovelier,
    And such my madness, Leonardo, was
    That one day I called in a painter who
    Has painted my scornful love on a card.

LEONARDO. Was it a good likeness?

COMENDADOR.   So good that later,
    Upon a full-size canvas he did paint
    Her image which I'll keep before my eyes,
    To charm me more than the original.
    It is ready: go to Toledo now for it,
    Since I may not the living image love,
    I shall live with the painted effigy.

LEONARDO. I'll serve you, though I grieve to see you woo

A woman who is sure to deny herself,
Until she knows what you intend to do.
Let me just speak a moment with Inés
And you will see how we shall settle all.

COMENDADOR. If she has all the powers that you say,
The world has no more interest for me.
(*Enter* LUJÁN *disguised as a reaper.*)

LUJÁN. Are you alone?

COMENDADOR.   Luján, Leonardo's here.

LUJÁN. A reward, my Lord, for I bring you good news.

COMENDADOR. If your desires to help me don't suffice
I assure you I have in Ocaña some estates.

LUJÁN. In reaper's clothes, my Lord, I went to Peribáñez,
And asked work as day laborer in his fields,
So from today I am in his house disguised.

COMENDADOR. Would I, Luján, were with you at daybreak.

LUJÁN. Tomorrow we reapers go to the fields,
But for your love there is a remedy at hand
For Peribáñez has gone to Toledo,
And left me free this night to act. As soon
As the reaping squadron are asleep around
The doorway, and as soon as I hear your sign,
Or the sound of your footsteps, the door I'll open
And guide you to the room, where you may see
That woman who has been invincible.

COMENDADOR. How can I, Luján, reward you for your help?

LEONARDO. Reason's the finest treasure of the soul.

COMENDADOR. What a simple method you have found for me
To rid me of my worst anxieties!
Now that the jealous yokel is not here,
And has tonight abandoned all to me,
If, when the reapers are asleep, you come,
And open the door to me, my hopes revive
That my mad love will end in victory.
A double share of good luck I have had,
For the yokel's gone and failed to pierce your mask.
Have you examined all the house with care?

LUJÁN. Of course I examined it and visited
The room of the sun whose rays consume your heart.

COMENDADOR. And did you go into her room to be
The Spanish Phaëton of a celestial sun?

What dread temerity! and was my angel occupied?

LUJÁN. Busy embroid'ring, seated on her dais,[9]
Not on a chair of rich brocade, though she
Might well have had one, but of blue leather,
Embossed with a gilt fringe on the edges,
Which instead of tassels, were on the corners cut.
And as throughout Castile the people say
That "ere August is old one feels the cold,"
And rain by now has fallen in our village,
Both wish to be gentle folk before the winter,
And all their walls they have decked with your hangings.
So I said when I saw your honored arms,
"That's no adornment, but Casilda's trophy,
For such has been the god of love's decree."

COMENDADOR. Nay, my arms warned you when that day they
      took
Possession of the conquest they had made;
For hanging where they do they've not surrendered.
But were they lives I would vow them well spent.
Go back now lest they notice you are here;
And while I now prepare me for the fray,
Night will descend and be compassionate.

LUJÁN. Will Leonardo go with you?

COMENDADOR.   That would be wise;
At all times it is comforting to find
A loyal friend at hand.   (*Exeunt.*)

(*The porch of* PERIBÁÑEZ's *home. Enter* CASILDA *and* INÉS.)

CASILDA. By my soul, Inés, you'll stay this night with me.

INÉS. It is only right that I should ask for leave.
Don't take offense; they're my parents, after all.

CASILDA. Lest they grow anxious I'll send word to them.
It is late I tell you.

INÉS.   Cousin, as you please.

CASILDA. No greater pleasure could you give to me.

INÉS. Of nights, Casilda, you are wont to sleep
With someone by you, hence your nervousness.
Your husband's absence I'll not compensate,
For he's as fine a youth in words and deeds
As ever breathed, but at the slightest noise

[9] The *estrado* or dais was a platform at the end of the room, on which ladies sat.

I swoon, at a sheathéd sword I quake,
At a naked blade I lose all consciousness.

CASILDA. There is no need to worry in this house.
The reapers sleep beside the entrance door.

INÉS. What is wrong with you, my dear, is loneliness,
You fear your cares will filch away your sleep.

CASILDA. You are right, for our anxieties are doors
Through which press all the jealous fiends of love,
And fear, and once we begin to fear,
We can no more sleep than we can relieve
Our love by jealousy.

INÉS.   Does he give you cause
While he is at Toledo?

CASILDA.   Can't you see,
My dear Inés, that jealousy's a breath
Of wind and may blow gusts from any quarter.

INÉS. I always heard that it came from Medina.[10]

CASILDA. And what about Toledo? Could it not
Come from there too?

INÉS.   Fair girls are there, I know.

CASILDA. Come in to supper.

(*Enter* LLORENTE *and* MENDO, *reapers.*)

LLORENTE.   Early to bed, early to rise.

MENDO. That's true. I think it is time to get some sleep.

CASILDA. Inés, the reapers are turning in.

INÉS.   We'll go.
Tell Sancho to keep a sharp eye on the orchard. (*Exeunt.*)

LLORENTE. The mistress of the house goes to the door;
She'll be chasing us as the master's not at home.

(*Enter* BARTOLO *and* CHAPARRO, *reapers.*)

BARTOLO. By sunrise I have to reap the meadow slope.

CHAPARRO. If sleep permits . . . God give you good repose,
Mendo and Llorente.

MENDO.   There'll be little rest.
We two with our sickles will go toilin' and moilin',
Now gatherin' into sheafs, now cuttin' and reapin'.

CHAPARRO. By heaven, Mendo, if it be worth a mention,
Honest work always makes a decent show.

[10] Medina del Campo, where there was a famous animal fair, was
famed for the beauty of its women. So too was Toledo, and was
often praised by Lope de Vega.

Come sit down all of you before we sleep
And let us sing a song or tell a tale.
We must have fun.

BARTOLO. Are you drowsy, Llorente?

LLORENTE. By heavens, Bartolo, I wish the dawn
Would come to me four times a year, no more.
(*Enter* HELIPE *and* LUJÁN, *reapers.*)

HELIPE. Is there room for us all?

MENDO. Welcome, Helipe.

LUJÁN. Do you think I might find a tiny place?

CHAPARRO. There'll be room for you: squat down by the door.

BARTOLO. We're all agreed we want to sing a song.

CHAPARRO. Or we might listen to a tale.

LUJÁN.   If anyone
Can spin a yarn, let him first join our group.

CHAPARRO. I wraps me in my cloak and down I sits.

LUJÁN. First have a song and I'll tell you the tale.
It's one that I have just remembered now.

MENDO. Sing.

LLORENTE. I'll start the tune.   (*They sing to guitars.*)
> *Trefoil, my Lord, that blooms in the dell;*
> *Trefoil, my Lord, how fragrant the smell!*
> *Trefoil of the lass who is fickle and vain,*
> *Trefoil of the lass who is fickle again.*
> *With her white widow's coif she looks so demure,*
> *But the minx wears a red petticoat as a lure.*
> *Trefoil, my Lord, that blooms in the dell!*
> *Trefoil, my Lord, how fragrant the smell!* [11]

LUJÁN. They seem to have fallen asleep.
Better not sing any more.

LLORENTE. I'd like to sleep but it will not be on clover.

LUJÁN (*aside*). What's halting me? The reapers are asleep.
O night, I now commend my love to you;
The whistles urge speed, I must open the door.
Is that you, my Lord?
(*Enter the* COMENDADOR *and* LEONARDO.)

COMENDADOR. Here I am.

LUJÁN.   Come in quick.

COMENDADOR.   I am inside.

[11] This charming song closely resembles one of the ballads in the
Romancero General of 1600 (f. 327 V.).

LUJÁN. They're dozing off. You now may safely pass;
Even if a cart passed they would not awaken.

COMENDADOR. Luján, I don't know the house,
Guide me to her chamber.

LUJÁN. Let Leonardo stay here.

LEONARDO. That suits me.

LUJÁN.   Follow me.

COMENDADOR. O love! O Fortune; do favor my quest.
    (*The* COMENDADOR *and* LUJÁN *enter the house;* LEONARDO
    stands watch watch behind the door.)

LLORENTE. Are you there, Mendo?

MENDO. What's up, Llorente?

LLORENTE. There are men in the house.

MENDO. Men?
I must confess I feared as much;
Is this the way then they respect
The good name of Peribáñez?

LLORENTE. I'm not sure; they're not common folk.

MENDO. How so?

LLORENTE. One wears a cloak with gold on it.

MENDO. Gold is it? Strike me dead
If it isn't the Comendador himself,

LLORENTE. Let's give a shout.

MENDO.   Better to hold our whisht?

LLORENTE. I suppose it would. How do you know
It is the Comendador?

MENDO. In Ocaña there's no other man
Would dare set foot in here,
Nor even think of doing so.

LLORENTE. That comes of wedding a pretty lass.

MENDO. She may be blameless?

LLORENTE. Quite so. They're coming back.
Pretend to be asleep.

COMENDADOR. Ho there, Leonardo!

LEONARDO. What's wrong, my Lord?

COMENDADOR. I lost the finest chance I ever had.

LEONARDO. How so?

COMENDADOR. That heartless woman has her window tightly
    closed.

LEONARDO. Call her.

COMENDADOR. If only there was nobody about . . .

They'll awake.

LEONARDO. They'll not awake, they are reapers;
And wine and weariness are padlocks
On reason and the external senses.
But hark! I hear them opening
The window at the door.

COMENDADOR.   All goes awry.

LEONARDO. Suppose it is she?

COMENDADOR.   It is she I'm sure.

(CASILDA, *with her face muffled, appears at the window.*)

CASILDA. Is it time to rise, friends?

COMENDADOR. My lady, dawn comes and it's time to reap,
But when you show your face, the Sun at once
Arises but to find itself eclipsed.
We all must sympathize with your sad plight,
When we observe your forlorn loneliness,
Surely your husband must not wish you well,
For to Toledo he has gone today,
Thus leaving you one dreary night alone.
If such were the luck of our Comendador
—Full well I know his love for you—
Though you repel and treat him scornfully.
I swear he would not thus abandon you,
Not even were the King to summon him.
For never among lovers has it been the case
To leave thus alone so fair a face.

CASILDA. Now you, good country man from far-off lands,
Who have come to our harvest as a guest,
Where did you pick up such malicious ways?
On with your leggings and off with your cloak,
Then with scythe on shoulder, and with gloves in belt,
Go forth at dawn for the day is calling you
Tie up the dried sheaves and don't harm the ears,
And when the stars come out go to your rest,
But don't poke your nose where you're sure to stumble.
The Comendador of Ocaña woos, I'm sure,
A high-born lady, not one in a smock
Of rough red homespun or a skirt of wool.
I'm sure she'll wear a forelock waved with curls,
And a gorgeous ruff of finest starchéd linen,
But not an uncouth coif upon her hair

Or a headdress all trimmed up with silver braid.
On holy days she'll go in state to Mass
In coach and pair or sedan chair lined with silk.
You will not see her riding from the fields
To the vines in lumbering waggon with side poles.
And she'll write him in cleverly worded letters
A thousand marvelous courtesies, but not
A mere rustic wife's scorn and curt refusal
Tricked and decked out with plenty of courtly lordships.
For him she'll wear her amber-scented gloves,
And she'll smell sweetly of perfumes and spices,
But not of wild thyme or fragrant lavender,
Or pennyroyal or the flowering bramble.
But even if the Comendador himself
Were to love me as he loves his own life,
And even if virtue and honor were
Nought but a delusion and a mockery,
I'd rather have Pedro on his dapple mare,
His beard stiff with frost and his snow-flecked shirt,
His crossbow athwart, and hanging from the saddle
A pair of rabbits or a brace of partridge,
And running behind his gray hound on the leash,
Than the Comendador in his silken cap,
With hood and shoulder puffs ablaze with gems.
And the ancient stone cross in the hermitage
More deeply stirs my heart to say my prayers
Than the red cross of the Apostle Santiago
That shines like a star on my Lord's braided doublet.
Go then, you reaper, else you'll rue this day,
For if my Peribáñez comes, I swear
You'll never see the light of another day.

COMENDADOR. I'm staying, mistress mine . . . mistress!
Casilda, my love, Casilda,
I am the Comendador;
Open, I entreat you.
Look! two strings of finest pearls
I have to give you, and a chain
Inlaid with many colors, heavier than my own.

CASILDA. Reapers of my house, it is time to rise;
Sweet-smelling dawn is summoning you to work:
Come raise your shouts of joyous merriment;

And he who culls most clusters by the eve,
Shall win the straw hat Pedro wears in the vines.
(*She leaves the window.*)

MENDO. Llorente, our mistress calls,

LUJÁN (*aside*). Flee, my Lord, flee quickly;
Or else the people will see you.

COMENDADOR. Ah what a cruel Libyan asp she is!
Even though I spend all my wealth,
My honor, my good name, my life,
I'll humble your pride and vanquish your wrath. (*Exit the* COMENDADOR, LUJÁN *and* LEONARDO.)

BARTOLO. Up with you quick, Chaparro, the dawn's at hand.

CHAPARRO. Come on, Helipe, it is very late.

HELIPE. By heaven, Bartolo, look at the peaks!
They're now bathed in the white light of the dawn.

LLORENTE. Follow me, good friends, lest our mistress say
Our sickles are idle as our master's away.
(*Exeunt, shouting gaily.*)
(*A room in a painter's house, at Toledo. Enter* PERIBÁÑEZ, *the* PAINTER *and* ANTÓN.)

PERIBÁÑEZ. Of all the holy pictures I have seen,
There is one that I'd like to see again,
Whether because it charms, or else perhaps
Because I'm a peasant like the girl portrayed.
Since you've agreed to repair our patron's statue,
May I have another look at that girl's portrait?

PAINTER. I agree with you: the girl is beautiful.

PERIBÁÑEZ. Take her off the nail; I want Antón to see her.

ANTÓN. I've seen her but I'd like to see her again.

PERIBÁÑEZ. Go, then, I pray, and fetch her.

PAINTER.   I'll go now.
(*Exit the* PAINTER.)

PERIBÁÑEZ. You'll see an angel.

ANTÓN.   I know why you gaze
At the peasant girl with such anxiety.

PERIBÁÑEZ. That is because of the costume she is wearing:
You're wrong if you think it delighted me.

ANTÓN. I suppose you thought that she was like your wife.

PERIBÁÑEZ. Do you believe Casilda is so fair?

ANTÓN. Pedro, you are her husband, and I think
It is fitter you should sing her praise than I.

(*Enter the* PAINTER *with the full portrait of* CASILDA.)

PAINTER. Here is the girl.

PERIBÁÑEZ (*aside*). And my dishonor too.

PAINTER. What do you think?

PERIBÁÑEZ.   Very fine. And you, Antón?

ANTÓN. In your eyes it is a token full of beauty,
    In the eyes of the world a work of art and grace.

PERIBÁÑEZ. Go, Antón, to the inn and saddle, I'll be there.

ANTÓN (*aside*). I may be a dunce but I know very well
    It's Casilda's portrait. Pedro's jealous mad.
    Farewell.   (*Exit* ANTÓN.)

PERIBÁÑEZ. Heaven has made none finer.
    What beautiful eyes! What a dainty mouth!
    From where, pray, came this lovely girl?

PAINTER. If you now fail to recognize that girl,
    Then I conclude that she's not well portrayed,
    For she comes from the village where you live.

PERIBÁÑEZ. From Ocaña?

PAINTER.   Yes.

PERIBÁÑEZ.   I know a bride, whom she
    resembles.

PAINTER.   I don't know who she is,
    But I'm sure that I painted her in secret,
    Not as I here present her, but upon a card.
    This is the copy I have made from it.

PERIBÁÑEZ. I know the man who had her portrait made,
    If I guess right, will you tell me the name?

PAINTER. I shall.

PERIBÁÑEZ.   The Comendador of Ocaña then?

PAINTER. As I am sure that she is unaware
    That one of Spain's most noble lords is now
    In love with her, I am convinced it is he.

PERIBÁÑEZ. Did she not know?

PAINTER.   You too ignored the truth.
    At first because of her fidelity
    It was no easy task to paint her picture.

PERIBÁÑEZ. Would you entrust it to me? I'd bring it to her.

PAINTER. But they have not yet given me the money,

PERIBÁÑEZ. I'll pay you the full amount.

PAINTER. The Comendador would rage and rant. His lackey
    I await tomorrow.

PERIBÁÑEZ. Does the lackey know?

PAINTER. Swift as a bolt he goes to vanquish her.

PERIBÁÑEZ. I saw him yesterday and wished to meet him.

PAINTER. Have you another order for me yet?

PERIBÁÑEZ. While you repair the saint, I'll come to see
This picture a thousand times.

PAINTER. As you please. Farewell.   (*Exit the* PAINTER.)

PERIBÁÑEZ. Alas, what horrors have I seen and heard
When heaven is angry and Time's out of joint?
If my wife's not a partner in this evil
How shall I tell her where she has done me wrong?
Who can ever judge a husband's jealousy?
Enough that the Comendador now woos my wife,
Enough that he robs me of my good name,
When it is he my good name should respect.
But I'm a vassal and he is my lord,
I live beneath his shelter and defense.
If he thinks he'll rob me of my good name
Then I shall have to rob him of his life;
For a wrong attempted means a wrong is done.
I was a fool to marry, but I thought, alas,
That with a lovely wife my soul would spend
A whole lifetime of pleasure, but I failed
To reckon that one day the might of wealth
Would gaze with envy and covet my love.
Deuce take the humble man, amen I cry,
Who roves the world in quest of a lovely bride!
Now Don Fadrique has my wife portrayed,
When to sketch her is a blow to my good name.
And if when painted my honor goes limping
Why then my good repute will run a risk,
Deuce take the humble man, amen, I cry,
Who roves the world in quest of a lovely bride!   (*Exit.*)
(*A room in the house of the* COMENDADOR. *Enter* LEONARDO
and the COMENDADOR.)

COMENDADOR. By letter, Leonardo, just arrived,
His Majesty commands me send at once
From Ocaña and its land some fighting men.

LEONARDO. What will you do?

COMENDADOR.   Let them make proclamation
And muster up to two hundred valiant youths,

To be divided in two companies,
A hundred peasants and a hundred squires.

LEONARDO. Were it not better if they all were squires?

COMENDADOR. Your wits, alas, do not keep pace with mine,
And thus, you stay far distant from my thought!
Peribáñez I intend to make the chief
And Captain of those hundred peasant lads,
And keep him absent by this stratagem.

LEONARDO. What strange ideas enter lovers' minds!

COMENDADOR. Love is but war, and all its thoughts but schemes.
Has he come yet?

LEONARDO.   Luján did say to me
That they expected him to dinner, and he found
Casilda full of anguish and distressed.
Then from Inés I heard she would not tell
Of all that took place on that famous night,
And in agreement with Inés she wished
To feign, that she might not upset her husband
So he beholding her so woebegone
Might not have courage to reveal his thoughts,
Though later he'd find plenty serving you.[12]

COMENDADOR. Hard-hearted woman, may a heavenly curse
Alight upon that moment when I fell,
Since then, my Leonardo, I have been
A haunting suppliant beside her door.

LEONARDO. Nay hush, my Lord, for Troy itself was strong,
Yet when it fell its walls were leveled flat.
Your peasant doxies are inclined to be
A trifle shy, and being of lower rank
They mostly answer "nay" when they mean "yea."
Do but send off her husband honestly,
And you will reach the crown of your delight.

COMENDADOR. May my good fortune hold; but by my troth,
Though I've been active in the lover's fray,
As all the world knows, yet today I'm scared.

LEONARDO. We should find out if Pedro will arrive.

COMENDADOR. Go, Leonardo, and search for Inés;
But don't walk up her street, or raise your eyes

[12] Leonardo here speaks ironically of Peribáñez's service to the Comendador.

To her window; don't loiter by her door.

LEONARDO. To show marked distrust is discourtesy,
  For no one ever loved without a hope.   (*Exit* LEONARDO.)

COMENDADOR. They tell a tale of a king who loved a tree,
  And of a statue that a youth did tend
  To whom by night and day he lisped of love.
  But he who loved a tree trunk or a stone
  Could still have hopes of reaching his desire,
  For he at last, when people were not nigh,
  Could kiss and fondle to his heart's delight.[13]
  Wretched am I whose fate it is to love
  The green ungrateful ivy clinging to a wall,
  Whose harshness I do try in vain to melt.
  Such is the end my fondest hopes foretell,
  But since I am so sure that I shall die,
  May Cupid therefore change you into stone.   (*Exit.*)

(*Enter* PERIBÁÑEZ *and* ANTÓN.)

PERIBÁÑEZ. You may go home, Antón, it's only right.

ANTÓN. And what of you? Haven't you a reason too?

PERIBÁÑEZ. I like to see my reapers; and I've come
  In the nick of time, for here lies tillage land.

ANTÓN. Casilda's surely finer tillage, man.

PERIBÁÑEZ. That's how it is; but I must give the men
  A plan of what they have to do for me,
  You go and see your wife and mine as well.
  Tell her I'm staying here to see our land.

ANTÓN (*aside*). A strange affair, but I don't want to let
  Him guess that I have understood his thought.
  May God be with you.   (*Exit* ANTÓN.)

PERIBÁÑEZ.   And protect your King.
  So grievous are my wrongs that I did make
  Pretense and thus go home at a late hour,
  How sad I feel! If my Casilda now
  Be blameless, why do I thus flee from her?
  Woe's me, beloved one, my evil lot

[13] This story, which Lope drew from Pero Mexia's *Silva de Varia Lección* (1500), originally came from Herodotus (VII: 31), who describes how Xerxes near Sardis found a beautiful plane tree which he presented with gold ornaments and placed under one of the gods. The legend is perpetuated in Handel's famous Largo from his opera *Xerxes*.

I do attribute to your peerless charm.
If you were not so fair you could not rouse
Such maddened love in our Comendador.
Here are my wheat fields and my threshing floors,
Yet fields and pastures I hoped to gaze upon
With heart rejoicing, when I lived at peace.
When I last saw you I had other hopes,
And when my heart rejoiced I planned to fill
To the brim my bins with your fair spikes of grain,
But now I must dissemble—(*Voices*)—for I fear
Their whooping cries though I must hear them sing;
But when another's instrument is playing
It is then one's soul begins to weep in earnest.
                    (*Shouts within as the peasants reap.*)

MENDO. Bartolo, make haste; the night will soon be here,
   For now the sun is just about to set.

BARTOLO. He always sups well who works well, I trow,
   So says the well known ancient Spanish proverb.

LLORENTE. I'll challenge you, Andrés, to swig four pints.

CHAPARRO. I'll give you two more challenges, Ginés.

PERIBÁÑEZ. Now all disturbs me, and there's nought but grief.

MENDO. Llorente, now sing of our master's bride.

PERIBÁÑEZ. What's left for me now? But I care no more
   For life, or even heaven itself, alas.
   Who will at last relieve me of my life?
   (*A reaper sings.*)

> *Ocaña's proud Comendador one day*
> *Peribáñez's lovely spouse did come to woo,*
> *But she, who's dainty as she's virtuous,*
> *Did answer thus to the Comendador;*
> *"I love more my Peribáñez in his plaid*
> *Than you, Comendador, in braided cloak."* [14]

PERIBÁÑEZ. I'll pluck up courage now I hear that song,
   For what this reaper sings must be the truth
   Of all that in my absence has occurred.
   How great a blessing heaven does bestow
   Upon the man who has a virtuous wife!
   I think the men are leaving their daily task.

[14] These lines, especially the last two (which Lope also incorporated in another play, *San Isidro labrador de Madrid*), came from the old ballad which inspired Lope to write the play.

Would that the earth could open at my feet!
Although, Casilda, you make great amends
To me for all, I still do suffer pain,
For when a woman's honor is the theme
Of song, then must it be of scant repute.   (*Exit.*)

(*A room in* PERIBÁÑEZ's *home. Enter* INÉS *and* CASILDA.)

CASILDA. How could you say such rank absurdities?

INÉS. Let me explain.

CASILDA.   How can I listen to such things?

INÉS. Cousin, you have not understood my words,
And pride in love for Pedro makes you now
Believe that Pedro is the one that's wronged.
What I must tell you is but my concern.

CASILDA. Yours?

INÉS.   Yes.

CASILDA.   I'm mad. If it's your concern, do tell.

INÉS. Leonardo, the Comendador's retainer,
Loves me and wishes me to be his wife.

CASILDA. Watch out, cousin, he may lead you astray.

INÉS. I know, Casilda, that I am his life.

CASILDA. Take heed, Inés, that men are sirens all,
And sing most sweetly when they would destroy.

INÉS. But I have here his signed certificate.

CASILDA. All words, like feathers, the wind will blow away,
And in Ocaña many ladies have
Rich dowries, but you are not of noble birth,
Nor wealthy.

INÉS.   Cousin, if such scorn you show
To our Comendador, then all my hopes
Are false, for you are hindering my relief.

CASILDA. Now see, Inés, how you beguile yourself,
Trying to feign that he's in love with you.

INÉS. If you are kind he will not harm your honor;
I don't say you should meet him at the door,
Nor stand beside the window when he comes.

CASILDA. On no account give countenance to him,
And I warn you not to mention him by name,
Else never more you'll set foot in my house;
It's after seeing, all the hearsay comes,
And foolish words do lead to evil deeds.

(*Enter* PERIBÁÑEZ *carrying saddle bags.*)

PERIBÁÑEZ. Wife!

CASILDA. My love!

PERIBÁÑEZ. Are you well?

CASILDA. I'm without you.

PERIBÁÑEZ. Are you well?

CASILDA. Now I see I am more than well, Inés.

INÉS. Pedro!

PERIBÁÑEZ. What is lacking now I have you both?

CASILDA. I am most grateful to our dear Inés,
Who has stayed with me since you went away.

PERIBÁÑEZ. When she weds, you will wear your fancy shoes,
And, as it's custom, I'll go new shod too.

CASILDA. What have you now brought for me from Toledo?

PERIBÁÑEZ. Desires in plenty, but they weighed so much
I could not bring you gems nor finery.
But I have brought you for your dainty feet
Open slippers tied with ribbons of silvery pink,
Two bonny girdles to hold up your skirt,
A yard and a half in length with silver clasps.

CASILDA. May heaven bless you a thousand years, my love.

PERIBÁÑEZ. While on my way I had a nasty fall
And it's a miracle I'm safe and sound.

CASILDA. God save us, husband, you do frighten me.

PERIBÁÑEZ. I fell from a slope upon a heap of stones.

CASILDA. What's happened?

PERIBÁÑEZ.   Had I not served our San Roque,
And said a prayer as I was falling off
My bay mare, it is dead I'd be this day.

CASILDA. I am in terror when I hear your words.

PERIBÁÑEZ. I promised him the object in my house
Of greatest value to adorn his shrine;
And so tomorrow take that coat of arms
Down from the walls, for we've scant use for it,
And hang it up instead, upon the wall,
On our saint's chapel in sign of gratitude.

CASILDA. Had they been tapestries of France, adorned
And woven of silk, and pearls, and precious stones,
I would not say a single word in argument.

PERIBÁÑEZ. It were best that hangings with another's coat
Of arms should not be blazoned on our walls,
Lest people start to murmur in the town

That a rustic should surround his simple bed
With hangings blazoned with device and arms
Of our Comendador. Such crests and plumes
Are out of place amidst the plow and spade,
Amidst the flail, the winnowing fork and hoe.
For our whitewashed walls should not display
Such silken crosses, but those made of grain,
And straw with poppies, camomile, and furze.
For one thing and one only I require:
To find before me painted images:
Of the Annunciation and the Assumption,
Of poor St. Francis with his stigmata,
St. Peter Martyr and St. Blas, the twin
Unrivaled doctors when my throat is raw,
And St. Sebastian and St. Roque, these,
And many other sacred images;
Now portraits—that is different, I say:
We might as well have ghosts upon the walls,
One ghost I saw which I would like to . . .
But I would not like anything at all.
Casilda, let us now sit down to dine,
And then do you prepare my bed for me.

CASILDA. Are you not well, my love?

PERIBÁÑEZ.   It's well with me.

   (*Enter* LUJÁN.)

LUJÁN. A servant from the Comendador has come.

PERIBÁÑEZ. From whom?

LUJÁN. The Comendador of Ocaña.

PERIBÁÑEZ. What does he want with me at such an hour?

LUJÁN. You'll soon find out if you but speak to him.

PERIBÁÑEZ. Are you, perchance, the reaper who last night
   Entered my house?

LUJÁN.   You don't remember me?

PERIBÁÑEZ. Where many men pass; it is not surprising.

LUJÁN (*aside*). This looks bad.

INÉS (*aside*).   He speaks with many meanings.

PERIBÁÑEZ (*aside*). So the Comendador's looking for me?
   Honor, you are ungrateful to my cares!
   If you are glass then even the best, alas,
   The merest blow can shatter into bits.

ACT III.

The Main Square in Ocaña. Enter the COMENDADOR *and* LEO-
NARDO.

COMENDADOR. Now tell me briefly, Leonardo, all
  That took place at Toledo.
LEONARDO.   Even if
  My tale's told briefly it will tax your patience.
COMENDADOR. Good news will even heal a mortal wound.
LEONARDO. His Majesty King Henry, called the Just,[15]
  Whom Cato emulates in equity,
  And Aristides, held in Madrid his court
  In the year fourteen hundred and six,
  When envoys came to say Granada's King,
  The Moor, had broken truce and had refused,
  Despite all promises and threats, to hand
  Back Ayamonte's fort or tribute pay;
  And so the monarch of Castile resolved
  To wage just war against him, and at once
  Assembled at Toledo all his fiefs
  And kinsmen from Navarre and Aragón
  As did befit the greatest king in Spain.
  The knights and prelates are assembled there
  With attorneys of the towns and villages
  To hold their councils in the Alcázar,
  And from Sigüenza's bishop seek advice,
  Who rules Toledo's holy church today.
  The see is vacant through the recent death
  Of the great prelate, Don Pedro Tenorio.
  Likewise Palencia's bishop there we find,
  Don Sancho de Rojas, the fair counterpart
  Of his famed ancestors; for him there waits
  Toledo's princely see; and next we find
  Don Pablo, Cartagena's bishop, who

---

[15] The following speech of Leonardo is, as Menéndez y Pelayo
pointed out (Vol. XIV, p. 70, of *Obras Completas*), a versified
version of the first chapter of the Chronicle of King Juan II (Logroño, 1517).

Is designate for Burgos, and again
The gallant Don Fadrique, who is now
The Count of Trastamara. Though he is
Titled Duke of Arjona, all the Court
Calls him and Don Enrique Manuel,
The King's first cousins, whose swords caused a blaze
Not of Granada but of Troy itself.
Don Lopez Dávalos, grandee of Spain,
By his good fortune and by his own arms
Castile's Condestable, glory of his house;
The Lord High Chamberlain, by blood descent
And by his own prowess, though I'll admit
His sire was one to leave such legacy,
Don Juan Velasco, worthy of all praise.
I'll mention one they call the Judge Supreme,
Don Diego López de Estuñiga,
And the Capitán-General of Castile, to wit,
Gómez Manrique, whose intrepid deeds
Granada and Castile have chronicled.
Nor should I pass by the judges of the Court
Of Oyer and Terminer, who protect the realm,
Pero Sánchez del Castillo, Rodríguez de Salamanca,
And Peribáñez . . .

COMENDADOR.   Stop . . . Peribáñez . . . halt . . .
My blood freezes when I hear that name.

LEONARDO. How droll! I name the Judges of the King
To you and one called Peribáñez,
And you think he's our Ocaña countryman.

COMENDADOR. Up to the present I was asking you
To tell me the causes of the King's campaign,
But I am now afraid to hear the tale.
And so, is His Majesty resolved to make
A campaign with the flower of Castile's knights
Upon the frontiers guarded by the fiefs
Of the Granadines, who still deny to us
Their tribute?

LEONARDO.   That is all I have to tell.

COMENDADOR. Well now, take note of one important point.
While you Toledo-wards your way did wend
My plan had reached its full accomplishment.
I spoke to Peribáñez and informed him

That I was pleased to nominate him now
A captain of a hundred countrymen,
And that he should straightway prepare himself.
It seemed that he felt honored, and it is true,
Unless it's honor wrapped in infamy.
But he was out to win it, and he spent
His little wealth on trappings and fine clothes,
And yesterday paraded in the square
His company. And Luján says today
He marches to Toledo with his men.

LEONARDO. Your way to fair Casilda then lies clear,
Though she be still as boorish and unkind.

COMENDADOR. Yes, but prolongéd absence must produce
On love the same effect that water does,
When many a year its course flows over stones.

(*Drums play.*)

LEONARDO. What mean those drums?

COMENDADOR.   They surely are his drums.
But your ensign is mustering the squires,
So go, my Leonardo, take your arms,
And that we may deceive him all the more,
You too, must sally forth with all your men.

LEONARDO. I hear them coming. Tarry here for me.

(*Exit* LEONARDO.)

(*Enter a company of farmers grotesquely armed, followed
by* PERIBÁÑEZ *with sword and a dagger.*)

PERIBÁÑEZ. I did not wish to leave without farewell
To you, my Lord.

COMENDADOR.   I esteem your courtesy.

PERIBÁÑEZ. I go to serve you.

COMENDADOR.   Say "the King my Lord."

PERIBÁÑEZ. The King and you.

COMENDADOR.   That is as it should be.

PERIBÁÑEZ. It is just that I should serve the King, and you,
For it's through you I have my honor now.
For how could I have ever so deserved
To find myself with my cloak, hood, and hoe
Promoted captain with short lance and flag
Of the King, whose royal ears had never heard
My name pronounced, and whose great stature far
Exceeds all five dull senses I possess.

May God, my Lord, preserve you many years.

COMENDADOR. And may He, Pedro, bring you happiness.

PERIBÁÑEZ. Am I correctly dressed?

COMENDADOR.   You are indeed.
There's now no difference 'twixt both of us.

PERIBÁÑEZ. There's only one thing I would wish . . .

COMENDADOR.   Speak out.

PERIBÁÑEZ. If you, my Lord, would gird on me my sword
That I might be honored.

COMENDADOR.   Hand it to me,
I'll dub you knight, for with such dash, I hope
You'll soon become a valiant officer.

PERIBÁÑEZ. In heaven's name, my Lord, I have it here,
Let your Grace gird it on.

COMENDADOR.   I'll do it now,
That you may wear it for my sake.

BELARDO. Down on your knees this instant, Blas, I say,[16]
They want to make of him a nobleman.

BLAS. Say, friend, did he fall short in anything?

BELARDO. In plenty if you don't quick bend the knee.

BLAS. Belardo, you who are advanced in years
Tell me, will they now hit him with your sword?

BELARDO. Sure I know more about my dappled ass
And its packsaddle, harness, and all its gear
Than I do of the how and why they arm
The Knights of Castile.

COMENDADOR.   You're already dubbed.

PERIBÁÑEZ. What else must I do?

COMENDADOR.   You must swear on oath
That you will serve Almighty God and King
With this your sword.

PERIBÁÑEZ.   This I do swear and vow
To bear it always in honor's defense,
So now at your behest I'm off to war
And you defender of this land remain.
Wherefore, though married recently, I leave
My house and wife, and I consign them both
Henceforth to your responsibility.
This I entrust to you, for it is more

[16] Belardo was the poetic name by which Lope de Vega frequently
introduced himself into his plays.

Than my own life with which I go to war,
For though I am so confident that none
Will do her wrong, I like to think
That you protect her, and being so wise
You know full well what Honor signifies;
For when Honor's at stake it can't be matched
With property, or even life itself.
And he who knows what his honor is worth
Can never possibly be robbed of it.
And you did gird me with my sword, my Lord,
Wherefore I understand what honor means.
Before this I was all but ignorant.
Now since this honor you have granted me
Makes us both equal, see that you guard it well,
Or I shall have cause to complain of you.

COMENDADOR. I now give you leave to complain of me,
If I should be disloyal to this trust.

PERIBÁÑEZ. March on, my men, and let there come what may.
(*He marches off arrogantly behind his company. Exit.*)

COMENDADOR. His way of speaking left me a bit perplexed
For now I'm sure he will begin to plot
How he may be avenged, or else complain.
But as I have my thoughts so charged with guilt,
With my own malice I now judge his words,
Whereas his words were said in innocence.
And even were it malice that I heard,
Who is the peasant could prevail against me?
You most rebellious and unthankful girl,
And may my passion die ere dawn shall break!   (*Exit.*)
(*A street in Ocaña, outside* PERIBÁÑEZ's *house. Enter above
on the gallery at the back of the stage* COSTANZA, CASILDA,
and INÉS.)

COSTANZA. And so at last your husband goes away?

CASILDA. Pedro's off to the front, but in the war
He has left at home I could win greater fame.

INÉS. Casilda, don't be so depressed; the rank
Of Captain is not given just any way.

CASILDA. Never, Inés, may you deserve such rank!

COSTANZA. Indeed, Inés, that is the very truth,
I've never seen commissions come our way,

For they belong to squires and noblemen.
But also I have been informed that he
Goes only to Toledo with the troops.

CASILDA. If this had not been so, could I have lived?

INÉS. I hear the sound of drums. It must be he!

COSTANZA. Pity those who go with him, but not yourself.

(*Enter* PERIBÁÑEZ *with the drum, flag and soldiers.*)

BELARDO. You see the damsels on the balcony,
When I see them I am young once again;
I'm no longer for them nor they for me.

PERIBÁÑEZ. Are you so old Belardo?

BELARDO.   Pleasure's gone.

PERIBÁÑEZ. But something's left beneath that homespun cloak.

BELARDO. I tell you, Captain, there was once a time
When in the sun and open air I played
The clown, the shepherd, and the sacristan,
But one year, when snow fell, I saw my hair
Was gray, so I took refuge in the church.

PERIBÁÑEZ. Why you've reached only three decades and nine.

BELARDO. You must add three more years the nurse did say,
Who weaned me, but I am sure she forgot,
For she had scanty memory, but way back
In the dark ages, my first jaw tooth came.

PERIBÁÑEZ. Already, I suppose, you went to school?

BELARDO. I could tell you on oath what I then knew,[17]
And thousands say I scarcely then could read,
But upon my word there's truth in it, I say;
For since to dance, to sing or play to me
Comes naturally, I know how to write
Without knowing how to read, a novel gift!

CASILDA. My dashing captain of my gloomy thoughts!

PERIBÁÑEZ. My lady of the balcony for whom
I hold the banner.

CASILDA.   Are you leaving now
Ocaña, sir?

PERIBÁÑEZ.   My lady, I must take
These soldiers to Toledo, they're my cares.

CASILDA. If they are soldered they'll no trouble give.

[17] A reference to the carping critics who were always finding fault with Lope de Vega.

If you're not jealous your honor has nought to fear.[18]
PERIBÁÑEZ. If I could be sure I'd not have such fears.
It's not for you I'm anxious, but because
Of him on whose behalf I lead the men.
If only my cares could be yours as well,
They would not go whither they are going now,
Nor I, my lady, be going with them too.
Security, which brings a moment's truce
In the grim war in which I find myself,
Now takes me to Toledo, and beyond
The world to desperate extremity.
And so I come to bid farewell to you,
And I leave you a guardian of yourself,
Because in you and with you I remain;
But from you I would now a favor beg
That ladies give new captains in the field,
When they await the trophies from their wars.
Do you not think I speak as though I had
A solemn mien and knightly courtesy?
Who would have said that a mere countryman,
Who yesterday had cut the stubble dry
With his steel sickle curved with tiny teeth,
Whose feet a-treading the purple grapes had made
The wine press overflow with dusky must,
And whose coarse hand the iron plow had grasped,
Would speak to you today in martial words,
Wielding his sword and decked in lordly plumes.
Learn now that I am noble and can do
Whatever I wish, for the Comendador,
Casilda, armed me; so this lesser thing,
When the time comes, as I suspect it will
Tonight, I reckon, will decide my life.
CASILDA. Your dark words I now fail to understand:
The favor, yes, I know it is due to you.
But what gift can a country girl bestow
Upon a captain?
PERIBÁÑEZ.   Don't so name yourself.
CASILDA. From me, my Pedro, this black ribbon take.

---

[18] Casilda makes a play on the words *soldar—soldados*. If Peribáñez's cares (i.e., jealousies) are well mended he need not worry
about his honor.

PERIBÁÑEZ. Is black the color, wife, you give me now?

CASILDA. Pray tell me are there omens in the war?

PERIBÁÑEZ. It is a token of despair and prophesies
Exile or mourning.[19]

BLAS.   Tell me, fair Costanza,
What token to a soldier do you give
For all his compliments?

COSTANZA.   I'll give you, Blas,
This leash of dog's hide, though you're setting out
For a place where dogs in plenty you will find
From which to fashion them.

BLAS.   God grant the Moors
Make them of my raw hide, if I don't kill
All those in battle whom I put to flight.

INÉS. Will you, Belardo, not request a favor?

BELARDO. Inés, as veteran, not as youthful swain,
From your hands I deserve a compliment.[20]

INÉS. Take my shoe.

BELARDO.   Nay, fair lady, pause a while;
A shoe-slap when delivered from a height
Will smart.[21]

INÉS.   Belardo, bring a Moor to me.

BELARDO. For days I've gallivanted after Moors,
But if one does not come to me in prose
From this day on I'll offer him in verse.[22]

(*Enter* LEONARDO *as Captain, with drum and banner and a
company of squires.*)

LEONARDO. Now march in order, soldiers, as I said.

INÉS. What's this?

[19] Black was the sign of banishment and exile as well as death.

[20] Belardo (Lope de Vega) had served in military expeditions
against the Azores in 1583, and with the Invincible Armada against
England in 1588.

[21] Women wore shoes with very thick soles and heels of cork, which
made them taller than men. According to Covarrubias, when they
were in a temper they were liable to pull off their shoe and inflict
punishment upon those who had offended them.

[22] Here Lope de Vega alludes to some forthcoming literary work,
probably his *Jerusalén conquistada*, an epic poem on the crusade
of Richard Coeur de Lion. That work he wrote in 1604, as he
refers to having finished it in a letter to the Duke de Sessa of
September 3, 1605.

COSTANZA. The company of wearied squires.[23]

INÉS. Our brawny farmers made a better show.

COSTANZA. Their cloaks are finer, not their bravery.

PERIBÁÑEZ. Ho there! let every man be all agog
To show his mettle, dash and elegance.

BELARDO. What if those cowards think they've beaten us,
Then let ours leisurely stroll in front of them.

PERIBÁÑEZ. Ho there! Let nobody advance: let lancer now
Follow crossbowman.
(*Each company wheels round the other, glaring at one another.*)

BLAS. Now the time has come,
Belardo, to show dash.

BELARDO. You hold your whisht!
Even the most decrepit age will find
In its own gallant spirit its relief.

LEONARDO. Enough! The farmers now vie with the squires!

BELARDO. You'll see those fellows running away like hounds.

BLAS. No stags could race faster once they perceive
A Moor near by. To name one were enough.

BELARDO. I saw them all run when we fought the bull.
(*Exeunt the farmers.*)

LEONARDO. So now they've gone away. Come here, Inés!

INÉS. Is it you, my Captain?

LEONARDO. Why have your cousins gone?

INÉS. Don't you yet know the reason? Why Casilda now
Is like a rock. Tonight she's in a huff.

LEONARDO. May our Comendador not see her then
For a while tonight.

INÉS. Hush! Mum's the word, I pray;
I'll fix his trysting when I am assured
That Pedro goes to rest.

LEONARDO. Then if you wish
To capture my affection, blind the eyes
Of that hard-hearted girl who is so niggardly
Protecting her honor. Our Comendador
Is like one at death's door since yesternight.

INÉS. Tell him to come to the street.

[23] According to Henri Mérimée, the edition of 1614 reads *cansados* (wearied). *Revista de Filología española* II, 1919, pp. 61-63. Other editions read *casados* (married).

LEONARDO.   What signal, pray?

INÉS. Whoever sings well.

LEONARDO.   So I'll say farewell.

INÉS. Will you come also?

LEONARDO.   I intend to hand
  Over to my ensign our brawny men,
  Then I shall meet you at our tryst.

INÉS.   Farewell.   (*Exit.*)

LEONARDO. Come sound the march, for now two suns have set.
                                              (*Exeunt.*)

(*A hall in the house of the* COMENDADOR. *The* COMENDADOR
  in a dressing gown and LUJÁN, *his lackey.*)

COMENDADOR. And so you saw him finally depart?

LUJÁN. Aye, he was riding on a goodly mare,
  One as swift in battle to o'ertake or flee.
  I wish you'd seen our Peribáñez lead
  His men, the sight would banish all your cares.

COMENDADOR. He is, I know, the best of company;
  But I, alas, prefer that of his wife.

LUJÁN. It's said, faint heart never won a fair lady.

COMENDADOR. Luján, the men will dine in the city
  Tomorrow.

LUJÁN.   If tonight they're billeted.

COMENDADOR. Neither the Captain nor his men should halt.

LUJÁN. Well as they're peasants and the day is short,
  And as the dance with beating drum beguiles,
  Still I am sure they'll march without a halt
  Right to Granada.

COMENDADOR.   How shall I pass the time
  That lasts from now till ten o'clock tonight?

LUJÁN. But it is already nearly nine. Don't fret
  And be so gloomy that when Fortune smiles
  Upon your plans, impatience mars your joy;
  Remember expectation, too, has charms.

COMENDADOR. I must, alas, when happiness delays,
  Still trust in hope, despairing all the while.

LUJÁN. And Leonardo, will he come with us?

COMENDADOR. Don't you see by my plan it's fixed that he
  Must wed Inés, for she must open the door.

LUJÁN. What signal will you give?

COMENDADOR.   It will be in song.

LUJÁN. What happens if they frighten off the game?
COMENDADOR. At first they will give us help, for in the noise
    No one will understand what's happening,
    Or the opening and the closing of the doors.
LUJÁN. Your plan's well laid and all has been foreseen,
    But yet I once heard of a family
    That gathered in a place to celebrate
    A wedding, and to eat their fill, and dance.
    The priest came, and the bridegroom, and with him
    The bridesmaid, and the groomsman, and as well
    The drummer with a handsome psaltery.
    But it turned out the bride had not said "yes,"
    For she cried they had brought her 'gainst her will.
    And so, when all had gathered in the church,
    The priest did ask, and she three times denied
    The question, so the marriage was dissolved.
COMENDADOR. Do you then mean to say that we, in spite
    Of all precautions, have left out Casilda's "yes"?
LUJÁN. I fear you shoulder a heavy enterprise,
    For she is hard, and her "yes" you did need.
COMENDADOR. Our plan is not so ill devised, and since
    Her boorish harshness will not yield to prayers,
    She must be tricked.
LUJÁN.   Perhaps you will succeed,
    But I'm inclined to think we're in the dark.
    (*Enter a servant and the musicians.*)
PAGE. The musicians have arrived.
FIRST MUSICIAN.   Here are, my Lord,
    Lisandro and Leónido till dawn.
COMENDADOR. My friends, give thanks that I entrust you with
    A theme that is both gallant and my own.
SECOND MUSICIAN. My Lord, you honor us.
COMENDADOR.   Has eleven struck?
LUJÁN. One, two and three . . . no more.
SECOND MUSICIAN.   You counted wrong.
    The clock struck eight.
COMENDADOR.   How comes it now
    That you should be so unwilling to tell
    The hours the clock so gladly gave to me.
LUJÁN. If you expect it's later, I'll count three.
COMENDADOR. One must not watch.

LUJÁN.   Do calm yourself and dine.

COMENDADOR. God send you a bad Easter when you say dine.

LUJÁN. Well, have a drink then.

COMENDADOR.   Is there snow?

PAGE.   There's none.

COMENDADOR. Share it between you both.

PAGE.   The cloak is here.

COMENDADOR. Show it to me. What is that?

PAGE.   A black cloth.

COMENDADOR. Whatever I see disturbs me. All those brutes
    Do mock me. Mourning? for what purpose?

PAGE. Do you want a colored cloak?

LUJÁN.   In love affairs
    The discreet lover never wears a cloak
    Of colors, for it is said that in a court
    Color oft gives a clue to judge a man.[24]

COMENDADOR. You fool, I'm all for color: are you servants
    here,
    Or else despotic duennas?

PAGE   See the color.

COMENDADOR. I go, my love, wherever you will guide
    My footsteps. Do but grant a night to me
    For all the days I've spent in servitude.

LUJÁN. Shall I go?

COMENDADOR.   Yes, as Leonardo will
    Not be with me. Musicians, tune your strings,
    Perhaps sweet music still may quench my fire.   (*Exeunt.*)
    (*A street. Enter* PERIBÁÑEZ.)

PERIBÁÑEZ. Lucky is the man who owns a mare,
    A beast that both can flee and overtake,
    For thus without discomfort he may ride.
    As soon as I had billeted my men,
    I then with speed unwonted, did return
    To Ocaña. Now how truthfully I could say:
    "What is my honor but a fragile reed?"
    And there's no reed so fragile as my honor,
    Which bends before whatever wind is blowing.

[24] In the days of Lope de Vega black was worn in the daytime, but for night adventures colored cloaks were worn. Luján, however, who is always cautious, thinks the colored cloaks might cause the Comendador to be identified.

But honor's reed is brittle, hollow, and
Devoid of substance, save some paltry leaves
With which it ornaments its hollow trunk.
The reed, alas, is all pomp and display:
It is fanciful, it's thin and breakable,
And when it is green it is for so short a time.
The fragile reed and honor too are full
Of knots, and they are only for the deaf,
And for my speechless neighbors in the town.
Here in Ocaña you sprang up with me,
When a fickle breeze was blowing through the town.
I'll cut you before you break, you fragile reed.
I thank my lucky stars for you, my mare,
Who have with such devotion carried me
Back to Ocaña. Blessed be the oats
And barley I so often gave to you!
I never did employ you in a cause
More honored, and it is now I reap my gain
For which I can't be grateful enough to you.
On other occasions you have carried me,
But I weighed little then; my honor now
Is greatly spurring me on, and if I am
So grateful it is for running all the course
While burdened by the insults heaped on me.
Let every man take pride in his trusty sword,
A coat of mail, and a friend of good repute,
One honored in the opinion of the world,
A goodly traveling cloak and other things;
But I swear a beast can give me wondrous aid.
O mare of mine! in less than one short hour
Three leagues gone! Why you even match the wind.
And if they paint the wind with wings, you shall
From this day onwards also have your wings.
And here is Antón's house, whose walls adjoin
My own, which bend their weight to ruin me.
I want to call, for now I think it's time
To do so. Ho! you in the house! Antón.

ANTÓN (*from within*). Ho, woman! Don't you think someone
    has called?

PERIBÁÑEZ. Peribáñez.

ANTÓN. Who knocks at such an hour?

PERIBÁÑEZ. Here I am, Antón.

ANTÓN. I'll go as I hear the voice,
No matter who it may be. Who is it?

PERIBÁÑEZ. It's Peribáñez.

ANTÓN. Who?

PERIBÁÑEZ. It is I
Whom heaven today chastised so cruelly.

ANTÓN. Full dressed I laid me down to sleep, for I
Had set my mind on rising with the dawn;
I'm mighty glad I am not in the nude.
How can I help?

PERIBÁÑEZ. By your leave through your house
I wish to enter mine; for certain things
So clear by day shadows become by night.
Now I suspect that in Toledo you
Heard some tales about me.

ANTÓN. Though I heard
I held my tongue, but I can reassure . . .

PERIBÁÑEZ. You need say no more. My Casilda is
An angel.

ANTÓN. You must shower gifts on her.

PERIBÁÑEZ. Let me be, brother.

ANTÓN. Do come in, I pray:
It is only for the news I've heard of her.

PERIBÁÑEZ. If I can only be quite sure of her,
I'll be forever hers, so help me God.

ANTÓN. Where are your men?

PERIBÁÑEZ. My ensign is with them.
All I have brought with me are my own woes,
And no small feat the mare has done to bring
Us both, for God's my witness, I've enough
Anxieties to drive me raving mad. (*Exeunt.*)

(*A street outside* PERIBÁÑEZ's *house. Enter the* COMENDA-
DOR, LUJÁN *with bucklers, and the musicians.*)

COMENDADOR. You minstrels may begin your singing now
In this place that the wind may help your song.

SECOND MUSICIAN. It is written.

COMENDADOR. How I hate what they call tun-
ing!

(*The Musicians sing:*)
> *At your door I was tossed by the bull,*
> *My bonny bride:*
> *And you never even cried: "Heaven help him."*
> *At your door I was caught by the bull,*
> *The bull of your wedding feast:*
> *Such a tossing he gave me the whole town laughed;*
>
> *And you full of dignity and full of mockery,*
> *My bonny bride,*
> *You never even cried: "Heaven help you."*

(INÉS *appears at the door.*)

INÉS. Stop it, Don Fadrique.

COMENDADOR.   Is it you, Inés?

INÉS.   I'm here.

COMENDADOR. Though it is but eleven I'm a soul in pain.
  May your bead win me pardon that I may
  Be freed from pain.[25]

INÉS.   Has Leonardo come?

COMENDADOR. He makes sure of Peribáñez. Do secure, Inés,
  My entrance and contrive that I may see
  My precious pearl. Leonardo'll soon be here.

INÉS. Will he be long delayed?

COMENDADOR.   Not long I trust.
  With such a cunning husband he could take
  No chances.

INÉS.   I believe that at this hour
  His wish to be seen in captain's uniform
  Is sure to keep him in Toledo still.

COMENDADOR. Perhaps this very moment he's asleep.
  May I go in? Do tell me if I may.

INÉS. Come in: I delayed in case Leonardo might
  Arrive.

LUJÁN. Luján, may he, too, enter?

COMENDADOR.   Now, Lisandro, cease
  your song. Farewell till dawn.

(*They enter the house. The musicians remain.*)

FIRST MUSICIAN. May Heaven favor your designs.

[25] According to popular superstition, the souls in Purgatory wandered at midnight. To one of the beads of the rosary the Pope granted an indulgence in favor of the souls in Purgatory.

SECOND MUSICIAN.   And we,
  Where shall we go?
FIRST MUSICIAN.   To bed.
SECOND MUSICIAN.   A pretty wench!
FIRST MUSICIAN. Silence!
SECOND MUSICIAN.   I must confess I'm envious.
                                                        (*Exeunt.*)
    (*A room in* PERIBÁÑEZ's *house. Enter* PERIBÁÑEZ.)
PERIBÁÑEZ. Over Antón's garden walls I made my way
    Into my house and found the doors of yard
    And threshold open: in the chicken house
    I wished to hide, but feared some cock might warn
    Them of my presence. By the corner light
    I watched the cock, but found him half-asleep
    Amidst his twenty or his thirty hens.
    "I am amazed that you so calmly sleep
    When your fortune's so doubtful: here am I
    Who cannot even protect a single wife,
    Yet you insist on guarding so many more."
    I can't sleep for I'm crazed with jealousy,
    And I suspect a cock with a crimson crest,
    For he has it emblazoned on his chest.
    At last like a thief I left and came in here,
    Where I saw my doves, models of wedded bliss,
    And watching their soft billing and their cooing,
    As they imparted through their beaks their love,
    I said: "May God's most weighty curse alight
    Upon the squab who now disturbs you twain."
    The geese now awakened, and the pigs
    Are grunting, the oxen bellowing, so the laws
    Of honor now cause widespread restlessness,
    On my behalf, and even the donkey roped
    To the manger brays; for I am master here,
    And all now see that the rope is throttling me.
    I long to weep; I'm sorry for myself
    And all my woes . . . but, if Casilda sleeps.
    Hush! I hear the sound of voices near.
    In this big sack of flour I'd better hide.
    If this should be the Comendador himself,
    He surely thinks I'm far away from here.   (*He hides.*)
CASILDA. I'm sure I heard men talk.

INÉS.   I'm sure you're wrong.
CASILDA. But you were speaking to a man.
INÉS.   Was I?
CASILDA. You were.
INÉS.   You heard him then?
CASILDA.   Take heed, my dear.
  If it is not malice, they must be robbers.
INÉS. Robbers! You frighten me.
CASILDA.   Then shout aloud.
INÉS. I shall not shout.
CASILDA.   I will.
INÉS.   Then you'll awake
  The entire neighborhood to no avail.
    (*Enter the* COMENDADOR *and* LUJÁN.)
COMENDADOR. My love is past endurance and no fear
  Restrains me, neither can I keep silence,
  I am your Comendador and Lord.
CASILDA.   I have
  No Lord save Pedro.
COMENDADOR.   As a slave I come,
  Although I am your Lord. Do pity me,
  Or else I'll have to say I found this lackey
  Who stands before you.
CASILDA.   Though I feared the ray
  I was not frightened by the thunderbolt.
  So then, my cousin, you have betrayed me!
INÉS. Come now: what madness is this, when you are
  A needy farmer's wife, your spouse a boor?
  Who would allow a prince to die of grief?
  For him it is matter of life and death,
  For you and your honor there is no such risk.
  You know Peribáñez to Toledo's gone.
CASILDA. O cruel and most heartless cousin, you
  Are changed from cousin to vile go-between.
COMENDADOR. Let me now see what I can do with her.
LUJÁN. The better course would be to leave them now:
  Alone they'll come to an understanding soon.
                                  (*Exit* INÉS *and* LUJÁN.)
CASILDA. I am a captain's wife, even if you are
  Comendador. But don't come near me, for
  Biting and kicking I'll . . .

COMENDADOR.   Softly and silently.
  (*Enter* PERIBÁÑEZ.)

PERIBÁÑEZ (*aside*). Alas, my honor! what awaits me here?
  I'm just a farmer and it were best to speak,
  But better still to kill him. Pardon me, (*Aloud:*)
  Comendador: my honor now becomes
  A patronage of greater weight than yours.
                 (*He wounds the* COMENDADOR.)

COMENDADOR. My God! You've killed me: do have pity, pray.

PERIBÁÑEZ. Do not fear, my love, come this way, and follow
  me.

CASILDA. Alas, I can't speak. I am terrified.   (*Exeunt.*)
  (*The* COMENDADOR *staggers to a chair.*)

COMENDADOR. Lord, by your sacred blood take pity now;
  My wound drives me to beg a vassal's pardon.
  (*Enter* LEONARDO.)

LEONARDO. Ah, there is chaos everywhere, alas!
  Inés, where are you hiding? My Inés!

COMENDADOR. I hear voices here. Who calls?

LEONARDO.   It is I.

COMENDADOR. Ah, Leonardo! can't you see me?

LEONARDO.   My Lord?

COMENDADOR. Yes, Leonardo.

LEONARDO.   What happened? Are you faint?

COMENDADOR. I'm dying, slain by him—I deserve my fate.

LEONARDO. You are wounded then? By whom?

COMENDADOR.   I do not wish
  Outcry or shouts of vengeance any more.
  My life is in danger, only in the soul
  I place my hopes. Let there be no extremes
  Or violence: I have been justly slain.
  Bear me that I may now confess my sins,
  And let us all our vengeance leave aside.
  I pardon Peribáñez.

LEONARDO.   Can it be said
  That a peasant slew you and that I refused
  To avenge your death? Alas! I grieve for that.

COMENDADOR. I vow he's not a peasant but a knight:
  For I myself did gird on him the sword
  With gilded guard.[26] He hasn't ill used his blade.

[26] The gilded guard was the insignia of an infantry captain.

LEONARDO. Let us go, and I'll knock at the chapel door
  Of Our Lady of Remedies.
COMENDADOR.   There's God alone.   (*Exeunt.*)
  (*Enter* LUJÁN, INÉS, PERIBÁÑEZ, CASILDA.)
PERIBÁÑEZ. Here you'll die, both of you.
INÉS.   Without a wound
  I'm dead already.
  (LUJÁN *and* INÉS *run across the stage.*)
LUJÁN.   O wretched Luján,
  Where will you hide?
PERIBÁÑEZ.   There's no reprieve for you.
LUJÁN. Why, Captain?
PERIBÁÑEZ.   You feigned to be a harvester.
INÉS. And why am I to die?
PERIBÁÑEZ.   You betrayed us all.
  (LUJÁN *runs to the edge of the stage, and then* INÉS *pursued*
  by PERIBÁÑEZ.)
LUJÁN. Alas, I'm done for!
INÉS.   Dearest cousin of mine!
CASILDA. No blood ties count when honor is at stake.
  (PERIBÁÑEZ *returns.*)
PERIBÁÑEZ. They both fell at the entrance.
CASILDA.   Just has been
  Their punishment.
PERIBÁÑEZ.   Casilda, will you stay
  With me?
CASILDA.   You know I'm yours for good or ill.
PERIBÁÑEZ. Upon the haunches of this frisky mare
  You shall behold Toledo's dawn with me.
CASILDA. Even on foot I'd go with you I say.
PERIBÁÑEZ. In all grim incidents a truce will last
  When there lies land between the battling sides,
  And harshness has not time to strike its blow.
CASILDA. May God have mercy on the Comendador.
  By his temerity he was undone.   (*Exeunt.*)
  (*The gallery of the Alcázar at Toledo. Enter* KING HENRY
  and the CONDESTABLE.)
KING. It gladdens us to see with what great joy
  Castile is mustering to our royal flag.
CONDESTABLE. Your Royal Highness, they abhor the sway
  The African in our fair Spain now holds.

KING. We mean to free all Andalusia,
  If our good army will but close its ranks
  Before inclement winter with its ice
  Freezes the fields and moves the earth to tears.
  And since the wide plain has sufficient space,
  Juan de Velasco, you must organize
  The stately armed tourney I have in mind.
  And let the fame of such a tournament
  Ring through the world and strike such awe in men,
  That even our gold-bearing Tagus may,
  As it flows through its adamantine gorge,
  See o'er the green fields a new Toledo rise
  With its rich tents and its gay pavilions.
  Let in Granada the usurping Moor
  Our blood-red flags and pennon start to fear,
  And turn his happiness to sad lament.
CONDESTABLE. Today you'll see me form the companies.
KING. The Queen whose presence I adore arrives.[27]
  On such occasions she inspires the troops.
  (*Enter the* QUEEN *and her suite.*)
QUEEN. If it is important, later I'll return.
KING. Even were it so, I beg you not to go,
  My lady, what can I discuss of peace
  That you could not give me advice about?
  And if it is of war that I am treating,
  When do I not take counsel, love, with you?
  How fares Don Juan?
QUEEN.   He weeps for lack of you.
KING. God guard him: he's a heavenly looking glass,
  Wherein those who departed see themselves
  Better portrayed than those of the present day.
QUEEN. Prince Juan's your son, and that alone endears him.
KING. But when we say he's yours, though he is ours,
  It is he reveals your virtue's legacy.
QUEEN. May Heaven make him fit to copy you.
  If that were granted to him and no more,
  He has been given all the good I wish.
KING. Knowing your generous love I well believe it.

[27] The Queen was Katherine, daughter of John of Gaunt, the Duke
of Lancaster of Shakespeare's *Richard II*. Her mother was Costanza,
daughter of Pedro the Cruel.

QUEEN. He is but two years old; I wish he were
Just old enough to follow this campaign
Under your banners.

KING.   Would that this were so,
And he would then begin to raise Christ's banner.
(*Enter* GÓMEZ MANRIQUE.)
What drums are these?

GÓMEZ.   Men from the Vera march
And from Extremadura.

CONDESTABLE.   From Guadalajara, too,
And Atienza people come.

KING.   And from Ocaña as well.

GÓMEZ. The lag is due to a tragic incident.

KING. What was it?

GÓMEZ.   People say who have just come,
That a farmer there has murdered Don Fadrique.

KING. Slain Don Fadrique! the greatest who ever wore
The Order of St. James.

QUEEN.   Is it true?

GÓMEZ.   Too true.

KING. My lady, those tidings grieve my soul.
How did such rank disorder ever occur?

GÓMEZ. Through jealousy.

KING.   Was it just?

GÓMEZ.   Madness it was.

QUEEN. Jealousy it was, for few alas are sane.

KING. And is the peasant captured?

GÓMEZ.   Later he
Fled with his wife.

KING.   What strange effrontery!
With such tidings Toledo welcomes me!
Is this the way Spain trembles at my law?
Now see you proclaim my edict in Toledo,
In Madrid, Segovia, Talavera and
Ocaña: those who take them alive or dead
A thousand crowns as income will receive
On the nail. Go then, and let no man conceal,
Or give them sustenance or other help
On peril of his life.

GÓMEZ.   I go.   (*Exit.*)

KING.   I trust

God's austere hand may shroud the heavens now.

QUEEN. You may be sure when fame of the promised gold
Reaches covetous ears the culprits will be found.

(*Enter a page.*)

PAGE. Here is Arceo who brings all complete
The Royal Standard.

KING.   Let him bring it now.

(*Enter* ARCEO, *one of the secretaries, with a red standard.
On it are the arms of Castile with a hand above holding a
sword, and on the other side Christ crucified.*)

SECRETARY. This, Sire, is the Royal Standard.

KING.   Show it to me.
I like it. And this captain likewise was
One whom I ransomed.

QUEEN.   What do the letters say?

KING. They say: "Judge thy cause, Lord."

QUEEN.   They are solemn words.

KING. They justly should cause fear.

QUEEN.   Let us now see
What's on the other side.

KING.   The Castle and
The Lion, and this blazoned hand that is
Now chastising.

QUEEN.   The writing?

KING.   Just my name.

QUEEN. What?

KING.   Instead of Third, Henry the Just.
I want that name to strike fear in the world.

(*Enter* GÓMEZ.)

GÓMEZ. The edicts now they do proclaim amidst
The city's lamentations.

QUEEN.   Even stones
Would feel pity.

KING.   Enough. What? can the hoes
Be compared to the crosses of St. James?
How could that be?

QUEEN.   Poor man, if he's not hiding
His outlook's grim.

KING.   I hereby take my oath,
I'll so chastise him that I'll affright the world.

(*Enter a page.*)

PAGE. A farmer here says he must speak with you.

KING. My lady, let us sit.

CONDESTABLE. A warning this.

(*Enter* PERIBÁÑEZ, *dressed as a farmer with long cloak, and his wife.*)

PERIBÁÑEZ. Allow me to kneel, Your Royal Highness, now.

KING. Speak out, I pray, and stay not on your knees.

PERIBÁÑEZ. How can I speak, Your Royal Highness, when
Words fail me and my brain is all awry,
Since I have gazed upon your royal face,
But since necessity forces me to speak,
And in your justice placing all my faith,
I shall start thus: Peribáñez am I called . . .

KING. Who?

PERIBÁÑEZ. Peribáñez from Ocaña.

KING. Slay him, guards,
Go slay him.

QUEEN. Not before my eyes, you guards,
Stand back, I say.

KING. You must respect the Queen.

PERIBÁÑEZ. As you do order them to butcher me
Will you not even hear me, Henry whom
The people call the Just?

QUEEN. Well said, take heed,
My Lord.

KING. You are right, and I had forgotten
That in disputes defendants must be heard,
And all the more so when they are so weak.
Continue.

PERIBÁÑEZ. I'm a man of peasant stock,
But my blood is unsullied and untainted
By Jew or Moor. I was the best among
My equals, and in all affairs they gave
First vote to me: Six years I bore the staff
Of office. I married that woman there.
Although she comes of peasant stock, her blood
Likewise is pure, and she is virtuous,
If Envy, reputation's minister,
Ever saw one. But alas it came to pass
That Don Fadrique, the Comendador,
The town of Ocaña's titled lord, began,

Like a mere stripling, to pay court to her;
Pretending I had done him services,
He honoréd my humble house and home
With some armorial hangings, which I found
Were laden with my own dishonor's weight.
He gave me as well a goodly pair of mules,
But not good enough to drag my honor's cart
Out of the mud of my own infamy.
And then one night, when I was absent from
Ocaña, he did try to rape my wife,
But he was in his fondest hopes deceived.
I came, I heard it all, and from my low
Walls I then took his coat of arms away,
Which might have served as cloak to fight the bull
I now was wiser to his purposes;
But calling me one morning he announced
That letters had come from Your Highnesses
Bidding him muster troops for this campaign.
At last a brave squadron of a hundred men
He gave me, and the title of captain too.
I left Ocaña with them; but as I knew
That my dishonor clearly shone at night,
I rode back on a mare, and reached my house
By ten o'clock at night, for I had heard
A squire once say it was good luck to keep
At home two good mares for emergencies.
I found my door battered down and all uncoifed
My wife, just like a simple little ewe,
Who finds herself in the clutches of the wolf.
She screamed, I came, I drew the selfsame sword
And dagger I had girded on to serve
Your Royal Highness, not for such sad deeds,
I pierced his heart, and then and only then
He let the white ewe go, for, shepherd-like,
I knew well how to snatch her from the wolf.
I came then to Toledo, where I found
That for my head they then were offering there
A thousand crowns; and so I have resolved
That my Casilda should conduct me here.
Grant this boon, I beseech Your Royal Highness,
For she it is who now should win the prize,

Since she'll be my widow, don't let her lose
So bountiful a prize: what do you say?

QUEEN.   I've wept.
That answer is enough for all to see
That this is not a crime but bravery.

KING. How strange that such a humble countryman
Should set so high a value on his name.
By the Almighty there's no reason why
He should be slain: We call this cruel justice.
And now I see so brave a man, I want
In this campaign to make him captain of
The very soldiers he took from Ocaña.
Henceforth his pay be given to his wife,
And carry out my word, and after this,
For his protection and his personal
Defense I give him leave to carry arms
Defensive and offensive.

PERIBÁÑEZ.   All do well
To hail our noble King surnamed "the Just."

QUEEN. To you most honest country girl I grant
Four dresses, that being a soldier's wife
You may appear in all your finery.

PERIBÁÑEZ. And thus, dear Senate, ends our tragicomedy,
Peribáñez and Ocaña's Knight-Commander.

PEDRO,
THE
ARTFUL
DODGER

❧❦❧

*Picaresque-Gypsy Comedia
in Three Acts*
by
MIGUEL DE
CERVANTES SAAVEDRA

(*1547-1616*)

❧❦❧

☙ DRAMATIS PERSONAE ☙

Pedro, the Artful Dodger (Pedro de Urdemalas)
Clemente, a youth
Clemencia and Benita, girls
Crespo, Mayor: father of Clemencia
Sancho Macho, Alderman
Diego Tarugo, Alderman
Lagartija, a farmer
Hornachuelos, a farmer
Redondo, a clerk
Pascual, a farmer
A sacristan
Maldonado, Count of the Gypsies
Musicians
Isabel, or Isabelica (whose name is shortened to Belica or Belilla by the Gypsies)
Inés, a Gypsy
A widow
A farmer who accompanies her
A blind man
The King
Silerio
A servant of the King
A constable
The Queen
A vagrant
Marcelo, an aged gentleman
Two actors with the author
A farmer
Three actors
Constable for plays

The text of *Pedro de Urdemalas* which we have used is from the edition of the *Comedias y Entremeses* of Cervantes by Rudolph Schevill and Adolfo Bonilla, Madrid, 1918, Vol. III.

ACT I.

Enter PEDRO, *the Artful Dodger, dressed as a yokel, and* CLEMENTE *as a shepherd.*

CLEMENTE. Pedro my friend, I know that I can trust
    Your native wit as well as your stanch friendship.
    For everybody knows that you possess
    Both qualities: in these I place my hopes.
    Your master's daughter, fair Clemencia,
    With whom I have to pick a bone, alas,
    Now shuns me and flees from my presence like
    A frightened doe before a hunter's shaft.
    The girl from Nature has received the gift
    Of loveliness, as you have seen, but when
    I thought that she was pliant, and about
    To yield to my entreaties, suddenly
    From lamb to tigress she became transformed,
    Because of lies about me she'd been told.
    And so I wonder, Cupid, why you aim
    Your arrows at me with such pitiless hate.
PEDRO. That's foolish prattle; tell me what you want.
CLEMENTE. Advice, dear Pedro, that is what I need.
PEDRO. Have you in your desires gone past the stage
    Of gentle toying, or attacked love's nest?
CLEMENTE. As you are well aware I'm a simple shepherd,
    You should intone upon a lower note,
    And phrase your sayings with less nicety.
PEDRO. I just ask if you're Amadis or Galaor.
CLEMENTE. I'm just Antón Clemente, a simpleton,
    And what you're saying is wide off the mark.
PEDRO. With folks like you I'll call a spade a spade.
    Have you not with Clemencia been alone?
    Or in a dark nook, where she let you take
    Some liberties which later worried her?
CLEMENTE. Pedro, the sky may fall, the earth may swallow
    me
    If my love be not pure as driven snow.
    Her father is a man of wealth and substance,

Hence he despises me because I'm poor,
And says I'm not his equal in my rank.
They say he only values men of wealth,
Such as Llorente and Pascual, and so
Why should I marvel that a woman's heart
Is always won by gold but not by love?
To add to my misfortunes, evil gossips
Have told Clemencia some foolish tales,
And so she now conceals herself from me.
If you, dear Pedro, do not make the peace
Between us both, I count myself as lost.

PEDRO. My wits have gone astray if I don't find
A swift relief for all your misery.
If, as I'm sure, my master is elected
The Mayor today, I guess that it was not
For nothing that he brought you over here
To talk about your destiny with me.
You'll see how I'll bring you your heart's desire,
Which selfish interest kept away from you.
But mark my words; before this can occur
You must first promise, give, and plead your case.
While this is brewing, turn your eyes, I pray,
Upon the bonds Love will impose on you,
For Phoebus even sighs and is disguised,
While he looks on Clemencia's golden hair,
And watches Cupid mirrored in its sheen.
Her cousin Benita comes with her, and like a star
Even rivals the sun with the light she sheds.
Clemente, take heed, if Clemencia comes,
To be a humble swain. As for myself
I intend to pay my homage to Benita,
As though she were already blessed by Heaven.
Now mind you pay her in exotic words,
A courtly tribute which will not displease her,
And of one thing be sure, that there's no woman
In the world who does not long to hear herself
Exalted to the skies as beautiful.
Stint not your praises and don't let your tongue
Be silent, then your Fortune's wheel will change.
(*Enter* CLEMENCIA *and* BENITA, *country girls, with their
pitchers as they go to the well.*)

BENITA. Why are you coming back, Clemencia?

CLEMENCIA. Why indeed, Benita? Not to find myself
    Near one who sickens me, a jackanapes
    Whose bearing contradicts his name.

BENITA.   I'll bet
    This is Clemente.

CLEMENTE.   Am I a basilisk,
    Or else some fleeting ghost that may arise
    In an uncouth hour when all our senses reel
    And we are terror-struck?

CLEMENCIA.   You chatterbox,
    You boaster, flatterer, and thorough liar!
    When did I ever give you pledges? When
    Did I ever lead you to believe, you fool,
    That I should never offend you? This you said
    To Jacinta, and you showed her the red ribbon
    I gave you: I see in your face it's true.

CLEMENTE. If I have said anything to displease you,
    May all my fortunes crumble into ruin!
    If I've not sung your praises to the stars,
    When I desired to tell you of my love,
    May Heaven turn my pledges all to silence:
    If I who proclaimed so stanch a faith in love,
    Yet when my life's course draws towards its close,
    Must be condemned, may Cupid find
    Nothing save leaden arrows in his quiver
    To fire at you, but golden shafts for me:
    And you they'll freeze and me they'll burn to ashes.

PEDRO. Clemencia, your father's here: I see
    He is bearing already his rod of mayor.

CLEMENCIA. He didn't win that gratis, for the sauce
    Had to be paid. Brother Clemente, hail!

CLEMENTE. How do we stand?

CLEMENCIA. Well.

BENITA. Let us be off then.

                    (*Exeunt* BENITA *and* CLEMENCIA.)

PEDRO. Be off, Clemente, and leave all to me.

CLEMENTE. In God's hands then.

PEDRO. So may He help you now.   (*Exit* CLEMENTE.)

    (*Enter* MARTÍN CRESPO, *the* MAYOR, *father of* CLEMENCIA,
    and SANCHO MACHO *and* DIEGO TARUGO, *aldermen.*)

TARUGO. Well, Martín Crespo, all's as right as rain:
　　You've won your office; not a vote astray.

MAYOR. Diego Tarugo, God knows what that rod
　　Of Mayor has cost me! What with butts of wine,
　　Capons in plenty, not to mention cattle.
　　Let him who doesn't know me now allege:
　　"He lusts for power."

SANCHO.   Oh, that's the rub: I'd like
　　To see what my own enemy would do.

MAYOR. But now it is your friend who rules the roost.

SANCHO. With you, Crespo, in the saddle all is well:
　　There'll be no double bribes and jobbery.

MAYOR. I take my oath, as long as I am Mayor,
　　I'll turn a blind eye when a woman comes
　　To me with gossip, and be deaf and dumb
　　To any nobleman who tries to frame me.
　　I'm all for rigorous severity.

TARUGO. I'm sure you'll be a Solomon on the throne,
　　Who sliced the child in half with his sharp sword.

MAYOR. I promise you that at any rate I'll stick
　　As closely to the law as I am able,
　　And I'll not change a detail in decrees.

SANCHO. I hope, with God's help, all will turn out thus.

MAYOR. May Fortune guide you, Sancho Macho, now,
　　For you're poised on the summit of her wheel.

TARUGO. It is time now to give your judgments, Crespo,
　　There must be neither fear nor favor, and
　　Let them be rigorous and also brief.
　　I disapprove of all delays. Good luck!

MAYOR. I must admit you are a worthy kinsman.
　　　　　　　　(*Exeunt* SANCHO MACHO *and* DIEGO TARUGO.)
　　Now, Pedro, as you're listening, why not
　　Congratulate me on my victory?
　　Now that I'm Mayor I do confess that all
　　Will be in vain unless you lend a hand,
　　And by your talents make me judge aright;
　　For I consider you a wiser man
　　Than priest or doctor.

PEDRO.   Well, experience
　　Will prove if that is true or false, for I

Can easily teach you a science which
Will bring you fame and reputation; why,
Lycurgus won't compare with you, and all
The lawyers in Athens will hang their heads.
I'll copy down for you two dozen judgments
Which will amaze them, each with its own variants,
Whether civil or private cases, you'll soon see.

MAYOR. From this day onwards, Pedro, you will be
No longer servant to me, but my brother.
Come now and show me how to set in train
All or part of what you've told me till now.

PEDRO. I promise you still more.

MAYOR.   I'm always ready.

                    (*Exeunt the* MAYOR *and* PEDRO.)

      (*Enter* SANCHO MACHO *and* TARUGO.)

SANCHO. Look here, Tarugo, I've a shrewd suspicion
That though you did congratulate our Crespo,
Your private thoughts were of a different hue.
It really is disgraceful that this town
Should have as Mayor the stupidest boob in all
The great wide world from Egypt to Castile.

TARUGO. Experience, dear alderman, will show
Us soon the true range of our Crespo's knowledge.
I shall not judge him until his first court
Has met, and as it is now due, I hold,
Sancho Macho, that we should listen to him.

SANCHO. I agree, though I am certain that the man
Is sure to show himself a simpleton.

      (*Enter* LAGARTIJA *and* HORNACHUELOS, *farmers.*)

HORNACHUELOS. Who knows if the Mayor's at home?

TARUGO. We're waiting for him.

LAGARTIJA. That means he is coming.

SANCHO. Here he is.

      (*Enter the* MAYOR *and* REDONDO, *the clerk, and* PEDRO.)

MAYOR. Most worthy aldermen!

REDONDO. Sit down, your worships.

MAYOR. No ceremony, gentlemen.

TARUGO. In courtesy you may exceed.

MAYOR. Let the clerk sit here, and on my right and left the
aldermen: And you, Pedro, sit behind me.

PEDRO (*aside to the* MAYOR). All is clear. Here in court you have enough judgments for all the cases that come up, even if you don't pay attention to what they say. And if by chance one should not apply, you have only to appeal to your consultant, myself, and I shall be well able to set you right, no matter what contingency arises.

REDONDO. Do you want anything, gentlemen?

LAGARTIJA. Yes we wish . . .

REDONDO. Say your say: the Mayor is here who will give judgment.

MAYOR. God forgive me for what I'm saying now, and let me not be accused of the sin of pride. I intend to give rigid justice, as if I were a Roman Sonador.[1]

REDONDO. You mean Senator, Martín Crespo.

MAYOR. That's all. Now state your case clearly, and as soon as I have taken cognizance of it in my mind I shall straightway deliver sentence with rectum and justice.

REDONDO. You should say rectitude, Your Worship.

MAYOR. Well that's that.

HORNACHUELOS. Lagartija lent me three royals. I returned two to him, there is still one owing, but he says that I owe him four in total. This is the lawsuit in short. Is this true, worthy Lagartija?

LAGARTIJA. True: but I myself find that either I'm an ass or Hornachuelos owes me four.

MAYOR. A fine case!

LAGARTIJA. There is nothing more in our suit, and I incur with whatever Mayor Crespo will decide.

REDONDO. You should say concur, that is all.

MAYOR. What do you say to this, Hornachuelos?

HORNACHUELOS. I've nought to say save that I admit to the Mayor.

REDONDO. Say submit, bad 'cess to my grandfather!

MAYOR. Let him say admit: what does it matter to you, Redondo?

REDONDO. Nothing.

MAYOR (*aside to* PEDRO). Pedro, my friend, go find me a judgment in the files—the one that's nearest.

REDONDO. Have you a judgment ready before you've seen the suit?

---

[1] Crespo says *sonador,* which means "noise-maker."

MAYOR. They'll see who is master here.

PEDRO. Read this judgment and mum's the word.

REDONDO (*reads*). "In the lawsuit between X and Y which I must judge, I condemn the said pig of Y to death, for it was the murderer of the said child of X." I'm blessed if I can make out who is this pig and who are those X's and Y's, or how it is possible to make all this square with the lawsuit of those two gentlemen here.

MAYOR. Redondo is right. Pedro my friend, put your hand in the bundle and pull out another judgment, it might be to the point.

PEDRO. As I am your consultant, I shall take the liberty of delivering a suitable judgment.[2]

LAGARTIJA. It suits me better than a new ass.

SANCHO. I say the consultant exaggerates.

HORNACHUELOS. A right judgment.

MAYOR. Well, Pedro, it is up to you: my honor now depends upon your imagination.

PEDRO. Let Hornachuelos first deposit twelve royals for me, the consultant.

HORNACHUELOS. The whole lawsuit is only for the half.

PEDRO. That is true: for the worthy Lagartija lent you three royals, and you paid him back only two. Wherefore you now owe four, and not, as you say, only one.

LAGARTIJA. That is right, exactly right.

HORNACHUELOS. I can't deny it: I'm beaten. I'll pay up the twelve royals with the four.

REDONDO. And I'll go defecate on Cato and Justinian.
O Pedro, the Artful Dodger, the famous highlander!
You're acting up to your name and pedigree.

HORNACHUELOS. I'll go for the money as fast as I can.

LAGARTIJA. I'm satisfied with winning my case.

(*Exeunt* LAGARTIJA *and* HORNACHUELOS.)
(*Enter* CLEMENTE *and* CLEMENCIA *disguised as a shepherd and shepherdess, masked.*)

CLEMENTE. Allow us to wear masks when we address
This solemn court.

MAYOR. Speak tied up in a sack

[2] The whole of this court scene recalls the interlude of Cervantes entitled *The Mayors of Daganzo*, and the judgment of Sancho during his short governorship.

For all I care. I'm in session to hear,
Not see.

CLEMENTE. The Age the ancients calléd golden
Now lives again among our people with
Their cult of justice. We see Crespo mayor.

MAYOR. Praise God; but lay aside that flatulence.

REDONDO. He meant to say flattery.

MAYOR. It is late; be brief, I pray.

CLEMENTE. I wish to state my case from beginning to end
In cultured language.

MAYOR. Speak on: I'm not deaf, nor have ever been.

CLEMENTE. Ever since my most tender years, beguiled
By my fatal star, unclouded by deceit,
I gazed upon the sun now veiled in mist,
And worshiped, and its rays did stamp themselves
Upon my soul and turn it all to fire.
And so I'm all ablaze, and yet today
I'm freezing like an iceberg, for a veil
Has now eclipsed me. My desires have found
Response, and Love allows my soul to feed
Its fancy, and this shepherdess I love,
Adores me too, but it is still a secret,
For her father like a tyrant holds her captive,
And there's no mother who might counsel her.
She gave her word and promise to be my wife,
But now she fears her father, who is rich,
May feel insulted by my humble state,
For in this age of tyranny it is
"The habit makes the monk," and he surpasses me
In wealth, but not in those virtues Nature gives.
I am as good as he is, even though I'm not
In wealth his rival, and I am devoid
Of evil, and no sluggard. Among honest men
Virtue is more than worth its weight in gold,
And so I ask that this girl may declare
Again that she consents to be my spouse,
For those whom God has joined together,
Let not man put asunder.

MAYOR.   My fair sun
Whom clouds have veiled, what do you say in answer?

CLEMENTE. Through modesty she will not speak, alas,

But she can make clear signs to show her will.

MAYOR. Are you his plighted spouse, my pretty maiden?

PEDRO. She has bowed her head: a sign that she agrees.

SANCHO. Well, Master Crespo, what is the decision?

MAYOR. Let a judgment be selected from my court.
You, Pedro, draw it out.

PEDRO.   This one I think
Will fit the case, for truth will always find
Sanction by short cut or by roundabout.
This judgment will tell and so I shall read:
(PEDRO *takes a paper from the desk and reads aloud:*)
"I, Martín Crespo, Mayor, hereby declare
That the ass should get his filly."

REDONDO. Your court desk is a lucky dip, and that
Judgment you have just given is a wonder.
Even though it was meant for animals,
It does show patent evidence of thought.

CLEMENTE. I'll bow my knee to you, for you're the pillar
That upholds the court where justice is enthroned.

MAYOR. Since this judgment of mine has given you
My heart, for that is what Clemencia is,
I welcome you with open arms, for since
The case is now decided I suppose
It will be carried out.

CLEMENCIA.   With such assurance,
Father, I'll take off my mask, and I'll kneel
At your feet. You were wrong to use
Such devious methods, for I am your daughter,
And not a ferocious monster. You have judged
At your sweet will, and if it is unjust,
I should attack your judgment; if it's just,
Then see that it is duly executed.

MAYOR. I have given my decision: You are right,
And let the world now learn from these events
That I judge not by passion but by law.

SANCHO. There is no one here who does not celebrate
Your unexpected joy.

TARUGO.   And everyone
Lauds Martín Crespo as a man of wit.

PEDRO. Our master knows that it is a special grace
When heaven gives a man a virtuous wife,

And the same is true likewise when a wife is given
A manly husband in whom courtesy
Is balanced by endurance. I am sure
Clemente and Clemencia will make
A happy union, and rejoice your heart
With offspring who will then perpetuate
Your honored name. And as tonight we hold
The feast of our St. John, we'll celebrate
The wedding also.

MAYOR.   Yes, you're wise indeed,
And all your brainwaves suit me, but the wedding
We'll hold another day. Tonight the entire village
Will romp and revel to its heart's content.

CLEMENTE. I do not care, as now Clemencia's mine,
And even the fondest hopes cannot compare
With full possession.

PEDRO. Hard work and wisdom always win the prize.

MAYOR. Let us be off; there's much to do tonight.

TARUGO. Good luck.

CLEMENTE. There's no need now for me to hope and fear,
When I shall visit you, my bride.

TARUGO. You have made a good choice, Clemencia.

CLEMENCIA. Let thanks be given to Heaven and to the man
Who planned the judgment.

PEDRO.   I have somewhat burdened
My conscience.   (*Exeunt.*)

(*Enter* PASCUAL, *pulling* PEDRO *by his smock.*)

PASCUAL. Dear Pedro.

PEDRO. What's up, Pascual? Do not think
That I have laid aside your remedy;
I hardly think of anything but it.
Tonight, however, is our St. John's Night;
And you know all the maidens in the village
Are longing to see signs of their future weddings.
Benita with hair billowing in the wind,
With one foot in a basin full of water,
And her ears agog, must wait till dawn to see
The evidence of her forthcoming marriage.
Now you must be the first to shout your name
In her street, but in such a way that she
Alone will clearly understand your name.

PASCUAL. You are the one who always had the fame
　Of being ingenious, so I'll follow suit,
　But after this, if you do what is needful,
　That scapegrace Cupid will not worry you.
PEDRO. I'll do my best: till then farewell, my friend.

(*Exit* PASCUAL.)

(*Enter a* SACRISTAN.)

SACRISTAN. No matter how quick you are, both of you,
　I've a handy loophole, and I'll easily
　Be able to steal a march on you two fools.

(*Exit the* SACRISTAN.)

(*Enter* MALDONADO, *the Count of the Gypsies. It is recommended that all who act the Gypsy parts should speak with a lisp.*)

MALDONADO. Master Pedro, God reward you!
　Where have you been?
　I've come to see if you're now resolute,
　Or if you're still a coward?
　I mean to say in other words
　If you are pleased to be
　Our comrade and our friend,
　As you once promised me.
PEDRO. I am.
MALDONADO. No reservations, eh?
PEDRO. None.
MALDONADO. Remember, Pedro, that our life
　Is free as the air we breathe,
　Unfettered as Nature,
　And the world provides for us,
　Hence we never lack
　What we ourselves can seek.
　The grassy sward gives us our bed,
　The sky above our canopy
　In every clime;[3]
　Our skin withstands the blazing sun
　No less than the icy blast.
　A padlocked orchard when we come,
　Offers its choicest fruits to us:
　No sooner do we spy amidst the vines

[3] This recalls the speech by the old Gypsy in *The Little Gypsy*, the Exemplary Novel of Cervantes.

The white and golden muscatels
Than the fairest clusters drop
Into the hands of our Romanichals,
Who cast their spells on the fruit of others.
Our muscles are hardened,
And we are brimful of the sap of life.
We revel in our loves
And have no rival suitors
To plague our hearts, and so we let
Love's passion surge within us
Without jealous pangs.
But now there is a maiden in our camp
Who is bashful with no one, and yet so lovely
That envy cannot find a flaw in her.
A Gypsy brought her to us secretly,
But her beauty and her purity
Proves that she comes of princely stock.
Though you, Pedro, may shun the yoke
That freedom curbs, this girl must be
Your bride when you and I
Have clasped hands on our friendship's pact.

PEDRO. But you, my brother Maldonado, now must learn
Why I am about to change my life. So heed
My words.

MALDONADO. I'm all ears. Do begin your tale.

PEDRO. A foundling too I was, or "son of the stone," [4]
And no father had I:
No greater misfortune a man may have.
I haven't a notion where I was reared,
I was one of those mangy orphans
At a charity school, I suppose: [5]
On a slum diet and scourgings in plenty
I learnt to say my prayers,
And to read and write as well:
But I learnt on the side
To snaffle the alms,
Sell cat for hare and steal with two fingers.

[4] So foundling children were called in Toledo. It was customary to
expose them on a slab in the Cathedral.
[5] This is one of the best picaresque ballads of Cervantes and rivals
the best of Quevedo's.

That life soon palled, so when I grew up
I sailed before the mast,
And served as a cabin boy;
Clad in canvas and tar
I sailed to the Indies and back again,
Without a groat to my name.
I shivered in the hurricanes,
And I sweated in the doldrums,
And Bermuda put the fear of God in me,
When I roamed its coast.
Then I gave up eating ship's biscuit
Mixed with lampblack and soot,
I foreswore too the devil's wine
Before St. Martin's feast came round:
And again I plodded
The banks of the Guadalquivir,
And I busied myself in its tides,
And back I was in Seville,
Where I took up the pilfering trade
Of basket boy, for I was down in my luck.
But there I picked up
Plenty of tithes
Without being a priest,
And I sampled a thousand things
That are forbidden here.
Then came the day when through a mishap
My job came to a sudden end,
And I took on the dangerous role
Of a whore's bully, and graduated
In the school of roguery,
Learning to pick a quarrel with the wind
And wound with my tongue as well as with my hand.
My master who was a tough egg,
Though a finger wizard,
One day made a studied assault
On a purse, but was caught
Red-handed with the swag
By a certain catchpoll,
And when he was racked
He wished to play confessor
Instead of martyr,

A martyr, I repeat, my Maldonado.
MALDONADO. What is that to me?
    Spout all that's in your mind.
    As you don't know the lingo.
PEDRO. The hangman flayed his shoulders
    Against his will,
    At which the poor fellow was peeved.
    According to one of the squealers,
    They took him for a ride in the galleys,
    Much to the distress of Chloe the climber,
    Who tore her hair,
    And Bovine Bessy, who
    Cried her eyes out.
    So finding myself minus the cover
    Of my Andalusian paladin,
    I was obliged to drop
    My job as whore's bully to the troops,
    Become a baggage man,
    And my luck gave me a swashbuckling soldier,
    One of those who march to the port
    Of embarkation and back again.
    O for the numbers of billeting tickets I cashed,
    O for the hens I choked!
    If Heaven doesn't pardon me,
    Hell will be my billet for sure.
    Life there taught me one lesson;
    For I found that a four-flushing soldier
    Always ends his days in the galleys.
    I halted a while with one of those gents
    On roguery's strand,
    But it's a dog's life
    With a thousand shocks,
    Though a hundred thousand may thrive on them.
    But for fear of finding
    Myself bound for Algiers,
    I made straight for Córdoba,
    Where brandy I peddled and orangeade,
    And I boozed in one day my whole month's pay.
    Of all the waters I have ever tasted,
    Firewater alone is a treacherous physic . . .
    The result was that my choleric master

Would have bumped me off with a blunderbuss,
But I made myself scarce, and by evil luck,
I landed next in the house of an Asturian.
He made rolled wafers and it was I who sold them.
But one day in a bout I gambled
Ten baskets full and lost them all.
I took to my heels with the speed of a hare,
And ran into a blind man whom I served
Ten months, and had they been ten years,
I'd now know more, I'm telling you,
Than Merlin, the wizard, ever knew.
I learnt the jargon;
How to be a bogus blind man,
And dash off prayers in a lively jingle,
But, alas, my friend the blind man
Gave up the ghost, leaving me
As poor as a church mouse,
Without a mite to bless myself,
Yet bursting with wisdom, and with a brain
As sharp as a razor blade fresh from the whetstone.
Then after a time as a muleteer,
I became the stooge of a cardsharper,
Who would swallow the kitty,
When he played his grand slam:
A great adept at the four-card trick,
And I have seen him with his one card
Clear the deck like a flash.
Past master he was at scraping cards,
Pin-pricking and marking them with black.
As a climax came his "Master John" trick,
With which he routed all his opponents.
Incomparable too with his luring tricks,
And when he slipped his winning card
In the deck, not even the lynx-eyed Cid
Would catch him napping or off his guard.
But every dog has his day, and no more,
And his house of cards came toppling down:
They clapped a notice across his nose,
So I left him and returned to the country,
Where as you see, I am serving the Mayor,
Martín Crespo, who loves me well,

More than he does himself, I know.
My name is Pedro, the Artful Dodger,
But a certain Malgesí,[6] the wizard,
When reading my palm one day did pause:
"My son," he cries in a solemn voice,
"You are destined to be a king,
A friar, pope, and a merry-Andrew,
Though you're no Romanichal.
Adventure in plenty will come your way,
To which kings will listen and like to hear.
Many a burden you'll have to bear,
But in the end the day will come
When you will accomplish all I've said."
Though I've little faith in all his prophecies,
Yet there's no doubt I am inclined
To be all that I had heard him say.
And now as you fit in with this prediction,
I repeat that I must be a Gypsy,
And henceforth I'll be a Romanichal.

MALDONADO. Pedro, the Artful Dodger, you are indeed,
The cornerstone and pillar of the Gypsies.
Come now and carry out your high resolve,
And be inscribed in the Romany company.
Can you now win the foundling maid,
And sweeten the bitterness of her heart?
If you can do this she will make you happy.

PEDRO. Let us go: I have no doubts in my mind.
And I hope my treasure I shall find.   (*Exeunt.*)
(*Enter* BENITA *with her hair down. She stands at the window.*)

BENITA. Come night and stretch your sable wings o'er all
The swains who are now in the wooing mood,
And hearken to their impassioned pleas,
For they say that across the sea the Moors
Chant your praises, so I to attain my wish,
Now keep my left foot in a basin full
Of clear cold water, and my ear agog.

[6] Malgesí, or Malagigi as he was called in Italian, was the cousin
of Rinaldo, the rival of Orlando (or Roland) in Ariosto's *Orlando
Furioso,* and was skilled in magic. The name is often used as the
exponent of magic.

You are the night, and such your sanctity
That even when a voice rings out, they say
That it is impregnated with good luck,
Which will descend on the one who hears it first.
I beseech you let a voice announce to me
That all my fondest hopes will be fulfilled.
(*Enter the* SACRISTAN.)

SACRISTAN. Without a doubt the damsel will be captured
By Roque, and it's he will win the game.
Even were she to defend herself, I'm sure
Rook's[7] luck calls him to enjoy so rich a prize.

BENITA. They say Roque, and I heard Roque as well,
But there is no other Roque here, except
The doltish sacristan. Let me now listen:
If Roque they will say once more, 'tis so.

SACRISTAN. For a rook is so powerful a piece
In chess that every damsel in the world
Would have to yield to him, and though he lives
Austerely he is rich in poverty.

BENITA. My good sir, I beseech you take this ribbon,
And do appear with it tomorrow morning.

SACRISTAN. I shall, fair lady, do what you request.
(*While* BENITA *is giving the ribbon to the* SACRISTAN, *enter* PASCUAL, *who seizes the latter by the neck and snatches away his ribbon.*)
Whichever of the two girls you may be,
Who dwell in this house, you even outshine Venus.

PASCUAL. What is happening? What have you to say,
Benita? Why do you give up your spoils
To a sacristan? This would indeed be grave,
If this were not St. John's Night. How comes it
That you, a bachelor in plain-song, try
To win a game that has been badly started?
Is this the shameless way you play your Matins?
And have a foolish girl's satiric jibes
Made you forget your singing and your chimes?
(*Enter* PEDRO.)

PEDRO. What's this, Pascual, my friend?

PASCUAL. The Sacristan

7 All through this scene there is a play on the word Roque, which means a rook in chess as well as a proper name.

And Benita wish to prove to me that she
Is thrice blest as a woman, and that he
Is a foe to every fraud: therefore to save
All trouble and to honor his compliment,
Before you witnesses I'll give him at once,
This ribbon and this drubbing for the nonce.

SACRISTAN. By the altar wine vessels I daily empty
To the dregs, I swear I never meant to play
A trick in earnest, but today I heard
That your Benita would let down her hair,
And so I came here to enjoy the show.
I named myself, she hearkened to the lure,
As one showing her pleasure at the first
Name which she heard: for the spell cast on the eve
Of St. John's Day arouses in all girls
A host of fickle fancies.

PASCUAL.   Why did she
Give you this ribbon?

SACRISTAN.   If I put it on,
She might then by its color know next day
Who I was.

BENITA.   Why, Pascual, do you prolong
Your questioning? Do you suspect me then?
I always notice that your wits improve
When it is to my disadvantage.

PASCUAL.   Aye,
May this home truth now mortify your heart,
Ungrateful girl, who still refuse to trust
In my plain frankness and sincerity.
The elm trees on the river bank, which have
Your name carved by my knife, will tell
You if I am a doltish man or not.

PEDRO. Benita, I'm a witness that there's not
A beech tree in that field without your name
Inscribed and consecrated to your fame.

PASCUAL. And when the shepherds gather, have you not
Heard me extolling my Benita's charms
To heaven, thus betraying my devotion,
Though my love I have always kept concealed?
What almond, apple or what cherry tree
With its fruits have I not brought to you

As gift before the birds could peck at it?
You know full well the other things that I
Have done for your own profit and fair name.
And on the branches of the trees which will
Adorn your door you'll see, O cruel maid,
The certain proof of all my faith in you:
You'll find perfumed verbena that contains
The rarest essences, and there's the rose
That gladdens hearts, and the victorious palm,
The harbinger of all good luck to men,
And you will see a slender wafer hanging
From the tall elm tree we've brought from the valley
To shed its gentle shade about your door.

BENITA. Do not imagine that your long harangue
Will ever persuade me to give you my hand,
For no one will I marry save the man
Whose name is Roque.

PEDRO.   You are right, I know,
But there's a remedy the Church confirms.
Pascual can be confirmed and change his name
From Pascual to Roque, and after that
He may, when both agree, then marry you.

BENITA. This way I do accept.

SACRISTAN.   Thanks be to God.
I find myself at last released from trouble.

PEDRO. You have, I promise you, Benita, played
Your part most gallantly, and I recall
The wise proverb that homely people quote:
"Wipe your neighbor's nose and then welcome him
Into your house." [8]

BENITA.   Now, Pascual, wear this ribbon,
Where I may see it.

PASCUAL.   I intend to make
Of it the treasure from which Iris fashions
The livery of the celestial rainbow.
But hark! The music which I ordered sounds
As they now bear the branches to your house.

PEDRO. With pleasure we shall wait.

BENITA.   Good luck to it.

[8] Teresa, the wife of Sancho Panza, uses the same proverb when speaking of María Sanchica. *Don Quixote*, Part II, Chapter 5.

(Sounds of varied music within, and the Zamoran bagpipe. Enter all with branches. CLEMENTE *and the musicians sing the following song:)*

> *"Pretty maiden tarrying*
> *At your lattice window*
> *Rejoice, your love draws nigh."*
> *Now tell the fair Benita*
> *That Pascual, the shepherd*
> *Tends his flock of cares,*
> *And he who is Clemencia's swain*
> *Vows himself her humble slave.*
> *As for the maid who is faint of heart*
> *And swoons for love,*
> *Do not forget her prayers,*
> *But hold her tightly by the hand,*
> *And whisper in her ear,*
> *Or speak in ringing tones*
> *That her fancy may be touched:*
> *"Pretty maiden tarrying*
> *At your lattice window,*
> *Rejoice, your love draws nigh."*

CLEMENTE. A lovely song well sung.
  Come now and deck this threshold
  On this side and the other.
  What are you doing here, Pascual,
  With your two companions? Come
  And help us now and our Benita
  To deck her portico:
  Our hopes have risen and we're all
  Impatient to know her.
  Put this branch of laurel here,
  And willow branches over there;
  Do not forget the scented jasmine,
  And the fragrant gilliflower.
  Let the floor be strewn with galangal,
  And topaze blooms of balmy mignonette,
  Let the empty spaces over there
  Be gay with garlands of sweet-smelling flowers.
BENITA. Once more, my dear friends, let the music play,
  For Clemencia listens, and you too, my Roque.

(*She leaves the window.*)
Let us have music again.

PASCUAL. My fairest maid,
Now doubly mine, we must beat tambourines,
And thrum guitars and start cross-capering,
That all the world may celebrate this feast,
For that's what my triumphant love decrees.

CLEMENTE. Let us all sing, for dawn is drawing nigh:
(CLEMENTE *and musicians sing:*)

> *The bramble and the hawthorn*
> *With which I did adorn*
> *My fair Benita's door*
> *Are sprouting flowers this morn.*
> *The gnarléd ash and the rugged oak,*
> *That crown the threshold of my love,*
> *Now turn into a leafy copse,*
> *And thorns and brambles blossom fast.*
> *On all sides even the tender plants*
> *Are vivid green, the fields are maying,*
> *The soul is jubilant, and lords*
> *And vassals feel blind Cupid's powers,*
> *When thorns and briars change to flowers.*
>
> (*Exeunt singing.*)

(*Enter the Gypsy maidens* INÉS *and* BELICA. *They may be played by those who have played* BENITA *and* CLEMENCIA.)

INÉS. This is all fancy's dream, Belilla, and
I must say I'm amazed: you dream, I suppose,
That you're a countess or a royal mistress.

BELICA. I am sad it is all a dream, Inés,
But do not irritate me by your words
Of blame, and let me follow my own star.

INÉS. You place too much trust in your own fair face,
Hence your presumption, but do not forget
That beauty when there is not quality
Rarely succeeds.

BELICA. My misfortunes, alas,
Do prove the truth of all that you have said.
How cruel is my fate! why did such thoughts
Of grandeur ever enter a Gypsy's mind?

INÉS. Alas, such thoughts are fashioned by the winds,

And Fate cares not a rap on whom they'll blow.
But you should shun such fancies like the plague:
Come learn the steps you have been practicing.

BELICA. Inés, by your nagging you'll drive me mad;
You are mistaken if you think that I
Am bound to follow your will as the law,
And I declare that only the King himself
Can make me dance.

INÉS.   In this way, dear Belilla,
It will not be surprising if you end
One day soon in the nearest hospital,
For you are not made to perform in life
So prominent a part. Go your way then,
In the Devil's name, to the kitchen and the hall,
Where you will flounder here and there at will.

BELICA. All that is not for me.

INÉS.   Why not? So you
Want pomp and circumstance, to rub your shoulders
With highborn ladies of the Golden Fleece,
And you would trample underfoot our Gypsy claim
To honor which we've proudly raised on high.
Before that, may I see you crazed with love
For some Romanichal who'll master you,
Or a hangman who'll take measure of your shoulders.
Have you the impudence to say, you hussy,
That a Gypsy girl should not wed a Romanichal?
May your child be poxed and come before its time,

BELICA. Inés, you're too long-winded and too dull
To fathom what I've said.

INÉS.   Though I am simple,
I see now what you will see later on.

(*Enter* PEDRO *and* MALDONADO.)

MALDONADO. So here you see, my brother Pedro,
The Gypsy girl I spoke to you about.
She is such a princess that I feel
I must give her to you as bride.
Come now, put on your Gypsy garb,
And set yourself to learn Caló.
Even if you don't learn our lingo,
You must be a Gypsy, I believe,
For you're the head of all your clan.

INÉS. Give us some alms, fair gentleman.

MALDONADO. As a farmer he is offended! How did you
  Not recognize him, Inés?

INÉS. You ask him, Belica.

PEDRO. If she asks I'll do anything.
  No matter what, and without pay,
  Just to serve those beautiful eyes.

MALDONADO. Won't my fair lady deign reply?

INÉS. My lord, see now the widow coming,
  Who is so miserly; the more
  She has, the more she covets.
  (*Enter a farmer's* WIDOW *accompanied by a* SQUIRE *who
  leads her by the hand.*)

INÉS. Alms, my lady, for the Blessed Virgin
  And her beloved Son.

WIDOW. Don't beg from me and don't insist,
  You shameless beggar, you should be
  Serving others.

SQUIRE. The world has come to such a pass
  That life becomes intolerable.
  We live in an age of vagabonds;
  Not a wench wants to serve,
  Every lad itches to sow wild oats,
  And there's no stopping him!
  If he's a boob, she's a pert hussy,
  These Romanichals are a profitless crowd,
  Brimful of malice and skulduggery,
  Trickery, coggery and chicanery,
  Fraudulent, double-faced, and hypocritical.
  Not a groat they give from their impious earnings
  To church or King.
  Masquerading as blacksmiths they delude and inveigle;
  And commit their outrages with impunity.
  And by your permission I must declare
  That there isn't a single ass in the meadow
  Who is safe from those rascally Romanichals.

WIDOW. Leave them and let us now be going,
  Llorente, it is getting late.
                    (*Exeunt the* SQUIRE *and the* WIDOW.)

BELICA. Take this as charity, but don't go on
  Making a poor mouth of your daily needs,

For there is sure to be another man
Like Gil or that Llorente who, instead
Of giving alms, will hurl insults at you.

MALDONADO. Do you see her, Pedro; she is said to keep
Ten thousand ducats underneath her bed,
In a pair of coffers which she calls her "angels."
She gloats upon them, for they are, I trow,
The apple of her eyes, which she must guard
At all hours, and in her soul she treasures them
As Absalom of old his golden hair.
Her only charity, a single royal,
She gives to a blind man every month, because
In the morning he knocks at her door and prays
To God for her husband and her relatives,
So that if they are now in Purgatory,
They may their glory win from the Consistory.
With this sole charitable work she hopes
To enter heaven without calamity.

PEDRO. My brain will find a way to inveigle her,
But you must find the names of her relations,
And friends, who have departed from this life,
Including even the servant or retainer,
And write them out for me. Then you will see
How easily I'll cure her stinginess:
With this "Big Trick" I'll show what I can do.

MALDONADO. I'll bring you daily every single name,
From her great-great-grandfather down to her
Latest grandson who has just passed away.

PEDRO. Let us be off and you will later see
What I'll do for our common interest.

MALDONADO. Where are you going, Belica?

BELICA. Wherever Inés wishes.

PEDRO. Wherever you go your thoughts will
Lead you towards the highest goal.

BELICA. Even if I ride on wings of fancy, Pedro,
Do not attempt to balk me of my wish,
For I have distant hopes that I shall reach
The goal I long for.

PEDRO.   I hope your good luck
Will match your peerless beauty; but come now,
My Gypsy maiden, we are proud of you.

ACT II.

Enter the CONSTABLE *for plays and dances;* MARTÍN CRESPO *the* MAYOR; *and* SANCHO MACHO, *the alderman.*

MAYOR. I want to tell you, Mr. Constable, about a young man who worked for me: he was a bright lad, and able to do a number of amusing tricks with cabbage stalks. He said that if by any chance the King should ask for dances, he strongly advised me to arrange one that would surpass the finest that had been given hitherto. He added, moreover, that women dancers were dull and out of fashion, and recommended me to introduce, as a novelty, a group of youths disguised as highland lassies, wearing plenty of bells on their arms and legs. So I have planned a ballet of twenty-four youths, which might, I am proud to say, be displayed in the Colosseum at Rome. I have already shown you the two best dancers.

CONSTABLE. Certainly the plot itself is excellent.

SANCHO. What our mayor suggests is all very vague, and the most any of us knows is that he obtained the idea from a young man who became his confidential adviser. But the latter has gone off and left us in the lurch, bad 'cess to him: we are lost without him, for all our brainwaves and bright ideas have vanished.

CONSTABLE. Is that young man such a know-all?

SANCHO. Why Solomon, King of the Jews, is no match for him.

MAYOR. Remember, when you see those dancers, that you are watching twenty-four performers, trained and disciplined to the highest degree. Everyone is vigorous and athletic. One of them, no mean performer, is Diego Mostrenco; another is Gil Perayle: each one is as proficient as a Flemish performing puppydog. And when it is Pingorrón who plays the guitar for them, they show their skill in every dance rhythm. Our new dance plan will be applauded by all. The sword dances will be performed in grim earnest, despite the husbandmen, the Gypsies, who will be green with envy, and the girls, who will feel insulted. What do you think, sir, of the physique and zest of both dancers?

CONSTABLE. If I may give my own sincere opinion, I never saw a worse display. I am afraid that if this is your novelty you will discover you have made a grave mistake.

MAYOR. You, too, I imagine must be suffering from envy, but in any case we intend to present twenty-four young dancers like those two, and I am convinced that novelties like these are bound either to surprise the public or make them laugh.

CONSTABLE. I've given my warning: farewell. (*Exit the* CONSTABLE.)

SANCHO. Mayor, carry out your own plan, and you'll be proved right. The dance is a novelty and will please the King.

MAYOR. I am sure of it. Come, Sancho, I'm bulging with confidence,
And I'm certain the dance will have a huge success.

SANCHO. You're right: but you'll return with a hollow bulge
I'm thinking. (*Exeunt.*)

(*Enter two blind men, one of whom is* PEDRO, *the Artful Dodger. The first blind man goes up close to the door, and* PEDRO *stands near him. The* WIDOW *appears at the window.*)

BLIND MAN. Blessed souls in Purgatory, be consoled by God.
And in a short time may you be relieved
Of all your sins and may the angel, like
A flash of lightning then descend on you,
And carry you upwards to receive your crown.

PEDRO. You souls, who have departed from this house
For Purgatory, may your easy chair,
Or hard seat at the Tribunal of God
Be given you without assessment, and
May your angel soar with you up to heaven
To see what happens there.

BLIND MAN. Brother, do go
To another door, for this belongs to me,
And you must not pray here.

PEDRO. For courtesy
I pray and not for reward, hence I am able
To pray anywhere without fear of a quarrel.

BLIND MAN. Have you, most honored blind man, never had
  Your sight?
PEDRO.   No, I'm blind from birth which took place
  In a tomb.
BLIND MAN. I had my sight once, but today,
  Owing to my sins, I see nothing but
  The unpleasant sights an unhappy man perceives.
  Do you know many prayers?
PEDRO.   So many that
  I'll answer this by word of mouth, though I
  Give them in writing to all, and precious few
  I hide away. The prayer of the lonely soul
  I know, and that of St. Pancracio,
  Which no one has ever seen, and prayers
  Of saints Quirce, Acacio, and the Spanish saint
  Olalla, and a thousand others which
  I have remodelled, and I also know
  Those of the helpers, which amount to thirty,
  And others of such excellence that I
  Have stirred up envy and bad feeling in
  The faithful, for I'm best among the best.
  I know cures for chilblains, jaundice, scrofula,
  And how to temper greediness in misers;
  I know one remedy to calm men's passions,
  And another which curbs curiosity.
BLIND MAN. I wish I knew them.
WIDOW.   Brother, wait a moment.
PEDRO. Who calls me?
BLIND MAN.   By the voice I think it is
  The lady of the house. To tell the truth,
  She is tight on her money, but she's rich.
  Her strong point is to give orders for prayers.
PEDRO. I always stay tongue-tied with one who is
  Too slow in giving, and I shall be mum
  To her demands unless she pays and prays.
  (*Enter the* WIDOW.)
WIDOW. As I stood at the window listening
  To your profession of your Christian faith,
  Your arguments and many prayers and cures,
  I wished that you could give me some

Of those prayers I might ask for, and let me
Assess their value.

PEDRO (*aside*).　　　If she will dismiss
The other blind man I shall tell her marvels.

WIDOW (*aside*). I shall get rid of him at once.

PEDRO.　　　　　　　　　　　　My lady,
I can't agree to say them in return
For gifts or otherwise . . .

WIDOW. Be off with you: and you, my friend, come later.

BLIND MAN. I'll come at three to say my daily prayers.

WIDOW. God be praised.

BLIND MAN. Cordial greetings, brother; if you were
Born blind, faked yourself blind, or whatever else,
If we communicate you must get to know
My house: though it is small and poor and pokey,
You'll find there an appreciative friend,
And a Segovian doubloon to bless yourself,
If you will give me some of your many prayers
And miracles for souls.

PEDRO.　　　　　　　　I shall turn up
And full of eagerness to know a house
So full of love and faith, and I shall pay
For my lodgings with the wonders I'll display.
I have forty miracles now up my sleeve,
Which I can show as I pass to and fro,
And I shall live as merry as a cricket.
(*Exit the* BLIND MAN.)
Now you, Marina Sánchez, hearken well
To this mission of mine which comes from heaven.
The souls of Purgatory have now gathered
In their consistory and have decreed
With forethought that their evil plight be known,
And they agreed that a soul of noted prudence
Should assume an old man's semblance, and appear
Before the world. And they instructed him
How he might now secure relief or freedom
For their sins. This soul in an old man's form
Is close at hand and carries on an ass
A silver mine of Potosí, so heavy
Is the load of doubloons carried by the beast,
Which relatives of the tormented souls

Bring forth in heaps, for when they learn
That souls are ling'ring in the throes of Purgatory,
All money bags and desks and safes are emptied,
And pregnant cat-skin purses pour in heaps
Their shining contents to redeem the souls.
This aged privileged soul will come, Marina,
This afternoon to show his list to you,
But I want all hushed up: you must receive
The soul alone, and hand him the amount
Demanded by your relatives, who are
Confined in the burning furnaces below,
And when all has been settled he will give
You a prayer that will increase your happiness.
All this service the soul offers in guerdon
To those who receive him frankly, and hand over
All their savings, remaining poor as Paul.

WIDOW. Blesséd blind man, now tell me, is this soul
Sending me this messenger?

PEDRO.   He places all
His trust in you and in your ancestry.

WIDOW. How shall I recognize him when he comes?

PEDRO. I shall make him assume my face and form.

WIDOW. Oh, what rewards I promise you for bringing
Such tidings!

PEDRO.   Now is the time to spend the money
You have amassed in the past, and practice fasts,
And floggings, for you must risk all, in hope
Of ransoming a single immortal soul
From its dire suffering, and speeding it
To a region where it will suffer pain no more.

WIDOW. Go now in peace and tell your ancient soul
That I await his coming with great joy,
And when he comes I'll give my heart and soul,
Which is my money, in humble Christian spirit,
For though I am of little consequence
I should be sad to see a relative
Of mine enduring heat and cold down there.

PEDRO. May your fame even surpass that of Leander,
And may no second Alexander tarnish it,
But rather may a swan now chant your praises
By the roving waters of Maeander, and

Soar o'er the mountains with you into Heaven. (*Exeunt.*)
(*Enter* MALDONADO *and* BELICA.)

MALDONADO. Here is the man, dear Belica, who will
Soon raise you up and set you on your feet,
His fame extends through all the countryside,
So full of wisdom, and so sharp as well,
That you would be astounded. He desires
To join our tribe because he is in love
With you and leaves aside all his other plans.
I beg you, treat him with sincerity,
For he's bound to be, if I am not mistaken,
The finest cattle thief the world has ever seen.
Among the tricksters he's an oddity,
But now he is preparing a Great Trick,
Which will win him fame with the Zincali.[9]

BELICA. You craftily turn all things to your profit,
But to my disadvantage; don't you know
That I'll refuse a husband who is not
Of rank to raise me to nobility?

MALDONADO. You now have given me the fullest proof
That you are lacking in all common sense,
And all the radiant beauty of your youth
You gamble away on this vain dream of yours;
For the greatest beauty lasts but a single day,
And withers before the Sun accomplishes
One single day's course; and I want to say,
That it is downright folly to believe
That beauty ever lasts more than the morning;
And sometimes it is foolishness to think
That beauty always makes a brilliant match,
For most people hold that a successful marriage
Is one between equals, so you, my mad
Gitana, should put a bridle on those fancies
That may exalt and yet diminish you,

[9] The Gypsies, being Oriental, developed the special picaresque technique of the gift of the gab, and their skill depended on flattery, persuasion and salesmanship. The Caló word for such trickery was *jonjanó*, which is the translation of the Spanish picaresque word *timo*. *Timo* only stimulates the covetous propensities of the *primo*, or victim, whereas *jonjanó* appeals to his imagination. Pedro's trick is thus a *Jonjanó Baró*, or Great Trick.

And don't, I pray, go gadding here and there,
Looking for what does not belong to you.
Marry your equal, that is the match I offer:
With this proposal I can promise you
Wealth, status, honor, standing and position.
(*Enter* PEDRO *dressed as a Gypsy.*)

PEDRO. My good friend, Maldonado, what is wrong?

MALDONADO. I must confess that I am all amazed
At the imperious claim this humble girl
Is making, for though she is of low state
Her claims are all ambitious, and I marvel
To see with what mad gusto she aspires
To soar aloft and even touch the sky.

PEDRO. She is right and you should not ridicule her.
It pleases me to see with what fierce pride
She brings her tools and drills her upward way.
I, too, who am dull-witted, have my fancies,
And dream of being Emperor and King;
Why there are times when I rave and believe
That I am master of the entire world.

MALDONADO. Well, tell me how you got on with the widow.

PEDRO. The whole affair has turned out very nicely,
Even better than I had ever thought.
She will be open-handed, or my name
Is not Pedro, but who are those I see
Dressed up as hunters and on revels bent?

MALDONADO. It is the King, I do believe.

BELICA.   Today
My longing for love will climb a rocky slope.
(*Enter the* KING *with a servant,* SILERIO, ***both in hunting
dress.***)

BELICA. Today my eyes will feast upon the scene
And give my soul a joyous sustenance.

MALDONADO. I am afraid your foolishness is bound
To end in trouble.

BELICA.   It is of no avail
For me to strive against my fate's decrees.

KING. Tell me, you gallant Gypsies, have you seen
A wounded stag pass this way?

BELICA.   Yes, my Liege,
A little while ago I saw it pass;

It had an arrow stuck in its right shoulder.

KING. It was a piece of lance.

BELICA. To flee in quest
Of new scenes brings but small relief to one
Who bears within her heart the iron barb
Of love's cruel shaft that feeds itself upon
Its victim's heart.

MALDONADO (*aside*). The girl will now, I'm sure,
Give proof of her madness.

KING. My Gypsy girl,
What are you saying?

BELICA. Your Liege, I say that love
And the hunter are both following the same
Victim; the hunter wounds the wild beast, and
Although it flies in terror it bears along,
No matter where it goes, the cruel wound.
Love wounds the heart with golden barb, and he
Who feels the pangs, even when he has lost his mind,
Still bears his suffering along with him.

KING. You're wise, my Gypsy maid; such qualities
Are rare.

BELICA. I am a Gypsy of gentle birth.

KING. Who is your father?

BELICA. I don't know, alas.

MALDONADO. My Liege, she is a madcap, and a host
Of foolish notions fills her head, though the airs
Of arrogance she gives herself do lend
A certain meaning to her words.

BELICA. And luckily
For me that is so; if I'm mad it is
Because your blindness thinks me so.

SILERIO. Can you
Tell fortunes?

BELICA. Not even a humble maid
Ignores her own misfortunes when she allows
Her dreams to soar on high above the clouds.

SILERIO. Why do you aim so high?

BELICA. It is not high,
But merely a little higher.

KING. You have charm,
And sense.

BELICA.   I put such trust in sense
  That I hope it will give me wings to fly
  Up to the sky.
SILERIO.   You really make me laugh!
KING. You frighten me. God help the man who tries
  To curb your whims.
SILERIO.   He means that for the Queen.
BELICA. It is unfortunate that one who now
  Has just arrived should haste away so soon.
                              (*Exeunt the* KING *and* SILERIO.)
PEDRO. My Belica, I now begin to see
  That I should be a fool to place
  My hopes of love in you: far better to
  Pursue another course; so I shall now
  Depart, good Maldonado, to conclude
  My Great Trick to transform that stingy widow
  Into my horn of plenty. I'll disguise
  Myself as hermit, and in humble garb
  Complete my Gypsy trick.
MALDONADO.   Then go your way.
  I have left there your disguise all prepared.   (*Exit* PEDRO.)
  (*Enter the* CONSTABLE *of plays and dances.*)
CONSTABLE. Who is here, Maldonado?
MALDONADO.   I am, sir.
CONSTABLE. God's blessing!
BELICA.   A well-spoken Constable,
  What a miracle! you are not from the village.
MALDONADO. You are right, he is from the capital.
CONSTABLE. We need a rustic ballet at the Court.
MALDONADO. Give us a little time.
CONSTABLE.   That is all right:
  The King departs two days hence from the Abbey,
  Where he now stays.
MALDONADO.   We'll do as you command.
BELICA. And is the Queen accompanying him?
CONSTABLE. I'm sure she will be with him.
BELICA.   Is she still
  As strict and jealous?
CONSTABLE.   They say that she is.
BELICA. Since she is Queen, and beautiful as well,
  Does that not give her lots of confidence?

CONSTABLE. Love in excess the senses drives awry,
  Even in those of highest moral worth.
BELICA. Love's ups and downs are close akin to fear.
CONSTABLE. How can so young a maiden know such things?
  I'll lay a wager your own heart is caught
  In Cupid's net. Well, I am off to do
  My rounds. Mind, Maldonado, you provide
  A first-rate dance, for every village has
  Its own particular dance.
MALDONADO.   Well I shall empty
  My sheepfold and she'll wear her finest dresses.
              (*Exeunt the* CONSTABLE *and* MALDONADO.)
      (*Enter* PEDRO *as a hermit, with three or four small rough
      canvas bags full of sand concealed in his ample sleeves.*)[10]
PEDRO. Here is the house of my blest widow,
  I mean, of that Marina Sánchez
  Who through her charity will soar
  On wings straight up to heaven.
  (*The* WIDOW *is at the window.*)
  Now Vicente del Verrocal,
  Her husband, will be ransomed
  From blazing flames, when she's aware
  That he is sizzling in the fire:
  Her son, Pedro Benito, soon
  Will cease the fearsome shouts
  He utters when he is toasted by
  Flames in the deep black maw of hell:
  And Martinico, her nephew,
  The man with the mole upon his face,

[10] We have followed Professor Casalduero's suggested rearrangement of the text of the following scene, which is obviously wrongly placed in the printed editions of the play.

  Pedro's last exit on page 133 was made with the intention of concluding his Great Trick and transforming the stingy widow into his horn of plenty. To which Maldonado replies that he has left his hermit disguise ready for him. As the text stands, Pedro comes back still dressed as a Gypsy, though he had expressly said that he was going out to change into a hermit costume. The scene of the widow and Pedro which is printed at the beginning of Act III should therefore be restored to Act II at this point, so that the episode of the Great Trick can be completed. J. Casalduero, *El Teatro de Cervantes*.

Will cease to moan when he sees us
Preparing his royal road to glory.

WIDOW. Father, wait, I am coming down,
And forgive me if I keep you waiting.

(*She leaves the window and descends.*)

PEDRO (*aside*). I give my thanks this day to Heaven,
Which is auspicious when I work;
I thank him who has made me enter
This narrow path, where, without fear
Of trouble, this tongue will free me
And give me honor and my profit too.
Now, Memory, don't fail me now,
Nor put impediment upon
My tongue, but rather prudently
Fill me with joy, then sadden me.
Now change my countenance, that I
May win that widow's confidence
Until I have her terrified,
And glad at heart, though penniless.

(*Enter the* WIDOW.)

WIDOW. Father, let me kiss those feet.

PEDRO. Stand back, most honored countrywoman,
Don't touch me; don't you see
That where humility resides,
Honor loses all its interest?
The souls that are in suffering,
And lacking all their happiness,
No matter how much they are tempted,
Never admit the ceremonies held
For human beings at the courts.
A Mass is more significant
Than four thousand hand-kissings.
This warning now your father gives you:
Henceforth such courtly greetings shun
And treat them all with mockery.
But before I tell you who I am,
I beg you keep this sack for me,
And this second one for the blind
And naked man, my load today.

WIDOW. Already, sir, I have heard who you are,
And I know full well that you wish

The souls should meet with mercy,
And not be harshly judged.
I know in what an honorable
Mission you are now engaged,
And in conclusion beseech you
To explain to me how my relatives
Will have eternal rest and pardon.

PEDRO. Vicente del Verrocal, your spouse,
With seventy crowns' payment will
Settle his account, and obtain
A thousand benefits from his mishap.
Your son Pedro Benito will
Leave his hiding place on paying
Forty-six crowns and no more;
With that you'll give him happiness
Beyond comparison, I know.
Your daughter Sancha Redonda, too,
Begs that your great generosity
May aid her: charity, alas,
Must be a rope to reach that cave
That is deeply buried in the earth.
She asks for forty-two gold crowns,
The round and simple ones, or else
Twenty-six doubloons with which they'll break
The iron manacles that fetter her.
Martín and Quiteria, your nephew and niece,
Are both sunk in a well and suffer
Agonies and cry most bitterly.
They beg for the doubloons of double face,
And they request the coins be offered
At the altar during divine service,
For Marina values them above all.
Then there's your uncle Sancho Manjón;
He agonizes in a lake
From cold and thirst, and cries aloud
To terminate his tribulation.
All he demands is fourteen ducats,
But cash-down in newly minted silver,
And I shall run the risk of carrying
The load upon my weary shoulders.

WIDOW. Have you yet seen my sister Sancha?

PEDRO. I saw her lying in a tomb
     O'ercovered with a plaque of bronze,
     A hard and heavy coverlet.
     And when I stood on it she said:
     "If you have pity for my sufferings,
     Which cry aloud, when you return
     To earth tell my cousin and sister
     It depends on them if we can leave
     The darkness and reach infinite light,
     For light in these dark realms of woe
     Is but the light of charity.
     No sooner will my sister hear
     Than she'll be ready enough to give
     Thirty florins, for she boasts
     She has common sense and is no sheep."
     Many I saw, and all your relatives
     And servants; every one now greets you.
     Some are of two ducats, others of a *maravedí*.
     When added up and written down
     In ink the sum total arrives
     At two hundred and fifty crowns.
     Don't be alarmed: that sack I gave you
     To hold, if my accounts are right,
     Was given me by a tavern-keeper,
     Rival of Cacus, but it was because
     His daughter lies amidst a heap
     Of firewood in the nether caves,
     And that her slender legs might not
     Be so afflicted by the fire.
     A mule boy handed me the second sack,
     Which I gave you. He was a rolling stone,
     A rascal, though a good-natured lad.
     The sacks are full of Tibar gold,
     Which must with subtle alchemy
     Transmute the toils and bitter gall
     Of all the souls into a sugar syrup.
     Come now, you giant among women,
     You are so strong, you are so good,
     Let no one contradict or try
     To prevent you lightening the woes
     Of all the tormented souls.

Undo the knot that smothers you,
And say in calm voice: "I shall, Lord,
Do all your holy voice ordains."
And when you put the money into
Their rough hands amidst the joy of all,
You'll see their merciless flames abate
At once, and dissolve into smoke.
What a sight to see at an untimely hour:
A soul in clogs dance through the air,
Pirouetting gaily, and from a slave
Become a lady! what praises you'll hear
On all sides, and at every hour
From every courteous soul to whom
Today you give its freedom!
(*She hands him back the sacks.*)

WIDOW. Hold them, and wait a while for me;
I'll go and I'll return later
With everything that you require. (*Exit the* WIDOW.)

PEDRO. May heaven favor your life,
And grant you peace, pleasure and rest.
Here is the strong woman of the Scriptures:
May you be fortunate, Marina,
In both your life and death.
Belilla, my fairest Gypsy girl,
You will enjoy the fruits
Of this my *Jonjanó Baró*
To the very last *maravedí.*
Even though my love-making
Is not to your liking, all this money
Brings in will be spent on the dance,
And on your person, for I don't
Want you to lose your hopes for lack
Of money and of finery.
(*The* WIDOW *returns with a cat-skin full of money.*)

WIDOW. Take it, venerable old man, and there
You'll find all that you asked of me,
And I shall even give you more.

PEDRO. Marina, you have given me your substance
With Christian charity: as soon as I pass
Over yonder hill I'll reach Rome in a jump,
And in the next reach the bowels of the earth;

And since I answer one who is myself,
Do take my blessing, for it cures the toothache,
And also guards against those who would try
To practice fraud, and gives you courage
If you should fear by night the prying eyes
Of sentries; even in the darkest halls
The weakest heart may stretch its wings
Without the slightest trace of fear.
(*He blesses her.*)
You carry with you now the blessings
Of the great Pedro, the Artful Dodger.   (*Exit* PEDRO.)

WIDOW. Most trusty commissary of the souls
Of those who are in constant agony,
For they say that the way to Purgatory
Is down hill, start your rolling way,
And reach in a trice the Gloomy Plain,
Or Valley of the Rueful Tears, and hasten
To accomplish all that my largess
Has enabled you. In every crown
You carry imprisoned my very soul,
And likewise in every *maravedí*, as
By enchantment. And here I'll remain,
For henceforth, alas, I shall be
Another soul in torment,
When later I find myself far from
The bag which I have handed up,
But, please God, borne up by my faith
I'll reach the region of the stars.   (*Exit.*)

(*Enter* SILERIO, *the* KING's *attendant, and* INÉS, *the Gypsy.*)

SILERIO. How churlish is the girl!

INÉS.   She refuses to change,
For she has a moody nature and excites
Herself with fancies that fill up her head,
And make her dream she is princess, or a queen.
She hates the Gypsies and treats them with scorn.

SILERIO. We shall now give her plenty of food for dreams,
For the King's in love and wants to pay her court.

INÉS. With love there is no fixed law; perhaps
As her thoughts aim so high, she now believes
A king is needful. I at least will do
What you have ordered me, and give

Her your message, simply to humor you.

SILERIO. I might compel you rather than request.

INÉS. When pleasure's mingled with uneasiness
    It tends to lessen rather than to grow.
    We first must organize our dance, and then
    We must talk, for the ladder of attraction
    Is now certain to rise up to the clouds.

SILERIO. There is another message I would give
    To you which is important.

INÉS.   Do tell me.

SILERIO. It is a secret, for the Queen is jealous,
    And the slightest sign of her displeasure will
    Disturb the King's pleasure, and we shall suffer.

INÉS. Be off, for now our Count is drawing nigh.

SILERIO. All the better: And let this lady's pride be humbled;
    I'll do all I can.   (*Exit* SILERIO.)
    (*Enter* MALDONADO, *and* PEDRO *disguised as a hermit.*)

PEDRO. Even if I painted what took place last night,
    It could not turn out more successful.

MALDONADO. Brunelo, the great Swindler, now must yield
    The palm to you: Your native wit gives such
    A mastery, and you make such great efforts
    That you are bound to triumph every time.
    You sally forth without the slightest trace
    Of trouble or dishonor, for in brain
    You rival Sinon, and as orator
    You beat Demosthenes.

INÉS.   My Lord, the King
    Expects to see us dance this afternoon.

PEDRO. Let Belica today parade my rich
    Good fortune and be Beauty's synonym.

INÉS. Our famous Pedro, you, perhaps, today
    May fashion for that wayward girl her luck.
    Let us start and rehearse our *Zambra* now,
    And in silken garments so bedeck ourselves
    That we shall dazzle everyone today.   (*Exeunt all.*)
    (*Enter the* KING *and* SILERIO.)

SILERIO. I repeat, my Liege, that very soon she'll come
    With the dancers.

KING.   My desires increase, alas,
    And they have now passed on beyond the bounds

Of honor. Prudence, though, now bids me think,
But I chafe at delays and blighted hopes,
And my desires increase; but promise me
You'll keep her hidden from the Queen.

SILERIO.   I'll do
As you wish.

KING.   You will blurt out all,
Why I am infatuated, and you'll say
A thousand other things, which will become
Accusing witnesses in your own mind.

SILERIO. If love were reasonable this would seem
Rank frenzy, but as this is never so,
I neither blame you nor do I excuse.

KING. I recognize my fault and blame myself,
Though I'm tardy and I make but paltry pleas.

SILERIO. The Queen is coming.

KING.   Do, I pray, be cautious,
And on the watch to help my further plans,
For she is jealous and has lynxlike eyes.

SILERIO. Today, I hope, you will enjoy the spoils
Of the fair Gypsy maid.
(*Enter the* QUEEN.)

QUEEN.   You here, my Liege,
Without me? I do not know what to say.

KING. I am rejoicing in the solitude
Of this delightful spot.

QUEEN.   Are you so worried
By my company then?

KING.   You should not say such things,
Else you'll exalt my good fortune to Heaven.

QUEEN. When I don't see you or your body's shadow
I am depressed, and my passion for you
Grows fiercer still, and though this may appear
To you mere folly, if you realize
That Love the despot rules me, you will be
More patient.

SILERIO.   The music, Your Royal Highness, plays
And the dancers are approaching.
(*The drums begin to sound.*)

KING.   We shall watch
Them from a point of vantage here, amidst

The flowers and roses.

QUEEN.   If that is your wish.

(*Enter* CRESPO, *the* MAYOR; *and* TARUGO, *the alderman.*)

MAYOR. Not speak to him? This is a sorry mess!
I swear I'll make a serious complaint
To the King for their shocking insults.

TARUGO.   Here is
His Reverence.

MAYOR.   Are you deceiving me?
Who is it?

KING.   It is I.
                              What have they done
To you, my good man?

MAYOR.   What can I reply?
Your pages have mocked all my efforts and
Have wrecked our dance; may I see all of them
Spitted with arrows and well gibbeted.
I'll speak out plainly and not bottle up
My rage, for such rank insolence is past
Enduring. Twenty-four young jackanapes
Turned up: all fellows of bulk and importance,
Giving themselves airs. I do not know why
Those pages are not given a public flogging.
They are the worst plague in the world, yet I
Through my outstanding zeal as Mayor did try
To coöperate with them, and I gave them
Both beards and bells, but I refused to show
Girls, as such a dance was not a novelty.
And I prepared a bell dance with the brothers
Of the girls, but when Your Liege's pages saw
The costumes, which were in modern gallant style,
Bedlam broke loose, and they tore them to bits,
And pelted them with mud, with the result
That they have wrecked the finest festival
Of dancing that has been seen in these parts.

QUEEN. Go gather them together, and I'll tell
The King to wait for them.

TARUGO.   Even if some
Were willing to return, they cannot be
Collected, for they are all reduced to pulp
After the drubbing and the fisticuffs.

QUEEN. Can't you bring even one of them? I'd like
    To see him.
TARUGO.   I'll see if I can bring him.
MAYOR. Tell them, Tarugo, that the King is waiting,
    And if Renco's less crippled than he was,
    Bring him, and if you can also Mostrenco,
    My nephew, and from him you can judge the rest.
    How many pages reared at court are damned!
    I thought that as they were in royal service,
    And were of gentle birth, they would show signs
    Of being well-bred, but I found instead
    That there is not a student's boarding house
    In any university that holds
    A tithe of the rascality that's seen
    Among your pages, and the tricks they played
    Upon us proved that though they've crosses on
    Their tunics, they have devils in their hearts.
    (TARUGO *returns and brings with him* MOSTRENCO, *who is
    wearing a strange woman's headdress with flaps that cover
    his ears and are tied under his chin; a skirt of green baize
    adorned with yellow, reaching to the knees, and leggings
    with bells; and a bodice. He plays the drum and must not
    move from the one place.*)
TARUGO. Here is Mostrenco, Crespo.
MAYOR. Play on, Pingarrón: his solemn mien
    Will show you what enthusiasts we are,
    And how inventive we are in our show.
    Get going, jig about, you silly fool,
    Or, next best, get yourself invited then,
    As if you were a musician or a peasant.
    Hello! who am I speaking to? My nephew.
    Do dance, I pray, a few steps for God's sake!
TARUGO. The Devil brought us here I do believe.
    Stand up and get a move on, blast your soul! (*He hits him.*)
MAYOR. You pages of Satan!
QUEEN. Don't ask, and stop hitting him.
MAYOR. Today you're driving us to ruin by
    Your mulish obstinacy.
MOSTRENCO.   I swear to God
    I cannot move a muscle.
SILERIO.   You must be

A ninny and a milksop!

TARUGO.   What is wrong?

MOSTRENCO. I've broken a toe of my right foot.

KING.   Let him be;
Go back to your village.

MAYOR.   If you, my Liege,
Wish to honor me, I am Mayor of Junquillos,
And if you punish your pages we shall
Bring you another dance which will excel
The last in costumes and inventiveness.

                    (*Exeunt* TARUGO, *the* MAYOR *and* MOSTRENCO.)

QUEEN. The Mayor exaggerates.

KING.   The costumes were,
I think, effective.

QUEEN.   The performance was
Well spoken and the dances well contested,
And the prize expected.

SILERIO. Here are the Gypsy dancers.

QUEEN.   Many are
Quite beautiful, and all are so well dressed.

KING (*aside*). A King who trembles at a Gypsy girl,
What a disgrace!

SILERIO.   My Liege, you'll see among
Those Gypsies a maiden who is beautiful,
Smart, and unusually chaste.

KING.   To gaze
At her will cost me dear.

QUEEN.   What now delays them?
(*Enter the musicians dressed in Gypsy fashion,* INÉS *and*
BELICA *and some Gypsy youths. The Gypsy girls, when
dancing, should be given all the adornment available, especially* BELICA. *With them enter* PEDRO, *dressed as a Gypsy,
and* MALDONADO. *They must have rehearsed two dances
and have drums.*)

PEDRO. May God protect Your Royal Highnesses,
Whom we, your humble Gypsies, celebrate
With our display of racial rhythmic grace,
And we wish that this dance of ours were decked
With silks and rich brocades, but our simple arts
And slender means win scanty guerdons; but
My fair Belilla with her flashing eyes,

Her grace and charm will banish all your cares,
And make you marvel at her peerless art.
You godlike daughters of the Gypsy race,
Come on and start your dance.

QUEEN. The Gypsy's good.

PEDRO. Ho there! You in the front, Belica!
Flower of the April moon, and you, Inés,
A famous dancer, who can add your luster
To this first dance and to a thousand more.
(*They dance.*)
Look how the dance flits rapidly, now see
You don't go wrong, but mind you keep strict time!
How dull your rhythm is, my Francesquilla!
Come on, Ginesa!

MALDONADO. Stretch the line crosswise:
Your arms like wings now beat the air; if this
Is not a heavenly dance I'm a saddled ass.

PEDRO. Come on, you elusive wagtails, Gypsy birds,
Now raise your arms and say that the camp is nigh.

MALDONADO. Keep your ears tuned to the thrumming harmony,
And like quicksilver let your twinkling feet
Weave patterns.

PEDRO. By God, the three are good!

MALDONADO. And even four of them are excellent,
But Belica beats all the rest in charm,
In beauty, and in noble dignity.

PEDRO. As they are not performing in a hall
I'm afraid they may collide with one another.
(BELICA *falls beside the* KING.)
Did I not say this would occur? Belilla
Has fallen just beside His Majesty.

KING. You eighth wonder of the world, it is only just
That I should raise you up, and with my hand
Learn that I offer you my heart as well.

QUEEN. This has been very well performed indeed.
The King, I see, has turned into a courtier.
How easily the King can level all
By laying in the dust his majesty,
And raising a fallen Gypsy up to heaven!

BELICA. In this he showed his greatness, for it would

Have been *lèse-majesté* for anyone
To stand so near my Liege in lowliness.
His greatness nobody could ever offend,
For majesty confirmed can never fail.
And in a certain manner I believe
That my fate has decreed I should receive
Marked courtesy from both Their Majesties.

QUEEN. I see; hasn't beauty now this privilege?

KING. Now come, my lady, do not make a fuss.
She is a happy soul and charms the eye.

QUEEN. Those fickle words clutch at my heart. Away
With yonder Gypsy girls to jail: I know
That beauty is a tyrant and will conquer
All hearts. Its strength is evident.

KING. Are you then jealous of a Gypsy girl?
You never should say such a dreadful thing.

QUEEN. This could be said if this girl had not been
So beautiful, and if you were not King;
But this is not the point, so yon three girls
Must be removed at once.

SILERIO.   A strange decision.

INÉS. My lady, do not be disturbed in mind,
Nor feel obliged to adopt measures that have
No truthful basis: if you would only listen
To what I have to tell, I shall not try
To escape from prison.

QUEEN.   Take them to my room,
But bring them after me.

                    (*Exeunt the* QUEEN *and the Gypsies.*)

KING. How rarely there is jealousy without
Its cruel toll!

SILERIO.   I now suspect
That the Gypsy whom I acquainted with your wish,
May, when she is speaking to the Queen, declare
What you intend to do.

KING.   In my sad state
There is nothing left for me to do but fear,
For the fateful raven cannot blacker be
Than its own wings. But come, and we shall try
To calm the jealous fury of the Queen,
And the discordant chaos of her mind.

(*Exit the* KING *and* SILERIO.)

PEDRO. We have well bargained and you have enjoyed
  The office.

MALDONADO. I declare I'll lose my wits,
  For I am, as it were, bewitched, with Belica
  In jail, and Inés who will insist on speaking
  To the Queen. It gives me much to think about.

PEDRO. It is all very worrying.

MALDONADO.   You are right.

PEDRO. I am not going to await the outcome,
  But now in time withdraw from the Gypsy tribe.
  A reverend bonnet and the clerical arm
  Will, if I'm not wrong, soon deliver me
  From troubles, Maldonado, so farewell.

MALDONADO. Stop! What do you want to do?

PEDRO.   Nothing at all.
  The die is cast, and I have frisky blood.
  I'll not allow them hold me longer here
  With ropes and cables.

MALDONADO.   You will drown yourself
  In shallow water: I never believed
  This would be your fate. In the past I thought
  You had enough valor to face an army.

PEDRO. That's mere talk; my strength lies in other ways.
  You have not yet begun to know my mind.
  But listen, Maldonado, a man should be
  Both prudent and devoid of rashness, for
  Prudence is needed to forestall the dangers.
  But best of luck.

MALDONADO.   You're going because you fear,
  But go your way.

PEDRO.   I know that there is cause
  For fear here, and when kings are in a rage
  Their passions go beyond the bounds of law,
  As their power is supreme.

MALDONADO.   If that is so,
  Let us be going then.

MUSICIANS.   We're all afraid,
  Good Maldonado.

MALDONADO.   I shall not deny it.   (*Exeunt all.*)

ACT III.

Enter the QUEEN *carrying in a small cloth some jewels, and with her enters* MARCELO, *an aged gentleman.*

QUEEN. Marcelo, without asking you to break
  A vow of secrecy you may have made,
  And as your life and fame are in no danger,
  I beg you to answer questions I may ask.
MARCELO. Where you, madam, command, there is no need
  To ask, so I pray you, ask me what you wish
  For my honor and my life lie at your feet,
  And that is what I wish for most of all.
QUEEN. These costly jewels, to whom do they belong?
MARCELO. Once they possessed an owner, and he was
  My master.
QUEEN.   I now wish to know how they
  Changed owners, and if they were given or robbed.
MARCELO. Well, since the earth now covers up the crime
  And the dishonor, if what honest love
  Has fashioned ever should be called a crime,
  I want to break a silence which no more
  Can harm or help the living or the dead;
  It even may be of consequence to all.
  One night, when all was sunk in gloom, and I
  Was on the terrace hoping to behold
  The lady whom Your Royal Highness gave
  To me as a spouse, when the Duchess Felix Alba
  —May God have mercy on her soul—cried out
  In agonized voice, saying: "May good luck,
  My Lord, attend you, whoever you are,
  If now you would show Christian charity,
  And succor a hapless lady who requires
  Your aid, and place this tender pledge of love,
  Nobler than fortunate, beyond harm's reach."
  With these words she let down by her fair tresses
  A white basket of fragrant wattles made.
  So saying she shut the window and departed.
  I there remained in dire perplexity

And anguish, for from within the basket came
The cries of a newborn child. See what a charge!
And what an hour to receive it! To cut short
My strange tale, I then left the city for
The nearest village on the top of yonder hill,
But Heaven, which assists men in their troubles,
Enabled me to find in the early dawn
A Gypsy settlement of humble huts,
And in return for many gifts and prayers,
A Gypsy woman, no longer young, agreed
To take the child; and when its swaddling clothes
She had unwrapped, amidst the napkins found
Those jewels, which I recognized at once,
As they all did belong to your brother.
I left the jewels with the child, who was
A lovely infant, a few hours old. I charged
The Gypsy woman to baptize the child,
And educate her, but she had to wear
The clean though humble garments of the tribe.
The strangest circumstance of all my tale
Is that when I related to your brother
What had happened, he said: "Dear Marcelo!
The child is mine, as are the jewels, and
The Duchess Felix Alba was her mother:
She is my pledge of love and my salvation.
The child arrived before her time, alas,
The mother was quite unprepared, and so
All faults in time come to the light of day."
And while I floundered in a maze, I heard
The church bells tolling everywhere, a sign
That some one of high rank had passed away.
Just then a page came up to me and said:
"My Lord, the Duchess Felix Alba suddenly
Did pass away last night: it is for her
That all the bells are tolling." When your brother,
Madam, heard these sad news he stood stock still,
As in a swoon, but then recovering,
He said as he departed: "Have the child
Brought up, and do not take away from her
The jewels: let them rear her as Gypsy
Without knowing the truth. This is my wish."

A few hours later he set off for the battle front
Where, wielding his lance 'gainst the Moorish foe,
He now forgets his loves and memories.
In notes he bids me go to see Belica—
That was the name the child was given by
The Gitana who reared her with a mother's care.
Your brother's plan I cannot fathom, nor
What he means by refusing to divulge
So strange and sad a story. They have told
The girl herself that she had been kidnaped
By a Romanichal, and she firmly believes
That she springs from a royal lineage.
On many occasions I have seen her do
And say things that make me believe she wears
A royal crown upon her head. The girl
Who suckled her has died and left her in
Her daughter's care, who though she is not so young
Or beautiful, is the one who had the jewels
In her trust, but she knows no more than what
Her mother knew, and she has no idea
Who are the parents of your gypsy niece.
Whose wisdom and whose peerless elegance
Have now become proverbial in these parts.
This, therefore, is my answer to your question,
Whether these jewels were given or stolen;
I am amazed to see them where they are.

QUEEN. Half of this curious story I have known,
And all you have said tallies with what I knew.
But would you recognize the fair Gitana
You speak of?

MARCELO.   Yes, of course, as I would myself.

QUEEN. Then wait a moment here till I return.

                              (*Exit the* QUEEN.)

MARCELO. I wonder who could have brought the jewels here.
What folly to believe that anything
Can be concealed from Heaven or from time.
Was I wrong to tell the story? Yes, I was,
For a hasty tongue allows no reasoning,
And is swifter to condemn than vindicate.

(*Enter the* QUEEN, INÉS *and* BELICA.)

QUEEN (*To* INÉS). Is this the gentleman who used to come

To visit your sister?

INÉS.   Why, yes, it is.
I heard him more than once speak with my mother.

QUEEN. With this proof, and with her close likeness to
My brother, I see a niece in front of me.

MARCELO. You may be sure of it, for this fair maid,
Whose hand you clasp in yours, is the pledge of love
Which your brother loves and should love the most.
If God on earth has made her noble through
Her famous father, Heaven ennobled her
Through her mother, and she herself deserves
The best of fortune through her loveliness.
(*Enter the* KING *and a courtier.*)

KING. It has been proved that jealousy does not
Exist unless there be insanity.

QUEEN. Without Love, Sire, you rather ought to say.

KING. The pangs of jealousy turn into madness,
But true love is devoid of them, for from
A cause that is good no wickedness can spring.

QUEEN. In me the opposite occurs, for when
I am jealous I am always suffering,
And it is my unbounded love for you
That has always kindled jealous pangs in me.

KING. If there is vengeance I have my revenge,
In watching how you have deceived yourself,
For your continual questions have become
Violent suspicions which may end with my
Conviction, yet if you consider well,
I am not of such paltry lineage
That I should have to do obeisance
To such a humble Gypsy maid today.

QUEEN. Look there, my Liege, and you will understand
How peerless loveliness may even wield
Still greater powers. Why, by my troth
I beg you gaze upon her beaming eyes.

KING. If you are so resolved to anger me,
Then you have not selected the best way.

QUEEN. Why is this? Are you then afraid to look
Upon a girl who is not only fair,
But also hopes that she will be my niece?

KING. What does this mean, tell me, Inés, I pray.

I now begin to fear they're mocking me.

INÉS. Be silent, Sire, you'll know the truth in time.

QUEEN. Do gaze at her serenely and then say
Whom does she resemble?

KING.   Her eyes, I think
Remind me of Rosamiro.

QUEEN.   More is needed,
For she is now your daughter, judge her thus.

COURTIER. Your Royal Highness is jesting?

QUEEN.   It is wrong
To draw such inferences from so clear
A truth.

KING.   If you're not joking, then why should
I not now wonder at this novelty?

QUEEN. Draw near the King I pray you, Isabel,[11]
And ask him to give you his hand to kiss,
Since you're my brother's daughter.

BELICA.   As a slave
I'll do obeisance.

KING.   Rise up, fair maid,
Your loveliness gives you the right to hope
For even greater things, but tell me now,
My Lady, how you ever heard this story.

QUEEN. The tale is brief and known to many, but
It cannot now be told; so let us go
To the city and while we are on the way
You'll hear it all.

KING.   Then let us go at once.

MARCELO. There is, Your Royal Highness, now no doubt.
The tale is clear as daylight, for her face
Declares its truth, and so do I who am
An actor in the play.

             (*Exeunt all with the exception of* BELICA *and* INÉS.)

INÉS. Now, Belica, since you have become at least
The Queen's niece it is time to have a thought
For us poor folk with whom you've lived till now.
Remember how we've gorged ourselves together,
And we have danced more than five other girls
Without self-pride. We've had our tiffs, and pulled
Each other's hair, but I respected you,

[11] The Queen gives Belica her full name for the first time.

And feared you. Now you've power, do good, I pray,
To our poor ragged Gypsies; if you do,
Your luck will far surpass the luckiest,
For it responds to all that is noble in
Your nature.

BELICA.   Do but give me now, Inés,
A petition and I'll send it on at once.   *(Exeunt.)*
(Enter PEDRO, *the Artful Dodger, in cloak and cap, as a
student.)*

PEDRO. Men say that it is her variety
Gives Dame Nature her radiance and beauty,
And I would certainly agree. To eat
The same food daily palls, and a single aim
Will even irritate the wisest man,
Just as one tires of wearing the same dress.
And so when there's variety we change
Our mind, and then our spirit rests. I'll leave
This world well tested when my time is up,
For I can say I've been a second Proteus.
Ye gods, what clothes I've changed, what jobs I've held!
What strange employments, what exotic tongues
I've spoken! now I'm a student on the run
From the Queen, and ready to face a host of risks
That spring from my unstable destiny.
But why rate oneself such a weathercock,
When it is the nature of our soul to keep
In eternal movement, so let God above
Cast me upon whatever shore He will.
(Enter a peasant with two hens.)

PEASANT. Today must be a Tuesday[12], that is why
I haven't sold them yet.

PEDRO.   Let us see them then.
Come here, pal: let me see. What is the fuss?
They're fine fat birds, and both show that you've been
Right open-handed. So good-bye and leave
The two of them. Look on them from afar,

---

[12] Classical authors regarded Tuesday as unlucky, because it was
the day sacred to Mars, the God of War, who causes the death of
relatives and friends. Hence it was unlucky to marry or travel on
Tuesdays. Cf., Jerónimo de Alcalá, *El Donado Hablador,* Vol. II,
Valladolid, 1626.

And say a prayer to them as honored relics,
And dedicate them to bucolic rites.

PEASANT. Provided you pay, you may make with them
An altar, or else relics, as you please.

PEDRO. The only holy payment for those birds
Would be to enable them to satisfy
The wishes of the worthiest Christian here.

PEASANT. In my opinion, sir, your plan will fail.
(*Enter two actors who are distinguished by the numbers
I and II.*)

PEDRO. What a malignant hypocrite you are!
You have not the intelligence to see
That the swarthy bloke you're talking to
Is worth a ransom when a prank's in view;
A man who is ready with a brace of hens
to ransom from Algiers two prisoners,
Who are safe and sound by the grace of God.

FIRST ACTOR (*aside*). This is a first-rate tale,
And the sacristan, whoever he is,
Is playing the part of high-brother.

PEDRO. Alas, self-interest rules the world;
nothing but envy and harshness:
Can such paltry requirements
Prevent you from ransoming
A couple of Christian captives
From those infidel tyrants?
May foul cannibals devour you!

PEASANT. Look here, Mr. Trifler,
Are my fowls monsters then?
Confound it all!
Because I wouldn't let you
Bamboozle me, is it?
And coax me into giving you
My poor nest egg?
Let rich folk, courtiers, monks,
And almoners ransom these Christians:
As for me, I haven't a stiver,
Save what I earn by my own two hands.

FIRST ACTOR. Let us back up this joke.
You are an ill-conditioned knave,
A vagrant and a fly-by-night,

And such a merciless ruffian
That there's no dealing with you.

PEDRO. May my vixen's malediction
And the curse of my bonnet and cap
Fall on you and your filthy brood,
And may I find you prisoner
In an underground cell in Fez,
And then we'll see if you'll enjoy
Seeing one who for two hens—no more . . .
O hearts of bronze, archives of Satan!
O wretched life now reduced to this,
That courtiers are begging for alms
From peasants and unholy folk.

PEASANT. Damn your soul! Give back my fowls!
I'm not the one to give alms.

FIRST ACTOR. How ignorant you are!
You do not know a thing
About the job of ransoming
A pair of portly solemn men!
I have already marked them down:
They're bearded and big-bellied,
Of ceremonious presence,
And they are genuinely worth
Well over three hundred ducats.
And for this brace of hens
I'll ransom them on the nail.
You see what a hard malignant heart
This wretched nincompoop possesses!
No wonder he was pupped beneath
The gnarléd branches of an oak.
There's nothing in such trashy folk
But poverty and greed!

PEASANT. Thank God there's a mayor or judge nearby.

(*Exit.*)

PEDRO. I have my tongue, I have my feet;
I'll wait and see.

FIRST ACTOR. So you're the traitor Galalón,[13]
One of those who are out to swindle
Their three times three.

[13] Galalón, Lord of Mayence, was the traitor in the *Chanson de Roland,* where he is called Guene.

SECOND ACTOR. Let him alone; why after all
   He left the pickings in the net;
   Let him go and good luck to him.
FIRST ACTOR. Well, what shall we do now?
PEDRO. As you wish, but first we must
   Pluck the ransom's feathers, then decide
   If there is a camp or tavern
   Where all may be consumed,
   And for my part I hereby renounce
   All claims that may pertain to it.
SECOND ACTOR. There is one major obstacle,
   We must rehearse first.
PEDRO. But tell me, are you actors?
FIRST ACTOR. Yes, for our sins we are.
PEDRO. Blessed are you both, my giants, like Mount Atlas,
   And my silver-veinéd hills of Potosí,
   You'll prop my dwarfish powers, so all my hopes
   Are centered in you.
SECOND ACTOR. What fierce squall has hit you
   And blown your wits away?
PEDRO. I must be an actor
   That Fame may sing my famous deeds
   For all the world to hear,
   So that they may be carried
   East and west, and even fly
   To the empty realms of Policea,
   And even further, in the name
   Of Nicolás, whose surname is de Ríos.
   That was the magician's name,
   Who taught me that the world was cruel,
   And though he was blind, he perceived
   That fraud and trickery today
   Hold undisputed sway.
   In cabins, and in palace halls,
   Amidst coarse blankets, and rich silks
   And satins my fame shall extend,
   Even though Pedro, the Artful Dodger,
   Has faded from men's minds.
SECOND ACTOR.   What you, Señor,
   Are ranting is just jargon and sheer gabble to us.
PEDRO. I should indeed be a fool to tell you now

My long life's story, but if my fortunes
Should improve when I am an actor, you
Will soon see all the talents I possess,
Especially my gift for playing tricks
In interludes, and clowning to the limits.
(*Enter another actor.*)

THIRD ACTOR. Have you not noticed that it is time to start
Rehearsing, for the King demands a play,
And the author has already been an hour
And a half expecting us: what carelessness!

FIRST ACTOR. If we now hasten, all can be put right.
Come now, my gallant, and I'll make of you
Today an actor.

PEDRO.   If I am made one
I'll show you soon that I can also be
An author with the tags I picked up, and
The luck the wizard Malgesí foretold
Is now to be fulfilled. I may
Be even Patriarch, Pope, Emperor,
As well as student, for a player's calling
Comprises every state, and, though his life
Is hard, it is in fact, both quaint and varied,
For quaint and various are its interests,
And even its worst critics never would
Describe it as an indolent profession.   (*Exeunt all.*)
(*Enter an author with the text of his play,* PEDRO, *and the
two actors who are numbered.*)

AUTHOR. You gentlemen are surely lax in conscience,
And I see signs ahead that I shall have
To lose my patience. Well, confound it all!
In twenty days could you not have rigged up
This play of mine? What have you now to say?
Yet all my fortunes do depend on it;
What irritates me most and drives me wild
Is to find that not one of you is absent
When it is payday, yet at rehearsal time
I have to go in search of the company
With dogs and ferrets, even with town criers,
But even then they don't appear.

PEDRO.   Can one
Who is not trickster and a chatterbox

Play it better than I if I wish to act it?

AUTHOR. If this pompous fellow be not boasting, he
    Should know a thing or two.

PEDRO.   I know all that comes
    Within the scope of an all-round actor, and
    I have the qualities an actor needs
    For his career, but these must be as rare
    As they are infinite. And first of all,
    Great memory; second, a fluent tongue;
    And third, he must not be devoid of grandeur;
    Good figure is essential, if he plays
    The part of gallant. He must never be
    Affected in his gestures, nor intone
    When he recites. And even when he plays
    The insolent, he must be careful, grave
    When he's an old man, rapid when a youth,
    In love complex, but raging when he's jealous.
    He must recite with such skill and intelligence
    That he transforms himself entirely into
    The character he represents, and to
    The lines he must give their significance
    Through his own expert knowledge of the language,
    That he may resurrect the tale that's dead.
    He must through terror move the crowd to tears
    From laughter, and as swiftly make them turn
    To tears again. Whatever aspect he
    May show the public, it must be the one
    They'll recognize as him. If he succeeds
    In this, he will be an accomplished actor.
    (*Enter the* CONSTABLE *of plays.*)

CONSTABLE. Why are you so slow? Have I then to wait
    Until you finish? clearly you don't know
    The palace news. I must say that the court
    Is so planet-struck I am going mad,
    While all await the King, the Queen, and niece.

AUTHOR. What niece?

CONSTABLE.   A Gypsy, they say, who is lovely.

PEDRO. I'm afraid it is Belica: Is it true?

CONSTABLE. So true that I know no more recent truth.
    The Queen now wishes to give some feasts for her.
    Come with me and you'll hear what's happening.

PEDRO. Great good is bound to come my way if you
　　Enroll me as one of your company.
AUTHOR. You are already admitted in the guild
　　Of our joyful diversions, for your rare
　　Good sense deserves a larger laurel crown.
　　But let us go now and we shall assess
　　Your original talent when we rehearse the play.
PEDRO. This will not help me, as you'll see in time.
CONSTABLE. Gentlemen, it's late.
AUTHOR.　　　　　　　　　　Who is missing?
FIRST ACTOR.　　　　　　　　　　　　　　No one.
　　　　　　　　　　　　　　　　　(Exeunt all.)

　　(Enter the KING *and* SILERIO.*)*
KING. Whatever dress she wears she shows her beauty:
　　She was my bane as Gypsy, now as lady
　　She prepares to kill me. Kinship, alas, does not
　　Diminish my desires, but on the contrary
　　It fans them, and my heart is set ablaze.
　　(Guitars sound.)
　　What music is that?
SILERIO.　　　　　　　It must be the players
　　Who go to dress.
KING.　　　　　　　The show depresses me:
　　Now that I'm alone with my desires I'd like
　　To face the surging billows of the sea
　　Of love, where I am floundering, but hark!
　　I fancy I hear them singing my sad tale,
　　A sign her memory will last forever.
(Enter the musicians singing the following ballad:)

　　　　　The Gypsies dance their roundelay
　　　　　The King's eyes are bewitched;
　　　　　The Queen, alas, is jealous,
　　　　　And packs the Gypsies off to jail.
　　　　　It was on Easter Sunday
　　　　　That Belilla and Inés
　　　　　Gave their Gypsy Zambra,
　　　　　All for the King;
　　　　　Poor Belilla in confusion
　　　　　Tripped and fell beside the King,
　　　　　And His Majesty with courtesy

> *Raised her to her feet again.*
> *But as Belilla's beautiful,*
> *With flashing eyes*
> *And skin that vies with the carnation,*
> *The Queen, alas, is jealous,*
> *And packs the Gypsies off to jail.*

SILERIO. They're all amazed and do not notice us.

KING. The theme of their song is astonishment.

FIRST MUSICIAN. Pray, silence all: His Majesty is here;
Perhaps indeed he may not like our song.

SECOND MUSICIAN. He'll like it, as it's new, and melancholy
In tone, and what it says is known to all:
That the Queen is jealous, and a woman has
The right to be jealous of her own spouse.

KING. How well you've understood it all! But may
The Devil himself make head or tail of it!
Silerio, my death and life come both
Together; what shall I do?

SILERIO.   You must show
A faith unshaken here, there only feigned.

(*Enter the* QUEEN *and* BELICA. *The latter is now dressed
as a lady of the Court. Enter* INÉS, *dressed as a Gypsy;*
MALDONADO; *the* AUTHOR; *the* MAYOR, MARTÍN CRESPO; *and*
PEDRO, *the Artful Dodger.*)

PEDRO. Illustrious Isabel, who was
Belica, Pedro, the famous Dodger,
At last lies prostrate at your feet,
So ready to plan his foolish deeds
That to win fame his name became
Pedro, the Artful Dodger;
Now that name he has changed
To Nicolás de los Ríos.
I now declare that you have here
Your Pedro, converted from a Gypsy
Into a famous actor, who will
Serve you in more ways than you
Can imagine if you now don't fail
To show those qualities of yours
That surpass all that others have.

Your claims and mine have been fulfilled,
But whereas mine were in fiction only,
Yours were in real earnest.
For there are countless fortunes
Men and women joke about,
That fashion men of straw,
As well as real men.
As actor I shall be the King,
When there is one in the play,
And you who listen to my words
Are already half a queen by law,
And by my merit as actor, I
Henceforth in jest can serve you.
In earnest you can do me favors,
Unless you follow the common herd,
Who run in quest of frivolous whims,
And if there be a thread of homespun
In your proud pedigree, it will
Always remain there as reminder
Of your own humble origin.
By your own goodness I'm convinced
That your heart never will be darkened
By the shadow of base ingratitude.
Relying on the Queen's good faith,
And on the feelings held by one
Whom you believed a Romanichal,
I beg you in the course of time,
To intercede with His Majesty,
To grant me a boon which I shall apply
According to my own sweet will.

KING.   I'll grant your boon at once, and you may ask
    What you desire.

PEDRO.   As my request is just,
    I shall not fear to ask. Since all agree
    That to be an actor is an occupation whose
    Sole aim is to teach and please, for this
    To be achieved one needs ability
    In plenty, hard work, curiosity,
    And one must know how to spend as well as save.
    Then no one should ever practice it unless

He has the essential skill that is required
To enable him to teach and satisfy
His public. First let everyone be tested,
As if all were to form a company:
But let the glibbest speaker take the lead,
Not just because of his light fancy, but
Because all those who follow him will try
To do their best, for no art is inferior
To the ends which it must struggle to attain.

BELICA. I shall persuade the King, my Lord, to grant
Your plea.

KING.   And others too if you but ask.

QUEEN. I now feel less disturbed when you are looking
At that girl, and all that you do for her
Rejoices me, and I am inclined to say
That both should be believed; but as she is
My niece, she comes between my jealousy
And you. With joy we'll see the comedy,
Since God has not allowed my jealousy
To turn it into tragedy. At once
I'll tell my brother what has happened here.   (*Exit.*)

KING. It is in my heart and I can touch it now,
For my imagination tries to reach
What is impossible.

SILERIO.   Don't be cast down:
Your kinship to her is not close; a way
Might still be found.

KING.   Meanwhile I'll die of grief.
                    (*Exit the* KING *and* SILERIO.)

MALDONADO. My Lady Belica, a moment's grace
I beg you: I am Count Maldonado.

BELICA. My state has now changed and I must not stay.
Dear Maldonado, pardon me, I pray,
And I shall speak with you another day.

INÉS. My sister Belica!

BELICA.   The Queen waits: let me go.
                    (*Exit* BELICA.)

INÉS. She has gone! If anyone had told me this
A while ago I should not have believed,
E'en if my eyes had seen it. Now may God

Protect us: what an ungrateful girl! And what
A shock!

PEDRO.   Life's mutability destroys
A thousand stabilities, includes
A thousand wrongs, and hoards a thousand gaieties.
And in one brief hour casts into oblivion
What it has learned in a thousand centuries.

MAYOR. What is it makes you now so cock-a-hoop?
What have you been up to?

PEDRO. I might have been undone,
If I had not looked to my own.
I have now changed my name and occupation,
Though it is not what I would wish,
For I have turned into a fabled monster.

MAYOR. You always were a legend,
And I came to get the prize
For the dance you taught us.
You then displayed your wit,
Your talents and your magnanimity;
And if there were no pages in the world,
I know your fame would reach world's end.
Clemente and Clemencia are flourishing,
And Benita and Pascual enjoy their lives.
(*Enter a courtier.*)

COURTIER. Their Majesties are waiting: you may start.

PEDRO. We may speak afterwards.

COURTIER. Take heed, they say you're late.

PEDRO. You see, gentlemen, that both Their Majesties
Are waiting inside, and there is no room
For all to see the play my author is
Presenting, for the Spanish halberdiers,
The German lancers and Burgundian guards
Prevent all boisterous groundlings from going in.
But tomorrow there will be another showing,
Which you will see right through for a tiny sum,
And you'll find that it does not end in marriage,
Or such trite and well-worn banalities.
Nor will you find a woman giving birth
In one act to a son, who in the next
Is already bearded and a doughty warrior

Striking and slaying to avenge his father,
And ending as King of a country that's not marked
In any known cosmography. Devoid
Of such nonsense and follies, he now shows
This comedy of artifice and skill,
Which I received directly from the hands
Of the one and only Pedro, the Artful Dodger.

THE
JEALOUS
OLD MAN

1615

Interlude

by

MIGUEL DE
CERVANTES SAAVEDRA

⊰§ DRAMATIS PERSONAE §⊱

Cañizares, an old man
His friend
Doña Lorenza, the wife of Cañizares
Cristina, her niece
Hortigosa, a neighbor
A young man, who does not speak
A constable
Musicians

The text of *El Viejo Celoso* which we have used is from the edition of *Comedias y Entremeses* of Cervantes, by Rudolph Schevill and Adolfo Bonilla, Madrid, 1918.

Enter DOÑA LORENZA; *her niece,* CRISTINA; *and* HORTIGOSA, *her neighbor.*

DOÑA LORENZA. It's a wonder, Señora Hortigosa, that my husband didn't lock the door; bad 'cess to him! I declare to God he has driven me daft! This is the first day since I married him that I've had a chance of colloguing with a soul outside the house. I'd like to see the old curmudgeon under the sod, and the man who tied me up with him!

HORTIGOSA. Come, come, my dear, no need to tear your hair and wring your hands. When the pot is worn out you can always buy a new one.

DOÑA LORENZA. That's the kind of rigmarole and proverb they dinned into my ears to bamboozle me. A thousand curses on his money—barring the crosses on the back—to hell with the jewels and all the finery he unloads on me and promises to give me. None of them have done me a pennyworth of good: what use is all that wealth when I'm as poor as a church mouse and famished in the midst of plenty?

CRISTINA. Indeed you're right, auntie; and as for myself I'd rather go about with a rag in front and one behind, provided I had a young husband, than see myself bedded and befouled by the rotten old scarecrow you took as husband.

DOÑA LORENZA. *I* took him, niece? Not on your life! I was delivered over to him by one whose word was law, and I as a dutiful girl was quicker to obey than to contradict. But I'm telling you if I had known as much then as I do now, I would have bitten off my tongue rather than say that three-letter word "yes" which will cost me three thousand years' repentance. But I suppose it was all in the cards and had to be, so it's no good crying over spilt milk.

CRISTINA. God bless us and save us, what a nasty old man he is! All the night long you hear him saying: "Hand me the chamber pot; put away the chamber pot: quick, little Cristina, warm up some cloths, I've a troublesome colic: fetch me those rushes, my gallstones are giving me twinges."

Sure there are more medicines and ointments in the bedroom than in a druggist's shop, and here am I who hardly know how to dress myself, obliged to be his nurse. Ugh! it turns my stomach! He's an old wreck, as moldy as he is jealous: there's no one alive more jealous than he is!

DOÑA LORENZA. That's the simple truth, niece.

CRISTINA. I wish to God this weren't the truth.

HORTIGOSA. All right, Doña Lorenza, if you follow my advice, you'll soon see how your luck will change. The young fellow I have in mind is as upstanding and sinewy as a mountain pine: he knows how to make love, and he's a model of discretion, and ever so grateful for all that's done for him. And seeing that the old curmudgeon's jealous nature doesn't give us a chance to write letters or get answers, it's up to you to cheer up and put on a bold face, and following my plan, I'll bring the young fellow to your room, ay, and shuffle him out of there too, even if the old blighter had more eyes in his head than many-eyed Argus, and had more clairvoyance than one of those wizards who are supposed to see seven leagues underground.

DOÑA LORENZA. As I'm a novice in such matters, I'm timid, and I'm against risking my reputation just for a lark.

CRISTINA. Dear auntie, your qualms remind me of the old ballad about Gómez Arias:

> My lord Gonzáles Arias,
> I prithee pity me;
> I'm but a tender maiden, and
> I've never been in such grave peril.

DOÑA LORENZA. Some wicked demon must be whispering in your ears, niece, you are so shameless in the things you say.

CRISTINA. I don't know who's prompting me, but I'm sure of one thing: if I were in your place I'd make no bones about doing everything Señora Hortigosa says, without missing one point.

DOÑA LORENZA. And where would my honor be, niece?

CRISTINA. What about the fun we'd have?

DOÑA LORENZA. And suppose we are found out?

CRISTINA. Suppose we aren't?

DOÑA LORENZA. Who'll guarantee we shan't be found out?

HORTIGOSA. Who? Why, careful planning, caution, and above all, boldness and my scheming.

CRISTINA. Now mind, Señora Hortigosa, that you bring us a lover who is clean-limbed, free and easy, on the bold side, and above all, young.

HORTIGOSA. The fellow I have in mind has all those qualities and two extra ones: he is rich and a good spender.

DOÑA LORENZA. Wealth doesn't mean a thing to me, Señora Hortigosa; I've more jewels than I need, and I'm all confused trying to choose between the different colored dresses in my wardrobe. In this respect I'm as happy as any girl can be, and long live Cañizares, say I, for he dresses me up like a doll, and I've more jewels to wear than you would find in a rich silversmith's shop window. If only he wouldn't nail up the windows, lock the doors, watch the house day and night, and drive away tomcats and dogs, simply because they are males, I'd do without his gifts and generosities.

HORTIGOSA. Is he then so jealous?

DOÑA LORENZA. Well, the other day they tried to sell him a piece of tapestry at a bargain price, but because it had human figures designed on it, he refused to buy it, and he chose another one of foliage pattern which was more expensive and not so attractive. There are seven doors to pass, in addition to the hall door, before one can get to my room, and every one of them has a lock and key. Bless me if I can find where he hides the keys at night.

CRISTINA. Auntie, I believe he hides the master key in the folds of his nightshirt.

DOÑA LORENZA. Don't you believe it, niece; I sleep with him and I've never seen or felt a key on him.

CRISTINA. But that's not all, for all the night long he's roaming all over the house like a ghost; and if any people are serenading in the street, he fires stones at them to drive them away. He's a nasty warlock, and he's an old man; that's the worst I can say of him.

DOÑA LORENZA. Señora Hortigosa, best for you to be off now; otherwise the old grumbler may find you with me; that would upset all our plans. But if you intend to do anything, do it as soon as you can: I'm so desperate that I've a mind to slip a rope around my neck and make an end for good and all.

HORTIGOSA. You'll soon cease to be depressed when your good time begins; then you'll revive and take a rosier view of life.

CRISTINA. I sincerely hope this happens, even if I have to lose a finger off my hand: I'm very fond of my dear auntie, and it drives me distracted seeing her so worried and woe-begone in the power of that doddering, dithery old dolt— I can't stop calling him old.

DOÑA LORENZA. Yet he is very fond of you, Cristina.

CRISTINA. Does that stop his being old? Besides, I've always heard that old men are fond of young girls.

HORTIGOSA. That is true, Cristina. Good-bye: I'll be back after supper. Now you, señora, consider carefully our plan: you'll realize that you stand to gain by it.

CRISTINA. Señora Hortigosa, please bring me a nice little friar for me to have some sport with.

HORTIGOSA. I'll bring the little girl the portrait of one to pin up.

CRISTINA. A picture of one is no good to me: I want a live lusty little one—a regular treasure.

DOÑA LORENZA. But suppose your uncle sees him?

CRISTINA. I'll tell him he's a ghost, and he'll be scared, and I'll have my fun.

HORTIGOSA. I promise you I'll bring you one. Good-bye. (*Exit* HORTIGOSA.)

CRISTINA. Now, auntie, if Hortigosa brings you a lover and me a little friar, and if uncle sees them, all we have to do is for all of us to seize him, choke him, and throw him down the well, or bury him in the stable.

DOÑA LORENZA. So that's the kind of girl you are: I believe you would do it too.

CRISTINA. Well, let the old blighter not be jealous then, and allow us to live in peace; we don't harm him, and we be-have like saints. (*Exeunt.*)

(*Enter* CAÑIZARES—*an old man—and a friend.*)

CAÑIZARES. My friend, when a man of seventy marries a girl of fifteen, he either is a fool or he wants to set out for the next world as soon as possible. No sooner did I marry this girl Lorenza, hoping to find in her a helpmate and a companion who would be at my bedside and close my eyes when I die, than I was overwhelmed by worries of every kind. I owned a house, but I landed myself with a household: I was lodged, but I am now dislodged.

FRIEND. Yes, my friend, you made a mistake, but not a great one; for as the Apostle Paul has said, it is better to marry than to burn.

CAÑIZARES. There was nothing in me to burn, my friend, for the tiniest flame would reduce me to ashes. I wanted companionship. I sought companionship, and I found companionship. May God help me.

FRIEND. Are you jealous, friend?

CAÑIZARES. Yes, of the sun that shines on Lorencica, of the breeze that touches her, of the skirts that cling to her limbs.

FRIEND. Does she give you cause for jealousy?

CAÑIZARES. Not in the least. She has no reason to, no way to, no time to, nor any place to. The windows, in addition to being fastened, are protected by bars and shutters: the doors are never opened: no woman of the neighborhood crosses my threshold, or ever shall as long as I am alive. Reflect, my dear friend: temptations do not enter the minds of women from taking part in festivals or processions or any public gatherings; where they stumble and come to grief is in the homes of their neighbors and friends. More wickedness is hidden by a bad woman friend than by the cloak of night itself, and more intrigues are planned in her house than in an assembly.

FRIEND. I am sure of it. But if Doña Lorenza never leaves the house, and no one enters it, what worries you then?

CAÑIZARES. Because Lorencica will soon discover what she is missing, and that will be a disaster, and such a disaster that the mere thought makes me afraid, and my anxiety drives me to despair, and my despair plagues my life.

FRIEND. It is natural for you to be apprehensive, for women would wish to enjoy the pleasures of matrimony to the full.

CAÑIZARES. My wife enjoys them doubly.

FRIEND. Ah, so there is the snag, my friend?

CAÑIZARES. Not at all: for Lorencica is more innocent than

a dove, and up to the present she has no notion of such complexities. Well, God be with you, my friend, I must be getting home.

FRIEND. I want to go with you, and meet your wife.

CAÑIZARES. I must remind you, friend, of the ancient Latin proverb that says: *Amicus usque ad aras,* meaning, "A friend as far as the altar," and implying that a friend is obliged to do any service for his friend except what is against the laws of God. So I say, my friend, *usque ad portam,* up to the door, for no one shall cross my threshold. So farewell, friend, and forgive me. (*Exit* CAÑIZARES.)

FRIEND. I have never in all my life seen a man more cautious or more senseless. He, doubtless, is one of those who go through life dragging their own rope after them for hanging: one of those who in the end die of the disease they are afraid of. (*Exit the friend.*)

(*Enter* DOÑA LORENZA *and* CRISTINA.)

CRISTINA. Aunt, uncle is very late, and Hortigosa is still later.

DOÑA LORENZA. I wish he'd never come, or she either, for he infuriates me, and she disturbs me.

CRISTINA. One must try anything once, auntie: if it turns out badly, give it the go by.

DOÑA LORENZA. Ah, niece! In this kind of affair, if I'm not mistaken, the danger lies in trying it at all.

CRISTINA. I must say, auntie, you've no guts: if I were your age no men would scare me, no matter how massive their attributes.

DOÑA LORENZA. Again, I repeat, and I'll say it a hundred thousand times, that Satan uses you as his mouthpiece. But what's that? How did the master get in?

CRISTINA. He must have let himself in with the master key.

DOÑA LORENZA. The Devil take his masteries and his keys.

(*Enter* CAÑIZARES.)

CAÑIZARES. Whom were you talking to, Lorenza?

DOÑA LORENZA. To Cristinica.

CAÑIZARES. Be careful what you say, Lorenza.

DOÑA LORENZA. I repeat, I was talking to Cristinica: who else could it be? Have I anybody else?

CAÑIZARES. I wouldn't like you to be talking aloud to yourself and saying things that might be harmful to me.

DOÑA LORENZA. I don't understand all your roundabout phrases, and I don't want to, and for goodness sake let us spend the feast in peace and amity.

CAÑIZARES. I wouldn't fight with you on St. John's Eve. But who's knocking so loudly at the door? See who it is, Cristinica: if it's a beggar give him alms and send him away.

CRISTINA. Who's there?

HORTIGOSA. Your neighbor Hortigosa, Cristina.

CAÑIZARES. Hortigosa, a neighbor? Heaven help me! Ask her, Cristina, what she wants, and give it to her, provided she doesn't cross the threshold.

CRISTINA. What do you want, dear neighbor?

CAÑIZARES. The very word neighbor gives me the creeps; call her by her right name, Cristina.

CRISTINA. What do you want, Señora Hortigosa?

HORTIGOSA. I want to beg a favor from Señor Cañizares: my very life and soul are at stake.

CAÑIZARES. Tell that lady, niece, that both of mine too are at stake, and more than that, to keep her from coming in here.

DOÑA LORENZA. Goodness gracious, what a weird person you are! Am I not here in front of you? Are people going to gobble me up with their eyes, or whisk me away through the air?

CAÑIZARES. Let her in and a hundred thousand devils with her, since you insist! Come in, neighbor. What a sinister omen that word neighbor is to me!

(*Enter* HORTIGOSA, *carrying a large hanging of tapestry and embossed leather. On the four leather corners are painted the celebrated knights Rodomonte, Mandricardo, Ruggiero and Gradasso. Rodomonte is represented as muffled in a cloak.*)[1]

HORTIGOSA. My dear sir, hearing of your noble reputation for charity, alms and good works, I have dared to come and beg you to do me the great favor and charity of buying from me this hanging. A son of mine is in prison because he wounded a cloth-shearer, and the magistrate has ordered the surgeon to give evidence in the case, and I have no money to pay him with; and the youth is in dan-

[1] These characters come from the Italian legend of Roland, as treated by Ariosto in his *Orlando Furioso,* a work that profoundly influenced Cervantes in *Don Quixote.*

ger of being liable for other fines, and there may be a lot of them, for he's a bit of a scapegrace; and I'd like to get him out of jail today or tomorrow, if possible. The tapestry is a fine artistic work, and it is brand new, but I can let you have it for whatever you are willing to give me, as it's a question of more importance than mere money, and I've sacrificed many such things in my life. Now hold up that corner, my lady, and let's unfold it, so that Señor Cañizares may see that I'm not cheating him. Hold it up higher, señora, and look how it hangs at full-length. And the paintings in the squares look as if they were alive.

(*As she raises the hanging to show it off, a young man slips into the room behind it.* CAÑAZARES, *meanwhile, who is examining the paintings, says:*)

CAÑIZARES. What a handsome Rodomonte! But what does such a muffled gentleman in my house? If he realized what I feel about such goings on and masquerades, he'd get a fright.

CRISTINA. Uncle, I've not the foggiest notion about muffled men and masquerades, but if one came into the house, Señora Hortigosa is to blame: may the Devil carry me away if I ever said or did anything to bring him in here. No, upon my conscience, it would be the Devil's own handiwork if my uncle were to blame me for his coming in.

CAÑIZARES. I'm well aware, niece, that Señora Hortigosa is to blame, but this is not surprising, for she doesn't know my prejudices, and how I loathe such paintings.

DOÑA LORENZA (*aside*). He's referring to the paintings, Cristinica, not to something else.

CRISTINA (*aside*). I am referring to the paintings. Ah, Heaven help me! My heart was in my mouth! I thought I was going to swoon!

DOÑA LORENZA (*aside*). Blast that blundering gaping mouth of yours! That's what comes of consorting with babes in arms.

CRISTINA (*aside*). What an idiot I was! I might have toppled over the whole house of cards!

CAÑIZARES. Señora Hortigosa, I've a rooted objection to muffled figures or those that are going to be muffled. Take this doubloon, which will see you through your difficulties, and leave my house as fast as you can, that is to say, this instant, and take your hanging away with you.

HORTIGOSA. I wish you a longer life than Methuselah of Jerusalem by the side of this dear lady . . . I don't know her name, but I entreat her to call on me at any hour of day or night; I'll serve her with my body and soul, and I'm certain that her soul must be as spotless as a cooing turtledove's.

CAÑIZARES. Señora Hortigosa, cut your cackle and be off, and stop passing judgments on other people.

HORTIGOSA. If you, my lady, need a little sticking plaster for female troubles, I have some infallible samples; or if your teeth ache, I know a few magic charms that check the pain in a jiffy.

CAÑIZARES. Cut it short, Señora Hortigosa; Doña Lorenza has no female ailments, and no trouble with toothache: all her teeth are sound as a bell, and no one has ever been pulled.

HORTIGOSA. She will have some drawn in time, if heaven is kind, for she will live a long life, and old age plays havoc with one's teeth.

CAÑIZARES. God help me, is there no way I can get rid of this pest of a neighbor? Hortigosa, you she-devil of a neighbor, or whatever you are, clear out to hell and leave me in peace in my home!

HORTIGOSA. Your request could not be more reasonable, so keep your hair on, dear sir, I'm off. (*Exit* HORTIGOSA.)

CAÑIZARES. Oh, those accursed neighbors! I'm singed by her specious words just because they were uttered by a neighbor.

DOÑA LORENZA. I do declare you're a boor and a savage. What did our neighbor say to make you so venomously spiteful against her? Why you even turn your decent actions into a mortal sin. You gave her two dozen royals trimmed with two dozen insults, you malicious, foul-mouthed slanderer!

CAÑIZARES. Tut, tut, it's an ill wind—and I suspect there's mischief in the offing. I don't like hearing you defend your neighbor so heatedly.

CRISTINA. Auntie, why not go into your bedroom to calm down; leave uncle alone, as he seems to get in a huff.

DOÑA LORENZA. I'll follow your advice, niece, and mind you, he won't set eyes on me for the next two hours. I'll make him drain the cup to the dregs, no matter how he tries to reject it. (*Exit* DOÑA LORENZA.)

CRISTINA. Uncle, did you not hear her bang the door? Why, I believe she is getting a prop to fasten it.

DOÑA LORENZA (*from within*). Cristinica, Cristinica!

CRISTINA. What do you want, auntie?

DOÑA LORENZA. If you only could see what a handsome young lover my good luck has brought me! Young, attractive, sleek, dark-haired, and his breath smells like orange blossom!

CRISTINA. Heavens! what madcap tomfoolery is this? Scold her, uncle, tell her she shouldn't say such naughty things even as a joke.

CAÑIZARES. Don't be a fool, Lorenza! I'm in no mood to put up with such jokes.

DOÑA LORENZA. This is no joke: I'm in dead earnest. There is no greater truth than this one for me this moment.

CRISTINA. Goodness gracious, what crazy childishness! But tell me, auntie, is my little friar there too?

DOÑA LORENZA. No, niece; but our neighbor Hortigosa will bring him along next time.

CAÑIZARES. Lorenza, say anything you wish, but don't utter again that word neighbor; I get gooseflesh when I hear it.

DOÑA LORENZA. And I'm all of a dither for love of my neighbor.

CRISTINA. Auntie dear, what crazy talk and childishness is that?

DOÑA LORENZA. Now I'm finding out what you really are, you accursed old man: up to today I've been fooled by you!

CRISTINA. Scold her, uncle! Scold her! She's a shameless hussy!

DOÑA LORENZA. I'm now going to wash the sprouting beard of my lover in a basin of scented manna water, for his face is truly angelic.

CRISTINA. Heavens! what mad talk, what foolishness! Tear her limb from limb, uncle!

CAÑIZARES. I won't tear her to pieces, but I'll tear down the door that hides her.

DOÑA LORENZA. No need to do so: I've opened it. Come on in, and you'll see that I've told you the honest truth.

CAÑIZARES. I know you're joking, but I'll come in, just to calm you down.

(*As* CAÑIZARES *enters the room, they throw a basin of water in his eyes. He starts to wipe his face,* CRISTINA *and* DOÑA LORENZA *both go for him, and in the confusion the lover escapes.*)

CAÑIZARES. By God, Lorenza, you almost blinded me! only the devil prompts horseplay that endangers a person's eyesight.

DOÑA LORENZA. Look what kind of man my ill luck gave to be my husband, the most suspicious man in all the world. Look how he believed my lying stories, just because he was so crazed by jealousy . . . truly am I to be pitied! I wish I could tear out my hair to chastize myself for marrying this old man! I'd cry my eyes out to wash away the faults of that cursed spouse of mine! See what value he sets on my honor and my reputation, when he tries to turn his foul suspicion into certainty, his lies into truth, jests into truth, and sport into cursing! Alas, my heart will break!

CRISTINA. Auntie, don't shout so loud, the whole neighborhood will be in an uproar.

(*Voices off stage.*)

CONSTABLE. Open the door! Open at once, or I'll break it down!

DOÑA LORENZA. Open it, Cristinica, and let everyone witness my innocence and the cruelty of this old man.

CAÑIZARES. I swear, I thought you were joking. Calm down, Lorenza!

(*Enter the* CONSTABLE, MUSICIANS, *and* HORTIGOSA.)

CONSTABLE. What's happening here? Who's quarreling? Who was shouting?

CAÑIZARES. It is nothing, Constable: just a tiff between husband and wife: it's soon over.

MUSICIANS. My companions and I, who are musicians, were next door at a betrothal, when we heard a hullabaloo, and we were startled, and we rushed over, thinking it was serious.

HORTIGOSA. I thought so too, as sure as I'm a sinner.

CAÑIZARES. The fact is, Señora Hortigosa, all this would not have happened but for you.

HORTIGOSA. That's it; my sins were the cause. I was born under an evil star, and people are always blaming me for what others do.

CAÑIZARES. Ladies and gentlemen, do kindly return to your homes. I'm grateful for your intentions. My wife and I have made up.

DOÑA LORENZA. Yes, I'll forgive him, provided he first of all begs this good neighbor's pardon for having had uncharitable thoughts about her.

CAÑIZARES. If I had to beg pardon from all the women of the neighborhood whom I think evil, I should never finish. Nevertheless, I now beg Señora Hortigosa's pardon.

HORTIGOSA. And I grant it here in presence of Pedro García.

MUSICIANS. Well, we didn't come here for nothing, I hope: so tune up, friends, let the dancer dance and let the reconciliation be celebrated in song.

CAÑIZARES. Good folks, I don't want any music: I count the song as already sung.

MUSICIANS. Well, even if you don't want to hear it:

> On St. John's Day if rain should fall,
> You'll have no wine and your loaves will
> be small,
> But if you quarrel on his feast
> they say,
> You'll live in peace for a year
> and a day.
> When wheat is golden and vines are in flower
> The farmer dreads the curse of a shower,
> But if there's a squabble on the Day of St. John
> It will bring peace till the year has gone.
> When the dog days blaze o'er the broiling plain,
> Men's tempers will rise beneath the strain;
> But autumn and winter bring peace as before,
> And everyone prophesies once more:
> If there are quarrels on his feast, we say,
> You'll live in peace for a year and a day.
> May all married couples when they mope,
> Find their gloom suddenly changed to hope;

All threat'ning clouds are swept from the sky
As the sun this morning dances on high:[2]
If there are quarrels on his feast, we say,
You'll live in peace for a year and a day. (They dance.)

CAÑIZARES. I sincerely trust you folks are now aware of all the troubles and tribulations a neighbor woman brought upon me, and you agree that I'm right to be on bad terms with the whole tribe of neighbor women.

DOÑA LORENZA. My spouse may shun the neighbors, but I kiss hand to all of you darling neighbors.

CRISTINA. And I too, but if my neighbor had brought me my dainty little friar, I'd have cherished her as a still better neighbor. So farewell, dear neighbors.

[2] According to an ancient Spanish folk tradition, the sun on the morning of St. John dances up the sky.

THE
PLAYBOY
OF
SEVILLE
1630

❧❦❧

Comedia
in Three Acts
by
TIRSO DE MOLINA
(1583-1648)

❧❦❧

◄§ DRAMATIS PERSONAE §►

Don Diego Tenorio
Don Juan Tenorio, his son
Catalinón, Don Juan's lackey
The King of Naples
Duke Octavio
Don Pedro Tenorio, Don Juan's uncle and Spanish Ambassador to Naples
The Marquis of La Mota
Don Gonzalo de Ulloa, father of Doña Ana
The King of Castile (Alfonso XI, 1312-1350)
Doña Ana de Ulloa
Duchess Isabel
Thisbe ⎤
Belisa ⎥
Anfriso ⎬ fisher folk
Coridón ⎦
Aminta ⎤
Batricio ⎬ peasant folk
Gaseno ⎦
Ripio, a servant
Fabio, a servant
Shepherds, musicians, etc.

The scene is laid in Naples, Tarragona, Seville, and Dos Hermanas, a little town on the road from Seville to Jérez de la Frontera.

The time: the fourteenth century.

The text of *El Burlador de Sevilla y Convidado de Piedra* which we have used is that of 1630, reproduced by Cotarelo y Mori in *Nueva Biblioteca de Autores Españoles,* Madrid, 1907, Vol. IX.

ACT I.

A room in the palace of the KING OF NAPLES.
Enter DON JUAN, *with face muffled in his cloak, and* ISABEL.

ISABEL. Here, Duke Octavio, there's a safer way.
DON JUAN. Duchess, my love, I'll swear my troth once more.
ISABEL. Then is my glory come! Will all your gifts,
    Your promises of lasting love come true?
DON JUAN. They will, my love.
ISABEL.   Then let me fetch a light.
DON JUAN. But why?
ISABEL.   That my heart may convince itself
    Of all the joy I feel.
DON JUAN.   I'll quench the light.
ISABEL. Heaven help me! Who are you; shame on you!
DON JUAN. Who am I? Just a man without a name.
ISABEL. You're not the Duke?
DON JUAN.   No.
ISABEL.   Help! The palace guard!
DON JUAN. Keep quiet, Duchess, do give me your hand.
ISABEL. Don't hold me, villain. Help, in the King's name!
    Help! soldiers, guards and servants of the King.
    (*Enter the* KING OF NAPLES *with a lighted candle in a
    candlestick.*)
KING OF NAPLES. Who is there?
ISABEL (*aside*).   The King, woe's me!
KING.   Who are
    you then?
DON JUAN. Who could it be? A man here and a woman.
KING (*aside*). Prudence now is my wisest plan.
    (*He turns aside so as not to recognize* ISABEL. *Aloud:*)
    My guards. Arrest the man.
ISABEL.   My honor's lost.   (*Exit* ISABEL.)
    (*Enter* DON PEDRO TENORIO, *Ambassador of Spain, and
    officers of the guards.*)
DON PEDRO. From the King's rooms we heard shouts; what
    is amiss?
KING. Don Pedro, you take charge of this arrest.

Use caution and identify them both,
But act with secrecy, for I believe
This may be an unpleasant business,
And if it is, the less I see the better.   (*Exit.*)

DON PEDRO. Arrest him now!

DON JUAN.   Just try to capture me!
I'm ready to sell my life, but at so high
A price, that one of you will rue the day.

DON PEDRO. Kill him.

DON JUAN.   Don't be misled. I am resolved
To die, for I come of a noble stock,
And of the suite of Spain's ambassador.
Let the man stand forth alone to whom I am
To hand my sword.

DON PEDRO.   Now all of you retire
And join that woman in the room nearby.   (*Exit.*)

DON PEDRO. We two are now alone; the time has come
To test your courage and your swordsmanship.

DON JUAN. My uncle, though I've courage, I am loth
To bring the matter to a test with you.

DON PEDRO. Who are you?

DON JUAN (*uncovering himself*). I'm your nephew, sir, I said.

DON PEDRO (*aside*). Alas, my heart! I fear treason's afoot.
(*Aloud:*)
What have you done, you crazy enemy?
What means your presence here in such a manner?
Tell me what you have done, foolhardy scapegrace!
Quick! Tell me or I shall slay you on the spot!

DON JUAN. My uncle and my Lord, I am still a youth,
And if you remember your own youthful loves
You'll pardon mine. If you compel me now
To blurt the truth I'll confess all. Disguised,
I cheated Isabel and have enjoyed
Her bed.

DON PEDRO. Hush! tell me how you cheated her.
Speak softly.

DON JUAN.   I made her believe I was
The Duke Octavio.

DON PEDRO.   You've said enough.
(*Aside:*)
If the King hears this I'm lost. What ruse will now

Enable me to extricate myself
From such a dangerous pass?
(*Aloud:*)
Now tell me, rogue,
Were you not satisfied to bring dishonor
Upon another noble lady back in Spain,
That you must now repeat the crime in Naples,
This time within the very royal precincts,
And with a lady of such princely rank.
Your father from Castile sent you to Naples,
Whose hospitable shore by the Italian sea
Welcomed you, but instead of gratitude
You bring upon the noblest lady here
Shame and dishonor. But there is no time
To lose, so tell me what you intend to do.

DON JUAN. I shan't attempt now to excuse my conduct:
To do so would but seem ill-omen'd fraud.
My blood, my Lord, is just the same as yours,
Shed it and let me pay the penalty.
Here at your feet, my uncle, I'll now kneel,
And here's my sword; I offer it to you.

DON PEDRO. Now rise, you rascal, and show you can fight.
Such meek humility but blunts my rage.
Would you dare jump from yonder balcony?

DON JUAN. I'm game, now that your favor gives me wings.

DON PEDRO. I'll help. Go to Milan or Sicily,
Where you may hide.

DON JUAN.　　　　　　　I'll dash away at once.

DON PEDRO. You give your solemn word?

DON JUAN.　　　　　　　　　　I promise, Uncle.

DON PEDRO. You'll soon hear from my letters what will be
The consequences of your escapade.

DON JUAN (*aside*). Truly it was a merry one for me.
(*Aloud:*)
I admit my guilt.

DON PEDRO.　　　　　Your hot youth played you false,
Go jump down now from yonder balcony.

DON JUAN. With such fair promises to back me up
I'll now set off to Spain with an easy heart!

(*Exit* DON JUAN.)

(*Enter the* KING OF NAPLES.)

DON PEDRO. I tried your orders, Sire, to execute
  But the man . . .
THE KING.   Is he dead?
DON PEDRO.   No, he has escaped
  The pitiless swords.
THE KING.   How?
DON PEDRO.   It was thus, my Lord.
  Scarce had you given orders, when without
  A word, he snatched his sword and, rolling his cloak
  Around his arm, he rushed with lightning speed,
  Attacking the soldiers, risking certain death,
  And leapt for life over the balcony
  Down into the garden. Your guards then set off
  In hot pursuit, and when through the door below
  They rushed, they found him writhing like a snake
  In agony; but when he heard the guard
  Cry "death," though he was bathed in gore, he fought
  His way with such heroic speed that soon
  He disappeared, to my astonishment.
  The lady whose name you'll be surprised to hear,
  The Duchess Isabel, has now retired
  To yonder room. She tells me it was the Duke
  Octavio by a trick did lie with her.
THE KING. What do you say?
DON PEDRO.   What she herself confessed.
THE KING (aside). Alas, poor Honor! You who are the soul
  Of man, why are you always placed
  In inconstant woman who is fickleness?
  (Aloud:)
  Ho there!
  (Enter a servant.)
SERVANT.   My Lord!
THE KING.   Bring me the lady now.
DON PEDRO. I see the guards escorting her draw nigh.
  (Enter ISABEL with guards.)
ISABEL (aside). How shall I ever face the King?
THE KING (addressing the guards).   Withdraw
  And guard the doors.   (Exeunt guards.)
                 Tell me, my lady, now
  What force or what ill-fated star made you
  Defile my palace by your wantonness.

ISABEL. My Lord.

THE KING.   Be silent; your tongue never can
  Excuse the grievous fault you have committed.
  The man with you was the Duke Octavio?

ISABEL. My Lord.

THE KING.   So Love, a mere babe, could with ease overcome
  Guards, servants, walls, and battlements, and pass
  Unscathed within.
                    Don Pedro, take this lady,
  Shut her up in a tower, and then arrest
  The Duke as well. I'll make him keep his pledge.

ISABEL. My Lord, I do beseech you turn and look
  Upon me.

THE KING.   As your offense was done behind
  My back, it is only your just punishment
  That I should turn my back upon you now.   (*Exit.*)

DON PEDRO. Come, Duchess, with me.

ISABEL.   There is no excuse,
  But if the Duke Octavio saves my name,
  Then my dishonor will thereby be less.   (*Exeunt.*)
  (*Enter* OCTAVIO *and his servant* RIPIO.)

RIPIO. Why are you up so early, sir, today?

OCTAVIO. Sleep cannot quench the flames that in the heart
  Love kindles, for he is not a child to rest
  Snugly 'twixt soft sheets with white ermine decked.
  When he retires to bed he stays awake,
  Already longing for the dawn, when he
  May rise from bed and play his merry pranks,
  As does a child. The thoughts of Isabel,
  O Ripio, banish all tranquillity,
  For as she has her mansion in my soul,
  My body keeps unending vigilance,
  Least I should ever fail to protect her honor.

RIPIO. With all respect, yours is a peevish love.

OCTAVIO. Why so, blockhead?

RIPIO.   It is foolish, I think,
  To love in your way. Won't you learn from me?

OCTAVIO. Have your way.

RIPIO.   Are you certain Isabel
  Loves you?

OCTAVIO.   Are you then still in any doubt?

RIPIO. No, but I ask—do you love her?

OCTAVIO.   Of course.

RIPIO. Should I not be "a fool of a well-known house" [1]
  To be so woebegone because I love
  A woman who loves me? if she did not
  Return your flame, you might then flatter her,
  Woo and adore her, and await the hour
  Of her surrender: But since both of you
  Love one another equally, tell me,
  What hinders you from marrying the girl
  At once?

OCTAVIO.   Such weddings are for laundry girls
  And lackeys.

RIPIO.   What's wrong with a laundry girl,
  Who is pretty and who scrubs and washes all
  The livelong day, who spreads her linen out
  For all to see, and patches, darns and charms
  Her friends, forever giving, for to be
  A giver is the first thing in the world.
  If Isabel be not a giver then
  Let us now see if she knows how to take.
  (*Enter a servant.*)

SERVANT. The Ambassador of Spain has just arrived.
  In arrogant tones he demands to speak
  With Your Grace. And if I am not deceived
  This means arrest.

OCTAVIO.   On what grounds? Show him in.
  (*Enter* DON PEDRO *with guards.*)

DON PEDRO. Who soundly sleeps must have his conscience
  clear.

OCTAVIO. When Your Excellency decides to call
  And favor me it were not right to sleep.
  Indeed I should an endless vigil keep,
  But tell me, pray, why you do visit me?

DON PEDRO. It was His Majesty who sent me here.

OCTAVIO. If the King, my master, now remembers me
  I'm glad to offer him my life, but first

[1] This is a parody on the descriptive phrase *hidalgo de solar conocido* (gentleman of a well-known house) which Don Quixote applied to himself.

Do tell me quickly what was the lucky star
That made His Majesty remember me?
DON PEDRO.   It was, alas, Your Grace's luckless star:
As the King's ambassador I have been charged
With a special mission for you.
OCTAVIO.   Tell me all.
I am all agog.
DON PEDRO.   I am sent to arrest you now;
Don't raise a riot.
OCTAVIO.   Are you arresting me
By royal warrant? For what cause, I pray?
DON PEDRO.   You know better than I do, though perhaps
I am mistaken. Anyway I'll tell
The reason why the King has sent for you.
It was the hour when night's black giants had
Folded their cerecloths and were fleeing the dawn
Pell-mell, and I was talking to the King
Of state affairs (the great always prefer
The shades of night) when suddenly we heard
A woman's frantic cry for help echo
Through vaulted halls and corridors. The King
Rushed out himself to see what had occurred,
And there he found the Duchess Isabel
Clasped in the lustful arms of a hulking man:
One so ambitious must a giant be,
Or a ruthless monster. The King then ordered me
To arrest the two of them, and I was left
Alone to face the man. I tried my best
To seize his sword, but he like Satan clothed
In human form, and wrapt in a cloud of dust
And smoke leapt from the balcony, and fell
At the foot of the slender elms that rise above
The elegant palace spires. The Duchess when
She was arrested at once blurted out
In presence of us all that you yourself
With promise of marriage had enjoyed her bed.
OCTAVIO.   What's that you say?
DON PEDRO.   The world already knows
That Isabel in a thousand ways . . .
OCTAVIO.   Leave me,
Don't say another word of Isabel

After such a vile betrayal, but suppose
All this were but deception to protect
Her honor? Why do you keep silent now?
You distill poisoned words that paralyze
My heart and force me to unseal my lips:
Just as the weasel in the mating time
Does through the ear conceive, and when its young
Are born, it's through the mouth they are brought forth.[2]
Could I believe that Isabel, my love,
Would so forget me as to cause my death?
But while our hearts are lulled in pleasant dreams,
Evil forever wakeful stands alert.
Still I have no misgivings in my heart,
And I can reckon all that has occurred
As whims and fancies gossip has whipped up
To rouse my fury, when my ear would hear,
And I should understand what eyes declared.
Marquis, I can't believe that Isabel
Has so deceived me and betrayed our tryst.
Must I not challenge, now my honor's hurt?
A man was found last night with Isabel
Within the palace: have I lost my mind?

DON PEDRO. Just as it is true that birds fly in the wind
And fish rise on the wave, and all things have
Four elements to share, and as all friends
Are loyal, and all enemies betray,
As night brings darkness, and the day brings light,
So every word I say is truth itself.

OCTAVIO. Marquis, I do believe your words, and I declare
There's nothing more can make my blood run cold,
When she whose constant love was all my faith
Has now shown mortal woman's fraility.
No more of this, the outrage I've endured
Is evident for all the world to see.

DON PEDRO. Then as you're prudent choose the wisest course.

OCTAVIO. My best plan is to absent myself a while.

DON PEDRO. Then, do make haste, my lord Octavio.

[2] Ovid in *Metamorphoses* (IX:306-321) tells the legend of how Juno punished Galantis—who had falsely announced that Alcmene had given birth—by changing her into a weasel and condemning her to bear her young through the mouth.

OCTAVIO. I'll sail for Spain and end my sorrows there.

DON PEDRO. By the garden gate you'll give the guards the
slip.

OCTAVIO. O fickle weathercock! O broken reed!
It makes my blood boil now when I reflect
That I must flee betrayal and depart
To foreign shores. Farewell, beloved land.
By night a stranger in the palace has
Enjoyed my Isabel: I shall go mad.　　　　*(Exeunt.)*
(The seashore near Tarragona. Enter THISBE *with a fishing
rod.)*

THISBE. Amidst all those fair fisher maids whose feet
Of rose and jasmine kiss the ocean's waves,
I am the only one immune to love,
The only one Love's tyranny to mock
And scorn his chains that hold the world enslaved.
Here where the sun lulls sleepy waves to rest,
Dispelling shadows by his sapphire flames,
And shedding o'er the fine-spun sandy shore
His joyful radiance, transforming them
To myriads of seeded pearls, atoms
Of golden sunbeams, and as I give ear
To plaintive warbling of the amorous birds,
And soft unending murmurs of the sea
Against the rocks, I ply my limber rod,
Which bends nigh double under the paltry weight
Of the foolish little fish that lashes the sea;
Or with my casting net, which in the depths
Will catch all those who live within
Their castellated conch shells; I rejoice
In my soul's freedom, for I've never yet
Been wounded by the poisoned asp of love.
Sometimes with other maidens I embark
In my frail skiff, and row through the foam and swell,
And when they rave and rant of lover's tiffs,
I laugh them to scorn: hence all envy me.
I'm blest a thousand times, Love, since you still
Exonerate me, though you don't despise
Such humble cots as mine, with its obelisk
Of thatch that crowns the roof and nests provides
For giddy turtledoves, though no cicadas,

And thus I keep my honor safe in straw,
Like ripening fruit, or glass, that it may be
Preserved intact. As for the fishermen
On Tarragona's silver shores, whose lights
Protect them from the pirate foe, they sing
My praises, but I treat them all with scorn,
Deaf to their sighs, and granite to their pleas.
Anfriso on whom heaven with bounteous hands
Bestowed the fairest gifts of body and soul,
Measured in words, and generous in deeds,
Modest in sorrow, and resigned to scorn,
Night after night he haunts my rustic door
In vain, through icy winds and rain, and snow,
And yet when I behold him on the morrow,
He's younger but more desperately in love,
And up he comes to me with fresh green boughs,
Which he had cut down from the towering elms,
And daily decks the roof of my thatched hut;
This is my leafy tribute in the dawn.
Still not content he comes again at night,
And serenades me with soft thrumming lutes
And rustic flutes, but all of this means nought
To me, for I possess a tyrant's power
To curb his love, and I gloat o'er his pain,
And glory in the flames that sear his heart.
But all the other girls go daft for him,
Whom I do hourly slay with my contempt.
Full well I know that Love decrees
That we should die of love for those
Who hate us, and have nought but scorn for those
Who love us, so I spend my youthful years
Without a care, and bask in flattery
Without the torments and intrigues of love.
But O you frivolous unmeaning words
That do but serve to drive my course awry,
My only wish is, like the fisherman,
To raise my rod and cast my line, and hook
To windward, so to bait the little fish.
But what do I perceive? Two men have dived
From the deck of yonder ship into the sea,
Before the waves can suck her down below.

For she has struck a rock, but keeps afloat,
Though now her poop has all but disappeared.
And like the peacock with despairing pride
Her billowing sails fan out in graceful tail,
As she begins to sink beneath the waves.
Alas, how pride rideth before the fall!
Lo, she heels over on one side, she's gone,
Leaving amidst the spindrift and the foam,
As relic her main topsail; let it serve
As cage to lodge a madman.[3]
(*Shouting is heard from within:* "Help, I drown!")

THISBE. One of the two men now assists his friend.
A brave deed! Now he hoists him on his back,
As once Aeneas did Anchises bear,
And now, like blazing Troy, the sea is raging.
Look how the man is buffeted by waves,
Yet cleaves his way towards the lonely shore.
Alas, upon the beach there's not a soul
To help these outcasts, but I'll raise a shout.
"Anfriso, and Alfredo, ho!" They hear
My voice, they're looking; now please God they'll come.
Miraculously both men reach the land,
And he who swam lies panting on the shore,
And his companion, thank God, is alive.
(*Enter* CATALINÓN *carrying* DON JUAN.)

CATALINÓN. Bravo the Canaan woman![4] we've reached land,
But briny water has a bitter tang:
At least a swimmer here will find escape.
Down deep it's rank folly even to try
In Neptune's stithy where he forges death.
Fancy God flooding us with so much water,
And forgetting to mix a like amount of wine!
But salty water is a fearsome brew
For one who is not born a fisherman,

---

[3] There is a play of words on *gavia* which meant, 1) main topsail
of a ship, and 2) a wooden cage for imprisoning a lunatic.
[4] A reference to Matthew, XV:22—"And behold a woman of Canaan came out of the same coasts, and cried unto him saying,
'Have mercy on me, O Lord, thou Son of David: my daughter is
grievously vexed with a devil.'" The exclamation is often used as
a ridiculous oath in plays.

If water, even fresh, is nauseating,
What must it be when it is salty too?
Oh, who could find me now a forge, and wine
In gallons, even if it is glowing hot?
If I recover from what I have drunk
From this day onward water I'll renounce.
To water such is my antipathy
That I'll not even look at holy water.
Alas, my master, he lies frozen there:
God help me, has he perished in the sea?
The sea's to blame for all our miseries.
It's only right to blame myself as well.
Bad 'cess to him who planted masts of pine,
Upon the seas and mapped its courses out
With logs of brittle wood, bad 'cess again
To that vile tailor who did sew the sea
With astronomic needle, origin
Of all disasters,[5] and my curses on
Jason and Theseus. Now my master's dead:
Who would believe it? Catalinón, alas,
Unhappy me, whatever shall I do?

THISBE. Tell me what ails you, friend, in all these woes?
CATALINÓN. Dear fisher maid, a deal of trouble and
The lack of much good luck. My master's dead,
Or so he seems to me.
THISBE.   No, he still breathes.
Go quickly call the fisherman beyond,
In yonder hut.
CATALINÓN.   I'll call them: will they come?
THISBE. They'll come, be sure of that. Who is this man?
CATALINÓN. He is the son of the King's High Chamberlain.
And goes to Seville, where, within a week,
If the King and I agree, they'll make me Count.
THISBE. What is his name?
CATALINÓN.   Don Juan Tenorio.
I'll be off.   (*Exit* CATALINÓN.)
(THISBE *holds* DON JUAN's *head on her lap.*)
THISBE. Gallant and handsome youth of noble brow,
Return, I pray, to life.

[5] This refers to the use of the compass (*aguja de marear*) by the
navigator, who is compared to a tailor.

DON JUAN.   Where am I now?

THISBE. Safe from all perils, in a woman's arms.

DON JUAN. I perished in the sea, but you are life,
　And I have now forgotten all my fears
　Of drowning, and the hellish ocean depths
　As I now soar skywards, and find myself
　In radiant heaven. A hideous hurricane
　Scuttled my vessel and cast me adrift
　To find refuge and shelter at your feet.

THISBE. You waste a great amount of breath for one
　Who but a moment past was at death's door.
　After such hardships you revive too fast,
　But if you rave and utter senseless words,
　I'm sure the thundering sea and riotous waves,
　That racked your helpless body, are the cause.
　No doubt your overdose of briny sea
　Adds too much seasoning to your saucy words.
　You say a lot even when you hold your tongue,
　And when as dead you lie upon the beach,
　You seem to have your senses all agog.
　Please God that all your words are not a lie!
　You seem to me the Grecian wooden horse
　The sea has now washed up to be my bane;
　For though you're dripping brine, you are afire,
　And though all wet you burn my very soul.
　What will you not consume when you are dry?
　You promise fire, and nought but fire, who knows?
　Please God that all your words are not a lie.

DON JUAN. Ah, would to God I'd perished in the sea,
　So had I in my senses been, not mad
　For love of you! the sea had swallowed me
　Amidst its silver waves that onward roll
　Forever, then had I not been so seared
　By flames of passion. You are like the Sun,
　Who shares with you his power; you're white as snow,
　And yet to ashes you now burn my soul.

THISBE. However frosty, you are kindling flames;
　Please God that all your words are not a lie!
　(*Enter* CATALINÓN, ANFRISO, CORIDÓN *and other fisher-*
　men.)

CATALINÓN. Here all have come.

THISBE. Your master is alive.

DON JUAN. It was your presence brought me back to life.

CORIDÓN. What orders?

THISBE. Coridón, Anfriso, friends . . .

ANFRISO. We seek by every means to gratify
You, fairest Thisbe, so give your commands.
As soon as your pink rosebud lips pronounce
The word to one of us who worships you,
He'll speed away like lightning over the plain
And mountain, or he'll plow the vasty deep,
Or dig the earth, or trample air, or wind.

THISBE (*aside*). How little did their flattering vows before
Impress me, and yet now I realize
That their lip-offerings were not all lies.
(*Aloud:*)
My friends, as I was fishing from your rock
I saw a ship sinking amidst the waves,
And two survivors swimming in the sea.
I pitied them and cried aloud for help
But no one heard. This man the raging sea
Escaped and carried on his back his friend,
A nobleman who had died. In my distress
I sent him at once to call on you for help.

ANFRISO. As we're all here, do give us your commands,
Though I had not expected such a message.

THISBE. Let us then take these young men to my hut,
Where we may gladly dry and mend their clothes,
And entertain them, for I know this act
Of charity will please my father so.

CATALINÓN (*aside*). She's ravishing.

DON JUAN (*to* CATALINÓN). Now keep your ears well
tuned.

CATALINÓN. I'm all ears.

DON JUAN. If she asks who I am, say
You do not know.

CATALINÓN. Tell me what I've to do.

DON JUAN. I'm crazed with love for the girl, this very night
I must enjoy her love.

CATALINÓN. What are your plans?

DON JUAN. Follow and mum's the word.

CORIDÓN. Anfriso, soon

The others will come here to sing and dance.

ANFRISO. Let us be off and set the place aglow
  With merriment.

DON JUAN.   I'm head over heels in love.

THISBE. You're able still to walk.

DON JUAN.   I'm suffering.

THISBE. You talk a lot.

DON JUAN.   You understand me well.

THISBE. Please God that all your words are not a lie.

(*Exeunt*).

(*The Alcázar at Seville. Enter the* KING OF CASTILE *with*
DON GONZALO DE ULLOA.)

KING. How did you fare, my lord Comendador?

DON GONZALO. At Lisbon I saw your cousin, King Juan,
  Massing his fleet of thirty ships for war.[6]

KING. What destination?

DON GONZALO. Goa, so he said.[7]
  But I guess it's some closer enterprise,
  Such as Tangier or Ceuta which he may
  Besiege this summer.

KING.   May God help his cause
  And Heaven increase his fame. What did you both
  Agree?

DON GONZALO. My Liege, he asks for Serpa and Mora,
  Olivencia and Toro, in return for these
  He'll give you Villaverde, Almendral,
  Mertola and Herrera, all of which do lie
  Between Castile and Portugal.

KING.   Let those
  Treaties be signed in due course, but tell me
  How have you fared on your journey. Are you now
  Worn out with traveling and short of pocket?

DON GONZALO. I'm not tired when I serve Your Royal Highness.

KING. Is Lisbon a fine city?

DON GONZALO.   In all Spain[8]

[6] John I, King of Portugal in 1385.

[7] Goa was not conquered by the Portuguese until the sixteenth century. It was called Goa Dourada.

[8] Portugal was united to Spain from 1580 to 1640. This is another
anachronism of Tirso de Molina.

The largest city; if you wish to learn,
I shall describe for you what I have seen.
KING. I'd like to hear it. Let my chair be brought.
DON GONZALO. Lisbon is the eighth wonder of the world.
From Cuenca's land which is the heart of Spain
The golden Tagus crosses half of Spain,
And flows into the ocean on the south
Of this fair city. But before it sheds
Its name and course it makes a port between
Two mountain chains, where ships and caravels
Of all the world can ride at anchor;
Such numbers of barques, brigantines, and sloops
From the Levant, that from the land it seems
As though a mighty city had been built
Of wooded pines where Neptune holds his sway.
Towards the side where sets the sun, two ports
Do guard the front, Cascais and Saint John,
The strongest bastions in all the world.
Just half a league from this great city lies
Belén, the convent of Jerome the Saint,
Whose emblems are the stone and guardian lion,
Where Catholic and Christian kings and queens
Have built their refuge for eternity.
And after this, beyond Alcántara,
The river flows a league towards the shrine
And convent of Jabregas. Nestling in
A valley it is circled by three hills,
Whose smiling beauty's unsurpassed
By any portrait painted by Apelles.
Seen in the distance they hang, as it were,
Like pearls in clusters in the sky above.
In that vast panorama we behold
Ten Romes thus multiplied in countless shrines,
Churches and palaces, and streets that lead
To manor houses, and commanderies
Renowned in art, in letters and in feats
Of arms, and balanced justice, but above
All else I saw her vast Hospital that stands
Upon the river bank and sheds afar
The quality of Mercy over all Spain.
And what I most admired in that vast pile

Of glorious granite was that from its roof
And pinnacle our eyes could gaze upon
Nigh seven leagues of country all around
And three score villages set by the sea,
And Odivelas convent in their midst,
Where I myself counted six hundred cells,
And twice six hundred blessed nuns.
From there on our way to Lisbon we behold
Full thirteen hundred manors with their parks
And gardens, which our Andalusian
Folk call *cortijos*, each with poplar groves,
And orchards. In the center of the city
Rucío stands, a stately builded square.
A hundred years ago the sea flowed over
The golden sands but now they've disappeared,
And thirty thousand houses take their place.
And so the sea, being thwarted in its course,
Has gone to nibble elsewhere at the coast.
There is a thoroughfare they call New Street,
Where all the treasure of the East we've seen
In heaps of such profusion that the King
Told me that a merchant there can count
His wealth by bushelfuls and not in coins.
The spot on which the royal palace stands
Assembles countless boats moored in the port
Laden with wheat and barley from the marts
Of France and England. The royal palace,
Against whose walls the flowing Tagus laps,
Has from its royal founder taken its name,
Ulysses, Conqueror of Troy. From him
The city draws its name Ulisibona,
And its heraldic arms are represented
By a great sphere on which are symbolized
The gory wounds that King Alfonso once
Received in battle against the invading Moors.[9]
In the Majestic Arsenal I've seen
All kinds of vessels, and among them stand
Most prominent those that did lead the Conquest,

[9] This refers to the battle of Ourique in 1139 against the Almorá-
vides, the Moorish invaders from North Africa. Alfonso was
crowned in 1140.

So high they loomed that when seen from the ground
Their mastheads seemed to me to touch the stars.
One custom of the city I observed,
That the inhabitants while they're at table
Can see the shoals of fish they are to eat,
Caught at their door, and wriggling in the net.
And every evening on the river bank
A thousand vessels dock, each piléd high
With varied merchandise and common goods,
Fruits of all kinds, and oil, and bread and wine,
Timber, and snow from Estrella's lofty peaks,
Which the hawkers carry on their heads, and sell
With raucous *cantilena* in every street
But why, my Lord, should I speak at such length?
If I were Lisbon's wonders to repeat
I might as well attempt to count the stars.
Lisbon now boasts a hundred thousand souls
And, Sire, if I may now conclude, a King,
Who kisses both your hands, then bade me wish
Success, good fortune to Your Majesty.

KING. I'd sooner listen to your vivid tale
Than see that city's grandeur for myself.
But tell me, have you children?

DON GONZALO.   Yes, my Lord,
I have a daughter who's so beautiful
That Nature herself marvels at her work.

KING. Then let me dower her and fix her marriage.

DON GONZALO. My will is yours. But who will be the groom?

KING. He is not here now; he's a Sevillian,
And his name is Don Juan Tenorio.

DON GONZALO. I'll go and break the news to Doña Ana.

KING. Now farewell, Don Gonzalo, and return
As soon as you can with the girl's reply.

(*Scene near Tarragona. Enter* DON JUAN *and* CATALINÓN.)

DON JUAN. Bring out the horses as they're for the road.

CATALINÓN. Although I'm just Catalinón, I am,
My Lord, a man of decent reputation.
And no one ever said "Catalinón
Is such and such," for I must tell you that
My actions do belie my milksop name.

DON JUAN. While those gay fishermen spend hours in song

And dancing, see that you make haste
To harness both the horses, for my plans
All do depend upon their galloping hooves.

CATALINÓN. So now your plan is to seduce poor Thisbe?

DON JUAN. Since it's my inborn nature to seduce,
Why do you ask what you have always known?

CATALINÓN. Too well I know you are the scourge of women.

DON JUAN. I'm mad about Thisbe, she's so fine a girl.

CATALINÓN. Fine payment for her generosity!

DON JUAN. Blockhead! Aeneas did the very same
To the Queen of Carthage.

CATALINÓN.   Such a wicked way
Of tricking women will end in your doom.
At the hour of death you'll pay the penalty.

DON JUAN. I've credit still to spare. How right they are,
Catalinón, to call you pigeon-hearted.[10]

CATALINÓN. Go your way, sir; when cheating women is
The order of the day, count me among
The lily-livered gang. But here she comes,
Unhappy maid.

DON JUAN.   Be off, and saddle the horses.

CATALINÓN. Poor girl! How generously we've repaid
Your hospitality!   (*Exit* CATALINÓN.)
(*Enter* THISBE.)

THISBE.   When I am not
By your side I feel absolutely lost.

DON JUAN. Your words do not convince me.

THISBE.   Why?

DON JUAN.   If you
Loved me you'd lessen my pain.

THISBE.   I am yours.

DON JUAN. What are you waiting for? What's in your mind?

THISBE. I've found at last in you Love's punishment.

DON JUAN. I promise to marry you, my love, you are
My life, I'll give you all, even my life.

THISBE. My birth is not the same as yours.

DON JUAN.   But Love

[10] According to Américo Castro, Catalinón was the augmentative of Catalina, which was often used with the same sense of "coward," just as *Maricón* meant an effeminate. Catalinón here objects to his master's dishonesty in stealing Thisbe's two horses.

Is like a King who levels all who come
Beneath his rule, and often it's his way
To match sackcloth with silk.

THISBE.   I almost could
Place all my trust in you, but I have heard
That men are deceivers ever.

DON JUAN.   You, my love,
Have not yet understood me: and today
My soul you have entangled in your hair.

THISBE. If you give me your solemn word that you
Will be my husband, I'll submit to you.

DON JUAN. Ó sparkling eyes that fascinate and slay,
I swear most solemnly to be your spouse.

THISBE. My love, remember, God exists and death.

DON JUAN. I've credit still to spare: as long as God
Allows me live, I swear to be your slave,
And here's my hand and word to prove my faith.

THISBE. I'll not be shy in paying, rest assured.

DON JUAN. My love, I can't contain myself for joy.

THISBE. Come now, and let my humble cabin be
Our bridal chamber, but till then, my love,
I pray you hide yourself between these reeds.

DON JUAN. But where shall I enter the hut?

THISBE.   Do come
And I shall show you.

DON JUAN.   How my heart rejoices!

THISBE. May your pledged word forever bind your soul,
If not, may God in Heaven punish you.

DON JUAN. I've credit still to spare, if it's till death. (*Exeunt.*)
     (*Enter* CORIDÓN, ANFRISO, BELISA *and musicians.*)

CORIDÓN. Ho there! call Thisbe and the other youths,
That our guest may in this secluded spot
Discover all the revels of the city.

ANFRISO. Thisbe, Lucinda and Atandria—come!
I've never seen such cruel maids as they.
Woe to the man who when he's amidst the flames
Remains a salamander. Ere the dance
Begins let our fair Thisbe now be called.

BELISA. We'll call her.

CORIDÓN.   Let us go.

BELISA.   To her cabin.

CORIDÓN. Can't you see she's still busy with her guests?
  They're lucky, and we all do envy them.
BELISA. Sing something till she comes, we want to dance.
ANFRISO (*aside*). Where can a jealous lover find relief?
  (*They sing*)

> *The girl went a-fishing one day,*
> *And she cast her nets in the shoals of the bay;*
> *When she pulled them up to reckon her gains*
> *No fish did she find but the hearts of her swains.*

(*Enter* THISBE.)
THISBE. Fire, O fire! I'm burning, burning!
  My cabin's all in flames! Now raise the cry,
  My friends! My tears will never quench the fire:
  My humble cot has become another Troy.
  Fire, oh fire! my shepherds, water, water!
  Take pity on me, Love, my heart's ablaze!
  For shame, my tiny cot, the squalid scene
  Of my own infamy! vile robber's den
  That sheltered and abetted all my wrongs,
  May blazing stars rain fearsome thunderbolts
  To blast and singe your thatched roofs, may the wind
  Blow ravenously and fan the writhing flames.
  O traitor guest! you have betrayed a woman!
  You were a cloud that rose up from the sea
  To overwhelm and drown my heart in woe.
  Fire, oh fire! Ye shepherds! Water!
  Take pity on me, Love, my heart's ablaze.
  It was I that always mocked and cheated men,
  But always those who cheat are in the end
  Themselves deceived, and that cavalier
  Seduced me after he had promised marriage,
  And he enjoyed me and profaned my bed.
  But I lent wings to his foul purposes.
  For I gave him the two mares I possessed,
  Which carry him far from me in headlong flight.
  Oh, follow, follow him. No, let him go,
  For in the presence of His Royal Highness,
  I'll cry aloud for vengeance. Fire, oh fire!
  And water! water! pity my blazing soul.   (*Exit* THISBE.)
CORIDÓN. Follow that fiend!

ANFRISO.   In silence I must bear
   My sad lot, but thank God through this foul fiend
   I am avenged against this thankless girl.
   But let us go in search of Thisbe now,
   Lest in her madness she may harm herself.
CORIDÓN.   Such is the end of pride and arrogance.
      (*Heard from within:* "Fire! Fire!")
ANFRISO.   She casts herself into the sea.
   Stop, Thisbe.
      (*Heard in the distance:* "Fire, oh fire, and water!
      Water! Have pity, love. My soul's on fire!")

ACT II.

The Alcázar at Seville. Enter KING OF CASTILE *and* DON DIEGO TENORIO *dressed as an old man.*[11]

KING. What do you say?

DON DIEGO. My Lord, I know the truth,
For I have just received a letter from
My brother, your ambassador. They found
Juan in the royal quarters, closeted
With one of the fair damsels of the court.

KING. What was her rank?

DON DIEGO. The Duchess Isabel.

KING. But what temerity! Where is he now?

DON DIEGO. I would not hide the truth from you, my Liege
Last night with one servant he reached Seville.

KING. You know, Tenorio, I've always shown
A high esteem of you. I'll get the full
Account of all that happened from the King
Of Naples, and we'll wed the truant youth
To Isabel, when we have soothed the pride
Of Duke Octavio, the hapless victim.
But first of all you must exile Don Juan.

DON DIEGO. Where to, Your Majesty?

KING. He must at once
Leave Seville for Lebrija. He may thank
His father's name his sentence is so light;
Meanwhile we must decide what tale to tell
To Don Gonzalo as my plan's upset.
His daughter's marriage must be set aside.

DON DIEGO. My Liege, I hope that you will order me
To bring prestige and honor to the child
Of such a father.

KING. I suggest a plan
To liberate me from the father's wrath:
I will appoint him palace seneschal.
(*Enter a servant.*)

11 The *barba* or old man was a stock character in the *comedia* and wore a gray wig and false beard.

SERVANT. A noble, Sire, has come from Italy.
  He says he is the Duke Octavio.
KING. The Duke Octavio?
SERVANT.   It is he, my Lord.
KING. No doubt your son's vile deed has reached his ears
  And he has come on vengeance bent, to ask
  That he be granted leave to challenge him.
DON DIEGO. My Liege, in your heroic hands my life
  I place, for my own life, alas, depends
  On that of my foolhardy son, who, though
  A youth, is gallant and is called by all
  Of his own age, the Hector of Seville.
  Though he has so many boyish pranks,
  His reason will mature. I beg you now,
  If there is time, to stop the fight.
KING. A father's honor is at stake, I know
  And I do understand, Tenorio.
  The Duke may enter.
DON DIEGO.   How shall I requite
  Your Majesty's great favors?
  (*Enter* DUKE OCTAVIO *in traveling clothes.*)
OCTAVIO. As pilgrim and exile, my Lord, I've come
  To kneel as suppliant before your feet.
  I've fled from a crazy woman and a man,
  Who have dishonored me.
KING.   Your innocence
  I am aware of, Duke Octavio,
  And so I'll write a letter to the King
  Of Naples to restore your privilege.
  Although your absence may cause you some loss,
  With his permission, pardon and consent
  I'll make a marriage for you at Seville.
  For though in looks an angel, Isabel
  Will seem to you quite ugly when compared
  With the girl that I shall give you for your bride.
  The great Comendador of Calatrava,
  Gonzalo de Ulloa, whom the Moors
  Laud to the skies in fear (for cowards ever
  Are wont to praise and flatter), has a daughter
  Whose virtue's worth a dowry by itself,
  Although I put her peerless beauty first,

For of the stars of Seville she's the sun.
She is the one I want to be your wife.

OCTAVIO. It is enough good luck for me to learn
That I have done what gives you pleasure, Sire.

KING (*to* DON DIEGO). See that the Duke is entertained and lacks
Of nothing.

OCTAVIO.   He, my Liege, who trusts in you
Will leave with both his hands well filled with gift
You're first of the Alfonsos, though eleventh!

> (*Exeunt the* KING *and* DON DIEGO.)

(*Enter* RIPIO.)

RIPIO. How did you fare, my Lord?

OCTAVIO.   The King was in
A gracious mood and listened to my wrongs.
A well-spent day, for I've out-Caesared Caesar,
I came, I saw, I conquered, and the King
Himself will choose my bride, and make my peace
With the King of Naples, and annul the law
By which I was deprived of privilege.

RIPIO. No wonder all Castilians call their King
The Bountiful. So now he offers you
A bride?

OCTAVIO.   A friend, and one from Seville too.
Seville, I would remind you, breeds bold men
Of brawn and valor, and is unsurpassed
For the grace and elegance of its fair maids;
Where else except in Seville would you see
Such nimble eye, such play of cloak and veil
Which, like a cloud, obscures the dazzling sun?
My happiness has routed all my woes.

(*Enter* DON JUAN *and* CATALINÓN.)

CATALINÓN (*aside to his master*). Don't stir, sir, there's the injured Duke at hand,
Fair Isabel's Archer, or horned Pan.[12]

---

[12] This is a characteristically Baroque reference to Greek mythology. Sagittarius—the Archer—was Chiron, the wise Centaur, who was wounded by his friend Heracles accidentally, and renounced his immortality. Zeus then placed him among the stars as the ninth constellation, Sagittarius. Isabel unwittingly injured Octavio. Capricorn, the tenth constellation, was the god Pan, who was changed

DON JUAN.   Pretend.

CATALINÓN (*aside*). When he betrays, he flatters him.

DON JUAN. As I left Naples under urgent orders
From my King, and as his will is my law,
I had no time to say farewell, Octavio.

OCTAVIO. For that, Don Juan, I must call you my friend:
Well, here we are in Seville, both of us.

DON JUAN. Who would have thought I'd find you in Seville,
Where I would serve you as I wish to do?
Who ever would exchange the charm of Naples
For any other city save Seville?

OCTAVIO. If I had heard such glowing words in Naples
And not in Spain I would have laughed with scorn.
But now Seville's to be my home I find
Your highest tributes are but underpraise—
But who is that?

DON JUAN.   The Marquis of La Mota.

OCTAVIO. I'll have to be discourteous . . .

DON JUAN.   Do say
If you, my Lord, should ever want my help;
My sword is at your service.

CATALINÓN (*aside*).   And if he
Should feel the urge he'll rape another girl
In your name too, for you're of good repute.

OCTAVIO. I am, indeed, pleased we have met.

CATALINÓN.   Good sirs,
If Catalinón is needed he'll be found . . .

RIPIO. Where?

CATALINÓN.   At "Little Birds," an excellent hostelry.

                                   (*Exeunt* OCTAVIO *and* RIPIO.)

     (*Enter the* MARQUIS OF LA MOTA *with a servant.*)

MARQUIS. All day I've searched the town for you in vain,
And here you are, Don Juan, while all your friends
Lament your absence!

DON JUAN.   It is you, my friend,
Who are indebted to me for that favor.

CATALINÓN (*aside*). He can be trusted if you don't allow
Him near a girl; in this, like a noble man,

---

into a goat. His horns connoted cuckoldry, always a source of
humor in the theater.

He is mighty cruel.

DON JUAN.   What's afresh in Seville?

MARQUIS. I'm afraid there have been many changes here.

DON JUAN. What women? Any fun?

MARQUIS.   Of course there is.

DON JUAN. And Inés?

MARQUIS.   ' She is off to Vejer, the veterans' town,
A jolly place for one brought up at court.
It was Time exiled her to Vejer.

DON JUAN.   To die.
And what about Costanza?

MARQUIS.   A piteous sight:
She's going bald and shedding eyelashes.
A Portuguese said she was old, but she
Cried out in anger that the gentleman
Had meant to call her pretty.

DON JUAN.   Yes, it's true.
The Portuguese word sounds like "old" in Spanish.
And what of Theodora?

MARQUIS.   I've been told
She has now cured herself of Gallic pox
By melting it away in streams of sweat,
And she's become so skittish and so coy
That yesterday she fired a tooth at me
Enveloped in a bunch of fragrant flowers.

DON JUAN. And what of Julia from the Candilejo? [13]

---

[13] Calle del Candilejo and the neighboring street called calle de
la Cabeza del Rey Pedro are in the fourteenth century part of
Seville and immortalize one of the nocturnal adventures of King
Pedro I, "the Cruel," who became the Spanish counterpart of
Harun-al-Rashid, the Commander of the faithful in *The Arabian
Nights.* The first of the two streets received its name from the
little lamp of the old woman in the window who saw the fight below at dead of night when one man was killed. It was King Pedro,
disguised, who killed the man, and the next day King Pedro, who
in Seville has always been called Pedro El Justiciero, accepted the
old woman's evidence when the King sat on the judgment seat and
called for witnesses. The old woman declared that the King had
committed the murder, for she recognized him by the creaking of
his joints, which was a known peculiarity of his: for this reason
the King ordered that his head should be set up in stone in the
street that bears his name.

MARQUIS. Today pommades and rouges plague her life.

DON JUAN. Does she still sell her favors as a whore?

MARQUIS. Aye, she is now a punk and sells them cheap.

DON JUAN. How's business in the slums of Brothel Town?

MARQUIS. There are courtesans galore.

DON JUAN. And the two sisters?

MARQUIS. Quite lively and that monkey-faced old bawd,
   Their mother, who reads them their catechism
   While they await their clients.

DON JUAN.   Whore of Satan!
   How is the elder girl?

MARQUIS.   Pure, undefiled
   But not a stiver to her name; she has
   One "saint" for whom she fasts.

DON JUAN.   All abstinence?

MARQUIS. Yes, she's a constant lover.

DON JUAN.   And her sister?

MARQUIS. She started better and makes thrifty use
   Of what's left over.

DON JUAN.   She must want to be
   A builder. But tell me your escapades,
   Your scandals, hoaxes, and your artful jokes.

MARQUIS. Pedro de Esquivel and I both played
   Last night a grim hoax, and tonight two more.

DON JUAN. I'll go with you and visit a certain nest,
   Where two "fresh eggs" are hatched for both of us.
   What of the terrace serenades by night?

MARQUIS. I won't as serenader catch my death,
   Yet when interred it is colder down below.

DON JUAN. How so?

MARQUIS.   I loved one who's beyond my reach.

DON JUAN. Does she not hearken to your suit?

MARQUIS.   She does,
   And truly loves me.

DON JUAN.   Who is she?

MARQUIS.   My cousin,
   Doña Ana, who has recently arrived.

DON JUAN. Where has she been?

MARQUIS.   In Lisbon with her father,
   In the Embassy.

DON JUAN.   Is she fair?

MARQUIS. She is
Most beautiful. She's Nature's masterpiece.

DON JUAN. If she is peerless, I must see her then.

MARQUIS. The sun has never seen such loveliness.

DON JUAN. If she's so lovely, go and marry her.

MARQUIS. The King has her betrothed, but no one knows
Who is the groom.

DON JUAN. Are you not in his favor?

MARQUIS. Yes, she now writes to me.

CATALINÓN (*aside*). Do not go on;
Don Juan, the greatest playboy in all Spain,
Is fooling you.

DON JUAN. You are the happiest man
In all the world. Entreat her, pester her,
Besiege her, woo her, and let all the world
Perish in flames.

MARQUIS. I am expecting now
The ultimate result.

DON JUAN. Don't lose the chance.
I'll wait here until you return.

MARQUIS. Do wait.
                    (*Exit the* MARQUIS *and the servant*).

CATALINÓN (*to the servant, as he goes*). Quadrado my round-
    bellied friend, farewell.

SERVANT. Good-bye.

DON JUAN. Well, here, my friend, we two remain,
Go shadow the Marquis, who has entered
The palace yonder.   (*Exit* CATALINÓN.)
(*A maidservant at a barred window speaks to* DON JUAN.)

MAIDSERVANT. Pst! Who are you?

DON JUAN. Who calls?

MAIDSERVANT. Listen, sir, I pray,
Since you are kind and prudent, and a friend
Of the Marquis, give this note to him; take heed,
It involves a lady's honor and her name.

DON JUAN. On my word as a gentleman, and his,
Good friend, I swear to give it.

MAIDSERVANT. That's enough.
Stranger, farewell.   (*Exit the maidservant.*)

DON JUAN. The voice has gone away.
What has just happened, does it not

Seem like enchantment? For the letter came
Borne by the courier of the wind. No doubt
It's from the lady the Marquis praised just now:
This windfall shows my halcyon days have come.
They all shout I'm the Playboy of Seville,
And the greatest pleasure life can ever give
Is to trick a woman and dishonor her.
By God, I'll open this and read it too,
And why not, pray, since I have left the square?
Suppose there were a trick? It makes me laugh.
Well, now the paper's open, and it's hers,
For here she signs it "Doña Ana." Look!
It says: "My faithless father secretly
Has promised me in marriage, and I cannot
Resist. I doubt if I can live a day,
For he, alas, has driven me to death,
If you still cherish my love, and my will
Respect, and if your love of me is true,
The moment now has come for you to show it.
To learn how I adore you come tonight,
And at eleven you shall find my door
Unlocked. There all your hopes will be fulfilled
In the enjoyment of the crowning bliss of love.
My love, I beg you wear a crimson cape,
So that tonight my maids may recognize,
And let you in. My trust, my love, farewell."
You hapless lover! Who has ever heard
Of such a strange adventure? Why, I can
Already laugh with glee at such a joke.
By God I'll now enjoy her through the snare
That lately netted Isabel in Naples.
    (*Enter* CATALINÓN.)

CATALINÓN. Here comes the Marquis.
DON JUAN.   Both of us tonight
    Have work to do.
CATALINÓN.   What new rascality
    Is in the offing?
DON JUAN.   This one is a delight.
CATALINÓN. I don't approve. You, sir, think we'll escape
    Being cheated in the end. But he who lives
    By cheating, one fine day will have to pay

Once and for all the price of all his sins.

DON JUAN. Have you turned preacher now, you insolent loon?

CATALINÓN. Right spurs on brave men.

DON JUAN.   Fear does cowards make
Like you. But he who serves must have no will.
He must all action be, words count for nought.
While serving, you are in a gambling game,
And if you wish to win the final trumps,
Act boldly, for who risks most wins the most.

CATALINÓN. No, he who acts and risks most, as a rule,
Will come to grief.

DON JUAN.   Now take heed what I say,
I'll not warn you again.

CATALINÓN.   I give my word
I'll carry out your orders from now on,
And chase elephants or tigers by your side.

DON JUAN. Hark! here's the Marquis.

CATALINÓN.   Must he be the quarry?

(*Enter the* MARQUIS OF LA MOTA.)

DON JUAN. Marquis, from the window there they handed me
A very courteous message for yourself;
I could not see who gave it, but I heard
A woman's voice. She says you are to go
Tonight in secret at the hour of twelve
To yonder door (*Aside:*) which will be open at eleven,
(*Aloud:*) And there you'll have possession of your love:
But you must wear a reddish-colored cape,
So that Leonorcilla's maids may know you.

MARQUIS. What is this?

DON JUAN.   They gave it at the window,
But who they were, I know not.

MARQUIS.   Dearest friend,
This message is a balm after my woes.
Through you alone my hopes may now revive.
On bended knee I give you heartfelt thanks.

DON JUAN. I'm not your cousin, so why kneel to me?
You are the one who must enjoy the girl.

MARQUIS. Such is my joy I am beside myself.
O sun, make haste and sink.

DON JUAN.   It's near its setting.

MARQUIS. Come, friends, let us away from here, and dress

Ourselves in evening clothes: I'm mad for joy!

DON JUAN (*aside*). That's evident, but at the midnight hour
You'll be still crazier.

MARQUIS.   My darling cousin!
Sweet guerdon soon you'll give me for my faith.

CATALINÓN (*aside*). By heaven, I'd not give a single mite
For that beloved cousin.   (*Exit the* MARQUIS.)

(*Enter* DON DIEGO TENORIO.)

DON DIEGO.   Don Juan!

CATALINÓN.   Your father calls.

DON JUAN. What are your orders, father!

DON DIEGO.   I wish, my son,
You were more sensible, good-natured, and enjoyed
A fairer reputation. Do you mean
Then hour by hour to hasten my decease?

DON JUAN. Why so downcast?

DON DIEGO.   Because of your excesses
And mad follies the King has ordered me
To ban you from the city, for he feels,
And justly too, indignant at your conduct.
Although you hid the truth from me, he knows
All details of your crime, which is so grave
That I scarce dare name it. How could you
Betray a friend, and cuckold him as well,
Within the precincts of the royal palace?
Unhappy son! May God now punish you
As you deserve. Take heed that God above,
Though He now turns a blind eye to your sins,
Must bring your fatal day of reckoning.
What awful doom must He reserve for those
Like you who've taken His great name in vain.
God is a pitiless judge when Death is nigh.

DON JUAN. When Death is nigh? I've credit still to spare
And have I not a lengthy road to go?

DON DIEGO. It will, alas, appear too short I fear.

DON JUAN. My journey now, which I must undertake,
To please His Majesty, is it as long?

DON DIEGO. Until you have repaired the insult done
To Duke Octavio, and all the fuss
And scandals you have caused with Isabel
In Naples have died down, the King requires

You go at once in exile to Lebrija,
A paltry sentence for so gross a crime.

CATALINÓN (*aside*). If he had also heard the tale of Thisbe,
The hapless fisher maid, the poor old man
Would even be more indignant, I am sure.

DON DIEGO. As all I do and say has no effect
On you, I leave your punishment to God.   (*Exit.*)

CATALINÓN. The poor old man is quite overcome with grief.

DON JUAN. Then floods of tears, that's how old men behave.
Let us go seek the Marquis, night's at hand.

CATALINÓN. Let us go. And now you will enjoy his bride.

DON JUAN. Tonight you'll see seduction's masterpiece.

CATALINÓN. I only pray to God we'll save our skins!

DON JUAN. Catalinón, beware.

CATALINÓN.   Why, sir, you are
The locust plague of women and they ought
To make the town crier proclaim your coming
With drum and trumpet and the warning words!
All maidens shun the man who outwits women,
And is the greatest playboy of all Spain!

DON JUAN. By Jove, you've given me a pretty name.
(*It is nighttime. Enter the* MARQUIS *with musicians singing;
he walks up and down the stage.*)

MUSICIANS (*singing*). *Who awaits a promised tryst today,*
                    Mopes in despair when there's delay.

DON JUAN. What noise is that?

CATALINÓN.   Musicians.

MARQUIS (*aside*).   Now it seems
The poet speaks to me.
(*Aloud:*)
                    Who's there?

DON JUAN.   A friend.

MARQUIS. It's you, Don Juan?

DON JUAN.   The Marquis, you?

MARQUIS.   Who else?

DON JUAN. I recognized your cape.

MARQUIS (*to the musicians*). Sing for Don Juan.

MUSICIANS (*singing*). *Who awaits a promised tryst today,*
                    Mopes in despair when there's delay.

DON JUAN. Whose house are you staring at?

MARQUIS.   Why, that belongs

216

TIRSO DE MOLINA

To Don Gonzalo de Ulloa, where my fairest dwells.

DON JUAN. Where do we go?

MARQUIS. To Lisbon.

DON JUAN. How if we
Are still in Seville?

MARQUIS. So you are surprised?
Why wonder if the dregs of Portugal
Live on what's best in Spain?

DON JUAN. Where do they live?

MARQUIS. In Serpent Street [14] you'll see Adam become
A Portuguese to woo the thousand Eves
Who haunt that sinful vale and offer us
Forbidden fruits and wheedle us of gold.

CATALINÓN. I should not like to walk by night along
That hellish street, for though by day you'll find
All fragrant as the honeycomb, by night
They void upon the street their filthy slops.
One night, alas, I did become a target,
And found I was befouled by Portugal.

DON JUAN. While you go up that street I'll step aside
And have a little sport. [15]

MARQUIS. Near here tonight
A bravo lies in wait for me.

DON JUAN. If you
Allow me, Marquis, I'll soon settle him.

MARQUIS. Now wrap this cloak around your arm, it will help.

DON JUAN. A good hint, come and show me now the house.

MARQUIS. To be successful, imitate my voice,
And way of talking. Do you see that lattice.

DON JUAN. I see it.

MARQUIS. Whisper "Beatrice" and enter.

DON JUAN. What kind of woman?

MARQUIS. Rosy and insipid.

CATALINÓN. She must then be a water-cooling jar.

MARQUIS. At the Cathedral promenade, we'll wait.

[14] Today it is called calle de las Sierpes, and starts at the spot where the celebrated jail stood in which Cervantes was imprisoned in 1597.

[15] Don Juan here refers to the hoax he plans for Doña Ana. The Marquis unwittingly assists Don Juan's plans by lending him his cloak, thus facilitating his entrance into Doña Ana's house.

DON JUAN.   Farewell.

CATALINÓN. Where are we going?

DON JUAN.   Hold your tongue, you fool!
We're going to play my trick.

CATALINÓN.   No one escapes
Your clutches.

DON JUAN.   I love complicated tricks.

CATALINÓN. So you threw your cloak to the bull? [16]

DON JUAN.   Not so,
The bull threw me the cloak.

> (*Exeunt* DON JUAN *and* CATALINÓN.)

MARQUIS.   The duenna must
Think I'm Don Juan.

MUSICIANS.   What an amusing trick!

MARQUIS. That is to win by error.

MUSICIANS.   All the world
Is nothing but error.

MUSICIANS (*singing*). *Who awaits a promised tryst today,*
                      Mopes in despair when there's delay.

> (*Exeunt.*)

(*A room in the house of* DON GONZALO.
DOÑA ANA *is within with* DON JUAN *and* CATALINÓN.)

DOÑA ANA (*within*). False friend: You're not the Marquis.
You've deceived me.

DON JUAN (*within*). I am, I tell you.

DOÑA ANA.   False foe, you are lying.
(*Enter* DON GONZALO *with drawn sword.*)

DON GONZALO. I hear my daughter Doña Ana's voice.

DOÑA ANA (*within*). Will no one kill this traitor here who has
Murdered my honor?

DON GONZALO.   Can such shamelessness
Exist in man? Her honor slain, woe's me!
And now her giddy tongue proclaims her woe
To all the world.

DOÑA ANA.   Now kill him.
(*Enter* DON JUAN *and* CATALINÓN *with drawn swords.*)

DON JUAN.   Who's there?

DON GONZALO. Base caitiff, by your tricks you've undermined

---

[16] This is a proverbial expression for risking all on a last effort, but
Don Juan takes it literally and makes a play on the words.

The barbican of my own honor's fort,
Of which my life was warden.

DON JUAN.   Let me pass.

DON GONZALO. Pass? You shall pass the point of my bare
   sword.

DON JUAN. You'll die.

DON GONZALO.   What odds?

DON JUAN.   I warn you I shall kill.
   (They fight.)

DON GONZALO. Die, traitor!

DON JUAN *(lunging at him with the sword)*. This is the way
   I die.

CATALINÓN *(aside)*. If I come out alive, no more deceits,
   And no more feasts.

DON GONZALO *(falling)*. Alas, you have slain me.

DON JUAN. You took your life.

DON GONZALO.   What use was life to me?

DON JUAN. Let us flee. *(Exeunt* DON JUAN *and* CATALINÓN.*)*

DON GONZALO. My chilled blood you have stoked up to fury.
   I'm dead and I have had my reckoning.
   My fury now will track you down, for you
   Are a traitor, and to be one signifies
   You're first of all a coward.
   (He dies. Servants enter and carry off the corpse.
   The street. Enter the MARQUIS OF LA MOTA *and musicians.)*

MUSICIANS. Midnight will soon be striking, and Don Juan
   Has not yet come. How cruel are the pangs
   Of those who have to wait!
   (Enter DON JUAN *and* CATALINÓN.*)*

DON JUAN.   Is that you, Marquis?

MARQUIS. Is that Don Juan?

DON JUAN. Here I am! Here's your cloak!

MARQUIS. What of your trick?

DON JUAN. It had a depressing end. A man was slain.

CATALINÓN. My Lord, flee from the corpse.

MARQUIS. And did you play your prank? What shall I do?

CATALINÓN *(aside)*. The joke's against you too!

DON JUAN. It was a costly prank.

MARQUIS. I'll pay the bill, but Doña Ana must
   Be complaining of me.

DON JUAN.   It is nearly twelve.

CATALINÓN. A pretty crisis now he'll have to face!

DON JUAN. Let's run.

CATALINÓN. No eagle will outstrip me now.

(*Exeunt* DON JUAN *and* CATALINÓN.)

MARQUIS. You all may go home. I'll go alone.

SERVANTS. God made the night for sleeping.

(*Exeunt servants.*)

(*Voices within the house:* "What a misfortune! what a woeful sight!")

MARQUIS. Heavens! I hear cries from the castle square.
  At such a late hour what can have occurred!
  An icy pang within my heart I feel:
  I see from here what looks like another Troy
  Ablaze, for hosts of flaming torches move this way
  In serried squadrons, making giant flames,
  And emulate the stars above, I must
  At once find out the reason . . .

(*Enter* DON DIEGO TENORIO *and the guards with torches.*)

DON DIEGO. Who goes there?

MARQUIS. One who would inquire the cause
  Of all this turmoil.

DON DIEGO. Seize him.

MARQUIS. Capture me!

DON DIEGO. Now sheathe your sword; the bravest man of all
  Is one who wins without recourse to arms.

MARQUIS. Is this the way to speak to me, who am
  The Marquis of La Mota?

DON DIEGO. Hand me your sword,
  The King has ordered your arrest.

MARQUIS. My God!

(*Enter the* KING *and suite.*)

KING. Throughout the length and breadth of Spain he must
  Not refuge find, not even in Italy,
  If he should flee there.

DON DIEGO. Sire, here is the Marquis.

MARQUIS. Your Highness, have you ordered my arrest?

KING. Take him away and stick his head upon
  A spike on the city walls: have you the base
  Effrontery to stand before me now?

MARQUIS (*aside*). Alas, how fleeting are the joys of love,
  The tyrant, though they come to us

With feet of lead. How wise the sage who once
Said: " 'Twixt cup and lip there is many a slip."
But I am puzzled by the King's mad rage.
(*Aloud:*)
I know not for what crime I am arrested.

DON DIEGO. Who knows better than you, my Lord?

MARQUIS.   I?

DON DIEGO.   Come!

MARQUIS. I am confused.

KING.   Try him now, and before
Tomorrow let the Marquis be beheaded.
As for the brave Comendador, with all
The pomp and ceremony that men pay
To royal or to sacred personages,
Let him be buried, and his sepulcher
Of bronze and varied stone be fashioned.
Let it there be surmounted by a bust
On which in mosaics and Gothic lettering
It will proclaim that vengeance is at hand.
The burial, the bust, and sepulcher
Shall all be paid by me: But where is Doña Ana?

DON DIEGO. She has sought refuge with Her Royal Highness.

KING. Castile today is mourning its sad loss,
And Calatrava misses its brave captain.   (*Exeunt.*)

(*The countryside near Dos Hermanas. Enter* BATRICIO *and*
AMINTA, *a betrothed couple. Also* GASENO—*an old man*—
BELISA, *and shepherd musicians.*)

MUSICIANS (*singing*).

> *When April's sun begins to shine,*
> *Clover blooms and the eglantine,*
> *But when Aminta shows her face,*
> *Her radiance gladdens every place.*
> *Now that the feeble sun at last has dawned,*
> *And shining gently kindles the frosty fields,*
> *Let us upon this blossoming carpet rest,*
> *Which like a bridal bower will welcome us.*

AMINTA (*to the singers*). Come, youths and lasses, raise your
voices now
And sing your tuneful songs to my betrothed.

SINGERS.   *When April's sun begins to shine,*
             Clover blooms, and the eglantine,
             But when Aminta shows her face,
             Her radiance gladdens every place.

GASENO. Right well you have solmized, and I believe
    It would compare with Kyries in church.
BATRICIO. The sun has shed over us its crimson light
    And turns the meadows and the woods to fire
    But when, Aminta, you begin to blush
    Your color even shames the April sun.
AMINTA. Batricio, you're false and flattering,
    Yet I must thank you, but if, like the sun,
    You will upon me shed your powerful rays,
    Then I deserve, through you, to be the moon.
    You are my sun through whom I wax and wane,
    Let dawn in haunting tones now sing your praises.

SINGERS.   *When April's sun begins to shine*
             Clover blooms and the eglantine,
             But when Aminta shows her face,
             Her radiance gladdens every place.

(*Enter* CATALINÓN, *dressed as a traveler.*)
CATALINÓN. Good sirs, there are guests who wish to attend
    The wedding feast.
GASENO.   They're welcome.
                                         Who is it?
CATALINÓN. Don Juan Tenorio.
GASENO.   The old one?
CATALINÓN.   No, Don Juan.
BELISA. His son must be a ladies' man.
BATRICIO (*aside*).   This is
    A bad omen. A gentleman and a rake
    Will spoil our pleasure and suspicions rouse.
    But who told him about our meeting here?
CATALINÓN. He's on the road to Lebrija.
BATRICIO (*aside*).   The devil 'twas
    Who sent him, but why should I fash myself?
    Let all the people in the world attend
    My homely wedding feast. Nevertheless

Our guest is a knight, and that's an evil omen.

GASENO. Let us from Rhodes then welcome the Colossus,
The Pope from Rome, and Prester John, and even
Our King Alfonso the Eleventh, and
His Royal Court, for in Gaseno here
They'll find good will and hospitality.
There are loaves of bread in mountains in the house,
And wine on tap that would overflow the river
Guadalquivir, and towers of bacon 'midst
Shy armies of the tinier birds
With which to baste the chicken and the pigeon.
The noble gentleman is welcome here
In Dos Hermanas. My white hairs are honored.

BELISA. He's the son of the High Chamberlain . . .

BATRICIO (*aside*).   A sign
Of evil omen for me, for they will
Place him next my bride. Though I have not yet
Enjoyed the bliss of marriage, I am doomed
By Heaven to be racked by jealousy,
To love, to suffer, and endure.

(*Enter* DON JUAN TENORIO.)

DON JUAN. By merest chance I was passing and was told
There was a wedding in the village, so
I too now wish to join the merry throng,
As I was fortunate to come this way.

GASENO. Your Lordship does us honor, I am sure.

BATRICIO (*aside*). And I, who am the host, say to myself
That you come in an evil hour.

GASENO.   Won't you
Make place for our distinguished guest?

DON JUAN.   I wish
With your permission to sit here.

(*He sits down next to the bride.*)

BATRICIO.   If you
Sit down before me, sir, you'll appear to be
The bridegroom.

DON JUAN.   If I were you, I'd not complain.

GASENO. He is the bridegroom . . .

DON JUAN.   I now beg your pardon
For my mistake and ignorance.

CATALINÓN (*aside*).   I pity

The hapless husband.

DON JUAN (*aside to* CATALINÓN.) He's in a rage.

CATALINÓN (*aside*). I'm aware of it; but if he has to be
The bull in this feast, should he not become
Enraged? I wouldn't give a cuckold's coin [17]
For his wife nor for his honor. Poor man,
You've thrown yourself into the Devil's hands.

DON JUAN. Can I believe, señora, that my luck
So favors me? I'm jealous of your husband.

AMINTA. You strike me as an arrant flatterer.

BATRICIO (*aside*). I was right to say before that at a wedding
A great man always brings bad luck.

GASENO.   Come all,
And let us eat and drink, so that my Lord
May have a moment to lie down and rest.
(DON JUAN *takes the bride's hand, but she draws it away.*)

DON JUAN. Why do you hide your hand?

AMINTA.   It is not mine.

GASENO. Let us go.

BELISA.   Sing again.

DON JUAN.   What do you think?

CATALINÓN. I don't think: I'm sure those boors are preparing
The vilest death for us.

DON JUAN.   Those flashing eyes,
That fair complexion, and white hands have set
Ablaze my heart, and are consuming me.

CATALINÓN. So you will brand her with your mark, and put
Her out to grass: she'll be your fourth.

DON JUAN.   Take heed;
They're staring at me.

BATRICIO.   An ill-omened knight
At my wedding.

GASENO.   Do sing.

BATRICIO.   My God! I'll die.

CATALINÓN. Let them sing, but soon they'll all rue the day.
                              (*Exeunt all.*)

[17] Cornado was an ancient Spanish coin of copper mixed with
silver, coined by Alfonso XI, worth less than a farthing.

GASENO's *house in Dos Hermanas.*
Enter BATRICIO, *pensive.*

BATRICIO. Jealousy, timepiece of care, whose hourly stroke,
   Though it be erratic, brings torments that kill,
   Cease from tormenting me, for it's absurd
   That, when love gives me life, you should
   Give death. What do you wish of me, Don Juan,
   That you torment me so? No sooner did
   My eyes behold him at my wedding than
   I said: "This is for me an evil omen."
   What lordliness to sit beside my bride,
   And not even to let me put my hand
   In my own plate! For every time I tried,
   He would push it away and say aloud:
   "What an ill-bred fellow!" and, when I appealed
   To others, and complained, they answered: "You
   Have nothing to complain of, and you should
   Not take this so to heart, or get so fussed:
   This must be courtier's manners, and genteel."
   For gentlemen indeed! not even in Sodom
   Would one behold another man beside
   The bride at table, while the bridegroom fasts.
   The other knave kept saying, when I tried
   To taste a morsel: "Don't you like the food?
   You're wrong." He then would snatch it off my plate.
   That was no wedding but a cruel jest.
   It's past enduring and must not be borne
   Among Christians; and now he has his fill,
   I wager, if he wants, he'll come to bed
   With us too, and when I approach my wife,
   He's sure to say: "How coarse this fellow is!"
   But here he comes, I can't stand it, I'll hide.
   Too late, it can't be done, he has seen me now.
   (*Enter* DON JUAN TENORIO.)
DON JUAN. Batricio.
BATRICIO. What orders, sir?

DON JUAN. I wish to say . . .

BATRICIO (*aside*). Does this mean more bad luck for me?

DON JUAN. That now for many days I've lost my heart
  To fair Aminta and enjoyed . . .

BATRICIO.   Her honor?

DON JUAN. Yes.

BATRICIO (*aside*). This is a clear proof of what I have seen,
  For if she did not love him, he would not
  Have gone to her house, and when all is said
  She is but a woman,
  (*Aloud to Don Juan:*)
                    but she is my wife.

DON JUAN. Aminta at last grew jealous or, perhaps,
  In despair at finding she had been forgotten
  By me, and yet was still another's wife,
  Wrote me this letter begging me to meet her,
  And in return I promised to enjoy
  What she had in her heart already granted.
  Look to your own life now, if you are wise,
  For whoever tries to hinder me shall die.

BATRICIO. If you leave it to my choice I'll agree
  To do what you want, for I do believe
  That honor and woman lose their luster when
  They are for ever on the lips of men.
  A woman who is talked about will lose
  More than she gains, for she is like a bell,
  Which is by its sound tested, and it is
  Well known that she whose name rings with the sound
  Of a cracked bell loses her reputation.
  As you destroy the happiness that love
  Had promised me, I do not want a wife
  Who is neither good nor bad, but like a coin
  Seen in the twilight; make her yours, my Lord,
  And live a thousand years. I'll try my best
  To resist, and undeceive myself, and die,
  For who would live amid such falsity?   (*Exit.*)

DON JUAN. Through his honor I have defeated him,
  For peasants clutch their honor with both hands,
  And in their thoughts give it preëminence.
  In life's vicissitudes we should believe
  That honor has fled from the city, and

Has taken refuge in the countryside.
But before I burn my boats and do the damage
I must pretend to find the remedy;
And so I'll have a word with her old father,
That he unwittingly may authorize
The ruse I plan. How well I've played my cards!
And so tonight his daughter I'll enjoy.
The night approaches, so I'll call on him.
O stars who shine upon my course, give luck
In this deception, and if death must be
My guerdon, let it tarry long in coming.   (*Exit.*)
  (*Enter* AMINTA *and* BELISA.)

BELISA. Your bridegroom comes, Aminta, now you should
    undress.

AMINTA. Of my sad marriage I don't know
  What to think, dear Belisa; all the day
  Batricio has been in tearful mood,
  And made scenes of turmoil and jealousy.
  What a misfortune! But do tell me, pray,
  Who is the gentleman who would deprive
  Me of my betrothed? Has shamelessness become
  A knight of Spain? I beg you leave me now.
  I am shamed and out of sorts; may ill befall
  That knight who robs me of my happiness.

BELISA. Be silent, for I think he comes this way.
  Who else would put his foot inside the house
  Of such a brawny bridegroom?
                       Fare you well.

BELISA. He'll soon forget his sorrow in your arms.

AMINTA. Please God my sighs his love may stimulate,
  And my sad tears seem gentle dalliance.   (*Exeunt.*)
  (*Enter* DON JUAN, CATALINÓN *and* GASENO.)

DON JUAN. Gaseno, hail!

GASENO.   I'd like to go with you
  To compliment my daughter on her luck.

DON JUAN. Tomorrow morning there'll be time enough.

GASENO. You're right: my soul goes with this maiden whom
  I offer you.

DON JUAN.   Say my wife: saddle at once.

CATALINÓN. When do we start?

DON JUAN.   At daybreak when the sun

Will rise half-dead with laughter at my trick.

CATALINÓN. There in Lebrija, sir, another bride
Awaits you. I must beg you settle quickly
This marriage first.

DON JUAN. This hoax is the best of all.

CATALINÓN. I only hope we'll save our skins from this.

DON JUAN. Why so afraid when my own father is
The Chief Justice and Royal Favorite?

CATALINÓN. God often is wont to take His vengeance on
Those Favorites, if they don't punish crime.
And He will often strike those who look on
At gambling. Now I've watched you play your game,
And I would not like a thunderbolt to fall,
And turn me to a heap of dust and ashes.

DON JUAN. Away with you and saddle me my horses;
Tomorrow night I shall sleep in Seville.

CATALINÓN. At Seville?

DON JUAN. Yes.

CATALINÓN. What are you saying now?
Reflect on what you've done, sir, and observe
That even the longest life is short in time
And there's hellfire beyond the gates of death.

DON JUAN. If you concede me such a long delay
You may yet be deceived . . .

CATALINÓN. Sir?

DON JUAN. Off with you!
You irritate me by your foolish fears.

CATALINÓN. More power to Turk, more power to Scythian,
To Persian, Libyan, Galician,
And Troglodyte, German and Japanese,
Even to the tailor with his golden needle,
Who does like the forlorn maiden in the song. (*Exit.*)

DON JUAN. Night in black silence stretches o'er the world,
And the Pleiades, 'midst starry clusters, tread
The Pole when at its highest in the sky.
The time has come when I must snare my prey.
Lust goads me onwards, how can I resist
This tempting moment? I must reach her bed.
(*Calling:*)
Aminta!
(*Enter* AMINTA *as from bed.*)

AMINTA. Who calls Aminta? Is it Batricio?

DON JUAN. I'm not Batricio.

AMINTA.   Then, who?

DON JUAN.   Look
And you'll see who I am.

AMINTA.   Woe's me, I am
Ruined; in my bedroom at such an hour
With you!

DON JUAN.   This hour is mine.

AMINTA.   Go back, I'll shout.
Do please respect the courtesy you owe
To my Batricio—you'll even find
In Dos Hermanas Roman heroines,
Emilias, and even Lucreces who
Will know how to avenge their cruel wrongs.

DON JUAN. Do listen to my words and hide the blush
Of your fair cheeks deep down within your heart.

AMINTA. Begone, my husband's coming.

DON JUAN.   I'm your husband.

AMINTA. Since when, pray?

DON JUAN.   From now onwards.

AMINTA.   Who arranged
The marriage?

DON JUAN.   My good fortune.

AMINTA.   And married us?

DON JUAN. Your eyes.

AMINTA.   With what authority?

DON JUAN.   With sight.

AMINTA. Does my Batricio know?

DON JUAN.   Yes, by now
He has quite forgotten you.

AMINTA.   Can he forget?

DON JUAN. Yes. I adore you.

AMINTA.   How?

DON JUAN.   With both my arms.

AMINTA. Unhand me.

DON JUAN.   How can I when, as you see,
I am dying of love?

AMINTA.   What monstrous lies you tell!

DON JUAN. Aminta, listen and you'll know the truth,
For you women are always friends of truth.

I am a noble knight, the scion of
The great Tenorios, the conquerors
Of Seville, and my father, second to
The King, is honored and esteemed before
All men at Court. And life and death do hang
Upon his lips. As I was traveling
By chance I saw you, for Love does at times
Steer the affairs of men in such a way
That he himself forgets they have occurred.
I saw you, loved you, and so scorched my wings
That now I am resolved to marry you,
Even though the King oppose it, and in rage
My father threatens he will hinder it.
I have to be your spouse. What is your reply?

AMINTA. I know not what to say because your truths
Are wrapped in such a mass of honeyed lies.
If, as the people know, I am betrothed
To my Batricio the bond is not
Annulled, even if he refuses me.

DON JUAN. As consummation never yet took place,
Whether through fraud or malice, it may be
Annulled.

AMINTA.   In my Batricio there was
Nought but the pure and simple truth.

DON JUAN.   Well then,
Give me your hand and let us plight our troth.

AMINTA. Are you not tricking me?

DON JUAN.   I should be tricked.

AMINTA. Then swear that you will keep your plighted word.

DON JUAN. I swear to your white hand that icy burns
To carry out my vow.

AMINTA.   And swear to God,
Who will doom your soul if you break your word.

DON JUAN. If I ever fail you in my word or faith
I pray God that as a punishment
I may be murdered by a man—(*aside*) a dead one,
For by a living man, may God forbid!

AMINTA. That oath now makes me your true wife.

DON JUAN.   My soul,
In this kiss I entrust my soul.

AMINTA.   My life

And soul belong to you.

DON JUAN.   Aminta dearest,
Tomorrow you'll encase your dainty feet
In shoes all gaily decked with silver soles,
Studded with nails of gold from Tibar's coast;
And your neck of alabaster I'll adorn
With necklaces of sparkling jewels, and
Your tapering fingers with pearl-mounted rings.

AMINTA. From now on, husband, my will bows, I'm yours.

DON JUAN (*aside*). You little know the Playboy of Seville.
(*Exeunt.*)

(*The shore at Tarragona. Enter* ISABEL *and* FABIO, *dressed as for the road.*)

ISABEL. To think that night has robbed me of my lover,
My only precious treasure in the world!
O cruel tyrannous truth, mask of the day,
O murky night, the day's antipodes,
Spouse of my dreams!

FABIO. What boots it, Isabel, to meditate
Upon your sorrows thus, when love is nought
But cunning, and will stir up anger when
He encounters scorn; when he who laughs today
Will probably tomorrow mourn his lot.
The sea is angry, and the storm unleashed;
The galleys, Duchess, have now raced for shelter
Beneath the tower that crowns this lonely shore.

ISABEL. Where are we now?

FABIO.   We are in Tarragona.
Soon we shall reach the city of Valencia,
The palace of the sun itself, where you
Will enjoy yourself some days, and then you sail
On to Seville, where you will see the world's
Eighth wonder. Though you lost Octavio's hand,
Don Juan is courtlier and of nobler stock.
Then why are you so downcast? It is said
That he has been already made a count,
I know the King himself intends to give
Your hand to him.

ISABEL.   My sadness does not spring
From marrying Don Juan, whose noble blood
Is known to all the world, but I shall mourn

My honor outraged until I shall die.

FABIO. Yonder I see a fisher maid who sighs
  As if her heart would break; I'm sure she comes
  To you for sympathy, so while I call
  Your suite, you two may make your sad lament.

(*Exit* FABIO.)

(*Enter* THISBE.)

THISBE. Out of Spain's roaring sea a column rose
  Of wingéd fire-waves and engulfed my home,
  A second Troy, but in dark stithy then
  The sea has stoked the flames and vomited them
  In scalding tears that overflow my eyes.
  Accursed be the ship that sailed across
  Your bitter crystal waters and was the cause
  Of Medea's woe; may curses, too, descend
  Upon the first who ever twisted hemp,
  And on the crosstrees spread the billowing sail
  Which would bring trickery and base deceit.

ISABEL. Why such forlorn complaints against the sea
  My lovely fisher maid?

THISBE.   I rail a thousand times
  Against the sea; but when it is rocked by storms,
  You must be happy if you can laugh at it.

ISABEL. I too have made complaints against the sea.
  But from where do you come?

THISBE.   From over there,
  Where you perceive those tempest-beaten huts,
  Over which the sea victoriously raged,
  Their humble walls have well-nigh crumbled away,
  But still their massive relics do provide
  A thousand crannies for the birds to rest.
  There I made myself a heart of adamant,
  But when I fell a victim to that monster
  Whom you see strutting here, my heart became
  Softer than wax when it is in the sun.
  Are you the fair Europa whom these bulls
  Bear off as prize? [18]

ISABEL.   They carry me to Seville

[18] The allusion here is to the abduction of Europa by Zeus, who
changed himself into a bull. According to the tradition, he took
her from Phoenicia to Tarragona, where he abandoned her.

To be wed, though it is against my will.

THISBE. If my mishap has moved your heart to pity,
And if you've been a victim of the sea,
Take me with you to be your humble slave;
For if my sorrows and my shame do not
Cut short my life, I wish to ask the King
For reparation of a wicked hoax.
Saved from the waves, Don Juan lay on the shore
Half-drowned and near to death, when I
Befriended him and kept him in my hut
Until his health returned, but he, vile guest,
Like a venomous viper lurking in the grass,
Bit me, and tricked me with his promises:
I yielded, woe's me, to his blandishments.
Unhappy the woman who puts trust in man.
At last he fled and left me to my fate,

ISABEL. Be silent, accursed woman, leave me now.
You have well-nigh killed me, but if it's grief
Compels you to speak, tell me your tale I pray.

THISBE. I would it were a tale.

ISABEL.   Accursed be
The woman who pins all her faith on men.
Who is to go with you?

THISBE.   A fisherman,
Anfriso, and my aged father, who
Will be the witnesses of all my wrongs.
No vengeance ever will satisfy my wrongs.
Come in my company. Accursed be
The woman who pins all her faith on men.

(*A church in Seville. In one of the side chapels is the tomb
of the Comendador Don Gonzalo de Ulloa with a statue
of the dead man. Enter* DON JUAN *and* CATALINÓN.)

CATALINÓN. All goes awry.

DON JUAN.   How so?

CATALINÓN.   Octavio
Has heard about your hoax in Italy.
The Marquis, too, is justly hurt. He says
The message which you said his cousin gave
Was false, and under cover of his cape
You played the trick that has besmirched his name

It is said that Isabel to Seville comes
To claim your hand, and it is said . . .

DON JUAN (*giving him a buffet*). Take this!

CATALINÓN. You have broken one of my wisdom teeth.

DON JUAN. Who told you, gossip, all these foolish tales?

CATALINÓN. They're true.

DON JUAN. I don't care if they are or not. Suppose
Octavio wants to kill me? Am I dead?
And have I not hands too? Where is our lodging?

CATALINÓN. A hide-out in a dark street.

DON JUAN. Very good.

CATALINÓN. The church is holy ground and sanctuary.[19]

DON JUAN. By daylight they may try to kill me here.
Have you yet seen the groom of Dos Hermanas?

CATALINÓN. I have seen him too: he is grim and sad.

DON JUAN. For a whole fortnight Aminta will not know
The trick I've played.

CATALINÓN. She has been so well hoaxed that she now calls
herself the countess.

DON JUAN. What a funny joke!

CATALINÓN. So funny she'll lament it many a year.
(*They catch sight of the sepulcher of* DON GONZALO DE
ULLOA.)

DON JUAN. Whose sepulcher is this?

CATALINÓN. Here Don Gonzalo
Lies buried.

DON JUAN. The same one I have killed.
They've given the old man a stately tomb.

CATALINÓN. This one was ordered by the King. What says
The lettering?

DON JUAN (*reads*): "Here, trusting in the Lord
For vengeance on a traitor, the most loyal
Of all knights lies buried."
I'll burst my sides
Laughing at this joke! So you'll avenge yourself
On me, you poor old man with beard of stone?
(*He pulls the statue's beard.*)

CATALINÓN. If I were you I would not pluck his beard,
For never did the men of such proud stock

---

[19] Those who fled from justice could take sanctuary in a church.

Let their beard be plucked while alive or dead.

DON JUAN (*to the statue*). Tonight I shall expect you at my inn
    For dinner. There we can arrange a duel,
    If you are still resolved to be avenged,
    Although, I fear, the fight will be one-sided,
    For with a sword of stone it's hard to fight.

CATALINÓN. Night approaches, sir, it's time for us to go.

DON JUAN. Surely your vengeance has been long delayed,
    And if you mean to wreak it, do not sleep,
    But if you still rely on Death for help,
    You may as well abandon all your hopes,
    For you grant me so long a lease on life.

(*A Room in an inn. Two servants of* DON JUAN *are setting a table.*)

FIRST SERVANT. All must be spick and span because Don Juan
    Is dining here tonight.

SECOND SERVANT.   The table's laid,
    But our Master is late, and once he starts
    To dawdle, God knows when he will come home.
    This drives me wild; the wine is growing hot,
    The food grows cold. But who will exact order
    From Don Juan, who's the acme of disorder?

(*Enter* DON JUAN *and* CATALINÓN.)

DON JUAN. Have you locked the doors?

CATALINÓN.   I've locked them as you ordered.

DON JUAN. Hello there! bring my dinner.

SECOND SERVANT.   Dinner's served.

DON JUAN. Catalinón, sit down.

CATALINÓN.   I like to sup
    More slowly.

DON JUAN.   Sit down, I tell you.

CATALINÓN.   All right,
    I'll accept the invitation.

FIRST SERVANT (*aside*).   He must be
    On a journey bound if he dines with his lackey.

DON JUAN. Sit down.

(*There is a loud knock on the door.*)

CATALINÓN.   I say! that was a mighty knock!

DON JUAN. I think someone has called. See who it is.

FIRST SERVANT. I'll go at once.

CATALINÓN. Suppose the officers
Of justice have arrived?

DON JUAN. What if it's so?
Don't be afraid.
(FIRST SERVANT *enters running, speechless with fright.*)
What's this? You're all a-quiver?

CATALINÓN. He has some dread news to report to you.

DON JUAN. If you don't speak you'll make me lose my temper.
What have you seen? Did some black devil cast
A spell upon you? Go at once and see
Who's at that door! go quick, I say!

CATALINÓN. I go?

DON JUAN. Yes, you, get going, move your feet.

CATALINÓN. They once did find my grandma dead and hang-
ing
From a tree branch, and from that day on
I dream her lost soul goes a-wandering.
I don't like hearing such loud knocks.

DON JUAN. Enough!

CATALINÓN. A fine time to do so!

DON JUAN. Won't you obey?

CATALINÓN. Who has the key?

SECOND SERVANT. The door is barred, that's all.

DON JUAN. What's wrong with you? Why won't you go?

CATALINÓN. Today
Is Catalinón's end. Suppose the raped
And ravished women come to take revenge
On both of us?
(*He goes out to the door and rushes back panic-struck,
stumbles, and falls, and gets up.*)

DON JUAN. What's this?

CATALINÓN. God help me! I am dead
And in their power!

DON JUAN. In whose power? come, do speak!

CATALINÓN. Oh, sir, I saw . . . there . . . there . . .
when I got there . . .
Who seizes one who snatches one away?
I reached the door, thereafter I was blind.
But when I saw it, I swear to God I saw.
I spoke, and said, "Who are you?" and it said . . .

I butted into it and saw . . .

DON JUAN.   Who was it, say!

CATALINÓN. I do not know.

DON JUAN.   How wine befuddles brains!
Give me that light, you chicken-breasted loon,
And I'll soon see who calls.

(DON JUAN *takes the candle and goes toward the door.*
DON GONZALO *enters and confronts him, in the form of the*
statue that was on the sepulcher, and DON JUAN *staggers*
backward, much perturbed, grasping his sword in one hand
and the candle in the other. DON GONZALO *walks toward*
him slowly, taking short steps, and DON JUAN *retires before*
him until they reach the center of the stage.)

DON JUAN. Who's there?

DON GONZALO. It's I.

DON JUAN. Who are you?

DON GONZALO.   I am he
Whom you invited here to dine with you.

DON JUAN. Why, there'll be food in plenty for us both,
And if you have brought guests along with you
The table's set already. Seat yourself.

CATALINÓN. God help me now, and St. Panuncio,
And our good St. Antón. Do dead men eat?
I'faith they must, for he makes signs he does.

DON JUAN. Sit down, Catalinón.

CATALINÓN.   Thanks, I have dined.

DON JUAN. You're all in a dither! Why such mortal fear
Of a mere corpse? Suppose he were alive?
What would you do? You lily-livered dolt!

CATALINÓN. Dine with your guest, sir! I've already dined.

DON JUAN. You madden me!

CATALINÓN.   God help me, sir, I stink.

DON JUAN. Come, I am waiting.

CATALINÓN.   I am dead with fear.
My buttocks have given up the ghost as well.

(*The two servants tremble with fear.*)

DON JUAN. Ho! You two there! what's wrong? you're all
    a-tremble!

CATALINÓN. I never could dine with a foreigner:
How, sir, could I dine with a guest of stone?

DON JUAN. A doltish fear! If he's of stone, what odds?

CATALINÓN. Suppose he cracked my skull.

DON JUAN. Be polite to him.

CATALINÓN (*to statue*). Are you all right, sir? Is the other life
A pleasant land? Is it all plain or mountain?
Does poetry win prizes there?

FIRST SERVANT. To all
The questions he is asked he noddeth "Yes."

CATALINÓN. And are there many taverns over there?
There must be if old Noah's there, I trow.

DON JUAN. Hello there! Pass the wine.

CATALINÓN. Lord Death,
In your far distant country do they cool
Their wine with snow?
(*The statue nods.*)
So there is snow?
A bonny country.

DON JUAN. If you want a song,
They'll sing for you.
(*The statue nods.*)
Then sing, I pray.

CATALINÓN. Lord Death's a man of taste.

FIRST SERVANT. A nobleman,
And fond of revelry.
(*They sing off-stage:*)

> *If you, my lady, day by day deny*
> *Possession of love's guerdon till I die,*
> *The lease on life you give me is too long.*

CATALINÓN. Either Lord Death now feels the heat, or else
He eats but little. I'm all shivers when
I touch my food. They're drinking little there,
So I'll make up for it. A toast of stone!
Ye gods! I'm less afraid already. (*He drinks.*)
(*They continue singing within:*)

> *If so far distant is the fateful date*
> *When I may all my lustful amours sate;*
> *Let life roll onwards as my lease is long.*
> *If you, my lady, day by day deny*
> *Possession of love's guerdon till I die,*
> *The lease on life you give me is too long.*

CATALINÓN. To which of all the ladies tricked by you
   Do they refer?
DON JUAN.   I scorn them all, my friends,
   On this occasion; why at Naples Isabel . . .
CATALINÓN. She, sir, is not deceived today, since you
   Will marry her, and rightly, but you tricked
   The fisher maid who saved you from the sea,
   And gave her sorry treatment for her pains.
   You cheated Doña Ana . . .
DON JUAN.   Hush, here's one
   Who for her paid the penalty, and now
   Awaits his turn for vengeance.
CATALINÓN.   He's a man
   Of mighty valor, and as he is made
   Of stone, and you of flesh, I like it not.
   (*The statue makes signs for the table to be cleared away
   and for* DON JUAN *and himself to be left alone together.*)
DON JUAN. Now take away the table, since he signs
   For all to go, and leave the two of us.
CATALINÓN. That's bad! For God's sake, sir, you must not
   stay.
   A dead man with one blow could fell a giant.
DON JUAN. Now get out all! . . . Were I Catalinón
   I might turn tail . . . go quick, he's coming near.
   (*The servants all go out, leaving* DON JUAN *and* DON GON-
   ZALO *alone together. The latter signs to* DON JUAN *to close
   the door.*)
DON JUAN. The door is shut and I await your pleasure.
   What do you want, you shade, phantom or ghost?
   If like a lost soul you're in pain, or if
   You seek some satisfaction or release,
   Do tell me and I'll give my word to do
   Whatever you command me. Are you in
   God's grace, or did I slay you when you were
   In mortal sin. Speak. I am anxious.
   (*The statue speaking slowly, as if from another world.*)
DON GONZALO. As a gentleman, then, will you keep your
   word?
DON JUAN. I am a man of honor, and I keep
   My word because I am a knight.
DON GONZALO.   Give me

Your hand, don't be afraid!

DON JUAN. What! I afraid?
If you were hell itself my hand I'd give.
(*He gives his hand.*)

DON GONZALO. Now by my hand and voice, tomorrow night
At ten o'clock I'll be awaiting you
For supper, will you come?

DON JUAN. I expected more.
Tomorrow I shall be your guest, but where
Am I to go?

DON GONZALO. To my own private chapel.

DON JUAN. Shall I go alone?

DON GONZALO. No, both of you, and keep
Your word as I have kept my word to you.

DON JUAN. By my troth I'll keep it, I'm Tenorio.

DON GONZALO. And I, Ulloa.

DON JUAN. I shall surely go.

DON GONZALO. I'll take your word. Farewell.
(*He goes toward the door.*) Farewell.

DON JUAN. Wait! I shall light you.

DON GONZALO. My soul needs no light,
As I'm in grace.
(*He walks out very slowly, gazing at* DON JUAN, *until he
disappears, leaving* DON JUAN *panic-stricken.*)

DON JUAN. God save my soul, my body's bathed in sweat!
My very heart now turns to ice within,
For when he took my hand within his grip,
So tightly did he squeeze it that I thought
I was in Hell. Never did I ever feel
Such heat. Yet when he spoke his voice and breath
Were like an icy blast from the abyss.
All such strange things do rage and multiply
Within our minds when we are sore afraid;
They're quite unreal, and to fear the dead
Is to possess a vile and caitiff soul.
If I am not afraid of living bodies
In the prime of life, with soul and wits aglow,
Why should I dream of fearing a mere corpse?
Tomorrow then I'll hie me to the chapel
Where it invited me, that all Seville
May celebrate, yet tremble at my valor. (*Exit.*)

(*The Alcázar at Seville. Enter the* KING OF CASTILE, DON DIEGO
TENORIO *and their suite.*)

KING. Has Isabel at last arrived?

DON DIEGO.   She is not pleased.

KING. Why? Does she not approve this match?

DON DIEGO.   She weeps,
   For her good name she lost.

KING.   But there must be
   Another reason why she is so sad.
   Where is she now?

DON DIEGO.   She lodges in a convent
   With the discalced nuns.

KING.   Then do bring her here.
   I want her at Court to assist the Queen.

DON DIEGO. If she Don Juan must marry, pray command
   That he appear before Your Majesty.

KING. Let him come here as gallant and betrothed,
   For I wish this to be widely known in Spain,
   That from today Don Juan Tenorio
   Is the Count of Lebrija, and it is his
   To hold and to possess with all its lands.
   If Isabel has lost a duke, at least
   She has won a count.

DON DIEGO.   For this great favor, Sire,
   I do obeisance.

KING.   You have deserved
   My favors richly, and I still do owe
   Greater rewards to you. Likewise today,
   Don Diego, we shall celebrate the match
   Of Doña Ana.

DON DIEGO.   With the Duke Octavio?

KING. It is not right that Duke Octavio
   Should be the one to vindicate her name.
   The Queen and Doña Ana now beseech
   That I should spare the Marquis' life, and since
   Her father's dead she does desire a husband.
   So if she lost the one she wins the other.
   Go now in secret to Triana first,
   And tell the Marquis I have pardoned him—
   For his injured cousin's sake.

DON DIEGO.   I behold

What most I have desired.

KING.   The marriage
Will take place tonight.

DON DIEGO.   All's well that ends well.
It will be easy to persuade the Marquis
That he is still enamored of his cousin.

KING. It would be wise as well to warn Octavio,
For the Duke with women always is unlucky,
And in his eyes they only represent
Good name and show. But I have heard it said
That he is very angry with Don Juan.

DON DIEGO. I'm not amazed, if he found out the hoax
That Don Juan played upon him and which caused
So much misfortune to us all. Here comes
The Duke himself.

KING.   Now do not leave my side.
You, too, are implicated in this crime.

(*Enter* OCTAVIO.)

OCTAVIO. Let me now bow before Your Majesty.

KING. Rise, Duke, put on your hat, what is your wish?

OCTAVIO. At your feet, Sire, I come to ask a favor,
One that is just and worthy to be granted.

KING. Provided it is just I swear to grant it.
What is it?

OCTAVIO.   Sire, in dispatches you have been informed
By your ambassador, and all the world,
Through idle rumor knows it, how Don Juan,
With Spanish arrogance in Naples did
One night—a bitter one for me—profane
A noble lady's sacred purity.

KING. Proceed not further, I know. What's your plea?

OCTAVIO. That you allow me fight him in the field,
For he's a traitor.

DON DIEGO.   No, his blood's too noble!

KING. Don Diego!

DON DIEGO.   Sire.

OCTAVIO.   Who are you who dare speak
Before His Majesty in such a way?

DON DIEGO. I'm one who's silent when the King commands,
Else would this sword of mine reply to you.

OCTAVIO. You are old.

DON DIEGO.   I once was young in Italy,
  And Naples and Milan have known my sword.
OCTAVIO. Your blood is frozen. I've not been, I am.
DON DIEGO. Well, I have been and I am.
  (*He puts hand to his sword.*)
KING.   Restrain yourselves!
  That is enough! Be silent, Don Diego.
  To my person you have shown disrespect.
  With you, Duke, when these weddings have been held,
  We'll talk about this matter at our ease.
  Don Juan is Lord of the Bedchamber and
  My man, and chip off this most ancient block,
  Mind you respect him.
  (*He points to* DON DIEGO.)
OCTAVIO.   I shall obey you, Sire.
KING. Don Diego, come with me.
DON DIEGO (*aside*). Alas, my son, with what ingratitude
  You have repaid my love.
KING.   Duke.
OCTAVIO.   My Liege.
KING. Your marriage will take place tomorrow.
OCTAVIO.   Sire,
  Let it take place then since it is your will.
                          (*Exit the* KING, DON DIEGO *and the suite.*)
  (*Enter* GASENO *and* AMINTA.)
GASENO. This lord perhaps will tell us where we'll find
  Don Juan Tenorio. My Lord, is there
  A certain Juan Tenorio, whose name must be
  Well known in these parts?
OCTAVIO.   Do you mean
  Don Juan Tenorio?
GASENO.   Yes, sir, Don Juan.
OCTAVIO. Yes, he is here: what do you want with him?
AMINTA. That young man is my bridegroom.
OCTAVIO.   How is that?
AMINTA. It's strange if you don't know that, being of
  The royal palace?
OCTAVIO.   Don Juan never told me.
GASENO. Can this be possible?
OCTAVIO.   It must be so.
GASENO. Countess Aminta's all a girl should be;

She comes of a God-fearing stock, and is
Stanch Christian to her marrow bones,
And the dowry she possesses from the farm
Makes her a fitter bride for count than marquis.
Don Juan took her from her Batricio,
And was betrothed to her.

AMINTA.   Why don't you say
That I was still a virgin when he took me?

GASENO. We're not in court and putting our own case.

OCTAVIO (*aside*). This must be another foul hoax of Don
    Juan
Which these good folk are blurting out to me,
Perchance it will help me to avenge myself.

GASENO. I'd like to see them safely wedded, as
The days are passing, otherwise I'll put
My case before the King.

OCTAVIO.   And you are right.

GASENO. Just reason and the law is all I want.

OCTAVIO (*aside*). I've now a chance that tallies with my
    thoughts.
    (*Aloud:*)
Today there is a wedding in the palace.

AMINTA. It must be mine!

OCTAVIO (*aside*).   I'll have to try a plan.
    (*Aloud:*)
Now come with me, señora, where you'll dress
In courtly robes, and then I'll introduce you
Into the King's apartment.

AMINTA.   By the hand
You'll lead me to Don Juan?

OCTAVIO.   This is the wisest course.

GASENO. Your plan comforts me.

OCTAVIO (*aside*).   So these worthy people
Will aid me to revenge myself against
That traitor Don Juan and the wrong he did
To Isabel.
    (*A street with a side view of the church where the* CO-
    MENDADOR *is buried. Enter* DON JUAN *and* CATALINÓN.)

CATALINÓN. How did the King receive you?

DON JUAN.   With more love
Than my father.

CATALINÓN.   Did you see Isabel?

DON JUAN. Also.

CATALINÓN.   How is she?

DON JUAN.   Like an angel.

CATALINÓN. Did she receive you well?

DON JUAN. Her lovely face grew pale and blushed by turns,
  Just as the snow-white rose at dawn
  Breaks through her prison to salute the sun.

CATALINÓN. So at last the weddings will take place tonight?

DON JUAN. Without fail.

CATALINÓN. Had they been held before, my Lord, you would
  Not have deceived so many, but you now
  Are marrying a wife with heavy charges.

DON JUAN. Do you wish to play the fool?

CATALINÓN.   You would be wise
  To wait until tomorrow, as today
  Brings bad luck.

DON JUAN.   What's the day?

CATALINÓN.   It is Tuesday.

DON JUAN. A thousand rogues and imbeciles go in
  For all such follies, but the only day
  I count unlucky and unprofitable
  Is when I'm short of cash. The other days
  I spend in laughter and in revelry.

CATALINÓN. Let us be off, it's late and you must dress,
  They're waiting for you in the palace now.

DON JUAN. Although we'll keep them waiting, near at hand
  There is another business to do.

CATALINÓN. What is that?

DON JUAN.   To sup with the corpse.

CATALINÓN.   What folly!

DON JUAN. Don't you know well I gave my solemn word.

CATALINÓN. But even if you broke your word, what odds?
  Why should a jasper statue demand an oath?

DON JUAN. The dead man could then say I was a coward.

CATALINÓN. But now the church is closed.

DON JUAN.   Knock loudly then.

CATALINÓN. The sacristans are sleeping: who will open?

DON JUAN. Knock at this side door.

CATALINÓN.   It's open.

DON JUAN.   Go in.

CATALINÓN. I'd sooner it were a monk with holy water.

DON JUAN. Now follow me and hold your tongue.

CATALINÓN. My tongue?

DON JUAN. Yes.

CATALINÓN. From all such feasts may God deliver me.

> (*They go in through one door and come out through another.*)

> (*The interior of the church. Enter* DON JUAN *and* CATALINÓN.)

CATALINÓN. How dark it is for such an enormous church.

Oh, sir, help! they're pulling me by my cloak.

> (*Enter* DON GONZALO, *as before, in the form of a statue.*)

DON JUAN. Who's there?

DON GONZALO. It is I.

CATALINÓN. I'm half dead with fear.

DON GONZALO. I am the Dead Man, don't be terrified.

I did not think that you would keep your word,

Since your pastime in life is hoaxing others.

DON JUAN. You then consider that I am a coward?

DON GONZALO. I do because that night you took to flight

When you had killed me.

DON JUAN. I fled to avoid

Being recognized, but here I stand before you.

Tell me at once what I have got to do.

DON GONZALO. I want you to have supper with me now.

CATALINÓN. We shall dispense with supper by your leave,

As cold meat must be all they ever serve,

And I don't see a kitchen anywhere.

DON JUAN. Let us sup then.

DON GONZALO. To do so you must lift

The lid off this tomb.

DON JUAN. If you ask for it,

I shall lift these pillars too.

DON GONZALO. You are brave.

DON JUAN (*Lifting one end of the tomb which folds back easily, showing a black table already laid*).

I still have strength and courage in my body.

CATALINÓN. This black table's from Guinea: are there none

To wash it?

DON GONZALO. Do be seated.

DON JUAN. Where?

CATALINÓN. Here come two coal black pages with the seats.
  (*Enter two figures in black with stools.*)
  So here they wear mourning and flannel made
  In Flanders.
DON GONZALO. Do be seated.
CATALINÓN.   Master, sir!
  I have already fed this evening.
DON GONZALO. Don't answer back.
CATALINÓN.   I do not answer you.
  (*Aside:*)
  God get me safely out of this in peace!
  (*Aloud:*)
  What dish is this, sir?
DON GONZALO.   Of scorpions and vipers.
CATALINÓN. How tasty!
DON GONZALO.   Such is our diet here. Won't you try
  it?
DON JUAN. Even if you gave me Hell's snakes I'd eat them.
DON GONZALO. I'd like to have the choir here sing for you.
CATALINÓN. What wine do they drink in this place?
DON GONZALO.   Try some.
CATALINÓN. It's vinegar and gall.
DON GONZALO.   We press it here.
  (*Singing offstage:*)

> Let all who meditate upon the ways
> Of God and His great punishments be warned,
> That there's no date but one day shall expire,
> No debt but has one day to be repaid.

CATALINÓN. How grim this sounds, but by the living Christ
  I understand the song: it speaks of us.
DON JUAN (*aside*). A block of ice has torn my breast asunder.
  (*Singing offstage:*)

> While in this world we live it's wrong to say;
> "My credit's large and I have time to spare."
> For very soon the hour for payment comes.

CATALINÓN. What's in this ragout, do tell me?
DON GONZALO.   Nails.
CATALINÓN. It must be fingernails of tailors then.
DON JUAN. Now I've supped, let them clear away the table.

DON GONZALO. Give me your hand—don't be alarmed—your
   hand.
DON JUAN (*he gives it*). Alarmed you say; I, alarmed? Here
   is my hand.
   I'm burning! Don't consume me with your fire.
DON GONZALO. It's nothing to the fire you sought yourself.
   God's wondrous ways, Juan, we can never fathom.
   And so He has decreed that you should pay
   The forfeit for your crimes into the hands
   Of one who's dead. This is God's justice, Juan.
   What ever man soweth, that shall he reap.
DON JUAN. I'm burning! Do not grip my hand so hard!
   I'll kill you with my dagger, but alas,
   In vain I weary, piercing empty air:
   Your daughter never was dishonored.
   She discovered how I had tricked her just in time.
DON GONZALO. That does not matter: your intention counts.
DON JUAN. Then let me call a priest to whom I may
   Confess my sins and purge them ere I die.
DON GONZALO. There is no way. You've thought of it too late.
DON JUAN. Oh, I am burning! Oh, I am consumed!
   I'm dying!   (*He falls dead.*)
CATALINÓN. There is not one who escapes.
   I, too must die to keep you company.
DON GONZALO. Such is God's justice: What a man has sowed
   That shall he reap.
   (*The tomb sinks with* DON JUAN *and* DON GONZALO, *amidst
   rumbling thunder.* CATALINÓN *extricates himself from the
   ruins.*)
CATALINÓN. God help me! Now the chapel's all on fire,
   And I am left alone to watch the corpse,
   And guard it, but I'll try to wriggle out,
   And sneak off to his father with the news.
   St. George and Holy Lamb of God, I pray,
   Let me in peace but reach the street alive.
   (*The Alcázar. Enter the* KING OF CASTILE, DON DIEGO
   TENORIO, *courtiers and attendants.*)
DON DIEGO. The Marquis, Sire, desires to bow the knee.
KING. Then let him enter: call the Count as well,
   I mean Don Juan Tenorio, that he
   Be kept no longer waiting.

(*Enter* BATRICIO *and* GASENO.)

BATRICIO. Why, Sire, are such delinquencies allowed,
    That even your servants deride the poor?
KING. What's that?
BATRICIO. Perfidious, detestable Don Juan
    The evening of our marriage stole away
    My young wife ere our bond was consummated:
    Here are my witnesses.
    (*Enter* THISBE *and* ISABEL.)
THISBE.   If you, Sire, now
    Deny me justice against Don Juan Tenorio
    I'll cry to God for vengeance all my days.
    When he was swept ashore at point of death,
    I gave him life and hospitality.
    But he requited all with lust and lies,
    And promises of marriage, and then fled.
KING. What do you say?
ISABEL.   All she has said is true.
    (*Enter* AMINTA *and the* DUKE OCTAVIO.)
AMINTA. Where is my husband?
KING.   Who is he?
AMINTA.   You don't
    Know even yet? Don Juan Tenorio,
    With whom I've come this evening to be
    His bride, for he owes me my honor, and
    Being noble he will not deny his word.
    Give orders, Sire, that we be wedded now.
    (*Enter the* MARQUIS OF LA MOTA.)
MARQUIS. It is high time, Your Majesty, to drag
    Some truths into the light of day: know then
    That Don Juan did commit the very crime
    For which Your Royal Highness sentenced me.
    False friend he was and cruel was his hoax.
KING. Could shamelessness be greater? Seize him now
    And have him executed later.
DON DIEGO.   Sire,
    In return for all my services let him
    Be arrested and compelled to expiate
    His foul crimes, so that Heaven itself on high
    May not hurl thunderbolts upon my head,
    Because I did beget so foul a son.

KING. So this is how my favorites behave!
  (*Enter* CATALINÓN.)
CATALINÓN. My lords, all hearken to the greatest marvel
  That ever happened in this world of ours,
  And slay me if what I say is not true.
  Don Juan, one afternoon, when making fun
  Of the Comendador, after he robbed him
  Of life and honor and of everything
  That makes a life worth living, pulled the beard
  Of the statue and with outrageous jibe,
  Invited him to dine. Ill omened was
  That invitation, for the statue came
  To dine with him, and asked him in return;
  And then (to cut the story short) when they
  Had finished supper, took his hand in his
  And squeezed until he took away his life,
  Saying: "God orders me to kill you thus,
  And punish all your crimes. So what a man
  Has sowed that shall he reap."
KING. What do you say?
CATALINÓN.   It is the honest truth.
  Don Juan dying said Doña Ana's honor
  Was spotless, for she found the hoax in time.
MARQUIS. For your good news I'll give you a thousand gifts.
KING. Just punishment from Heaven has descended.
  Now let them all be married, since the cause
  Of all their miseries has passed away.
OCTAVIO. As Isabel's a widow I desire
  To marry her.
MARQUIS.   And I shall wed my cousin.
BATRICIO. And we shall all of us wed our own girls,
  For now the Guest of Stone is ended.
KING.   Let
  The tomb now be transferred to San Francisco,
  Madrid's great church, where these events may be
  Remembered for all time.

THE
MAYOR
OF
ZALAMEA

❦

Comedia
in Three Acts
by
PEDRO CALDERÓN
DE LA BARCA
(1600-1681)

❦

◆§ DRAMATIS PERSONAE §◆

King Philip II
Don Lope de Figueroa
Don Alvaro de Ataide, captain
Pedro Crespo, a farmer of Zalamea
Juan, his son
Isabel, his daughter
Inés, his niece
Don Mendo, a poor nobleman
Nuño, his servant
A clerk of the court
Rebolledo, a soldier
Chispa, his mistress
A sergeant, soldiers, farmers, a drummer, royal suite, etc.

TIME: the sixteenth century. The events of the play have to do with the invasion of Portugal by Philip II in 1580. The scene is laid at Zalamea, and its neighborhood, in the province of Estremadura in southwestern Spain, seventy-four miles from Badajoz.

The texts of *The Mayor of Zalamea* which we have used are those of Max Krenkel in Vol. III of the *Klassische Bühnendichtungen der Spanier*, Leipzig, Barth, 1887, and of Hartzenburch, Vol. XII of the *Biblioteca de Autores Españoles*, 1848-1863.

ACT I.

Country near Zalamea. Enter REBOLLEDO, CHISPA *and soldiers.*

REBOLLEDO. God blast these forced marches from place to place without even wetting one's whistle!

ALL. Amen!

REBOLLEDO. Are we raggle-taggle Gypsies that we have to go careering about the country like this, trudging after a furled flag and a drummer boy . . .

FIRST SOLDIER. At it again?

REBOLLEDO. At last there's silence, and that accursed drum has stopped its deafening din.

SECOND SOLDIER. Cheer up, Rebolledo, don't be downhearted; we'll soon reach the village and you'll see how soon you'll forget your fatigue.

REBOLLEDO. What odds if I'm dead beat this moment? Even if I'm alive when we get there, God knows if they'll billet us. I bet you the mayors will besiege the quartermaster, saying that it were best for the men to push on further, and they'll give the needful palm grease. The quartermaster's sure to reply that there's nothing doing as the men are dead beat. But if there's any cash in the municipal court he'll say: "Gentlemen, orders have just come that we mustn't halt here, so march on right away!" And so we wretched blighters without more ado obey the order, which is as profitable for him as a sleek monastic order, and as beggarly for me as a ragged order of friars-errant. But I swear to God that if I reach Zalamea alive, and they try by fair means or foul to move us on, they'll march without me: it will not be the first time in my life I've given them the slip and deserted the ranks.

FIRST SOLDIER. It's not the first time either that a poor devil of a soldier has lost his life for doing so; especially today when I know that Don Lope de Figueroa has assumed command, a man reputed to be as brave and lion-hearted as they make 'em, but as merciless a fiend, and as great a blasphemer as could be found in the wide world, one who'd condemn his dearest friend to death without troubling to inquire too closely into the case.

REBOLLEDO. Have you heard what he says, gentlemen? Well, I'll do what I say.

SECOND SOLDIER. Fancy a soldier making such a boast.

REBOLLEDO. I'm not worried about myself, but I'm sorry for that poor little girl who has come along with my estimable self.

CHISPA. Señor Rebolledo, don't be fretting on my behalf: I'd have you remember I was born with a beard on my heart instead of on my chin, and girlish fears I consider a blot on my escutcheon. I've come with you on active service, ready to toil and moil for honor's sake. To tell the truth, if I had only thought of living in clover I'd never have left the Alderman's house, who had lashings of everything, I tell you; why every month they handed out presents galore; and there are aldermen who give a free lunch in addition to the month's pay. Well, I decided to say farewell to all that and come here to march and suffer with Rebolledo, but without being a burden to him. Why hesitate now and wonder what to do?

REBOLLEDO. Heaven be praised: you're a paragon of women!

SECOND SOLDIER. That's only too true. Long live Chispa!

REBOLLEDO. Hurrah for Chispa! And hurrah again if only she sings a ditty or ballad to clear the air and charm away all our weariness after marching up hill and down dale.

CHISPA. Now my castanets are summoned, let them answer that petition.

REBOLLEDO. I'll lend a hand, too. Now that all have been summoned, let my comrades pass sentence.

FIRST SOLDIER. God's truth, they have approved with acclamation.

(REBOLLEDO *and* CHISPA *sing.*)

CHISPA.

> *I am titiri, titiri, tina,*
> *I'm the flower of rascally song.*

REBOLLEDO.

> *I am titiri, titiri, tina,*
> *I'm the flower of rascally song.*

CHISPA.

> *Let the ensign go off to the war,*

> *And the captain embark as well.*

REBOLLEDO.
> *Kill Moors by the hundred if that's what you wish,*
> *But I know they've never done me any harm.*

CHISPA.
> *Be off now, and let them draw up the breadboard*
> *To the oven and bake till I've eaten my fill.*

REBOLLEDO.
> *Come now, my hostess, kill a fine fat hen*
> *For a surfeit of mutton is hard on the men.*[1]

FIRST SOLDIER. Stop a moment, comrades: so charmed were our ears that I'm sorry to see yonder church tower, for surely that is where we are to halt.

REBOLLEDO. Is that Zalamea?

CHISPA. I know it by its belfry. No need to be sorry the song should end: you'll have plenty of opportunities for enjoying my singing; that is my enjoyment; other women weep for a mere trifle, but I sing for a mere trifle, and you'll hear me sing a hundred ballads.

REBOLLEDO. Let us halt here, for we'd better wait until the sergeant comes with the order which will decide whether we have to march into the village or break ranks.

SECOND SOLDIER. Here he is coming alone; but the Captain too is waiting.

(*Enter the* CAPTAIN *and* SERGEANT.)

CAPTAIN. I've good news for you, gentlemen; we're not leaving this village, and we shall be billeted here until Don Lope arrives with the troops left behind at Llerena. Today an order came for all preparations to be made, and we are not to leave for Guadalupe until the whole regiment is here, and he will come later. You may all, therefore, have a few days rest.

REBOLLEDO. You certainly deserve a reward for your good news.

ALL. Hurrah for our captain!

CAPTAIN. Your quarters are ready, and the quartermaster will give out the lodging tickets when they turn up to receive them.

---

[1] This refrain, which is repeated several times, foreshadows the denouement of the play.

CHISPA. Today I intend to find out why in heaven's name he
    sang that rogues ballad:

> Come now, my hostess, kill a fine fat hen,
> For a surfeit of mutton is hard on the men. (*Exeunt.*)

(*A street. Enter the* CAPTAIN *and* SERGEANT.)

CAPTAIN. Well, sergeant, have you the lodging tickets re-
    served for me?

SERGEANT. Yes, sir.

CAPTAIN. And where am I to stay?

SERGEANT. In the house of the wealthiest man in Zalamea,
    a farmer who, they say, is the haughtiest man in the world,
    and has more pomp and circumstance about him than an
    Infante of León.

CAPTAIN. It is natural for a rich peasant to be vain.

SERGEANT. They say his is the best house in the village, and
    to tell the truth, I chose it for you, not because it is the
    best, but because in Zalamea there is no prettier girl . . .

CAPTAIN. Speak.

SERGEANT. Than his daughter.

CAPTAIN. Pooh, no matter how pretty or how vain she may
    be, surely she must be a mere peasant wench with ugly
    hands and feet?

SERGEANT. Fancy anybody in the world saying the like of
    that!

CAPTAIN. Who would say the contrary, blockhead?

SERGEANT. What pleasanter pastime in the world is there
    than to toy with a country lass, when love is not an obliga-
    tion, and it is just to while the time away and observe how
    she never manages to give a timely answer?

CAPTAIN. Well, that is something that never in my life ap-
    pealed to me, not even temporarily; for if I note that a
    woman is not elegant and well dressed, she is not the
    woman for me.

SERGEANT. Well, sir, she'd do me, aye, and so would any
    doxy who is ready for a lark. Let us go there; by God,
    I'll have a fling at her myself then.

CAPTAIN. Do you know which of the two is right? He who
    adores a beauty and says when he sees his love: "That is
    my lady," and not, "that is my country lass"? If the woman

we love is called lady, it is then obvious that in the case of a country lass the name lady is unsuitable. What noise is that?

SERGEANT. A man who has dismounted from a lean horse at the corner of the street yonder. In face and figure he's the dead image of Don Quixote, whose adventures Miguel de Cervantes wrote.

CAPTAIN. What a freak!

SERGEANT. Let us go, sir; it is time.

CAPTAIN. Take my kit first to my lodgings and come back to report to me. (*Exeunt.*)

(*Enter* DON MENDO *and* NUÑO.)

DON MENDO. Here is the dappled horse?

NUÑO. He's more dun[2] than dappled: why he can't move a leg.

DON MENDO. Did you tell the lackey to walk him up and down for a while?

NUÑO. Fine fodder that for the poor beast!

DON MENDO. Nothing is so restful for an animal.

NUÑO. I pin my faith on fodder.

DON MENDO. Did you say that the greyhounds were not to be tied up?

NUÑO. They'll rejoice, but not the butcher.

DON MENDO. Enough: well, as it has struck three I'll stick my toothpick in my hat and put on my gloves.[3]

NUÑO. Suppose they think your toothpick is false?

DON MENDO. If any man dares as much as to insinuate that I have not dined on pheasant, he lies in his inwards and I'll sustain that here and everywhere.

NUÑO. Wouldn't it be better to sustain me than that other man, for after all I serve you?

DON MENDO. What foolish words! But tell me, haven't the soldiers arrived in Zalamea this afternoon?

NUÑO. Yes, sir.

DON MENDO. I feel sorry for the peasantry and villagers when I think of the guests they are expecting.

2 Play on words. *Rodado* means "spotted brown," or "dun," and "done."

3 In the seventeenth century a Spanish dandy wore his toothpick in his hat.

NUÑO. I'm sorrier, far sorrier for those they don't expect . . .

DON MENDO. Whom?

NUÑO. The nobles; don't be alarmed; do you, sir, know the reason why nobody is billeted in the houses of the nobility?

DON MENDO. Why?

NUÑO. For fear they may die of hunger.

DON MENDO. God rest my worthy lord and father's soul in peace, for leaving me so great a patent of nobility, all blazon'd azure and gold, and exemption for my lineage.

NUÑO. I'd have preferred if he had left a little of the gold apart.

DON MENDO. Though now, when I come to think of it, if the truth must be told, I have no cause to thank him for having begotten me noble, for I would never have let myself be begotten on any account except as a noble.

NUÑO. How could you have helped it?

DON MENDO. On the contrary, very easy.

NUÑO. How so, sir?

DON MENDO. You of course are ignorant of philosophy, and so you don't know the principles.

NUÑO. Yes, sir, I do: I've learnt the first course and the dessert since I have been dining with you; and at this very moment yours is a divine table, without beginning, middle, or end.

DON MENDO. I don't mean those principles. You must know that he who is born is the essence of the food which his parents have eaten.

NUÑO. Did your parents then eat? you, at any rate did not inherit that knack.

DON MENDO. Afterwards this is converted into flesh and blood. Thus if my father had eaten onions, he would straightway have begotten me with a stinking breath, and I should have said: "Take care, it is not right to fashion me from such nasty filth."

NUÑO. Now I see the old proverb is true.

DON MENDO. What?

NUÑO. That hunger sharpens the wits.

DON MENDO. You imbecile, am I hungry?

NUÑO. Don't lose your temper; if you're not hungry, you may be, for it is already three o'clock in the afternoon, and there's no clay that more completely removes stains than your saliva and mine.[4]

DON MENDO. Is that a sufficient reason why I should go hungry too? Let the clodhoppers be hungry; we are not all alike, and a nobleman is not obliged to eat.

NUÑO. I wish I were a nobleman!

DON MENDO. No more of this; we are now entering Isabel's street.

NUÑO. If you're so stanch and faithful a lover of Isabel, why don't you ask her father for her hand in marriage? If you do that, you and he will at once solve all your difficulties; you'll eat and he'll make his grandchildren noblemen.

DON MENDO. No more, Nuño; hold your tongue. Do you think that just for money I would debase myself by accepting a mere plebeian as father-in-law?

NUÑO. Well, I used to think that it was important to have a plain man as father-in-law, but they say there are other pitfalls that trip up sons-in-law. Well then, if you are not going to get married, why do you make such a show of your infatuation?

DON MENDO. Without my marrying the girl is there not that abode of peace, the convent of Las Huelgas at Burgos, where I may take her, in case I get really displeased with her? Watch if you can see her.

NUÑO. I'm afraid, if Pedro Crespo catches sight of me . . .

DON MENDO. What harm can anyone do to you who are my servant? Do what your master orders you to do.

NUÑO. I'll do his bidding, even if I don't sit down to eat with him.[5]

DON MENDO. Servants and squires are chock-full of proverbs and pretexts.

NUÑO. Good news! she appears at the window with her cousin Inés.

DON MENDO. Lo! in the beauteous East, crowned with diamonds, the sun doth echo itself and dawneth in the afternoon.

[4] The ancients believed that the saliva of one who had fasted possessed magic properties.

[5] A reference to the proverb "Do your master's bidding and sit down beside him at table," quoted by Sancho Panza in *Don Quixote*, Part II, Chapter 29.

(ISABEL *and* INÉS *at a window.*)

INÉS. Look out of this window, cousin, so may God protect you; you'll see the soldiers entering the village.

ISABEL. Don't ask me to stand at the window while that man is in the street, Inés; you know how I loathe the very sight of him.

INÉS. He certainly has developed a remarkable craze with his courting and wooing antics.

ISABEL. I wish he'd spare himself and me the trouble.

INÉS. I think you're foolish to take it so to heart.

ISABEL. What am I to do?

INÉS. Laugh at him.

ISABEL. Bitter is the laughter that comes from displeasure.

DON MENDO (*below the window*). Up to this very instant I could have sworn on the word of a nobleman (which is an inviolable oath) that day had not yet dawned; but however strange this may seem it has not occurred until now, when a second day comes with your dawn.

ISABEL. I have told you many times, Señor Mendo, that you waste your time with your love declarations and the foolish antics you make every day before my window.

DON MENDO. If only pretty women knew how much their beauty is enhanced by anger, scorn and indignation they would wear no other face paint than indignation. Go on, my lovely one, grow angrier and lovelier, I do entreat you.

ISABEL. Even if my angry words serve but to little purpose, Don Mendo, at least let my actions prevail on this occasion. Inés, go in and slam the window in his face. (*Exit.*)

INÉS. You, sir knight-errant, who are forever entering such jousts as champion, will find it no easy task to face a challenger.[6] Adieu! May love provide for you. (*She slams the window. Exit.*)

DON MENDO. Inés, it is ever beauty's privilege to have the last word. Nuño! Humiliation, alas, is the lot of all who are born poor!

(*Enter* PEDRO CRESPO.)

PEDRO CRESPO (*aside*). I can never go in and out of my

[6] All through this scene Don Mendo suggests the vision of Don Quixote, and the terms of knight-errantry are used. Inés, however, uses *aventurero* ironically in its secondary sense of "worthless upstart."

street without seeing that solemn-faced squireen strutting
up and down.

NUÑO (*aside to his master*). Here's Pedro Crespo, sir, let us
turn aside; he's an ill-conditioned fellow.

(*Enter* JUAN CRESPO.)

JUAN (*aside*). Whenever I come home I find this ghost
haunting my doorstep, wearing gloves and hat pulled down
like a swashbuckler.

NUÑO (*aside to his master*). Here comes his son.

DON MENDO. Keep calm; don't become confused.

CRESPO (*aside*). Juanico is here.

JUAN (*aside*). Here is my father.

DON MENDO (*aside to* NUÑO). Dissemble. (*Aloud:*) Pedro
Crespo, God be with you.

CRESPO. God be with you. (*Exeunt* DON MENDO *and* NUÑO.)
(*Aside:*) He has taken it into his head to be stubborn: One
of these days I'll make it hot for him.

JUAN (*aside*). One of these days I'm going to become angry.
(*Aloud:*) From where have you come, father?

CRESPO. From the threshing floors. This afternoon
I went to see my harvesters at work
In the fields where pile after pile of unthrashed grain
Seem from afar to rise like hills of gold,
Aye, gold of many carats, since the Assayer
Is all our heavenly firmament above.
And while the gentle breeze blows o'er the floor
The winnowing flail selects, and on one side
Leaves all the grain, and on the other chaff.
And so even there the humblest path leads on
To what is of greater value: may God grant
I may store this in granaries before
Some fierce tornado scatters them all awry,
Or some tempestuous whirlwind blows them down.[7]
Now come, Juanico, what have you been up to?

JUAN. I scarcely know how to tell you, Father, without
Rousing your indignation. I've played two
Games of pelota this afternoon, and lost
Both of them.

CRESPO.   That's all right if you've paid up.

JUAN. I didn't pay as I had not the money;

[7] Another prophetic hint of the catastrophe in the play.

I've come to ask you, Father . . .

CRESPO.   Listen to me:
There are two things that you must never do:
Never promise what you cannot fulfill,
Never gamble more money than you have in pocket,
Lest, if by chance the money were not there,
Your reputation might thereby be damaged.

JUAN. Your advice is sound, but I must pay you back
In your own coin, so here is another proverb:
"When one in need of money doth beseech
It is not the time to lecture him and preach."

CRESPO. You surely have scored well off me this time! (*Exit.*)
(*The courtyard and portico of* PEDRO CRESPO's *house. Enter
the* SERGEANT.)

SERGEANT. Does Pedro Crespo live here?

CRESPO. Have you any orders for him?

SERGEANT. Yes, I have to bring to his house the kit of Don
Alvaro de Ataide, Captain of the company that has been
billeted in Zalamea this afternoon.

CRESPO. Say no more: my house and all my property is at
God's and His Majesty's service, and that includes the captains who act in their name. Until his room is prepared
leave his kit here, and go tell his Honor to come when he
will, and we shall all be at his service.

SERGEANT. He will be here directly. (*Exit.*)

JUAN. Now that you are well off, Father, why do you submit
to these billetings?

CRESPO. How can I avoid them or get exempted?

JUAN. Simply by buying a patent of nobility. Tell me sincerely, do you think there's a soul who doesn't know that
I'm just a simple farmer, though my stock is untainted? Not
one, I'm sure . . . Now what do I gain by buying a patent
of nobility from the King if I can't buy gentle blood with
it? Will anyone think that I'm more of a gentleman than I
am now? No, it is absurd. What will they say then? That I
am noble because I have paid five or six thousand royals.
That is money but not honor; for nobody can buy honor.
Let me illustrate this by a commonplace instance. A man
who has been bald for untold years decides at last to wear
a wig. Does such a man, in the opinion of ordinary people,

cease to be bald? No, for what do they say as they look at
him? So-and-So knows how to wear his wig. All know that
he wears a wig, even if they don't see his bald pate: what
does he gain thereby?

JUAN. Gain? Why, he relieves his discomfort, banishes his
irritation, and feels no longer the annoyance caused by
sun, ice and wind.

CRESPO. No make-believe honors me. If I had such a defect
I'd stay at home. My grandparents and my parents were
peasants; let my sons remain peasants. Call your sister.

JUAN. She's coming.

(*Enter* ISABEL *and* INÉS.)

CRESPO. My child, the King, our master, God bless him, is
on his way to Lisbon, where he is anxious to be crowned
as legitimate monarch of the country: hence all this military display and marching of troops, and the ancient regi-
ments of Flanders will descend to Castile under the command of Don Lope who, I'm told, is the Spanish Mars.
Today soldiers will arrive at my house, and it is important
that they should not see you: so, my child, you must immediately withdraw to the attic, where I used to have my
quarters.

ISABEL. I was on the point of asking you, Father, to give me
permission to do likewise; I know only too well that if
I remain here below I'll hear nothing but foolish remarks
and nonsense without end. My cousin and I will stay above
in that room, without anyone, even the sun itself, being
any the wiser.

CRESPO. God protect you. Juanico, you stay here, and welcome our guests, while I go and collect the wherewithal
to entertain them. (*Exit.*)

ISABEL. Come, Inés.

INÉS. I think it's foolish to shut a girl up if she herself does
not want to be shut up. (*Exeunt* ISABEL *and* INÉS.)

(*Enter the* CAPTAIN *and the* SERGEANT.)

SERGEANT. Here, sir, is the house.

CAPTAIN. Now bring all my kit from the guardroom.

SERGEANT (*aside to the* CAPTAIN). I want first of all to take
a look at the peasant wench. (*Exit.*)

JUAN. Welcome to this house. We are indeed honored, sir,

in having such a cavalier as yourself for a guest, I assure
you. (*Aside:*) What a dashing fellow! I'm longing to try
on the uniform.

CAPTAIN. I thank you, my lad.

JUAN. You must forgive the lack of comfort. My father
wishes this were a palace to house you. He has gone to
prepare your meal, for he wishes to entertain you. I'll be
off now to make ready your room.

CAPTAIN. I am grateful to you for all your kindness.

JUAN. I'm always at your service, sir. (*Exit.*)

(*Enter the* SERGEANT.)

CAPTAIN. Well, Sergeant, where's the country lass you spoke
of?

SERGEANT. By Heaven, sir, with that object in view I've looked
all over the place, in the kitchen and the parlor and I can't
find her.

CAPTAIN. I'm sure the old clodhopper has hidden her.

SERGEANT. I asked a maidservant, and she told me that her
master had locked the girl up in the attic, forbidding her
to come down here: he's hugely suspicious, she said.

CAPTAIN. Tell me of a clodhopper who isn't suspicious.
Speaking personally, if I saw her before me now, I wouldn't
cast an eye her way. But just because the old fellow has
put her under lock and key I've a longing to catch a
glimpse of her.

SERGEANT. What reason can we give for going in there that
will not rouse suspicions?

CAPTAIN. I've now a craze to see her, so I must find an
excuse.

SERGEANT. The trick needn't be so ingenious, provided you
see the girl, and whatever it is, she'll appreciate it.

CAPTAIN. Pay attention then.

SERGEANT. What is it?

CAPTAIN. You've got to pretend . . . but no, here comes a
soldier who's more wide-awake and will do the job better.

(*Enter* REBOLLEDO *and* CHISPA.)

REBOLLEDO (*to* CHISPA). I'm resolved to speak to the Captain
and try my luck with him.

CHISPA. Then speak out and make him feel he's under an
obligation to you, and that it's not all foolishness and moon-
shine.

REBOLLEDO. Lend me a bit of your common sense.

CHISPA. Such as it is, I wish it would help you.

REBOLLEDO. Wait for me here while I tackle him. (*Coming forward*) Please, your worship . . .

CAPTAIN. I'll do all I can to help Rebolledo, I like his spirit and his liveliness.

SERGEANT. He's a great fighter.

CAPTAIN. Well, what can we give him?

REBOLLEDO (*comes forward*). I have lost all the money I possess, have possessed and ever shall possess, for as a poor man I take the oath in present, past and future tenses, so help me God. Let your worship grant me a trifle towards meeting my expenses, so that this day the Ensign may give me . . .

CAPTAIN. Well, out with it, what's the request?

REBOLLEDO. I want him to give me the management of the game of pigeon holes or troll-madam;[8] for I'm a man of honor, even though I'm laden with debts today.

CAPTAIN. I'm of the opinion that's a fair request, and I'll inform the Ensign that it is granted.

CHISPA (*aside*). Oh, the nice Captain! If I can only hear them all call me Troll-Madam!

REBOLLEDO. I'll go and give him the message then.

CAPTAIN. Wait a moment. I want first of all to trust you with a little scheme I have prepared which I hope will relieve me of anxiety.

REBOLLEDO. Let your worship tell me what's afoot: just say the word and it's as good as done.

CAPTAIN. Listen. I want to get into that attic to see if a certain person is there who is trying to give me the slip.

REBOLLEDO. And why doesn't your worship go up yourself?

CAPTAIN. I don't want to do this in a strange house without a valid excuse. But if you and I pretend to quarrel you can run away from me up there. I'll draw my sword and pursue you in a rage. You in your alarm must break into the room where the person I'm looking for is hiding.

REBOLLEDO. It's all as clear as daylight to me.

CHISPA (*Aside*). The worthy Captain is now so charming to

[8] The most popular soldiers' game was *el boliche*, which was similar to the French *Trou Madame* or the Shakespearean Troll-my-dames (*Winter's Tale*, IV: 2). It was like our bagatelle.

my Rebolledo that they'll all be calling me from today Troll-Madam herself.

REBOLLEDO (*Raising his voice*). By Heaven! those living expenses have been granted to a wretched cowardly robber, and when a man of honor begs for them he is refused!

CHISPA (*Aside*). Ah! the balls are beginning to rattle!

CAPTAIN. Why do you speak to me in that tone?

REBOLLEDO. Why shouldn't I get annoyed? Am I not in my rights?

CAPTAIN. That's not the way to speak to me; be thankful that I tolerate such insolence!

REBOLLEDO. You are my captain: that's my only reason for my forbearance: but God be my witness, if I had my cane in my hand . . .

CAPTAIN (*putting hand to his sword*). What would you do?

CHISPA. Hold, sir. (*Aside.*) He'll kill him.

REBOLLEDO. Change your tone.

CAPTAIN. Why don't I run this insolent rascal through the guts? (*He draws his sword.*)

REBOLLEDO. I only retreat out of respect for your commission.

CAPTAIN. Even if you retreat I'll slay you.

CHISPA. He has made a mess of everything as usual.

SERGEANT. Hold, sir.

CHISPA. Listen.

SERGEANT. Wait.

CHISPA. Now they'll never call me Troll-Madam.

(*Exit the* CAPTAIN *pursuing* REBOLLEDO: *the* SERGEANT *follows the* CAPTAIN. *Enter* JUAN, *sword in hand, followed by his father.*)

CHISPA. Come quickly, all of you.

CRESPO. What has happened?

JUAN. What is up?

CHISPA. The Captain has drawn his sword on a soldier, and is chasing him upstairs.

CRESPO. Is anything more elusive than fortune?

CHISPA. All of you go up after him.

JUAN (*Aside*). It was useless hiding my cousin and my sister. (*Exit.*)

(*The attic of the same house.* REBOLLEDO *runs into* ISABEL *and* INÉS: *later the* CAPTAIN *and the* SERGEANT.)

REBOLLEDO. Ladies, a church has always been considered

sanctuary, so today let this room be sanctuary as it is the abode of love.

ISABEL. Who is pressing you then?

INÉS. Why do you burst in here?

ISABEL. Who is after you?

(*Enter the* CAPTAIN *and the* SERGEANT.)

CAPTAIN. I must slay this rascal: by God, if I thought . . .

ISABEL. Restrain yourselves, if only because this poor man has sought my protection; but men like you are duty-bound to protect women, not for what they are, but as women. Surely being officers you will not deny us such a plea.

CAPTAIN. No other sanctuary but that of your peerless beauty would deliver this man from my fury; for you I would even sacrifice my life. But consider that on such an occasion as this it is not right that you should slay me with your beauty in return for my sparing him the sword.

ISABEL. Good sir, if your graciousness in granting our request makes us for life your debtors, let not your guarantee for his safety so quickly waver: I beseech you let that soldier go free: I would not have you dun me now for payment of a debt which I so gratefuly incurred.

CAPTAIN. Your wit, I see, matches your loveliness, for both combine in perfect harmony. (*He kneels.*)

(*Enter* CRESPO *and* JUAN *with swords drawn, and* CHISPA.)

CRESPO. What means this, sir? I feared I'd find you slaying a man, and now I discover . . .

ISABEL (*Aside*). Heaven protect me!

CRESPO. You courting a woman. Noble you must be, and no mistake, when your rages can so quickly cool away.

CAPTAIN. One who is born with noble obligations must perforce attend to them, and I out of chivalrous respect for this fair lady laid aside my fury.

CRESPO. Isabel is my daughter, a simple farmer's daughter, but no lady.

JUAN (*Aside*). By heaven! It then was all a trick to enter her room! I'm really ashamed that they should imagine they have deceived us. This must not be. (*Aloud:*) I think, sir, you might have shown due appreciation of my father's desire to serve you, instead of giving him such offense.

CRESPO. Who has asked you, young fellow, to meddle in this business? What offense has there been? If the soldier annoyed him, why shouldn't he have pursued him? My daughter is very grateful to you for having pardoned him, and I am, likewise, for your consideration towards her.

CAPTAIN. Naturaly there was no other intention, and you should mind what you say.

JUAN. I know what I'm saying.

CRESPO. Why do you speak thus?

CAPTAIN. It is only because you're here that I don't chastise this youth.

CRESPO. Not so fast, Captain, I may treat my son as I please, but you may not do so.

JUAN. I'll take it from my father, but not from anyone else.

CAPTAIN. What would you do?

JUAN. I'd die rather than lose my good name.

CAPTAIN. What kind of good name has a mere peasant?

JUAN. The same as yours; there would be no captain if there were no farmer.

CAPTAIN. My God! it degrades me to listen to such insolence.

CRESPO. You see I'm standing between both of you. (*They draw swords.*)

REBOLLEDO. Christ Almighty! Chispa, there'll be murder!

CHISPA (*shouting*). Here is the guard!

REBOLLEDO. Don Lope! (*Aside:*) Keep your eyes peeled!
(*Enter* DON LOPE DE FIGUEROA, *elegantly dressed, with a cane, soldiers, and a drummer.*)

DON LOPE. What is all this commotion? Is this what I find today on my arrival? What has happened?

CAPTAIN (*Aside*). What an awkward moment for Don Lope de Figueroa to arrive!

CRESPO (*Aside*). By God, the young fellow held his own with the best of them.

DON LOPE. What's amiss? What has happened? Speak, I say, otherwise I swear to God I'll throw the whole lot of you, men, women and household, into the street. Isn't it bad enough making me climb up here with the pain in my gouty leg—Devil mend it!—instead of saying to me: "This has happened?"

CRESPO. This is nothing, sir.

DON LOPE. Speak, tell the truth.

CAPTAIN. The fact is that I, Don Lope, am quartered in this house: a soldier . . .

DON LOPE. Go on.

CAPTAIN. A soldier's behavior obliged me to draw my sword on him. He fled in here, and I went in after him to where these two farmer's daughters were closeted. Their father and their brother were annoyed that I entered their room.

DON LOPE. I've arrived at the right moment I see, and I'll settle everything this day. Who was the soldier, tell me, who caused his captain to draw his sword?

REBOLLEDO (*Aside*). Am I to be the scapegoat for all?

ISABEL. This was the man that came running in here.

DON LOPE. Give him two turns with the rope.

REBOLLEDO. What kind of turns are they going to give me, sir?

DON LOPE. Turns with the rope.

REBOLLEDO. I'm not the man for such turns.

CHISPA (*Aside*). This time they'll cripple him.

CAPTAIN (*Aside to* REBOLLEDO). I say, Rebolledo, on your life, mum's the word: I'll see you are set free.

REBOLLEDO (*Aside to the* CAPTAIN). How am I to avoid speaking? If I keep silent they'll tie my hands behind me and hoist me on the rope as if I was a bad soldier. (*Aloud:*) The Captain ordered me to sham the quarrel so that he might have an opportunity for coming in here.

CRESPO. Now you see how right we were.

DON LOPE. You certainly weren't right in exposing this village to the danger of total destruction. Hullo there! drummer! Beat all troops to quarters. Let no one leave all day under pain of death. And to relieve you people of this obligation, and you of this annoyance, and to satisfy both parties, do you, Captain, choose other quarters. I'll stop here until we move on to Guadalupe where the King is staying.

CAPTAIN. Your orders, sir, shall be carried out. (*Exeunt the* CAPTAIN, *the soldiers and* CHISPA.)

CRESPO. Go in there. (*Exeunt* ISABEL, INÉS, *and* JUAN.)

CRESPO. I must, sir, offer you my most sincere thanks for preventing me from ruining myself.

DON LOPE. How could you have ruined yourself?

CRESPO. By killing a popinjay who thinks that not even the smallest offense . . .

DON LOPE. My God, do you know he's a captain?

CRESPO. By God, even if he were the general himself and
insulted me, I'd slay him.

DON LOPE. I warn you that if anyone dares touch even the
hem of the garment of one of my private soldiers, by God,
I'll hang him.

CRESPO. And I warn you likewise that if anyone dares poke
his finger at my honor, by God, I too will hang him.

DON LOPE. Are you aware that you are bound by your status
to submit to these obligations?

CRESPO. As far as my property is concerned, yes, but not as
regards my honor. My property and my life are His Majesty's, but my honor is my soul's own patrimony, and that
is God Almighty's.

DON LOPE. I swear to God there's truth in what you say!

CRESPO. I swear to God it is true, for I've always believed
it so.

DON LOPE. I'm weary after my journey, and this leg's the
devil and plagues me with clamors for rest.

CRESPO. And who says nay to that? 'Tis the same devil gave
me a bed on which your leg may rest.

DON LOPE. But tell me, did that same devil make that bed
of yours
As well as give it?

CRESPO.   Of course he did.

DON LOPE. Then I'll unmake it, for, by God, I'm tired.

CRESPO. Then rest, in Heaven's name.

DON LOPE (*aside*).   He's a stubborn cuss
That peasant, and he swears as well as I do.

CRESPO (*aside*). That Don Lope's a crotchety customer.
We'll not break bread in peace together.

ACT II.

A street. Enter DON MENDO *and* NUÑO.

DON MENDO. Who told you all this?

NUÑO. Ginesa, her maidservant.

DON MENDO. So the Captain, you say, after that disturbance
in the house, has fallen in love with Isabel, whether in
earnest or by design?

NUÑO. Aye, and so little time does he spend in his quarters
that he's becoming like ourselves: all the day haunting her
door, sending her messages by the hour through a mean-
eyed little orderly who is his go-between.

DON MENDO. That will do: there's too much gall in all your
news to take in all at once.

NUÑO. Especially when you've no fodder in your belly to
give you strength to resist.

DON MENDO. Do let us talk seriously, Nuño, for once.

NUÑO. Would to heaven it were all in fun!

DON MENDO. And what does Isabel answer?

NUÑO. The same as she does to you. I tell you Isabel is a
goddess, peerless in beauty; her sky's not clouded by
earthy vaporings.

DON MENDO. May God give you some decent news for me.
(*As he utters the exclamation he buffets* NUÑO *in the face.*)

NUÑO. May He give you the toothache, you've broken two
of mine. But you were quite right to try to replace them,
for as a set they're of precious little use to me here. Here's
the Captain.

DON MENDO. By God, if Isabel's honor were not in jeopardy,
I'd slay that Captain.

NUÑO (*aside*). In your brain you'll do the deed.

DON MENDO. I'll hear from within. Here he comes.
(*Enter the* CAPTAIN, *the* SERGEANT, REBOLLEDO. DON MENDO
and NUÑO *are within.*)

CAPTAIN. The passion I feel is not just love, it's an obsession:
it's anger, rage and fury.

REBOLLEDO. I wish, sir, you never had seen that pretty peasant wench who has you so distracted.

CAPTAIN. What did her maid tell you?

REBOLLEDO. Don't you know her answer?

DON MENDO (*Aside to* NUÑO). Now is the moment for it. Since night is already spreading its dark shadows, come and help me arm before discretion counsels a more moderate course.

NUÑO. God save us, sir, what arms have you, save those that are emblazoned on the glazed tile over your door?

DON MENDO. I am sure there is the wherewithal for such affairs of honor in my armory.

NUÑO. Let us be off before the Captain hears us. (*Exeunt.*)

CAPTAIN. Fancy a peasant wench protecting her virtue like a highborn lady! Not one pleasant word did I extract from her.

SERGEANT. That kind of girl, sir, doesn't fancy a gentleman like you. Were a peasant lad to court her she would take notice of him. All the same your complaints are unreasonable. If you have to leave tomorrow, why imagine that a decent girl would look with favor on you after one day's courtship?

CAPTAIN. In a day the sun lights up the world and sets;
In a day an entire kingdom is recast;
In a day a rock becomes an edifice;
In a day a battle's lost, a victory's won;
In a day the sea is calm but storms do rage;
In a day a man is born and breathes his last;
Then surely my love in one day could see,
Like a circling planet, shadow and light at once;
Like an empire, suffering and happiness,
Like a dark forest, both wild beasts and men,
Like the vast ocean, calm and turbulence,
Triumph and ruin, as the grim-faced war,
And life and death, as one who is master
Of all his senses and his faculties:
And since this passion in one day had time
To make me so unhappy, why should it
Not have time in one day to give me joy?
Is it the law of nature that good luck
Should be created slower than ill luck? [9]

[9] The Góngoristic speech of the Captain is a further Calderónian reminiscence of Cervantes, for the same idea is expressed by Sancho Panza in *Don Quixote*, Part II, chapter 19.

SERGEANT. Do you mean to say that one look at the girl
  Can drive you into such a paroxysm?
CAPTAIN. What other cause was there except that I,
  After scheming to see her did then see her?
  Once and for all a tiny spark becomes
  A roaring conflagration, and just once
  A sulphurous volcano may erupt
  Into a yawning abyss of fire; just once
  A ray of lightning sets the heath ablaze;
  Once and for all the oldest blunderbuss
  Spits forth its venom and the victim dies.
  Surely then love, which burns with fourfold fire
  From mine, and conflagration, blunderbuss
  And lightning ray, will once for all erupt,
  Dumbfound, consume and wound, and lay me low?
SERGEANT. Did you not say that peasant girls were ugly?
CAPTAIN. My trusting confidence was my undoing.
  A man who knows a danger looms ahead
  Goes well prepared to make his own defense;
  But he who thinks that he is all secure,
  Runs greater risks when danger faces him,
  Because it comes upon him unawares.
  I expected to find a peasant wench,
  But found instead a peerless goddess here.
  Alas, Rebolledo, what would I give
  To catch a glimpse of Isabel again.
REBOLLEDO. We have a soldier in the company,
  A noted singer, and there is my helpmate
  Chispa, who now presides as Troll-Madam:
  No woman is her equal in street ditties
  Let us, sir, hold a singsong 'neath her window,
  Then you will see the girl and speak to her.
CAPTAIN. Don Lope's a guest; I shouldn't like to wake him.
REBOLLEDO. How can he ever sleep with his wounded leg?
  But if, sir, he ever gets word of it,
  The blame would fall on us, but if well muffled
  You mingle with the troops, you won't be blamed.
CAPTAIN. Were there still greater obstacles, my pangs
  Of love would easily surmount them all.
  Assemble all the men tonight, but do
  Not let them know that I have ordered it.

Isabel, what cares I suffer for your sake! (*Exeunt the* CAP-tain *and the* SERGEANT.)

CHISPA (*from within*). Take that!

REBOLLEDO. Chispa, what's up?

CHISPA. There's a poor devil whose face I've slashed.

REBOLLEDO. What was the quarrel about?

CHISPA. It was over trying to cheat me of my dues for the hour and a half I spent watching him like a hawk, while he was throwing the balls, to see whether his throws were "odds" or "evens." In the end I became wearied and I slashed him with this. (*She pulls out the dagger.*) Now while he's having it out with the barber in points and stitches, let us go to the guardroom and I'll tell you the whole story.

REBOLLEDO. You're a nice one to be cross when I'm out for a spree!

CHISPA. Why should one disturb the other? Here is the castanet: what's to be sung?

REBOLLEDO. That will be after nightfall, and high-class music too. Let us be off, don't delay. The guards are about.

CHISPA. I'll be famous forever all over the world as Little Chispa, the Troll-Madam. (*Exeunt.*)

(*A room in* PEDRO CRESPO's *house which looks on to and communicates with a trellised garden. A window on one side. Enter* DON LOPE *and* CRESPO.)

CRESPO (*from within*). Lay the table for Don Lope in the passage:
  Here, sir, I'm sure, your supper will taste better.
  Indeed, the only saving grace of these
  Hot August days are the cool evenings.

DON LOPE. This is a pleasant and a peaceful nook.

CRESPO. It is a tiny garden, large enough
  For my girl Isabel to play about.
  Pray now be seated and enjoy the calm
  Of this retreat in which the gentle breezes,
  Rustling through boughs and tender-leavéd vines,
  Murmur in rhythm with this fountain's song:
  It is a gittern of silver and of pearls,
  Where pebbles are chords tuned on frets of gold.
  I crave your pardon if our music here
  Be only played on instruments without

The sound of human voices to delight
Your ears, but this is because our minstrel birds,
Who warble sweetly, will not sing at night,
Nor can I force them to perform for me.
There sit you down and ease that lasting pain.

DON LOPE. Alas, I cannot and there's no relief for me, God help me!

CRESPO. I say "Amen" to that.

DON LOPE. Heaven grant me patience: You may sit down, Crespo.

CRESPO. Since you give me permission, sir, I shall. (*He sits down.*) But you might have avoided doing this.

DON LOPE. Do you know, Crespo, I have noticed that your rage yesterday made you beside yourself.

CRESPO. Nothing in the world makes me beside myself.

DON LOPE. Then how comes it that yesterday, without my telling you to sit down, you sat down, and in the biggest armchair there as well.

CRESPO. Because you did not ask me to sit down: now you ask me, I hardly like to do so. I like to be polite to one who treats me with politeness.

DON LOPE. Yesterday you cursed and ranted; you're now in a more tactful mood.

CRESPO. I always answer, sir, in the same tone as I'm spoken to: yesterday you were off-key, so I had to be likewise. For I believe it is the wisest policy to swear with the swearer and to pray with the saint. I'm all things to all men, and on this occasion I must inform you that I could not sleep a wink last night thinking of your leg, with the result that this morning I had a pain in both legs: As I was not sure which one ails you, both hurt me; wherefore tell me, I pray you, which one it is, so that I may only have a pain in one.

DON LOPE. You will agree that I have some justification for my curses, when I tell you that for thirty years, during which I have served in war in Flanders through winter's frost and summer's sun without rest, I have never known what it is to be a single hour without pain.

CRESPO. God grant you resignation to bear it!

DON LOPE. What's the use?

CRESPO. Let Him not grant it then.

DON LOPE. To hell with it! and may two thousand devils take me in tow!

CRESPO. Amen! If they don't it is because you're too good for them!

DON LOPE. Christ Almighty!

CRESPO. I swear to God I'm sorry for you!

(*Enter* JUAN, *who brings the table.*)

JUAN. Here is the table.

DON LOPE. Why are my servants not here to serve me?

CRESPO. With your permission, sir, I took the liberty of telling them not to serve you, for in my house, please God, you shall want for nothing.

DON LOPE. Well, as no servants are to appear, then please allow your daughter to dine with us.

CRESPO. Juan, bid your sister come immediately. (*Exit* JUAN.)

DON LOPE. My poor health, I think, places me beyond suspicion.

CRESPO. Even if your health were as good as I could wish, I should feel no anxiety. You offend my love, for nothing of the kind worries me. I warned my daughter not to enter here, lest she might hear silly nonsense from the soldiers, but if they were as courteous and as chivalrous as you are she would have been the first to serve them.

DON LOPE (*Aside*). How shrewd the old boy is! and how cautious, too.

(*Enter* INÉS, JUAN *and* ISABEL.)

ISABEL. What are your orders, sir?

CRESPO. Don Lope wishes to honor you: it is he who invites you.

ISABEL. Let me serve you, I beg you.

DON LOPE. Nay, I wish you to honor me by being my guest. (*Aside:*) What a comely girl!

ISABEL. We girls should wait on you.

CRESPO. Sit down and do what Don Lope orders.

ISABEL. The merit lies in obedience.

(*They sit down. Guitars are played off-stage.*)

DON LOPE. What is that?

CRESPO. Your soldiers must be singing and dancing in the street.

DON LOPE. The toils of war become a heavy burden without

a little relaxation now and then; a soldier's life, you know, is mighty strict, and one must give free rein.

JUAN. Nevertheless, it is a fine life.

DON LOPE. Would you like to go in for it?

JUAN. Yes, sir, if I might serve under Your Excellency.

(*A soldier is heard from within:* "Better sing from here.")

REBOLLEDO (*within*). Here goes a song to Isabel; to wake her up, throw a pebble at her window. (*Sound of a pebble hitting the window.*)

CRESPO (*Aside*). The music is for a special window: patience. (*A voice sings within.*)

> *Hail, rosemary, you fragrant pledge of Spring,*
> *Today your azure blossoms gaily sing*
> *Love's paean to my fairest Isabel.*
> *Before your blossoms wither, comes the bee*
> *To sip their life, ere it fly away,*
> *And with it fashion in his tiny cell*
> *Love's guerdon for my fairest Isabel.*

DON LOPE (*Aside*). As for music, that will pass; but it is scandalous impudence to throw stones . . . and to go serenading the house where I'm staying . . . Better hide my feelings on account of Pedro Crespo and the girl. (*Aloud:*) What tomfoolery!

CRESPO. They're lads. (*Aside:*) If it were not for Don Lope I'd soon make them . . .

JUAN (*Aside*). If I could only get that old shield which is hanging in Don Lope's room . . . (*He makes for the door.*)

CRESPO. Where are you going to, my boy?

JUAN. I'm going to get them to serve the dinner.

CRESPO. The boys out there will bring it.

(*Soldiers, inside, singing.*)
> *Awaken, Isabel, awaken.*

ISABEL (*Aside*). Heavens above, what have I done to be exposed to such treatment?

DON LOPE. This is intolerable; it is a shame! (*He overturns the table.*)

CRESPO. Well, I should say so! (*He overturns the chair.*)

DON LOPE (*Aside*). My impatience carried me away. (*Aloud:*) Isn't it a shame when one's leg hurts so?

CRESPO. That's what I was saying.

DON LOPE. I thought it was something else, as you overturned the chair . . .

CRESPO. As you overturned the table, I had nothing else to overturn but what was nearest to hand. (*Aside:*) Honor, let us hide our feelings.

DON LOPE (*Aside*). If I were only in the street! (*Aloud:*) Well now I do not want to dine. You may withdraw.

CRESPO. Well and good.

DON LOPE. God be with you, young lady.

ISABEL. Heaven protect you.

DON LOPE (*Aside*). My room is by the door leading into the street, isn't it? And isn't there a shield in it?

CRESPO (*Aside*). The yard has a door hasn't it—and haven't I an old sword somewhere?

DON LOPE. Good night.

CRESPO. Good night. (*Aside:*) I'll shut in my children from the outside.

DON LOPE (*Aside*). I'll wait until the house is quiet.

ISABEL (*Aside*). Heavens! how badly the two of them pretend they are vexed!

INÉS (*Aside*). Each is trying to deceive the other.

CRESPO. Ho there, son!

JUAN. Yes, Father.

CRESPO. Your room is on that side. (*Exeunt.*)

(*The street outside* CRESPO's *house. The* CAPTAIN, *the* SERGEANT, CHISPA, REBOLLEDO *with guitars, soldiers. In one corner* DON MENDO *in old armor, with* NUÑO. *It is dark.*)

REBOLLEDO. Let us stand here: now take your places all of you.

CHISPA. Is the music coming?

REBOLLEDO. Yes.

CHISPA. Now I'm in my element.

CAPTAIN. That wench hasn't opened the window yet!

SERGEANT. They hear all right from within.

CHISPA. Wait.

SERGEANT. I'll pay for it.

REBOLLEDO. Just until I can see who's coming.

CHISPA. Can't you see the armed horseman over there?

ĐON MENDO (*Aside, to* NUÑO). Do you see what's happening?

NUÑO. No, I can't see people, but I can hear.

DON MENDO. Heavens above! who could tolerate this?

NUÑO. I can.

DON MENDO. Do you think Isabel will open the window?

NUÑO. She'll open.

DON MENDO. She won't, clodhopper.

NUÑO. She won't then.

DON MENDO. What cruel pangs are caused by jealousy! If I could only drive the miscreants helter-skelter out of this with my sword; but I must hide my misfortunes until I see if she's to blame for all this.

NUÑO. Well, let us sit down here.

DON MENDO. All right: then I'll be unnoticed.

REBOLLEDO. That fellow over there is sitting down, unless he is some ghostly soul wandering about the earth in quest of the cane jousting he had played in life, with his shield over his shoulders. (*To* CHISPA) Raise your voice.

CHISPA. Already the air is carrying it.

REBOLLEDO. Now let us sing a fine rousing ballad that'll make her blood tingle.

CHISPA. I shall.

(*During the singing of the following song* DON LOPE *and* CRESPO *enter at different sides with shields and swords and begin to lay about them.*)

CHISPA (*sings*).

> There was once a certain Sampayo
> Of old Andalusian stock,
> An arrogant braggart and head of his band,
> And a red-headed ruffian to boot.
> One night as he strutted.

REBOLLEDO (*speaks*). They mustn't blame him for the date: it must have been Monday—hornday for husbands.

CHISPA (*sings*).

> One night as he strutted from pub to pub
> He found his moll La Chillona
> Dead drunk in a snug with the Squealer.
> Now the Squealer, as ballads relate,

> *Though a boozer, was quick on the draw,*
> *A hot-headed fellow from top to toe,*
> *Who could stretch his man in the wink of an eye.*
> *And so while the Squealer is cursing his moll,*
> *His sword like a flash cuts right and left.*

CRESPO (*speaks*). It must have been like this.

DON LOPE (*speaks*). It was thus, I'm sure. (DON LOPE *and* CRESPO *slash at the soldiers with their swords and at* DON MENDO *and* NUÑO, *putting them to flight.* DON LOPE *returns.*) What courage! They've all fled save one.

(CRESPO *returns.*)

CRESPO (*Aside*). The one who is left must be a soldier.

DON LOPE (*Aside*). Not even this one will escape without uncorking the claret.

CRESPO (*Aside*). I want him to have a taste of my sword too.

DON LOPE. Why don't you run off with the rest?

CRESPO. Away with you, you'll soon run faster. (*They fight.*)

DON LOPE (*Aside*). By Heaven, he fights well!

CRESPO (*Aside*). By God, he knows his business!

(*Enter* JUAN *with a sword.*)

JUAN (*Aside*). I hope to heaven I meet him.

(*Aloud:*) I'm at your side, sir.

DON LOPE. Is that Pedro Crespo?

CRESPO. Here I am. Is that Don Lope?

DON LOPE. Yes, here is Don Lope. Didn't you say you were going to bed? What does this mean?

CRESPO. My only excuse is that I'm doing what you did.

DON LOPE. This was an indignity to me, not to you.

CRESPO. Let us not beat about the bush; I went out to fight to keep you company.

SOLDIERS (*within*). Let us wipe out these clodhoppers.

CAPTAIN (*within*). Mind . . .

(*Reënter the soldiers and the* CAPTAIN *with swords.*)

DON LOPE. Am I not here? Wait. What is the meaning of this riot?

CAPTAIN. The soldiers were enjoying themselves in this street, singing without creating a disturbance, when a quarrel broke out, and I am stopping it.

DON LOPE. Don Alvaro, I appreciate your prudence, but to-day this village is in an ugly mood, and I don't want to

impose further severe restrictions. As it is now dawn, order
your company out of Zalamea for the whole day. See that
my order is carried out, and don't let such scenes occur
again; otherwise, by God, I'll establish order by the sword.

CAPTAIN. Your orders shall be carried out directly. (*Aside:*)
Alas, my pretty country girl, you'll cost me my life.

CRESPO (*Aside*). Don Lope's a stubborn bloke! We'll now
agree. You two come with me: don't be caught alone.
(*Exeunt.*)

(*Reënter* DON MENDO *and* NUÑO, *who is wounded.*)

DON MENDO. Is your wound serious, Nuño?

NUÑO. Even if it was a mere scratch I could do without it.

DON MENDO. I've never in my life felt so sad.

NUÑO. Neither have I.

DON MENDO. I was in my rights to be enraged. In his fury he
hit you on the head, did he not?

NUÑO. My whole backside's hurt. (*A drum is heard from
within.*)

DON MENDO. What's that?

NUÑO. The company is now marching out.

DON MENDO. I am in luck, for now the Captain will cease to
be jealous.

NUÑO. They'll be away all day.

(*Enter the* CAPTAIN *and* SERGEANT *from one side.* DON
MENDO *and* NUÑO *are on the other side of the stage.*)

CAPTAIN. Let the day pass, marching with all the company
until sundown, but remember that when that shining orb
disappears behind the briny Spanish ocean I shall expect
you in the wood yonder, for I must find my life's treasure
this day after the setting of the sun.

SERGEANT (*Aside, to the* CAPTAIN). Hush! here comes one of
the eccentrics of the village.

DON MENDO (*Aside, to* NUÑO). Try to pass by without letting
them notice that I am so cast down. Mind, no trace of
feebleness, Nuño.

NUÑO. Do you expect me to be plump and stout? (*Exeunt*
DON MENDO *and* NUÑO.)

CAPTAIN. I have to return to the village, for I have bribed a
maidservant to spy out a favorable opportunity when I
may speak to that fair assassin. My gifts have prevailed
upon her to second my attempt.

SERGEANT. If you must return you'll need to be well accompanied: there's no trusting those clodhoppers.

CAPTAIN. I know that. You can select some men to return with me.

SERGEANT. I'll carry out your orders, but suppose Don Lope returns and recognizes you?

CAPTAIN. Aye. Because of that fear my love affair went astray on the last occasion, but Don Lope today must depart to prepare the whole regiment's stay in Guadalupe. I heard this just now when I went to take leave of him, for the King will soon arrive, as he already is on the way.

SERGEANT. Your orders, sir, will be carried out. (*Exit.*)

CAPTAIN. Remember that my life's at stake.

(*Enter* REBOLLEDO *and* CHISPA.)

REBOLLEDO. Reward me, sir, for good tidings I bring.

CAPTAIN. What can they be, Rebolledo?

REBOLLEDO. I may well deserve it; I'm only telling you . . .

CAPTAIN. What?

REBOLLEDO. That there's an enemy about, not one to fear though.

CAPTAIN. Who is it? Tell me at once.

REBOLLEDO. That youth, Isabel's brother. Don Lope asked the father for him, so the lad is off to the war with him. I ran into him in the street. He was most elegant and cock-a-hoop, a loutish farm hand still, but valiantly aping the soldier; so the old fellow is the one who'll give us trouble yet.

CAPTAIN. All goes well, and if the servant girl turns up trumps I shall speak to my love this night.

REBOLLEDO. I do not doubt it.

CAPTAIN. I'll return from the march, for I must put in an appearance with the troops who are seen marching out. You two must come with me. (*Exit.*)

REBOLLEDO. We're mighty few, God help us, even with two more, aye, even with an extra four or six more.

CHISPA. If you are returning there, what am I to do? Devil knows what will happen if I run into the man in whom the barber-surgeon put the stitches.

REBOLLEDO. I don't know what to do with you. Haven't you got the guts to join me?

CHISPA. I've no proper garments, but I have the guts, that's sure.

REBOLLEDO. You'll have clothes galore: in any case, there are those of the Captain's page who has gone.

CHISPA. I'll join him.

REBOLLEDO. Let us be off, the regimental flag is passing.

CHISPA. Now I see why I sang the song: "A soldier's love ne'er lasts an hour." (*Exeunt.*)

(*Enter* DON LOPE, CRESPO *and* JUAN.)

DON LOPE. For many reasons I am grateful to you, but above all because you gave me your son to make him a soldier: I thank you from the bottom of my heart.

CRESPO. I give him to you as a servant.

DON LOPE. I'll take him with me as a friend, for I've been deeply impressed by his spirit, his easy manner, and his fondness for arms.

JUAN. I'll always be your humble servant, and you'll see how I shall serve you and obey in everything.

CRESPO. I beseech you, sir, to pardon his shortcomings, for in the hedge-school he was trained, and the best books he has read are the plow and harness, shovels, hoes, and winnowing fans. It was precious little he learnt there of that refinement of the city, which is the fashion of the age in which we live.

DON LOPE. As the sun is beginning to set, I want to depart.

JUAN. I'll see, sir, if your litter has arrived. (*Exit.*)

(*Enter* ISABEL *and* INÉS.)

ISABEL. Should we not take leave of one who has been so attentive to us?

DON LOPE (*to* ISABEL). I could not depart without kissing your hand and begging you to be kind enough to forgive me for temerity which calls for pardon, for it is not the price that moves the gift but the service rendered. This locket, though set with precious diamonds, is a poor gift for you, but I beseech you to keep it and wear it as a medal for my sake.

ISABEL. I should be very sad that you should think that by so rich a gift you requite our hospitality, for we are your debtors through the honor you bestowed upon us.

DON LOPE. That is not payment but sincere affection.

ISABEL. Only as token of affection, not as payment, can I ac

cept it. I recommend my brother to your care, as he has
been so fortunate, but he does deserve to be your servant.

DON LOPE. Again I repeat, you need have no anxiety on his
behalf; he goes with me.

(*Enter* JUAN.)

JUAN. The litter is ready.

DON LOPE. God be with you.

CRESPO. May He be with you too.

DON LOPE. My worthy Pedro Crespo!

CRESPO. My lord Don Lope, the redoubtable.

DON LOPE. Who would have said that day when first we met
that we would end by being such great friends?

CRESPO. I would have said so, sir, if I had known that you
were . . . (*He speaks as* DON LOPE *goes.*)

DON LOPE. Tell me, I pray.

CRESPO. That you were such a good-natured crank. (*Exit*
DON LOPE.)

CRESPO. While Don Lope gets ready, listen, son, before your
cousin and your sister to what I'm going to say. By the
grace of God, Juan, you come of honorable and unblem-
ished, though humble, stock; bear both those facts in mind,
so that you may never so humble your pride and spirit as
to become distrustful of yourself and unable to raise your
status by prudent judgment, nor yet become puffed up
with haughtiness and lower yourself thereby. Bear both in
mind with modesty, for being modest you will maintain
your dignity and yet consign to oblivion many a rub that
chafes a haughty spirit. How many have effaced the memory of some defect by behaving modestly! while others
without a blemish have been credited with one simply because they were disliked. Be courteous in your manner to
all and generous of your purse, for it is the hat and ready
money make best friends; and all the gold the sun gener-
ates in the Indies or the sea engulfs is not as valuable
as your own good name. Do not speak ill of women; I tell
you the meanest of them deserves our respect, for do they
not bring us into the world? Beware of being embroiled
in a quarrel unless the cause be just, for when around me
I see the number of youths who are taught in schools of
arms the art of dueling, I say to myself again and again:
"This school is not the one we need," for I argue that a

man should not be taught how to fight skillfully and elegantly, but rather why to fight at all; and I believe if but one master were appointed to teach not how but why one fights, all would send their sons to him. So now you have sufficient money for the journey, and for getting a couple of suits made when you reach your permanent quarters. With Don Lope's patronage and my blessing I trust in God I'll see you return with honor and advancement. Farewell, my son; it saddens me to say the word.

JUAN. Your words will remain graven in my heart as long as I live. Your hand, Father, and, sister, let us embrace. Now that Don Lope, my Lord, has gone I'll have to overtake him.

ISABEL. Would that my arms could hold you back.

JUAN. Cousin, good-bye.

INÉS. I can't speak, for my eyes have paralyzed my voice. Farewell.

CRESPO. Go quickly; as I look at you I feel your going all the more: yet it must be, for I've given my word.

JUAN. Heaven protect you all.

CRESPO. God be with you. (*Exit* JUAN.)

ISABEL. Father, you've been very hard on him!

CRESPO (*Aside*). Now that he's not present I'll be able to speak more calmly. (*Aloud:*) What could he have done at home except be a good-for-nothing waster all his life? Let him go and serve the King.

ISABEL. I'm sorry he had to leave by night.

CRESPO. Traveling by night in summer is pleasanter than by day. Besides, he must overtake Don Lope as soon as possible. (*Aside:*) I break down when I think of the boy, though in public I make the best of it.

ISABEL. Come, Father, let us go in.

INÉS. As we have no soldiers about, let us stay a little longer and enjoy the breeze here on the porch. The neighbors will soon be about.

CRESPO (*Aside*). True: I'm not going in, for from here I imagine the long white road and I see my son on the way. (*Aloud:*) Inés, bring me a seat.

INÉS. Here is a bench.

ISABEL. They say that this afternoon the Town Council elects its officers.

CRESPO. Yes, that takes place always in August. (*They sit.*)
  (*Enter the* CAPTAIN, *the* SERGEANT, REBOLLEDO, CHISPA *and
  soldiers with faces muffled in their cloaks.*)

CAPTAIN (*aside to his men*). Walk softly. You, Rebolledo, go
  and warn the maidservant that I'm in the street.

REBOLLEDO. Right. But look, there are people at her door.

SERGEANT. By the moon I think it is Isabel herself.

CAPTAIN. It is she: my heart, not the moon, tells me so.
  We've come at the right moment. If only we are auda-
  cious, our adventure will be worth while.

SERGEANT. Will you listen to a bit of advice?

CAPTAIN. No.

SERGEANT. I'll not give it. Go your own way.

CAPTAIN. I'm ready to risk all: I must carry off Isabel. You
  all at the same time with your swords prevent them from
  pursuing me.

SERGEANT. We're at your back and under your orders.

CAPTAIN. Remember that we must all meet in the neighboring wood. It is on the right hand as you leave the village.

REBOLLEDO. Chispa.

CHISPA. Well?

REBOLLEDO. Hold these cloaks.

CHISPA. When a fight's in progress, I imagine the best course
  is to look after the clothes, though the proverb refers to
  swimming.[10]

CAPTAIN. I must get there first.

CRESPO. I think we've enjoyed the place enough. Let us go
  into the house.

CAPTAIN (*Aside, to his men*). Now is the moment, come on,
  friends.
  (*The soldiers rush at the three: they hold* CRESPO *and* INÉS,
  and overpower ISABEL.)

ISABEL. Villain! Father! what is this?

CAPTAIN. I'm mad, mad for love! (*He carries her off.*)

CRESPO. How clearly you treacherous rascals saw that I was
  unarmed!

REBOLLEDO. Off with you, otherwise you'll be killed this instant. (*Exeunt plotters.*)

[10] The proverb is: *La gala del nadar es saber guardar la ropa* (The
best part of swimming is knowing how to look after the clothes),
meaning that, in a crisis, the best course is to avoid danger.

CRESPO. Now my honor's gone, why should I go on living?
If only I had a sword; it is no use pursuing them sword-
less, and if I rush off to get it I'll lose sight of them. What
shall I do, elusive fate, what shall I do? In any case, one
can but die once.

(*Enter* INÉS *with a sword.*)

INÉS. Here, uncle, is your sword.

CRESPO. You've brought it in the nick of time. Now my
honor's intact, as I have my sword and now can chase
them. (*Exit.*)

(*Enter* CRESPO *and the* SERGEANT *fighting,* REBOLLEDO *and
the soldiers; later* ISABEL.)

CRESPO. Release your prey, you cowards! I must regain her
or lose my life.

SERGEANT. You haven't a chance; there are many of us.

CRESPO. My woes are infinite and every one of them fights
for me . . . (*He falls.*) But the earth gives way.

REBOLLEDO. Kill him!

SERGEANT. That were downright wickedness to take away his
life as well as his honor. Better gag and bind him in the
wood, so that he may not raise the hue and cry.

ISABEL (*within*). Father, help!

CRESPO. Daughter!

REBOLLEDO. Carry him off, as you said.

CRESPO. Daughter, only my sighs, alas, can follow you. (*They
carry him off.*)

(ISABEL *and* CRESPO *within; later* JUAN.)

ISABEL (*within*). Woe's me!

JUAN (*appearing*). What voice is that?

CRESPO (*within*). Alas!

JUAN. I heard a moaning cry at the entrance to the wood.
My nag stumbled in its swift course and fell with me, and
I blindly followed it through the undergrowth. I hear sad
voices on one side and groans on another, but they are
indistinct and unrecognizable. But two unfortunate people
are in danger and call out for help: one is a man and the
other a woman: I'll follow the latter. In this way I'll obey
my father, who gave me two pieces of advice: "Fight when
the cause is just, and respect women." So then, I'll honor
women, and I'll fight in a just cause.

ACT III.

Within a wood.

ISABEL (*weeping*). Oh, never may the light of day arise
    To remind me of my shame, as in the gloom
    I linger; oh, you fleeting harbinger
    Of countless stars, I pray you never yield
    To Dawn that even now is hovering over
    Your azure fields, nor let her try
    With tears and laughter to obliterate
    Your peaceful image, but let tears instead
    Of laughter be the order of the day.
    And you, O greatest Orb of all, delay
    Your coming hither, and remain amidst
    The ocean foam; for once let elusive night
    Prolong her flickering empire; be it said
    That your divinity will hear my prayers,
    For she will hearken to her own resolve
    And bow to none: why then do you insist
    On sallying forth to find in my sad tale
    The vilest deed and fiercest tyranny
    That ever Heaven could in warning quote
    As proof of man's eternal infamy?
    But now, alas, I know, your tyranny
    Is cruel, for though I entreated you
    To halt your coming yet awhile, my eyes
    Behold your fairest orb appear above
    The mountains; woe is me, I am distraught
    And harassed by misfortunes without end,
    And now as well as my anxieties
    You come too as a plotter in your rage
    Against my honor. What am I to do?
    Where must I go? For if my wandering feet
    Turn towards my home, I should but stain afresh
    My aged father's name, whose only joy
    Lay in my honor's moonlike purity.
    But now, alas, the moon is in eclipse
    And foully stained. And yet, if through my love
    For him and my fears, I return not home,

I expose myself to all who will cry out
That I was accomplice in my own dishonor,
And in blind folly was content to leave
Foul slander arbiter of innocence.
What wrong did I do? Was it then so wrong
For me to flee as fugitive away
From my own brother? Should I not have let
His arrogant passion slay me when he learned
My sorry destiny: I'll call him now
To hasten hither like an avenging fiend
In all his fury and to slaughter me.
Now let the echo once or twice repeat
My agonized cries . . .

CRESPO (*within*).   Murder me once more,
   For it is not pity thus to spare the life
   Of one bereft of all life's happiness.

ISABEL. What voice is that which I can scarcely hear
   Or recognize?

CRESPO (*within*) Come slay me now, I pray,
   If you are forced to pity.

ISABEL.   Heavens above!
   Another is invoking death; can one be
   Even so unhappy that despite himself
   He lives?
   (*She thrusts aside the leafy boughs and discovers* CRESPO
   bound.)
               But what do my eyes now behold?

CRESPO. If one who timidly now plods his way
   Through this thick forest, and would do a deed
   Of mercy, may he come and slay . . . Ye gods!
   What do my eyes behold?

ISABEL.   My hands are bound
   To an unyielding oak tree . . .

CRESPO.   Moving heaven
   By her sad cries for help.

ISABEL.   It is my father!

CRESPO. My daughter comes.

ISABEL.   O my beloved sire
   And father.

CRESPO.   Come, my daughter, loose these bonds.

ISABEL. I dare not, dearest father! once the bonds

That bind you I untie I'll never dare
To tell you of my woeful misery.
For once your hands are free to wreak revenge
And discover all your honor gone,
Your rage will spur you on to slaughter me,
And so before I loose my hands I wish
To tell you all the story of my woes.

CRESPO. Hold back, my Isabel, I beg you stop.
Do not go on; misfortunes, Isabel,
When we count them need not be ever told.

ISABEL. There are many things that you should know, and I
Perforce must make you angry when I speak
And rouse your vengeance ere you hear my tale.
Last night, dear Father, as I sat at peace
Beneath your shelter, wherein I had spent
Till now my maiden years, lo! all at once
Those rascals, who made up their minds to storm
Our honor's bastion with effrontery,
Abducted me, and like the ravenous wolf,
Did tear me from your bosom like a lamb.
The Captain, our ungrateful guest, when he
Entered our house, began to introduce
Dissension and betrayal. He was first
To seize me, while his sundry accomplices,
Who fight beneath his banner, helped his flight.
This dense and hidden wood outside the town
He planned as place of safety; are not woods
Forever refuge for the tyrannous?
But here distraught and mad with grief I looked
Upon myself again and yet again,
While still I heard your voice, but then it died
Away behind me, for the wind which bore
Your cries grew fainter and still fainter, till
What had been distinct arguments before,
Were now no longer voices but mere noise;
And when the wind had wafted them away
They were not even noise but confused sound,
As when, while we retire, a bugle sounds,
And its note echoing floats after us.
The wretch then seeing there was no pursuit,
And not a soul about for my defense,

For even the Moon was wrapt in murky shade.
(A cruel and revengeful one, you are!)
Again, woe's me! he insisted, and again
A thousand times, and tried with treacherous words
To plead his violent love. Who would not be
Amazed at one who should attempt to turn
His foul offense to love? accursèd be
The man, accursèd thrice, who tries by force
To win a heart, for he does not observe
That love gives no trophies of victory,
Save affection which from beauty must be won.
For if with soulless passion we make love
To offended beauty, then we do but love
A beauty that is lifeless. With what prayers
And requests, now haughty, now in humble tones
Did I attempt to move him, but in vain,
For he was—here may I be mute awhile—
Proud—may my tears cease to bedew my eyes;
And insolent—let my heart groan with woe;
Discourteous—may my tears now flow afresh;
Brutal—let envy close her ears this day;
Shameless—may my breath falter as I speak;
Ruthless—may I wear mourning in my shame.
And if my voice errs, let my actions tell;
In shame my face I hide; and I lament
That I have suffered such indignity;
In rage I wring my hands, and anger wells
Up in my heart: what happened is for you
To understand, for my words fail me now.
Let it suffice to say that my complaints
And prayers for Heaven's justice, not for help,
Were echoed and reëchoed by the winds.
The Dawn arose, and with her as my guide,
I heard a noise amidst the leafy boughs,
And looked again to see who it could be.
It was my brother: Heavens above! Oh when,
Unlucky fate, has your assistance come
So speedily to one unfortunate?
But through the dusky twilight as he gazed
He saw the injury ere he'd been told,
For sorrows are lynx-eyed and pierce without

The need of words; he then unsheathed his sword,
Which you did gird upon him on that day.
The Captain, seeing help had at last arrived
On my behalf, drew forth his glittering steel,
And each did meet the other hand to hand:
The latter wards off and the former thrusts;
And I, while both did valorously fight,
Was terror-struck, and in despair because
My brother knew not if the fault was mine,
And not to risk my life to justify
Myself, I turned back: through the underbrush
And thickets of the wood I fled, but not
So swiftly that I did not make of boughs
A tangle latticework, for as I fled
I wished to see what happened, and just then
My brother wounded the Captain, who fell,
And tried to follow with a second blow,
But those who now came looking for the Captain
Were eager for revenge, and then the youth,
Observing that they were a troop, at once
Took to his heels, and they made no attempt
To follow him, for they were more inclined
To offer help instead of punishment.
And so they bore the Captain in their arms,
And marched towards the town unmindful of
His wicked deed; for in what has occurred
They were resolved to bring help where they thought
It was needed urgently. There as I watched,
Crazed by the toll of my anxieties,
And blind with terror and with agony,
I fled up hill, down dale, through brush and briar,
Till at last I fell before your feet, my father,
To tell you my sad story ere I die.
And now you know my tale it is time to draw
Your sword, and my hand shall unloose your bonds;
One bond alone's enough to bow my neck.
Your daughter kneels before you in her shame,
But you are free and can avenge us both,
For you shall by my death your glory win;
And men will say that in your daughter's blood
You have your own dead honor now revived.

CRESPO. Rise, Isabel, rise up, my child; no more
  Must you remain upon your knees, and if
  Almighty God had not such sufferings
  And trials sent to plague and persecute,
  Mankind's good fortune had been valueless.
  It is by such means that He teaches us;
  Let us then bravely stamp them on our hearts.
  Come, Isabel, let us depart at once,
  And homewards wend our way, for Juan I fear
  May be in danger, and we must now make
  Supreme efforts to trace his whereabouts
  And rescue him.

ISABEL (*aside*).   My fortune smiles, for this
  Is passing prudence, or else crafty cunning.

CRESPO. Come.   (*Exeunt.*)
  (*A street at the entrance to the town. Enter* CRESPO *and*
  ISABEL.)

CRESPO. By all that's holy! if the captain's wound
  Has caused him to return here, then it is well,
  As far as I'm concerned, if he should die
  Of that first wound to save himself another,
  And a thousand more, for my anxieties
  Will not end till I rid the world of him.
  But come, my daughter, and let us go home.
  (*Enter the* CLERK *of the court.*)

CLERK. Pedro Crespo! Good news! A reward for news!

CRESPO. What news, clerk?

CLERK. The Corporation have elected you mayor, and, mark
  my words, sir, you enter on your judicial duties with two
  important functions today: the first is the King's visit. They
  say His Majesty will spend all today or tomorrow here;
  the other concerns some soldiers who have secretly smug-
  gled in that captain whose company was here yesterday.
  He has been wounded, and they want him to receive im-
  mediate attention, but they don't say who wounded him:
  so if this matter can be attested judicially it will be all to
  the good.

CRESPO (*aside*). Heavens above! Here was I dreaming of revenge, and now the black rod of justice makes me master
  of my honor: how can I now transgress the law, when at
  this very hour I'm set as judge to see that others do not

transgress it? Events like this are surely not seen every day. (*Aloud:*) Well, clerk, I'm extremely grateful to my fellow members of the Corporation for the honor they have done me.

CLERK. You are to come to the Town Hall and take possession of the rod of office. Then you can start the judicial investigation.

CRESPO. Let us go. You, Isabel, return home.

ISABEL. May heaven take compassion on me! I must go with you.

CRESPO. Child, remember your father's now Mayor: he will see justice is done you. (*Exeunt.*)

(*The* CAPTAIN's *lodgings. Enter the* CAPTAIN *wounded, and the* SERGEANT.)

CAPTAIN. The wound was of no consequence: why did you bring me back here?

SERGEANT. How could we know it was but a grazing wound before it was cured?

CAPTAIN. Now that the cure has been provided, it is wise to remember that it's not worth while today risking one's life to get a wound healed.

SERGEANT. Wouldn't it have been worse if you had been left to bleed to death?

CAPTAIN. Now that I'm as fit as a fiddle it would be a mistake to hang about here. Let us be off before they get wind that we are here. Are the others here?

SERGEANT. Yes.

CAPTAIN. Let us make a dash for it before those yokels get to know that I'm here, otherwise we'll have to come to blows.

(*Enter* REBOLLEDO.)

REBOLLEDO. The officers of the law are here.

CAPTAIN. What have they to do with me?

REBOLLEDO. I repeat that they are here.

CAPTAIN. I'm pleased to hear it. Now that they know that I'm here I need have no fears that the villagers will lynch me. The magistrates are in duty bound to hand me over to the Council of War. Though it is a troublesome affair, I am perfectly safe.

REBOLLEDO. No doubt the fellow has lodged a complaint.

CAPTAIN. I've thought of that.

CRESPO (*within*). Guard the doors, and let no soldiers, who might by any chance be here, go out: if any tries to leave, kill him.

CAPTAIN. Who dares to come in here? (*Aside:*) Ye gods! What is this?

(*Enter* PEDRO CRESPO, *with his staff of office, and farmers.*)

CRESPO. Why not? Does justice then need more permission than I am aware?

CAPTAIN. Justice indeed! Even if you are a magistrate since yesterday, your office has no jurisdiction over me.

CRESPO. In Heaven's name, sir, don't excite yourself; I've only come here on business, with your permission, and I want to have a talk with you alone.

CAPTAIN (*to the* SERGEANT *and* REBOLLEDO). You both may leave.

CRESPO (*to the farmers*). You too may go as well. (*Aside to the* CLERK:) Keep an eye on those soldiers.

CLERK. I'll keep my eye on them. (*Exeunt the farmers, the* SERGEANT, REBOLLEDO *and the* CLERK.)

CRESPO. Now that I, as magistrate, made use of my dignity to oblige you to hear me, I shall now lay aside my staff of office, and as a simple man I wish to tell you my troubles. (*He lays aside the staff.*) And as we are alone, Don Alvaro, let us speak unequivocally without ever letting our inner feelings burst the bonds of silence. I am an honorable man, and were I to choose my birth, I would not overlook (God is my witness) even the tiniest defect of mine, provided I could fulfill my aims in life. I have always enjoyed esteem among my fellow men, and the Corporation and the Council think well of me. As regards property, I'm comfortably off, in fact, thank Heaven, I'm the wealthiest farmer in all the villages of the district, and my daughter, as far as I know, has been brought up modestly and with decorum, and bears an unsullied name among the people. She is her mother's image, God rest her soul! I believe, sir, it is sufficient guarantee that I am wealthy and have none to slander me; that I am unassuming and have none to censure me, and this, mind you, in a small community, where our only failing is to be only too aware of the failings and defects of others: and would to God, sir, that they remained content with knowing

them. That my daughter is beautiful, what better proof
than your infatuation? Even though I could, in saying this,
with deeper sorrow deplore this fact. This, sir, is the story
of my misfortune. Let us not drain all the poison, but let
the dregs be left to make us suffer. But Time, sir, must
not be allowed to have its own way with everything. We
too must help to hide its shortcomings. The wrong, you
see, is great and I must have redress. Even if I try to hush
it up, I cannot: God knows were it possible to keep the
secret entombed in my own heart I would not come on
purpose bent as I do today, but would have given it all
up and acquiesced in suffering rather than speak out. But
if I seek redress for an injury that cries to heaven, it is
vengeance, not retribution. And so, considering all con-
tingencies, there is but one way which will not be amiss
for both of us. It is that you should take all my wordly
fortune, and I shall not retain a *maravedí* for me or my
son: I'll bring him here to kneel before you; and we'll beg
for alms from passers-by, when there's no other way to
nourish our bodies. And if you wish you may straightway
brand an S and a nail upon us both today, and sell us into
slavery.[11] That sum of money, in addition, I'll offer you as
dowry for my daughter, if you will but restore to her the
honor you have robbed. In doing this you will not tarnish
your own name, for what your children, sir, may lose by
being my grandchildren, they will surely gain by being
your children. For as the Castilian proverb—an apt one
too—says: "It is the horse carries the saddle." Consider
well what I am asking now. (*He kneels.*) I bend the knee
to ask it, and as my tears flow on my hoary beard its white
hairs seem to melt away like snow in water. What do I
demand? My honor, which you stole from me; and though
it is mine, yet I ask it back so humbly, that it seems that
what I ask is not mine but yours. And mark well that I
have power as magistrate to take the law into my hands
and redress my grievance and restore my name; I would

[11] *Poner una S y un clavo* (to put an S and a nail) refers to the
pictorial placement on documents of an S drawn with a nail
(clavo) through it. There is a play on the words *esclavo* (slave)
and S *clavo*.

have none of this, but only what you give me of free will.

CAPTAIN. I have not the patience, tiresome and prolix old man, to put up with more: You may be thankful I don't slay you with my own hands this instant, for what you are and for your son as well. I don't do so because I want you to be beholden to Isabel's beauty. If you seek to avenge your honor by arms, I have little to fear; if it is as magistrate, by law, you have no jurisdiction.

CRESPO. So my distress then leaves you cold.

CAPTAIN. Who would heed the idle tears of old man, child or woman?

CRESPO. So sorrow and suffering deserve no consolation.

CAPTAIN. Enough consolation that you're still alive.

CRESPO. Kneeling on the ground I cry out to you to give me back my honor you have robbed.

CAPTAIN. How irritating the old man is!

CRESPO. Mind, I am now the Mayor of Zalamea.

CAPTAIN. You have never had jurisdiction over me: the Council of War will send for me.

CRESPO. Is this your only answer?

CAPTAIN. Yes, you doddering old fool!

CRESPO. There is no remedy then?

CAPTAIN. Except silence, which is your best plan.

CRESPO. No other?

CAPTAIN. No.

CRESPO. By God you'll pay for this! Hello there! (*He rises and picks up the rod of office.*)

CLERK (*within*). Sir!

CAPTAIN (*Aside*). What are these yokels up to?
(*Enter farmers.*)

CLERK. What are Your Worship's orders?

CRESPO. Put the Captain under arrest.

CAPTAIN. Here's a pretty state of affairs! you can't do that to me—to an officer in His Majesty's service.

CRESPO. We'll see. You'll not leave this place except under arrest or dead.

CAPTAIN. I warn you I'm a captain.

CRESPO. Do you take me for a dead mayor then? Off to prison with him.

CAPTAIN. I'm defenseless so I have to let them take me. I'll complain to the King for such unjust treatment.

CRESPO. So shall I about the other affair. It is a mercy he's nearby. He'll hear us both. Hand over your sword.

CAPTAIN. There's no reason why . . .

CRESPO. But if you're under arrest?

CAPTAIN. Treat it with respect then.

CRESPO. With all due respect. Take the Captain, constables, with due respect to the cell, and with due respect clap on him a pair of handcuffs and a chain, and take mighty good care of him with due respect, but don't let him have word with any soldier. Put the two others in the jail too, but apart. For later the officers of the law, with due respect, may get a confession from them. And if I get sufficient evidence, with all the respect in the world I'll hang you by the neck until you're dead, so help me God!

CAPTAIN. If you give a peasant a mule
The dolt thinks he is fit to rule. (*Exeunt the farmer-constables with the* CAPTAIN.)
(*Enter* REBOLLEDO, CHISPA *and the* CLERK.)

CLERK. This soldier and the page are all we could find. The other fellow got away.

CRESPO. This is the rogue who sings: with a gurgle in the throat he'll trill no more in this life.

REBOLLEDO. Surely, sir, there's no crime in singing.

CRESPO. I'm sorry it's a virtue, so sorry, in fact, that I've an instrument here that will make you sing more sweetly. Make up your minds to squeal . . .

REBOLLEDO. What?

CRESPO. About what took place last night.

REBOLLEDO. Your daughter knows better than I do.

CRESPO. Or you'll swing.

CHISPA (*aside, to* REBOLLEDO). Rebolledo, make up your mind to deny each detail; if you deny, you'll be the theme for a ballad I'll sing.

CRESPO. Who else will sing for you?

CHISPA. They can't torture me.

CRESPO. And why not, pray?

CHISPA. That's fixed: it is not laid down in my law.

CRESPO. What's your reason?

CHISPA. A fine big one.

CRESPO. Out with it.

CHISPA. I am in the family way.

CRESPO. What a shamelessness! My temper is getting the better of me. Are you not the Captain's page?

CHISPA. No, sir, my stirrups are too long.

CRESPO. Prepare yourself to spill the beans—all you know.

CHISPA. We'll spill even more than we know, for it will be worse to die.

CRESPO. In that case both of you will escape the rack.

CHISPA. If that's so, and as I came into the world to sing, by heaven I must sing.

   (*She sings.*)

> They wish to torture me.

REBOLLEDO (*sings*). *What do they wish to give me?*

CRESPO. What are you up to?

CHISPA. I want to tune up from here, as we are going to sing.

   (*Exeunt.*)

   (*A room in* CRESPO's *house. Enter* JUAN.)

JUAN. After my duel in the wood, when I
  Wounded the traitors, so many came
  Upon the scene that I was forced to flee
  Through the undergrowth, but no trace could find
  Of my unhappy sister, so I took
  The risk of coming home, that Father may
  Now give me counsel what I have to do
  To vindicate my honor and my life.

   (*Enter* INÉS *and* ISABEL, *who is very downcast.*)

INÉS. I beg of you to calm yourself, your sorrow
  Will end by killing you.

ISABEL.   Alas, Inés
  Who has told you that I don't loathe my life?

JUAN. I'll tell my father . . . (*Aside:*) Alas, I am sure
  It's Isabel; why do I tarry now?   (*He draws his dagger.*)

INÉS. My cousin!

ISABEL.   Brother!
               What will you do now?

JUAN. I would avenge the wrong that you today
  Have done to me, my honor and my life.

ISABEL. Remember, brother.

JUAN.   I must slay you now,
  May God protect my soul.

   (*Enter* CRESPO *and farmers.*)

CRESPO.   But what is this?

JUAN. Father, she must now atone for all
　　The wrongs done, she must pay the penalty.
CRESPO. Enough, enough; how foolish and how rash
　　To risk your head in coming.
JUAN (*seeing the rod of office*). What is this?
CRESPO. So here you are, yet not long since you have
　　Wounded a captain yonder in the wood.
JUAN. If I am guilty, Father, of this crime,
　　It was in fair defense of your good name . . .
CRESPO. Come now, Juan, I have heard enough of this.
　　Hello there! take him also prisoner.
JUAN. Can you behave with such severity
　　Towards your son?
CRESPO.　　　　　　　　Aye, and I would likewise
　　Act towards my father with severity.
　　(*Aside:*)
　　In this way I can guarantee Juan's life,
　　But now they'll think that never stranger form
　　Of justice has yet by man been devised.
JUAN. Now listen well. When I struck down that rogue
　　I was resolved to slay my sister too.
CRESPO. I know, but it is not enough for me
　　To know as Crespo. I must also know
　　As Mayor, and I must even report on it.
　　Until the trial proves your innocence
　　Or guilt, I'll have to hold you prisoner.
　　(*Aside:*)
　　Your exculpation I shall find, I'm sure.
JUAN. No one will take the trouble to divine
　　Your purpose. But now that you've lost your honor
　　You arrest the one who would restore it to you,
　　And protect the rascal who has ruined you.
　　　　　　　　　　　　　(*They escort him away.*)
CRESPO. Now come here, Isabel, and sign your name
　　To this complaint which you are lodging now
　　Against the man who has dishonored you.
ISABEL. But you who did insist on secrecy
　　Are now about to publish it abroad.
　　As you have not been able to avenge
　　My wrongs and yours, let silence cover all.
CRESPO. No. Since my duties as the Mayor will not

Allow me satisfaction to obtain
As I would wish, I must arrange it thus.   (*Exit* ISABEL.)
Inés, now lay aside my rod of office;
As he refused a friendly settlement
He'll now be forced to accept the evil way.   (*Exit* INÉS.)

DON LOPE (*within*). Halt! Halt!

CRESPO.   Who is dismounting at my
        door? Who is it?

DON LOPE.   Pedro Crespo, here I am;
    When I had half the distance gone I felt
    Compelled again to come here, where distress,
    I fear, awaits; surely it were not right
    That I should halt elsewhere, since you're my friend.

CRESPO. Thank heaven I find favor in your eyes.

DON LOPE. They tell me that your son has not been seen
    Over there.

CRESPO.   You will soon be told the cause;
    But do be kind enough to tell me why
    You are, my Lord, so mortally upset.

DON LOPE. Disorder's rampant, and no man, I say,
    Has ever conceived more flagrant foolishness.
    A soldier on the road caught up with me
    And gave me tidings. I'm beside myself
    With rage, I must admit.

CRESPO.   Do tell me all.

DON LOPE. He told me that a whipper-snapper mayor
    From here has clapped a captain into jail.
    By God! I swear that accurséd leg of mine
    Did never hurt me on a journey till
    Today when it delayed my coming here
    In time to make him pay the penalty.
    By Christ, I'll beat the shameless man to death.

CRESPO. Well then, I believe, you have come here in vain,
    For the Mayor, I'm sure, will not let that take place.

DON LOPE. I'll beat him all the same, you may be sure.

CRESPO. A bad solution; nor do I believe
    There's any man who'd give such poor advice.
    Do you not know why he arrested him?

DON LOPE. I do not; but whatever cause there was—
    The wronged one must be judged by me alone;
    For I, too, know how to decapitate,

If it be needful.

CRESPO.   You don't understand,
What is a mere mayor's status in a town.

DON LOPE. Don't tell me he can be more than a boor.

CRESPO. A boor he may be, but if he insists
With stubborn will to strangle the accused,
By God, he'll carry out what he has planned.

DON LOPE. By God, he shall not; and if you perchance,
Are wont to see him, tell me where he lives.

CRESPO. He lives very near here.

DON LOPE.   Well then, tell me who
The Mayor is.

CRESPO.   I am he.

DON LOPE.   By God, I did
Suspect as much.

CRESPO.   By Heaven, as I've said.

DON LOPE. Well, what I have said, I've said, that is all.

CRESPO. And I, my Lord, what I've done, I have done.

DON LOPE. But I have come here for the prisoner,
And to chastise this gross intemperance.

CRESPO. I hold him captive here for what occurred.

DON LOPE. Do you know he's in service of the King
And I am his judge?

CRESPO.   Are you not aware
That he did kidnap from my house my daughter?

DON LOPE. Do you know that my rank is arbiter
Of such a case?

CRESPO.   He robbed me of my honor,
Shamelessly in a wood?

DON LOPE.   Do you not know
That my own jurisdiction in command
Soars high above yours?

CRESPO.   Are you not aware
That I besought him with my pleas for peace,
But he refused?

DON LOPE.   You stray within the bounds
Of another authority, say what you will.

CRESPO. He strayed within the bounds of my good name,
Which were not under his authority.

DON LOPE. I'll know how to make full atonement for
What has occurred and I promise redress.

CRESPO. I never asked a soul to do what I
    Could not do for myself.
DON LOPE.   But I must take
    The prisoner, for I'm in honor bound.
CRESPO. And I have here examined all the case.
DON LOPE. What is a case?
CRESPO.   Some sheets of paper which
    The case requires to be judicially
    Investigated.
DON LOPE.   I shall go for him
    To prison.
CRESPO.   I shall not prevent your going;
    But take note that an order has been given
    To shoot at sight the first one who gets there.
DON LOPE. As I've been trained such bullets to await,
    We'll take no chances in today's affair.
    Hello! you soldier! go, fly like the wind
    And to all companies that have these days
    Taken their quarters and are on the march,
    Give orders that they must at once set out
    In right good order, and in squadrons march
    With cannons loaded and with tinder lit.
A SOLDIER. There was no need to order out the men,
    For hearing what had taken place they have
    Already made their entry in the town.
DON LOPE. Well then, by God, I'll see if they hand up
    The prisoner or not.
CRESPO.   Well then, by God,
    I'll be the first to do what must be done. (*Exeunt.*)
    (*A room in the prison. We hear* DON LOPE, *the* CLERK,
    CRESPO, *soldiers, all off-stage. Drums sound.*)
DON LOPE. Here, soldiers, is the prison, where they hold
    The Captain; if they don't deliver him
    At once, set fire and burn it to the ground,
    And if they do defend it, burn the town.
CLERK. Even if they break the jail down, they'll not free
    The Captain.
SOLDIERS.   Death to all the villagers.
CRESPO. Why should they die? Oh, why? Is there no way?
DON LOPE. They have received help; break the prison down
    Come on, my men, break down the door, I say.

(*Enter the soldiers and* DON LOPE *on one side: on the other
the* KING, CRESPO, *farmers and suite.*)

KING. What means this row? Is this how you behave
When I arrive?

DON LOPE.   All this, Your Majesty,
The most foolhardy yokel ever known
Erstwhile provoked, and had you not arrived
So quickly you'd have found a feast
Of bonfires gaily burning everywhere
Throughout the town.

KING.   What has occurred?

DON LOPE.   A mayor
Has taken a captain into custody,
And when I went for him they would not hand
Him over to me.

KING.   Who's the Mayor?

CRESPO.   I am.

KING. And what is your excuse?

CRESPO.   This case in which
The crime is duly proven worthy of death,
For here a maiden was kidnaped and raped
In a deserted wood, and he refused to wed
The victim, though her father did entreat
With peaceful plea.

DON LOPE.   This is the Mayor who is
Her father.

CRESPO.   That matters not in this case,
For if a stranger were now to accuse,
Should I not do him justice? Yes, I should.
So why today should I not do the same
For my own child as I would for the rest?
Besides which, as I have a son of mine
Locked up in jail, it's true I would not give
More than just ear to my poor daughter's claim
Since all the ties of blood had equal weight . . .
Consider if the case be well drawn up,
Or if there's one to say that I have done
An evil act, or have suborned a witness,
Or if there's any written word beyond
What I have said; if so, put me to death.

KING. It is well substantiated, but you have

Not full power to carry out the sentence,
For that's the function of another court,
And so hand up the prisoner at once.
CRESPO. It were wrong, Your Majesty, for me to hand
    Him over, for there's only one court here,
    And every sentence that this court decrees
    It carries out.
KING.   What then do you propose?
CRESPO. If then Your Majesty does not believe
    That this is true, look yonder and behold
    There is the Captain.
    (*They open a door and the* CAPTAIN, *who has been stran--
    gled, appears seated on a chair.*)
KING.   Why so rash an act?
CRESPO. Your Majesty did say the sentence was
    A just one, then it is rightly carried out.
KING. Could not the Council execute the sentence?
CRESPO. All kingly justice in one body lies:
    And if that body should have many hands,
    What are the odds then if this hand or that
    Should have to kill, what matter if the one
    Who has succeeded in the most should fail
    In the least?
KING.   If this is so, why did you not
    Have him beheaded as a captain and—[12]
CRESPO. A Knight? The nobles here, I would remind
    Your Majesty, are so God-fearing that
    Our public hangman has not yet been taught
    How to decapitate, but it's the dead
    Should lodge complaint: yours the authority.
    The rest of us are not concerned with it.
KING. Don Lope, what's done now can't be undone.
    The Captain's fate was so well merited,
    That if there's been an error in the least
    Matters not when the rest has been achieved.
    Let not a single soldier here remain,
    And make the troops march on without delay,
    For I must soon arrive in Portugal.

[12] According to the Spanish social code, a caballero had the privilege of being beheaded: garroting and hanging were reserved for
the rest of the population.

Here in this town I do appoint you mayor
In perpetuity.

CRESPO.   The King alone
Could thus know how to do honor to justice.

                           (*Exit the* KING *and his suite.*)

DON LOPE. And you may thank your stars the King arrived
In the nick of time.

CRESPO.   By Heaven, had he not
Arrived there was already no redress.

DON LOPE. Would it not have been wise to speak
With me and hand over the prisoner,
For then your daughter's honor you'd have saved?

CRESPO. A convent she already has selected,
And she has now a husband who does not
Distinctions make in rank.

DON LOPE.   Then hand to me
The other prisoners.

CRESPO.   Take them at once.

DON LOPE. Your son is missing, and because he now
Serves under me, he must not stay in jail.

CRESPO. I also want, my Lord, to punish him
For his past disrespect when he did wound
His captain; though his honor, it is true,
Bound him to help his sister, still he could
Have given her help in another way.

DON LOPE. My Pedro Crespo, call him now.

CRESPO.   He's here.
  (*Enter* JUAN.)

JUAN. Let me now offer you, my Lord, my thanks.
Henceforth I shall be your servant forever.

REBOLLEDO. I now intend never to sing again.

CHISPA. Well, I shall sing whenever I behold
The rack which I so narrowly escaped.

CRESPO. And so the author ends this truthful tale,
And asks you to forgive all his defects.

THE

MYSTERY PLAY

OF

ELCHE

or

FEAST OF ELCHE

❧❦❧

Music Drama
in
Two Acts

❧❦❧

ACT I.

La Vespra (the Eve), *August 14th.*

SCENE 1.

The Blessed Virgin, the Angels, and the two Marys enter by the church door and proceed up the andador, *or sloping platform, to the stage. They pause, and Our Lady kneels on two cushions of crimson velvet which are laid on the platform, and sings the first* cobla.

OUR LADY. Sisters, who love me so tenderly,
Do not, I beseech you, leave me this day.
THE TWO MARYS. Blessed Virgin, Mother of God,
We shall stay beside you,
And wherever you go,
We shall accompany you.
OUR LADY (*chanting*). How sad, alas, is our mortal life!
How cruel and unjust the world!
Woe's me, what shall I do?
When shall I see my dearest Son?
(*She sighs as she ends her chant and advances slowly up the sloping platform. She stops at each of the three little symbolical stations of the Cross which are fixed to the columns of the nave of the basilica on the Epistle side. At the first, which represents the Agony in the Garden, she chants:*)
O Holy Garden of Gethsemane,
Where the Lord was taken!
How brutally they treated you,
The Lord of Israel!
(*At the second, representing the Crucifixion, she chants:*)
O sacred bough most honored of all,
And best of all trees in the world,
On you was shed the blood
Of Him who wished to redeem the world.
(*At the third station she chants:*)
Most holy and hallowed sepulcher,
Honored for all eternity,

Because in you was laid to rest
He who created Heaven and Earth.
(*Our Lady and her escort mount the stage.*)

SCENE 2.

Our Lady kneels by her deathbed. The two Marys and the Angels sit on a bench on the far side of the bed. They do not move from there until the end of Act I. The two Marys, however, must be able to act as understudies for Our Lady, in case the boy taking the part should fall ill.

OUR LADY. My heart suffers grievously for my beloved Son,
Such are my pangs of sorrow that I long for death.

(*The organ plays and the church bells peal to announce the arrival of the angelic messenger from heaven. Slowly a globe shaped like a pomegranate descends from the lofty roof of the basilica, and its leaves begin to open amidst the plaudits of the multitude, when they see the Angel within. The organist watches carefully the opening of the pomegranate so as to be ready to give the lead, and when the wings of the pomegranate are raised horizontally the opening above in the sky closes, the church bells are hushed, and the Angel scatters glittering star dust upon the crowd beneath. He then chants the following:*)

All hail, Imperial Virgin,
Mother of our heavenly King,
I bring you bliss and blessings
From your all-powerful Son.
Your Son, whom you love and miss so grievously,
Awaits your coming with impatience,
When He will exalt you.
And He says that on the third day
He will in the celestial kingdom
Crown you Queen of the angels.
And He orders me to bring you this palm
And deliver it to you in name,

That it may be borne before you
When you are carried to your grave.
(*A sacristan dressed as an Apostle loosens the metal belt
binding the Angel to the pomegranate, and hands him the
palm which is in the pomegranate. The Angel, holding the
palm in his right hand, walks over to the bed of Our Lady,
makes three bows, holds the palm crosswise and touches
his forehead with it before he hands it to Our Lady. He
kneels before her. The Blessed Virgin replies to his saluta-
tion by touching her brow with the palm before she chants:*)
Fair radiant Angel, hearken to me now,
I would beseech you to grant me a boon,
If I perchance find favor in your sight:
Do not, I pray, deny me this request:
With all my heart and all my soul I wish
If it were possible, before my death,
To gather all the Apostles around this bed
That they may bear my body to the tomb.
(*The Angel rises, genuflects and walks towards the pome-
granate, accompanied by the other Angels. He enters the
pomegranate and as he is carried aloft he chants the fol-
lowing farewell to the Virgin:*)
The Apostles will not delay,
And soon they will come
For God who is Almighty
Will bring them all at once.
And as it is your wish, Blessed Virgin,
The Almighty says He wishes them to come
To be your consolation at this hour.

SCENE 3.

*While the pomegranate soars up to heaven, the Knights-
Elect* (caballeros electos) *and the Standard-Bearer, who
symbolize the link between the leaders of the community,
the Church, and the performers, go down to the church*

door by the andador *to meet St. John, and they accompany
him up the* andador *when he enters. He is dressed in white,
has brown hair and carries with him a copy of the Gospel.
He is young and hearty and rouses the enthusiasm of the
public. He looks around, searching for Our Lady, and
finally he sees her in bed. He bows three times before em-
bracing his adoptive mother, chanting as follows:*

ST. JOHN. My fervent greetings to you, Blessed Mother,
And all honor and eternal glory.
And may the Lord of the thunder
Give you consolation.

OUR LADY. Alas, my dearest son John,
Truest son of God, console yourself;
My heart is at rest, and joyful am I
At your arrival.
My son John, take, I pray, this palm,
And see that they bear it in the procession
When they carry me to my grave.

*(These last lines of Our Lady are often omitted. She si-
lently hands the palm to St. John, who places it across his
brow as before. He then sings the following:)*

ST. JOHN. Alas, how sad is our mortal life!
How cruel and unjust the world!
Woe's me! where shall I go?
What a pitiful fate! What shall I do?
O Blessed Virgin, Imperial Queen!
In what sorrow you leave us!
Without any head or guiding spirit.

Ye Apostles, my brothers!
Come all of you and let us mourn!
Today we lose our beloved,
The guide and counselor of our faith.
Without your help, most Blessed Lady,
What shall we do? What consolation find?
Our hearts as well as our eyes will weep.
And we shall sigh as long as we live!

*(St. John sings those verses, moving from one side of the
deathbed of Our Lady to the other, and he turns toward
the door of the church, as though summoning the Apostles.
While St. John chants those words the Knights-Elect go*

down the andador to meet St. Peter, who enters carrying in his right hand the keys of Heaven, symbol of the power conferred upon him by Jesus. By tradition and ordinance St. Peter must be a priest, and to him falls the task of burying Our Lady. He is dressed in a yellow robe with a royal-blue cloak. He advances up the sloping platform to the stage and kneels to Our Lady and embraces her as St. John has done. He then embraces St. John, and then chants the following to the Virgin:)

ST. PETER. Humble Virgin, most honored flower,
Mother of our Redeemer,
All blessings and eternal glory
May you receive from Almighty God!

SCENE 4.

The Knights-Elect go out to welcome the rest of the Apostles, who advance up the sloping platform as St. Peter finishes his song. They advance in pairs amidst the applause of the multitude, and when they reach the death-bed of the Virgin they kneel as the other two had done, and embrace them in turn. They surround the bed. Not all the Apostles mount the stage, for according to the Consueta of 1625 three of them, including St. James, remain at the foot of the andador. St. James is dressed as a pilgrim, in a purple or brown habit, and he wears the broad-brimmed hat of the pilgrim to Santiago de Compostela, the scallop shells, and he carries the long staff and gourd. These three Apostles sing one of the most celebrated songs of the whole festival, the so-called Ternari, or motet for three voices. It is sung twice, the first time at the foot of the andador near the door, the second time at the foot of the stage.

THE THREE APOSTLES. O power of the heavenly Kingdom!
(First time.) Lord of all creation!
Truly it is a great wonder
That we should all meet here together.

For we have come here from foreign parts
Through many a town, o'er many a mountain,
Spirited here in less than a moment.
(*Second time.*)
To our great joy without mishap
We are here in a flash:
Truly this is a great wonder
That we should all meet here together.
(*At the end of the* Ternari *the Apostles mount the stage,
repeat the same genuflections and embrace as the others
and take their places around the bed of Our Lady. Then
begins the* Salve (*Musical No. VIII*) *under the direction
of the choirmaster, who is dressed as an Apostle and stands
amidst the singers. The Apostles and the choirmaster stand
at each side of the bed. First on the right is St. John with
the palm. He sings the alto part: then comes the* Tiple *or
treble, and behind him, the choirmaster, and the altos of
the choir. On the other side are St. Peter, who is solo bass,
and the remaining basses and tenors. They sing:*)
THE APOSTLES. Hail holy Queen and Princess,
Mother of the King of the Angels,
Protector and pleader for sinners,
Consoler of the afflicted.

Almighty God, your Son,
To console us in our woes,
Gathers us all together
In your saintly presence.
Purest of all women and without sin,
Protector and pleader for sinners,
Consoler of the afflicted!
(*The first line of the above song "Hail holy Queen and
Princess" is sung softly by the Apostles kneeling. They
then rise and sing the rest standing. When they reach the
fugal part of the song, at the entry of each voice the
singers genuflect. At the end of the song St. Peter sings:*)
Almighty God, what is this I see?
Is there some hidden mystery
In our meeting here
That God wishes to reveal to us?
(*Then Our Lady, who at this solemn moment has been*

given a lighted candle, answers St. Peter, *explaining the divine mystery:*)
My beloved sons have arrived,
And the Lord has brought you all
That my body may be entrusted to you
And you may bury it in Josaphat.

SCENE 5.

Our Lady falls back dead. At this moment, at a sign from the priest, master of ceremonies, the organist plays, and the sky above opens, and the Araceli *or "sky-altar" hovers above in the air. While the public all gaze at the Angel-Minstrels in pink and green kneeling at the foot of the celestial altar, down below on the stage the boy playing the part of the Virgin disappears below by a trap door and his place in the bed is taken by a small statue representing her soul. One of the Apostles (the sacristan) places four lighted candles at the four corners of the bed, and meanwhile the* Araceli *descends, and the Apostles, who are standing, sing the following motet, one of the most ancient in the play:*
"O saintly and most glorious body
Of our blessed Virgin immaculate,
Today you will be laid to rest,
And you will reign on high."
(*This is one of the most difficult passages of the drama owing to the necessity of synchronizing the descent of the* Araceli *with the singing of the motet, which is one of the slowest in tempo, by the Apostles. As soon as the Apostles have finished their song the Minstrel-Angels in the* Araceli, *after opening their handkerchiefs and scattering glittering tinsel, sing their motet to the following words:*)
Spouse and Mother of God,
You will follow us angels
And sit upon the royal throne

In the kingdom of Heaven.
Because in your womb once did lie
He who created heaven and earth,
You shall be exalted
And wear the finest of all crowns.
Apostles and friends of God
Take up this sacred body
And carry it to Josaphat
Where she wishes to be buried.

(In the Araceli *the Men-Angels are grouped above, and the one on the right plays the guitar, and the one on the left carries a harp. Below them are the Child-Angels, who mark the rhythm on guitars that have no strings, and in the midst of the sky-altar stands an Angel who, according to ordinance, must be a priest, wearing his alb. The* Araceli *comes to rest half within the sepulcher, which opens in the stage, the music stops, and the Apostle-Sacristan hands to the priest the little statue representing the soul of Our Lady which the latter will carry up to heaven in the sky-altar. Again the* Araceli *floats in the air—pink and green and gold. The music continues until the altar reaches the top of the rope at the gate of heaven. So ends the first act of the drama.)*

ACT II.

Feast of the Assumption, August 15th.

The two acts are differentiated by the inhabitants of Elche, who call Act I "The Day of the Angel," and Act II, "The Day of the Coronation"—i.e., the two culminating scenes. In the morning of August 15 there is a procession in which all the characters in Festa take part. The performance takes place at 5 P.M.

SCENE 1.

Enter the two Marys and their escort of Angels, who remain near the entrance, while the other Angels and the choirmaster (dressed as an Apostle, as in Act I) proceed up the sloping platform to the stage. One by one they genuflect to the statue, kiss its feet and group themselves around the bed. Then St. Peter, St. John, and St. James stand in front of the sepulcher and sing another Ternari:

THE THREE APOSTLES. My brothers we ought to go
And ask the Marys devoutly
Whether they wish to come with us
To lay Our Lady in her sepulcher.
(Another Apostle joins them and they go down the andador to where the Marys are standing. They sing as follows:)

THE FOUR APOSTLES. We come to ask you to go with us
To bury the Mother of God the Creator
Who has done so much good for us.
Let us therefore set out together
With love and joy in our hearts,
For God our Redeemer and the Virgin Mary.

THE MARYS AND ANGELS. Hail and all welcome to you,
You kinsmen and beloved friends!

We are all ready to go
And lay Our Lady to rest.
(*The company now mount the stage, and the Marys and the Angels sit on the bench, and St. Peter, taking up the palm which St. John had left on the bed of Our Lady, offers it again to him singing as follows:*)
Come, John, take the precious palm
And carry it before her who is now in glory.
For such was the wish of the Blessed Virgin,
Before she soared to heaven.
Flower of virginal beauty,
Temple of humility,
Wherein the holy Trinity
Entered and found protection.
We beg of your most saintly body
To remember for evermore
The yoke that binds us to the earth
When you are raised heavenwards.

SCENE 2.

The Apostles now rise and intone the Psalm "In Exitu Israel" preceding the burial of the deceased. Only the first verse is sung, for it is interrupted by the Jews. We now come to the most dramatic scene in the drama entitled "La Judiada," composed by Maestro Ribera in the sixteenth century. While the Apostles are singing, a group of Jews suddenly appear at the main door of the basilica. They are important personages, and at their head are the Great Rabbi and a Pharisee. They advance halfway up the anda-dor *and see the Apostles singing psalms to the dead body. They shout and call excitedly to their companions, who arrive in hot haste, and all of them decide to prohibit the honors that are to be paid to the deceased, and they arrogantly order the Apostles to abandon the dead woman. From the* andador *they sing a motet in dialogue:*

THE GREAT RABBI. This great novelty
PHARISEES. Dishonors us.
ALL. Let us tread our way carefully.
PRIESTS. Do not tolerate such falsehood.
ALL. Do not tolerate such falsehood.
THE GREAT RABBI. We are not willing
PHARISEES AND PRIESTS. That you should bury this woman
ALL. Rather do we order you
     In solemn terms to abandon that body.
THE GREAT RABBI. And if you do not so as we wish,
PHARISEES. We all shall force you
ALL. By Adonai to abandon her.

(*Before this motet ends St. Peter and St. John have descended the sloping platform to stop the Jews, and a fierce struggle ensues. St. Peter, when attacked, struggles with the leader of the Jews, and puts his hand to his sword. The Jews repel the Apostles and mount the stage, but when they attempt to seize the dead body of Our Lady, they all remain paralyzed, with their hands rigid and unable to move. The Jews cry "Miracle!" and fall on their knees before the Virgin, who even when dead manifests her power. Meanwhile the motet continues:*)

O God Adonai
Who grants the powers to Nature,
Succor us, O mighty one!
Protect us, O fount of wisdom!
Such a miracle never was performed
By human creature.
Help us St. Peter,
For you have the power!
We all repent
In our hearts,
We beseech you, O Lord
To grant us protection!

(*St. Peter and St. John, seeing the Jews have repented, address them in the following moving* Ternari:)

You Jewish Leaders, if you believe
That the Mother of the Son of God
Was truly a virgin undefiled
Before and after
She was delivered of her Son.

(The Jews answer in the following motet:)
We all believe
That She is the Mother of the Son of God.
Baptize us all at once,
For we wish to live in that faith.
(St. Peter at once baptizes them all, sprinkling them with the hyssop. The Jews rise up astonished to find that suddenly after baptism their paralysis and rigidity have gone.

SCENE 3.

Their singing now becomes a paean of joy owing to the miracle, and we have a further inspired dramatic song composed by Maestro Ribera.

THE GREAT RABBI. Let us sing, brothers!

SCRIBES. How shall we sing?

PHARISEES AND PRIESTS. With acclamation.

ALL. Let us offer thanks and praise
To the humble Mother of God.

ALL. All our life long
We must serve her,
For her infinite goodness
Has protected us.

THE GREAT RABBI. Let us all sing.

SCRIBES. We all praise her.

PHARISEES AND PRIESTS. With acclamation.

ALL. Let us give thanks and praise
To the humble Mother of God.

(When the "Judiada" has ended, the interrupted funeral of the Virgin proceeds. In this all take part. At the head of the procession goes the Cross carried by the sacristan, then a double file of Apostles and Jews carrying lighted candles. Then come St. John carrying the long palm and another Apostle the thurible. Both precede the bier containing the body of Our Lady, over which rises the pallium. Behind follows St. Peter officiating as priest, and last

of all the two Marys and the Angels. During all this cere-
mony the choir sings the psalm "De Exitu Israel." The pro-
cession marches around the stage clockwise, then the statue
is laid upon the bed, and the Apostles and the Jews kneel
and sing one of the most beautiful songs in the drama—
No. XXII, by Maestro Luis Vich, who was a native of
Elche and organist of the Church of Santa María where
the Mystery is performed:)

Before this glorious body
Of the pure and blessed Virgin
Enters the sepulcher,
Let us willingly adore.
Gazing with contrition and sorrow
Upon the image
Of the pure and blessed Virgin,
In attendance upon the Creator,
Believing that the image
Of the pure and blessed Virgin
Has such majesty
Let us all willingly adore.

(Again the psalm "In Exitu Israel" is sung, and Apostles,
Jews, the Marys, and Angels, all in order of hierarchy,
make their bows to the image and kiss its feet. While this
takes place the sacristan-Apostle piles up before the sepul-
cher opposite the sloping platform the cushions in an
inclined plane and over them he lays two large coverlets.
After the Adoration the Apostles take up the image and lay
it upon this inclined bed, leaning its head against the rail-
ing of the sepulcher. Still singing "De Exitu Israel" the
Apostles and Jews do obeisance to the Virgin, and then
they raise up the bed with the statue and lower it into
the sepulcher. The organist plays loud chords, and the sky
above opens, the Araceli descends slowly, and the Apostles
and Jews fall to their knees around the tomb. As the Ara-
celi slowly floats down the Angel-Minstrels sing the follow-
ing song:)

Rise most glorious Queen,
Mother of God Almighty,
Come, you will be crowned
In the heavenly mansion.
Rejoice, for here you will see

Him whose Spouse and Mother you are,
And you will also see the Father
Of his beloved Son and God Eternal.
There you will be sad no longer,
And you will intercede for Sinners
And reign eternally,
Gazing upon Almighty God.

SCENE 4.

On the Araceli *are grouped five figures, namely, the four
Minstrel-Angels, and the priest, who holds in his hands the
"soul" of the Virgin. He is the envoy of God, and descends
bearing the soul of Our Lady that it may unite with her
body, and she may rise to eternal life in heaven in her
Assumption, surrounded by the choir of Angels. When the*
Araceli *reaches the stage and disappears within the sepulcher the Angels cease singing. After some moments we
hear the thrumming of the guitar of the Minstrel-Angel and
the* Araceli *soars again into the air, bearing in addition to
the angels, the statue of Our Lady, but it remains poised
above the nave, for down below a dramatic incident in the
drama takes place. At the main door of the church appears
St. Thomas, the missing Apostle. He stands at the foot of
the sloping platform and sings in resounding voice:*
O what a terrible shock!
Woe's me, what a misfortune
That I was not present
At this saintly sepulcher.
(*He advances up the* andador, *and, as though for the first
time, he catches sight of the Virgin, who is soaring into
heaven; he ceases lamenting and addresses her in pleading
tones:*)
I beseech you, O most glorious Virgin,
Mother of Almighty God.
Do consider me excused

As the Indies delayed me.

(*St. Thomas, who wears a green habit and a red cloak,
makes the most dramatic entry in the whole play: he is
dumbfounded at the news of Our Lady's death. He had
been wandering in far-off countries, and had not heard the
sad news and thus was the only one of the Apostles who
was not present by her deathbed. As the play draws nearly
to its climax with the coronation of the Virgin, the excitement of the audience grows. Above the vast multitude the
Araceli floats in the air pink and green and gold—a rainbow bridge linking heaven and earth, recalling Calderon's
lovely simile of the Cross hovering above the world. In
response to their celestial harmony there comes the full-
throated resonance of the choir below, swelling to a great
volume of sound in the Grand Fugue for four voices. As
soon as St. Thomas embraces the Apostles the Coronation
hymn begins, and all eyes now gaze at the roof of the
church where another sky-altar appears, called "The Coronation." On it are kneeling Minstrel-Angels, as in the Araceli, and another priest, who represents God Almighty,
holds in his hands the crown for Our Lady. The words of
the Coronation Hymn are as follows:*)

All hail to you on your arrival
To reign for all eternity,
For you will be crowned by us
with a glorious diadem.

SCENE 5.

*As the music soars higher and higher, so does the emotion
of the people rise to a climax, until even the chorus is
submerged by the booming of church bells and the tumul-
tuous murmurs of the multitude. The Coronation Hymn is
virtually the end of the performance, for most in that multitude have come simply to see the Coronation, as they
superstitiously believe that they will have luck for a whole*

A NOTE ON THE MUSIC OF
THE MYSTERY PLAY OF ELCHE

ACCORDING to legendary tradition, the celebrated liturgic drama was discovered together with an image of Our Lady, in an ark which floated to the east coast of Spain and was picked up by a coast watcher on December 29, 1376. None of the documents of the fourteenth century, alas, have survived, for the church in Elche where they were preserved was destroyed in 1672. The ancient statue, which was said to have floated to the coast in the ark, perished in the holocaust of 1936. The *Festa* in its original form was the only example extant of a primitive Spanish lyric drama which was entirely sung, and it may, therefore, be considered the forerunner of opera, which did not appear in Italy until several centuries later.

The music of the Mystery Play of Elche consisted of primitive melodies with Mozarabic influences, but upon this basis the three masters of the sixteenth century—Antonio de Ribera, Ginés Pérez and Lluis Vich—wove elaborate polyphonic numbers. And that polyphonic music, in its turn, adapted itself to the style of the local singers of Elche, who learned it through the tradition handed down from father to son. There is, in fact, in the musical play as we hear it, an astonishing mixture of childlike simplicity and subtle sophistication, which in the ordinary theater would disturb and spoil the effect of the work as a whole, but which we accept in the reverential atmosphere of the church, owing to the overwhelming influence of the folk spirit. There is the complete fusion between the original chanted medieval drama and the florid polyphony of the sixteenth century, and the sense of unity is produced by the folk singers whose mannerisms and peculiarities of style recall the polyphonic brotherhoods of folk singers today in the villages of Murcia, called

Auroros or dawn-singers, who sing their *Correlativa* and *Salves* during Holy Week every year.

According to the account of the *Festa* given by José Pomares Perlasia, which is by far the most authoritative, we know that the performance of the Mystery Play passed under the direction of the Municipal Council of Elche on March 11, 1609, and in 1625 Soler Chacón made a copy of the original *Consueta*, which was submitted to the Inquisition in 1632 for approbation. It appears that in those days the *Festa* was frowned upon by the Bishop of the diocese of Orihuela, owing to the supposed irreverence of the public who assisted, and there was grave danger that the play would be prohibited by the Holy See, in accordance with the decrees of the Council of Trent, which had suppressed theatrical representations in church. Pope Urban VIII, however, in view of the deeply devotional character of the Mystery Play at Elche, granted in 1632 a Rescript authorizing its performance under the direction of the Confraternity. In 1740 the city of Elche itself took the Mystery under its wing and appointed commissioners, its standard-bearer and knights-elect to represent the community.

Although there were originally four *consuetas* or texts of the play, only the fourth is extant—that arranged in 1709 by El Beneficiado Lozano based upon the *Consueta* of 1639. It is significant that the natives of Elche themselves have always presented and sung annually the *Festa*, as they call it, with songs and chants that have been transmitted orally. The tradition has been preserved by the successive choirmasters and organists who have taught the performers the ancient style, which still in places preserves the ancient Mozarabic chant and the grace notes or *zuak* of Arabic music, inherited from the Moors, who had occupied Elche until 1265.

As an illustration of the Hispano-Moslem elements that pervade the *Consueta*, here is the moving passage from the chant of Our Lady as transcribed by José Pomares Perlasia: [1]

[1] J. Pomares Perlasia, *La "Festa" o Misterio de Elche.* Elche, 1956.

The musical effect produced by the singing of the angels on the sky-altar floating in space above us is indescribable. Playing their instruments and singing, they seem like a group painted by Beato Angelico bringing with them the ethereal harmony of the heavenly choir. The music echoes through the lofty church, mingling with the harmony of the organ,

and in the distance we hear the booming of the bells. The
song the angels sing is "Esposa e Mare de Deu" (Spouse and
Mother of God):

Cobla 35 · Es - po - sae Ma - re de Déu a nos àn - gels se - gui -

reu Seu - reu - - - - - en ca - di - ra Re-al en lo

Reg - ne ce - les - ti - al

The Best of the World's Best Books
COMPLETE LIST OF TITLES IN
THE MODERN LIBRARY

A series of handsome, cloth-bound books, formerly
available only in expensive editions.

MISCELLANEOUS